"Should be required reading for all those committed to winning the battle against one of the world's biggest problems."
    —Lamar Alexander, President, the University of Tennessee and former Governor of Tennessee

"Congratulations to Ira Lipman for authoring a book on crime protection that is logical, intelligent, and non-exploitative."
    —Michael Douglas, actor and film producer

"With all the press headlines about crime, with all of us folks in government worrying and talking about it, why was I surprised to read a straightforward, clear piece of writing that actually helped people understand how they could protect themselves against crime?
    "Thank you, Ira Lipman, for doing that."
    —Neil Goldschmidt, Governor of Oregon

"*How to Protect Yourself from Crime* is an impressive and timely book that addresses modern-day problems, particularly with working parents who have children coming home to an empty house. Until we find a proven alternative to this lifestyle, this is the answer to parents' fears. It offers very concrete advice that will allow parents to teach their children how to be safe and secure. This book is a must for all parents; it should be in every home."
    —Tipper (Mrs. Albert) Gore, child advocate and author of *Raising PG Kids in an X-Rated Society*

"A great book. Should be in the home of everyone. If you apply the wisdom contained herein, you will be safer and much more comfortable whatever your environment.
    "Read it, use it, and be better off."
    —H. Stuart Knight, Director, U.S. Secret Service (retired)

"A well-documented and clearly written guidebook for making our communities safer. Ira Lipman offers the best compendium of crime prevention information available today."
    —Barry Krisberg, Executive Director, National Council on Crime and Delinquency

"Not only did I learn from this book, but I enjoyed reading it. Very informative."

—Karl Malden, President, Academy of Motion Pictures Arts and Sciences

"The third edition moves this most comprehensive, well-organized text into the next century, covering precautionary information about contemporary and future criminal activity. This easy-to-read guide to self-protection contains essential information for everyone. The recommended awareness and prevention tips will enhance the safety and security of all those who practice them."

—George B. Sunderland, Manager, Criminal Justice Services, American Association of Retired Persons

"From securing your home and neighborhood crime prevention techniques to preparing for overseas travel, Ira Lipman stresses that through proper planning, it is possible to react correctly to virtually any problem one might face. . . . His book answers the victim's lament, 'If I had only known.' Knowing what to do, in advance of a situation, will greatly reduce the probability of becoming a victim. I would recommend *How to Protect Yourself from Crime* right along with the basic first-aid text as required reading for personal survival."

—Robert C. Trojanowicz, Ph.D., professor and Director, School of Criminal Justice, Michigan State University

"A careful analysis of research on crime and the wisdom of someone who has significantly advanced personal and corporate security in our country are combined to produce the most comprehensive, balanced, and useful guide to crime prevention I have ever read. In a time when many citizens, especially in our largest cities, seem to accept crime as an unavoidable aspect of their environment, this book presents an alternative—reasoned self-protection."

—Charles F. Wellford, Ph.D., Director, Institute of Criminal Justice and Criminology, the University of Maryland at College Park

HOW TO PROTECT YOURSELF FROM CRIME

HOW TO PROTECT YOURSELF FROM CRIME

IRA A. LIPMAN

CONTEMPORARY
BOOKS

CHICAGO · NEW YORK

Library of Congress Cataloging-in-Publication Data

Lipman, Ira A.
    How to protect yourself from crime / Ira Lipman. — 3rd ed.
      p.   cm.
    ISBN 0-8092-4244-3
    1. Crime prevention.   2. Dwellings—Security
measures.   I. Title.
    HV7431.L56   1990
    362.88—dc20   89-38777
                                     CIP

For Barbara, Gus, Josh, Benjamin, and my parents, with love

This is a revised and updated edition of *How to Protect Yourself from Crime.* This title was first published in hardcover by Atheneum Publishers in 1975, was published simultaneously in Canada by McClelland & Stewart Ltd., and was reprinted in paperback by the Law Enforcement Assistance Administration in December 1980. Portions appeared in *Reader's Digest* in August 1981. The second edition was published by Avon Books in 1981.

Copyright © 1989 by Ira A. Lipman
All rights reserved
Published by Contemporary Books, Inc.
180 North Michigan Avenue, Chicago, Illinois 60601
Manufactured in the United States of America
International Standard Book Number: 0-8092-4244-3

Published simultaneously in Canada by Beaverbooks, Ltd.
195 Allstate Parkway, Valleywood Business Park
Markham, Ontario L3R 4T8 Canada

Contents

Foreword

Crime, like death and taxes, exists in every society. The amount and character of crime and the distribution of victims vary over time and place. Every citizen is aware of these generalizations.

But most citizens are uninformed about the specific theories of the causes of crime, the details of the operation of the criminal justice system, or the scientific studies of the modes of crime prevention and treatment of the offenders. Criminology is a scientific discipline of knowledge. Criminology is the scientific study of crime, criminals, and society's reaction to both.

As a criminologist, I have attempted to study delinquency, criminality, law enforcement, and punishment of criminal behavior in as scientific a way as my educational training has provided.

Criminologists have analyzed abstract theories of crime and punishment, and have produced detailed historical reviews and elaborate quantitative, highly sophisticated statistical studies of patterns of crime, personalities of criminals, and the effectiveness of prevention and therapeutic programs.

For nearly twenty years, criminologists also have been carefully studying the victims of crime, ever since the focus on victims was creatively introduced by Bernard Mendlesohn, an Israeli scholar, and by Hans Von Hentig, a German scholar who escaped from the Nazi period. There has developed a new subfield of criminology known as victimology and a World Society of Victimology has been created, devoted to the scientific study of victimization, especially of victims of crime. Studies in victimology have been legal, philosophical, sociological, cross-cultural, macroeconomic, psychological. All of this scientific research has been enlightening and has shown the importance of the relationship between the criminal and his or her victim.

The pragmatic analysis of how we, as individuals, might best protect ourselves against crime, against becoming victims of crime, has been neglected by criminologists and victimologists. That vacuum has now been greatly filled by this third edition of Ira Lipman's *How to Protect Yourself from Crime.*

I first came to know Ira Lipman over a dozen years ago when he sought my advice on some matters associated with his private security organization, Guardsmark. I immediately perceived him as an intelligent, humane person who knew his business well, who knew the problems of crime and the practical way of managing those problems on a day-by-day basis in business, in private institutions, and in the private lives of individuals. I came to know the efficiency and the effectiveness of Guardsmark, one of the largest private security organizations in the country. I admired Ira Lipman's managerial capacities and his understanding of the criminological literature he had begun to absorb.

Because of my respect for his pragmatic acumen and intellectual integrity, I, as President of the American Academy of Political and Social Science, encouraged him to be a special editor of *The Annals*, the bimonthly publication of the academy. The issue he edited, "The Private Security Industry: Issues and Trends," Volume 498, July 1988, has been one of our most highly regarded and widely distributed volumes in the recent history of the academy.

This third edition of *How to Protect Yourself from Crime* is the most comprehensive treatment of the topic I have ever read. I can think of no significant concern of individuals or groups that is not covered in this volume with thoroughness, precision, and accuracy. I mention accuracy especially, because the descriptions of various kinds of crimes and the recommendations for protection against them are solidly, firmly based on the best available evidence in the scientific literature.

On controversial issues, such as owning and using guns, discussions are carefully balanced and must be applauded. The checklists at the end of each chapter are especially useful as reminders of the details. These lists should be consulted on specific occasions, such as taking a vacation or a business trip, moving a residence, or traveling overseas. All of these summaries should be reread as time and circumstances permit and require.

This is not an alarmist book, but there are alarming changes occurring in the amount, character, and violence of crime in our nation. For example, the chapters on robbery and rape are outstandingly grounded in scientific research and provide the best guides to prevention and protection to be found anywhere.

To be alert to these changes, to be aware of protective strategies is useful to our capacity to reduce our being victimized and to our ensuring greater safety and the "pursuit of happiness" for us all.

How to Protect Yourself from Crime is the best antidote to criminal victimization I can recommend to my family, my friends, and all citizens of America.

Dr. Marvin E. Wolfgang
Professor of Criminology and of Law
University of Pennsylvania

Preface to the Third Edition

In the dozen or so years since *How to Protect Yourself from Crime* was written, thousands and thousands of ordinary people have benefited from a very special protection against the ravages of crime. We began our protective efforts with one central message in mind: crime is so pervasive that it defies traditional controls. Police ranks then, as now, were stretched too thin to control the vast numbers who had selected crime as a career. We said then, as we do now, that if there is a recurring theme running through this book, it is that we are making crime too easy for the criminal. In fact, not only are we victims of crime, we are also, in effect, accomplices.

During the intervening years, our crime experience grew, moderating slightly in the early 1980s. Then crime rates fell, and fell substantially. In 1983, a 7 percent decline, following declines of 3 percent in 1982 and less than 1 percent in 1981, signaled to some the end of the "Great Crime Wave" of the twentieth century. Crime rates continued to fall—if not precipitously, at least steadily. Our experience with crime continued to move favorably. Then, in 1985, the trend reversed—crime rates climbed a bit. The following year saw the largest increase in six years. The upward trend continued through 1987 for an overall increase of 13 percent for the three-year period.

Many observers were not surprised. The turnarounds, downward in 1980 and upward in 1986, were predictable. It was a simple matter of demographics.

One of the major contributors to the Great Crime Wave was that there were more young people (the group most likely to commit crime) than ever before. But in the early 1980s the Baby Boomers were getting older, marrying, and settling down.

The consequent drop in crime rates led some to anticipate a long period of relative freedom from crime. Unfortunately, a number of factors mitigate against this hope. What we have seen in the crime turnarounds of 1985 and 1986 is the vanguard of the children of the Baby Boomers. We are witnesses to the emergence of the Baby Boom Aftershock.

The members of this generation are starkly different from their parents. They are conservative, pampered, accustomed to getting what they want, and, according to the nation's leading criminologist, they tend, much more than their fathers and mothers, to be vicious and brutal.

Perhaps we need to accustom ourselves to continuing periods of viciousness and brutality. If we view ourselves realistically, we must conclude that we are vicious and brutal. In a quarter of a century (1969–1984), we have seen serious crime increase 40 percent. *We have seen violent crime increase by more than 60 percent.*

A book like *How to Protect Yourself from Crime* is therefore all the more needed today. Its primary function is to nudge you into a positive, preventive approach by taking the first steps for you. Where possible, the stress is on psychological and physical readiness—that is, preaction rather than reaction.

To understand how to protect yourself, you'll need to be clear about some of the terms used repeatedly in this book:

- *Robbery* is the taking of money and/or other valuables under the threat of physical harm or force, with or without a weapon. An example is a holdup at gun- or knifepoint.
- *Burglary* is breaking and entering with no personal threat involved and usually no confrontation between burglar and victim. The traditional "second-story man" is an example of a burglar.
- *Theft* or *larceny* is the act of stealing, in which neither illegal entry nor the threat or use of force is present. Shoplifting is an example of theft.

Each year the Federal Bureau of Investigation (FBI) publishes statistics dealing with eight classifications of personal crime. Three are considered crimes against property: burglary, larceny, and auto theft. Four are considered crimes against the person: murder, forcible rape, aggravated assault, and robbery. (Clearly, robbery is a crime directed at property as well as the person, but there is the threat, at least, of bodily harm.) Arson was recently added to the list, but at this point much of the information is too incomplete to be reported.

It's somewhat consoling to learn that nearly nine of every ten crimes, as defined by the FBI, are crimes against property—that is, incidents during which the victim and the perpetrator do not come face to face. In reading this book, bear in mind that you are unlikely ever to be subjected to a violent crime against your person. Though the possibility does exist, there is no reason for undue alarm.

The sharp rise in many types of crime in recent years is illustrated by the following extrapolations of FBI statistics:

- In 1965 you would have had to live 20,000 years to be considered a probable murder victim. By 1973 your likelihood of being murdered had almost doubled—you would have had to live only 10,750 years. By 1980 this figure had been reduced to less than 10,000 years. By 1986, your survival odds actually improved by more than 10 percent.
- To be considered a probable rape victim in 1965, you would have had to live 8,295 years. By 1973, this fell to 5,000 years; and by 1980, only 2,680 years. Figures for rape victimizations in 1986 were virtually the same as those of 1980: 2,666 years.
- In 1965, you would have had to live 1,400 years to be considered a probable robbery victim. By 1973, your likelihood of being robbed had more than doubled—you'd have had to live approximately 548 years. By 1980, this figure had dropped to 396 years. The year 1986 saw your odds of robbery victimization improve a bit—to every 444 years.
- You would have had to live 906 years in 1965 to be considered a probable victim of aggravated assault. Here, too, your odds nearly doubled in 1973—the figure dropped to 500 years. But by 1980, your probability of being assaulted had nearly tripled—the figure had dropped to 335 years. In 1986, your chances of being seriously assaulted increased substantially, compared with the preceding year, to once in 289 years.
- You would have had to live 152 years in 1965 to be considered a probable burglary victim. By 1973, the life span had come down to a very realistic one: 83 years. In 1980, it was even more realistic: 59 years. Burglars fell on hard times during the early 1980s—from once in 59 years, to once in 74 years, a substantial improvement for the forces of law and order.
- In 1965 you would have had to live 76 years to be considered a probable victim of larceny. By 1973, the likelihood of suffering

larceny had become once in 46 years, and by 1980, once in 31 years. Larceny/thefts, which can be reasonably anticipated every 33 years, if the results of 1986 are any barometer, are much the same as was the case six years earlier. Putting these larceny statistics in perspective, we find that during our biblically allotted three score years and ten, we can expect to be ripped off at least two times.

These figures show quite clearly how our crime rate has changed—very much for the worse—over the intervening years. So great has this increase in criminal activity been that we can now expect murders at the rate of one each twenty-five minutes, a rape each six minutes, a robbery every fifty-eight seconds, and an assault each thirty-eight seconds. Property crimes occur at even faster rates: a burglary each ten seconds, a theft each four seconds, and a motor vehicle theft every twenty-six seconds. The statistical improvement during the first half of the 1980s clearly seems to have been an anomaly. Furthermore, the ensuing reversal of that trend can be expected to usher in another crime wave of great magnitude.

Earlier remarks attributed the bulk of our crime problems to the Baby Boomers and stated that the Baby Boom Aftershock also will be a serious challenge to the forces of law and order. Realistically, this demographic bomb is by no means the only cause. Other important contributors are our national involvement with drugs, especially cocaine; a lack of trust in many of our national leaders; and serious concerns about the economy. Solving the problems ahead requires a fresh approach. We can no longer depend on the old approaches, which failed us in the past.

As you read this book, you will notice there is no mention of specific brand names, and for a very good reason. Today's best door lock or alarm system may not be the best next year, and almost certainly will not be five years from now. Thus, if and when you purchase security devices, the only way to be sure you are getting the best available equipment is to consult an accredited expert.

Nevertheless, this book does unhesitatingly recommend certain types of equipment—dead bolts, for example. This particular type of lock has been around for centuries and probably will remain for many more centuries. From time to time, one or another manufacturer may come up with a seemingly superior product, but it usually is essentially a dead bolt because nothing superior in principle is even on the horizon.

However, even when you do read a recommendation for a certain type of equipment, you should still let an expert select and install it.

This book attempts to strike a balance in its recommendations because some readers will have greater security requirements than others, and price will be a bigger determinant for some than for others. Following the recommendations exactly would thus leave some readers underprotected, some overprotected, but most readers adequately protected. If you have any doubts, an expert will be able to resolve them for you.

A complete solution to our crime problem is not just around the corner, and until and unless we reach that point, most of the responsibility for your protection is yours. You needn't arm yourself or organize a vigilante group. Nor should you undertake unrealistic acts of "heroism" that may in fact increase your peril and loss. Instead, simply take a series of commonsense preventive measures.

How to slow down a potential criminal or influence him or her to seek another "mark" (or, better yet, deter that person altogether) is probably the major lesson that this book has to offer. For example, it is estimated that half of all auto thefts result from keys left in the ignition and that one-fourth of all illegal entries into homes are made through unlocked doors.

We can't expect somebody else to take care of our security needs. We must handle them ourselves. Read this book carefully and often, and periodically review the security checklists at the end of each chapter. Teach your family good security practices, and reinforce the messages so that you and yours can respond automatically in an emergency. Add notes of your own to fit security precautions and practices to your lifestyle. Before we can completely protect ourselves from crime, we must, in many respects, change our attitude toward it. We must be vigilant, we must be prepared, and we must endure the inconvenience that simple and sensible day-to-day precautions entail. Self-protection is a way of life. Good security practices not only make life safer but make compensation easier if a crime does occur.

The third edition of *How to Protect Yourself from Crime* has been thoroughly revised and updated. For example, new developments in computer security required a complete rewriting of the chapter dealing with this subject. Also, the present volume contains many new crime subjects and ways to protect yourself and your family from these forms of harm. The intention is to provide security guidelines for a variety of criminal acts, no matter how subtle and regardless of who is responsible—even members of your own family. The new topics include abuse at day-care centers, abuse of the elderly, school and campus security, teen suicide, alcohol abuse, security in hospitals and nursing homes, compulsive gambling, multiple murders, investment fraud, and security issues when moving to another city. This book even includes a chapter on how to plan for your future protection into the twenty-first century, which is not really very far off.

This book offers two types of suggestions: routine, day-to-day preventive measures to decrease your exposure to crime, and practical, step-by-step recommendations to guide you through the unhappy and sometimes bewildering experience of being a crime victim. May you never need to put the latter suggestions to use, but genuinely learn to protect yourself from crime.

Acknowledgments

Reflecting my position as chairman and president of Guardsmark, Inc., my name on the title page of this book simply reflects the names of the many Guardsmark people responsible for this collective effort. The fine work of those who assisted with the first and second volumes was greatly enhanced in this third edition by the efforts of Dr. Bernard Cohen, noted criminologist and sociologist. Dr. Cohen was ably assisted by Susanne M. Loftis of Guardsmark. I am grateful to all those who made this project possible.

PART ONE

SECURITY IN YOUR HOME

1
Doors and Windows

Walter, a machinist and bachelor, came home from work Thursday night and discovered that he had been visited by a burglar. "A window was all busted out," he commented, "so I knew right away that somebody had been inside." He went into his small rented house and found a wreck—the whole place was in shambles. His TV was gone, as were his VCR and stereo, some cash, and a few other possessions. No arrest was made, nor did Walter recover any of his possessions.

DOORS

The easiest way for someone to enter your home is simply to open an unlocked door. In fact, this is the way that many houses are illegally entered. Very few families take the number one precaution of locking exterior doors at all times, whether someone is home or not. Children who are in and out of the house all day leave doors unlocked, as do people who step next door for a neighborly visit.

An example will illustrate just how hazardous an unlocked door can be. A woman was in her house, not particularly concerned that her back door was unlocked, since she had a large dog in whose presence she felt absolutely secure. Sure enough, an intruder entered through the unlocked door, and sure enough, the dog sprang to the attack, badly mauling the intruder. Unfortunately, the intruder was a two-year-old who lived next door.

While doors should always be locked, this in itself is actually small defense against the determined criminal. Here's why:

• Doors often have small glass or light plywood panels, which can

1

easily be broken or cut with a rasp or a keyhole saw. Someone could then open the lock very easily by simply reaching through the hole.

- A door that doesn't fit its frame properly can easily be forced open by wedging a tire tool or prying bar between it and the frame and then "spreading" the door away until the bolt moves free from the strike (the hole in the door frame that the bolt slides into when the door is locked).
- Some older homes and apartments have doors that open outward. These can often be opened simply by removing the hinge pins and lifting the entire door from the frame. The Multi-Lock, mentioned later in this chapter, is useful in protecting doors of this type.
- Certain locks can be easily picked, removed, or destroyed.

It is virtually impossible to prevent someone from entering your home through an outside door if that person is really determined to do so and has enough time and skill to accomplish the deed.

If you can't entirely eliminate the possibility of someone's breaking into your home, then what's the next best thing to do? Make breaking in as difficult and as time-consuming as possible. And if the burglar still succeeds, at least you will have forced him or her to destroy the lock or a part of the door, or in some other way to leave clear evidence of illegal entry. This will be very important when you file an insurance claim to recover your loss. If nothing else, it will at least minimize the likelihood of your claim's being denied on the grounds of negligence.

Strengthening Doors

Strengthening doors—and these comments apply to all outside doors— is not difficult. First, the door itself should be as sturdy as possible. A hollow-core metal or solid wooden door is best.

For aesthetic purposes, however, many prefer doors with heavy glass or wooden panels. These types of doors offer considerably less protection than those just mentioned, but there is one thing in particular that you can do to make them more secure: double-cylinder locks should always be installed on such a door. This kind of lock requires a key to open it from the inside as well as from the outside, which prevents an intruder from unlatching the lock by reaching through broken glass or a hole in a wooden panel. That much delay—unless the burglar is especially determined—will very often send an intruder off to easier pickings. A word of caution, however: in the event of fire or other emergency, double-cylinder locks can delay occupants from getting out of the house.

Consequently, a key to the inside lock should always be kept conveniently at hand.

There may be a reason why one of these measures won't be practical. For example, your landlord might not want to replace an existing door or permit you to do so, or you, as a tenant, might not want to go to the expense of installing a really good door on someone else's property. In this case, consider reinforcing your door with a sheet of steel or heavy plywood. It may not be a thing of beauty, but it might save your TV and VCR.

In securing all outside doors, be particularly meticulous with those that offer an intruder cover—such as doors inside vestibules or enclosed porches. Here a criminal could work at leisure, safe from observation by neighbors or passersby. Be aware that these protected areas often are of less sturdy construction than other parts of your home. Ideally they should be finished off with exterior walls as sound as the rest of the house.

Every exterior door should fit its frame snugly. Most don't. Housebuilders sometimes take shortcuts by making the openings oversized, and even a well-fitted door can develop problems as a house settles on its foundation. The best way to remedy a poor fit is to reinforce the door frame or to replace the door with one that fits. If you don't want to go to that much expense, at least use locks with bolts that slide a minimum of one inch into the frame, or attach a common thumb lock with a long bolt to the inside face of the door. Or better yet, ask a locksmith about an L-shaped metal strip that can be attached to a door frame to protect an

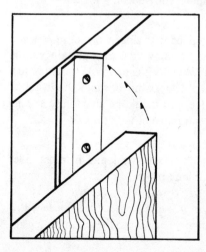

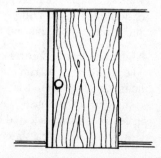

An L-shaped metal strip makes a door jimmy-proof.

inward-swinging door from being jimmied with a crowbar. A flat plate attached to an outward-swinging door can be used to cover such an opening, but it should be attached with flat bolts or nonretractable screws so that it cannot be removed from the outside.

Storm doors are excellent energy savers, and when equipped with adequate locking devices, they add an element of security by introducing an additional delay factor. The glass and/or wrought-iron features serve as another deterrent.

Chain Locks

In general, chain locks are not effective in preventing someone from entering your home. A good kick might easily pull the lock away from the wall. Furthermore, the chain itself can be cut with a hacksaw or a bolt cutter. To maximize the effectiveness of such locks, anchor them with long screws or, better yet, bolts. A wedge-shaped rubber doorstop inserted beneath a door can add substantial additional protection against unwanted entry.

One advantage of a chain lock is that, when it is engaged, it indicates to a burglar that someone is at home, generally causing the burglar to move on. One distinct disadvantage of a chain lock is that a burglar, once inside your house, can become relatively free from being surprised on the job simply by engaging the lock him- or herself.

The value of a chain lock is thus debatable, but on balance a good one is worthwhile, if for no other reason than its effect of delaying entry into your house. Also, if you have solid doors without peepholes, a chain lock allows you to speak to visitors without fully opening the door.

Peepholes

A solid exterior door should be equipped with a peephole (or interviewer or optical viewing device) simply to allow you to ascertain who is outside before you open your door. Ideally, the peephole should have a wide-angle lens. If at all practical, a convex mirror should be installed opposite the door. With this device, you should be able to see anyone attempting to hide beyond the vision range of the peephole.

Night Latches and Doorknob Locks

The night latch or rim spring latch commonly found in most older houses, and the cylindrical lock or lock-in-knob found in many apartments and newer houses, do not offer a great deal of security. The lock-in device is easily defeated by prying the entire assemblage loose with a crowbar. Night latches are very common because they are inexpensive and convenient and because they can be engaged simply by slamming the door shut. But often they can be opened by sliding a credit card or similar piece of plastic into the gap between the door and the frame.

Newer night latches have protection to prevent the "credit card" entry into a structure. This represents little, if any protection, however, as doors of this type can often be compromised by forcing them open with a screwdriver. This can be prevented by equipping the lock with an effective dead-latch plunger, which prevents pushing back the latch's beveled edge. Unfortunately, the faceplate can be pried loose and the cylinder removed quite easily. Thus, this type of lock isn't considered a satisfactory locking device.

Dead Bolt Locks

The remedy for these problems is a dead-bolt lock. Such a lock usually features a square-faced (rather than beveled) bolt, which is engaged from the inside by the second turn of a key, or else is operated by turning a thumb knob. Unquestionably, the dead bolt is superior to the common night latch inasmuch as it cannot be forced open with a knife blade, spatula, or similar implement. The shape of the bolt and the pressure required to move it in any way other than through the normal use of a key or knob make these burglar tools useless. If the bolt is long enough (a one-inch throw is recommended), the door becomes most difficult to jimmy open. Either a variation on this theme, the rim- or surface-mounted vertical dead-bolt lock, or the ring-and-bar lock is an even more effective protection measure. For high-risk applications, the Multi-Lock is a dead-bolt lock that, when engaged, bolts into all four edges of the door frame.

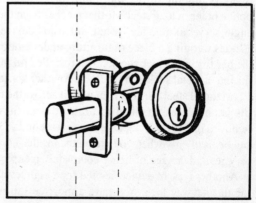

A dead-bolt lock is your best security buy.

A dead bolt is, dollar for dollar, the best means of defense that you can enlist in securing your home. You definitely should install one on each outside door either in place of or supplementary to whatever locking devices you are now using. A number of excellent dead-bolt locks are on the market.

Other Locking Devices

There are a number of virtually pickproof locks available, but they are expensive and, except in the most extraordinary of circumstances, unnecessary for the average homeowner. Few burglars are skilled at picking locks, so unless there are items of unusual value in your home, installing pickproof locks generally would constitute overprotection.

Push-button combination types of locks are also generally available and are secure from lock pickers, but a drawback is that the combination can be "read" even from great distances. Such locks are therefore much more effective for interior security than for exterior use.

No lock can prevent a door from being opened through the application of brute force, especially if there is a weak door frame. The wooden door frame itself can present a problem. In many cases when a forced entry is made through a door, the dead bolt itself has held but the door frame around the strike plate has splintered. This can be overcome by ensuring that there is proper bracing in the wall behind the door frame. If you push against the door frame on the strike-jamb side and it bends outward, it is not well supported.

The proper combination for preventing the wooden door frame from splintering without determined attack is by using a high security strike box or plate and screws long enough to anchor the strike device into two-by-fours bracing in the wall immediately behind the strike device. A police brace, a long steel bar that reaches from the floor to the door at an angle, serves as an effective anti-intrusion device in much the same way as does wedging a piece of furniture under a doorknob. The top edge of the bar fits into a lock mechanism installed on the door, and the bottom fits into a metal socket in the floor. Another version of the police brace is a horizontal steel bar that is mounted across the center of the door. This fits jamb braces attached to both sides of the door frame. It can be removed or put back in place in a few seconds. Of course, these devices can be used only when you are on the inside. They do, however, have the very real advantage of being completely pickproof.

Another type of device favored for a high level of home security is the tubular keyway lock. You have almost certainly seen the round locks found on many vending machines. Perhaps you have even seen the service person open the vending machine, using a small cylindrical key. This locking device has the advantage of being extremely difficult to pick and, for all intents and purposes, impossible to force open with a screwdriver or wrench. Other locks have similar advantages, and the configurations of the various available locking devices are many.

Sliding Doors

Of all the doors giving access to your house, probably the most hazardous are the patio doors—typically of the sliding-glass type. In general, such doors have locks that are none too effective. Even if they hold up against an intruder, a piece of glass can easily be cut or broken from the doors and the locks disengaged.

One safeguard is to attach locks with vertical bolts that fit into holes in the floor and upper frame and hold the door in place when it is engaged. Another safeguard is to substitute the panes of plate or tempered glass with polycarbonate or other shatterproof glass, or other types of impact-resistant glazing material. An inexpensive auxiliary means of securing such doors is to cut a broom handle to fit the track in which the doors slide. Thus, even if the lock were forced, the door would not slide open.

These highly susceptible openings into your home may be further protected by inserting screws into the upper track of the door assemblies. Properly placed, these screws can prevent the lifting and removal of an entire door, glass, frame, and all.

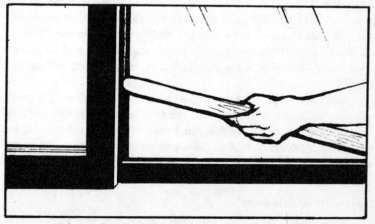

A broom handle cut to size helps secure sliding doors.

WINDOWS

The primary aim of window precautions is to secure permanently every window that is not needed for ventilation. Windows that are used for ventilation or as an emergency exit, particularly those on the ground floor, should be secured by the installation of key-operated locks, which are easily available from hardware stores and locksmiths.

Key-operated windows and locks add security.

As a general rule, an intruder will not break a window—first, because the noise would be likely to attract attention and, second, because the sharp edges present the risk of injury. This does not mean, however, that he or she will not remove a small piece of glass with a glass cutter and reach through to unlock the window. Thus, the use of laminated glass or the special impact-resistant plastics developed for such applications as schools and store windows is an excellent extra precaution—if you can afford it.

In many homes, glass is held in windows by putty. Few people seem to take into account how severely this material deteriorates with age and exposure to the elements, making panes relatively easy to remove with no more than a pocketknife. Usually a contractor will replace all putty when painting your house, but double-check to make sure that this is done.

Double-Hung Windows

The windows of many older homes are of the so-called double-hung construction, made of two panels, one or both of which slide up and down. A two-piece device, resembling a butterfly, locks it shut. This lock can be rather easily opened by sliding a thin piece of metal, such as a knife blade, vertically through the crack separating the two sashes.

Windows become considerably more secure when a hole is drilled completely through the lower window sash and halfway through the upper while the window is in the closed position. A bolt, inserted into the hole resulting from the drilling, will effectively lock the windows in the closed position only. Similarly, nails or bolts may be driven into the window tracks to prevent the window from being raised high enough to admit an intruder. For maximum security, such stops should be employed on both sides of the tracks, to make removal more difficult and time-consuming for a potential intruder.

A nail in the window track is a simple precaution.

When a window has been "frozen" shut by paint and is not needed for ventilation, a simple antiburglar precaution is to leave it that way.

Window Guards

Screens made of chain-link fencing are widely used for protecting windows, particularly in industrial applications. Aluminum curtains are available from suppliers of security hardware in sizes suitable for window protection. Bars (horizontal, vertical, or a combination of both) are similarly available. These may be enclosed in a frame attached to the window frame, or they may extend through the frame and into the walls.

For windows opening onto fire escapes, fire department regulations usually prohibit the installation of permanently placed bars or guards, but folding or hinged guards may be used on these openings if they are not locked in place. For residential application, however, these items will be considered by many to be aesthetically unappealing. Metal window guards, also called burglar bars, may be more pleasing to the eye, but, like nails in window tracks or paint-frozen windows, they could hinder you when evacuating a building threatened by fire or other danger.

Lockable folding metal screens provide excellent security, yet still provide for emergency evacuation of the home, as long as the key to unlock the screens is readily at hand. It should not be placed within reach of a would-be intruder on the outside.

Storm windows, in addition to being valuable savers of energy—and thus money—provide an impediment to the would-be intruder. Although they can usually be removed with little more than a screwdriver, this takes time and can create noise, which will generally send the typical intruder on to easier targets.

Casement Windows

Casement windows are more secure than most double-hung windows in that they are opened with a geared-crank arrangement and often are too small to allow human entry even when they are successfully opened. Intrusion is usually possible only after smashing or cutting the glass. For those who want to be doubly sure, a number of key-operated locks are available for casement windows.

Windows Above Ground Level

Second-story windows pose less of a problem than do ground-level windows, but they still require attention because they may be accessible from the outside staircases, from fire escapes, from the roofs of porches, or even from trees. You should never store ladders where they are available to a potential intruder.

In some city areas, windows may be near enough to neighboring buildings to allow a plank to bridge the gap between the structures. In some high-rise apartment buildings, an intruder might gain access by lowering him- or herself from a rooftop or higher floor to an unprotected or open window. Protection in these cases can best be accomplished through the same measures as for ground-level windows—it being a matter of personal judgment to decide how much security is necessary relative to installation costs.

In evaluating your window security, also pay special attention to basement and storeroom windows, attached garages, ventilation exhausts, access to crawl spaces opening into partial basements, coal chutes, storm cellars, attics, and all other spaces that give access to little-used areas inside the house.

In all your door and window security precautions, remember that a very important consideration is that there must be definite evidence of forced entry if you are to recover theft losses on your homeowner's insurance policy. Similarly, it is difficult to substantiate a claim for loss when you file income tax returns without indisputable evidence that the loss was sudden and unexpected.

Garages and Outbuildings

Garage doors that lead directly into the house are, in fact, entry doors, in the same way as the front door. However, they represent a more serious threat to your security, because an intruder, hidden from sight in the garage, could leisurely breach your security and attack your assets or your family. At the very least, such an opening should be protected by a solid-core door, a dead-bolt lock, secure hinges, and, if warranted, an intrusion alarm.

Obviously, you should keep your garage locked shut whenever practical. A ten-minute trip to the grocery could result in an intruder's use of your unprotected ladder to gain access to a substantially more unprotected upstairs nursery.

All garages should be protected with *good* padlocks. A good padlock has a hardened (or, better yet, a stainless) steel shackle (the loop). This should be no less than $9/32$ inch in diameter. It should have a double locking mechanism (heel and toe), a five-pin tumbler, and a key-retaining feature. This last feature, sometimes difficult to find, prevents you from removing the key unless the lock is engaged. Cane bolts and sliding hasps, installed on the inside, are inexpensive but highly effective means to increase the security of your garage.

Roll-up garage doors require two good padlocks for acceptable security, one on either side of the door. Sometimes upward pressure on one side of the door will cause the other side to rise enough for someone to crawl under. Many garage door assemblies, electric or mechanical, have predrilled holes on the tracks for a padlock, which, of course, will substantially increase your safety and perhaps your peace of mind.

Window-Unit Air Conditioners

A particularly vulnerable illegal-access location that is often overlooked by the homeowner is the window-unit air conditioner. One way to thwart the potential intruder here is to ensure that a unit is secured by long screws to both the window and the window frame. When this is not possible, consider placing a bar across the face of the unit, again ensuring that it is very firmly secured to the window frame and/or to interior walls.

Doors and Windows: A Checklist

1. Exterior doors should be locked at all times.
2. All outside doors, including enclosed porch or vestibule doors, should be protected.
3. Every outside door, without exception, should be equipped with a dead-bolt lock.
4. Doors should be sturdy. If they are not, they should be replaced or reinforced.
5. Glass doors and glass- or wood-paneled doors should be equipped with double-cylinder locks.
6. If the walls of enclosed porches are inadequate to prevent through-the-wall entry, they should be made secure. At the least, brightly light such areas.
7. Doors should fit frames snugly even if this means reinforcing the frame or replacing the door.
8. Locks with extra-long bolts can offer additional protection.
9. Chain locks, especially cheap dime-store versions, provide little security. Such devices should be limited to permitting the partial opening of a door to establish the identity of a visitor.
10. Peepholes—ideally with wide-angle lenses—should be installed in all solid exterior doors.
11. Patio and sliding glass doors, should be secured with vertical-bolt locks and equipped with shatterproof or impact-resistant panes. A length of broom handle cut to fit the door track can provide an effective, inexpensive auxiliary "lock" for such doors.
12. All windows should be equipped with adequate locking devices, preferably key-operated, and should be kept locked at all times.
13. Iron window guards can offer protection, but provision must be made to allow the use of some windows for emergency evacuation of the building. Interior removable or folding guards are recommended for this purpose.
14. Casement windows, though less hazardous than double-hung windows, nevertheless require adequate locking devices, preferably key-operated.
15. Windows above ground level require less protection than ground-level windows only if they are generally inaccessible. If in doubt, protect them as if they were at ground level.

16. Windows used for ventilation should be lockable both in closed and in partially open positions.

17. All wall openings large enough to admit a person should be protected.

18. Putty securing windowpanes should be periodically checked and replaced as necessary.

19. Impact-resistant glazing material, though expensive, can be an effective burglar deterrent.

20. Roll-up garages require two locks, one on each side of the door, because upward pressure on one side will raise the other side enough for a person to slide under through the opening.

21. Some garage door assemblies have holes predrilled in the tracks. Padlocks inserted through them will provide excellent and relatively inexpensive protection.

22. Cane bolts and sliding hasps, also used for the garage, are inexpensive and highly effective auxiliary locking devices.

23. Doors of attached garages should be equipped with locking devices as secure as those protecting the front door.

24. Attached garages are especially hazardous because if the security of the garage is breached, an intruder could gain entry to the house with little chance of being seen.

25. Garages often contain tools, ladders, and other equipment that would make breaking into the house relatively easy.

26. All garages should be protected with good padlocks that have the following features: hardened shackle, $9/32$ inch or greater shackle diameter, double locking (toe and heel), and a five-tumbler key-retaining feature.

27. Window-unit air conditioners should be adequately anchored to prevent their removal; otherwise, these unprotected openings through the walls would easily admit intruders.

2
Interior Security

"It's kind of embarrassing," a police spokesperson said. "We brought a couple to the station Friday on a shoplifting charge, and after they left, we discovered three police payroll checks worth nearly two thousand dollars missing from a partially opened drawer."

There are a number of commonsense rules that will offer you a considerable amount of protection inside your home.

DON'T ADMIT STRANGERS

First of all, don't admit anyone into your home until you know who it is. And determine who it is before you open the door. If you have a peephole or glass panels in the door or a window nearby, you can see visitors. If you have a solid door, fit a good chain lock to the door, and always use it. As an added precaution, keep at hand a wedge-shaped rubber doorstop available at variety or discount stores to slip beneath the door. This will give your chain lock some assistance if a caller tries to crash through the door. Also, since he or she will probably recoil from the initial thrust, it will give you a chance to slam the door and seek help.

If you live alone, consider installing an intercom so that you can communicate with front-door callers without opening the door. If you live in an apartment equipped with a buzzer to admit callers at the outside door, use it discriminately.

A few simple steps will keep a would-be intruder away from your door. A radio is an excellent crime fighter. Placing it so that it may be heard from outside the front door will lead an aspiring thief to believe that someone is at home. Another radio, this one near the rear of the

14

place, will add to the thief's plight. Tuning the radios to different stations could easily lead him to believe that two persons, at least, are in the structure. The burglar would probably seek an easier target.

On the other hand, leaving your drapes drawn during the day tells a thief one of two things—either you are not at home, or else you're simply not concerned about the security of your home. This laxity would send him looking avidly for an open door or window or some other easy way into your home and belongings.

Return now to your front door, where you are confronting a caller. Once you have determined your visitor's identity from what you are told, don't believe it! Assume the caller is lying, and make him or her prove his or her identity. Insist on two or three items of clear identification. This applies even to a person in police uniform. Even though a police officer with a warrant, if denied admittance, can forcibly break into your home to carry out the task described in the warrant, you are always entitled to see proper identification.

If a visitor in another kind of uniform appears—to read your gas or water meter, for example—ask him or her to wait while you call the utility company to determine if readings are being taken in your neighborhood that day. Beware the door-to-door salesperson. Call your neighbors on either side to see if they have been visited. If they haven't, the caller will probably be gone by the time you put down the phone.

Don't trust any casual or unexpected caller. Ask for a business card, driver's license, or other identification. If you are still suspicious, suggest that he or she call for an appointment. An unexpected caller might actually be a potential thief or a con artist (see Chapter 30).

Many legitimate businesspersons—such as insurance agents, stock-brokers, and others making direct-to-the-public sales—will call you in an attempt to set up an appointment to see you at home. If you do agree to an appointment, be sure to check with the caller's office, using the phone directory number rather than the number given to you by your visitor.

DON'T BE LURED AWAY FROM YOUR HOME

The ways in which burglars or confidence tricksters attempt to gain admission to homes are legion. Many of them are equally skilled at getting people out of their homes.

For example, a friend's purse was stolen at a restaurant. The next day she received a call from a woman who apologized profusely and said that she had taken the purse by mistake. The caller indicated that she was at work, but that if the victim would care to meet her at a convenient location, she would be happy to return the purse. Naturally the friend was overjoyed at the prospect of recovering her property—to the point of even buying lunch for her benefactor. When she returned home, she found her home burglarized. It had been entered by an accomplice, who had duplicated a key from the one in the victim's purse.

CHANGE LOCKS

Whenever you mislay or otherwise lose keys, get your locks changed. Entirely new hardware is rarely necessary, and usually a residential lock's pins can be realigned on the site by a locksmith and a new key made at minimal expense.

The friend in the preceding story had a hard time recovering her loss on her homeowner's insurance because there was no evidence of forced entry. She could have avoided the burglary simply by keeping her house keys separate from any form of personal identification. Failing that, she should have taken the trouble to have had her locks changed immediately. She still might have lost her TV, stereo, silverware, and Oriental rug, but at least she would have had an easier time recovering on her insurance because there would have been proof of a genuine forced entry.

HOUSEHOLD INVENTORY

Another form of burglary insurance is a household inventory. Set aside a Saturday or Sunday to go through your home, room by room, and list every item therein, noting also the approximate value of each and, where possible, serial numbers. Use a form like the inventory sheet provided on pages 30–31. Items of extraordinary value such as jewelry, silverware, and art objects ideally should be photographed. Then take the inventory to your insurance agent, and discuss your existing coverage, not forgetting items that need separate scheduling for adequate insurance protection.

Keep this inventory list up-to-date, and retain a copy in your safe-deposit box or nonbank depository or with a trusted friend or relative. Do not keep a copy at your office or anywhere else where it might serve as a shopping list for a burglar.

A growing number of people seem to prefer the nonbank depository type of safe-deposit boxes for protection of valuables. These facilities scorn traditional "banker's hours," with many remaining open around the clock. Many are better protected at night than are banks, which typically would not be protected by armed personnel. Perhaps even more important, however, is the convenience of round-the-clock access to your valuables.

Another way to protect your belongings is to etch your name or Social Security number onto them with an electric pen that has a hard tip capable of scratching most metals. These pens are easily available—call or visit your local police, because many let you borrow these instruments.

Identifying all items of value that are likely to be stolen, such as TV sets, stereo equipment, radios, cameras, binoculars, and so forth, makes life a lot tougher for burglars. One reason is that etching makes your household goods harder to fence. Also, etched goods must be defaced to remove evidence of etching. An honest person wouldn't buy such defaced property, and fences would either not handle damaged goods at all or only at ridiculously low prices. Finally, if a thief is caught with etched merchandise in his or her possession, he or she is practically convicted then and there. Some thieves are smart and will avoid etched property entirely—that's really the best reason for etching household items.

Some of your assets defy etching, though, and other protective measures may be necessary to protect you from the thief. Paste copies of expensive gems may fool your adversary; marking the skin side of furs (after loosening the lining, of course) may lead to a recovery if your mink or sable is retrieved by police. Some auto manufacturers may attach unique identifiers to automobile components. You may protect your vehicle's highly desirable, easily removed accessories by etching. CB radios, T-tops, and similar items particularly need such protection.

Operation Identification is a nationwide project encouraging citizens to mark their property as a tactic to combat burglary and theft. In one large city, burglary rates for Operation Identification households were eighteen times lower than those of nonparticipants. A major reason for the success of projects like these is the character of the participants. People who join a communitywide crime prevention activity like Operation Identification are the same ones who install adequate lighting and good dead-bolt locks and who use and practice overall self-protection.

Many people attach decals to their front doors advising welcome and unwelcome visitors that the premises are protected by a patrol service, alarm service, or other type of security device. In many cases, the homeowner purchased only the decal. No other services or devices were added to the security of the structure. A really accomplished thief would not be fooled—it's his or her profession. A young thief, just starting to make his or her mark, might. So the decal won't hurt anything and may help. However, it is usual for a thief to return to the scene of the crime, and if once burned, the thief just might feel he or she has a score to settle with you.

Many police departments throughout the country have specialists who advise on ways to improve the security of homes and belongings. By all means, make use of these services, if they are available to you. If no such service is offered, check with newspapers, civic leaders, elected officials (particularly those who may be facing an election soon), and others who may be in a position to spread the protective message. Don't underestimate the power of radio talk show hosts either.

HOME SAFES AND SECURITY CLOSETS

Some people take the sensible precaution of using a small safe to protect valuable items. It can be especially effective against fire. However, most home safes can be physically removed by a skilled and determined burglar and thus do not offer a great deal of protection against theft. Also, most such safes cannot protect items like furs.

Some of these objections can be overcome, of course. A small safe may be hidden, bolted to the walls or floor, or otherwise made a permanent addition to a structure. Setting the safe in concrete in the basement is one approach. Installing an alarm on a safe is also a fine additional security measure.

One excellent alternative to a safe is the home security closet. This requires lining the floors, walls, ceiling, and door of a suitable space with fire-retardant or fire-resistant material and then providing adequate locks for the entry door. Usually an ordinary closet door must be rehung because the hinges of most are on the outside. Bracing or otherwise strengthening the door frame also will usually be necessary so that it cannot be removed along with the door.

It would be difficult, if not impossible, to construct a safety closet with walls as impenetrable as those of a safe. Thus, an alarm system is highly recommended. Fire-resistant building materials and adequate locking devices are generally available, so an accomplished handyman could fabricate his or her own elementary security closet. For a more sophisticated installation, consult a general contractor or bank vault/safe installer.

CREDIT CARDS

Some years ago a friend had the unpleasant experience of having his pocket picked, losing a case containing a number of credit cards and his driver's license. Fortunately he kept a record of his credit card numbers. He immediately notified each of the companies of the theft by telephone and followed the calls with confirming telegrams. This prompt action assured that the card issuers were notified before any bogus charges. Thus, our friend was spared any liability for subsequent purchases made with his cards. This freedom from responsibility was important, because in the time required to notify all the firms honoring the credit cards, charges amounting to tens of thousands of dollars were made on his stolen cards.

The impact of credit cards on the nation's economy staggers the imagination. The available purchasing power is enormous. Total credit limits are more than twice as great as the nation's entire amount of money in circulation. Furthermore, the increasing use of credit continues unabated. Even the federal government is "going plastic." Federal agencies expect credit card transactions by citizens to reach $6.5 billion by 1991. Anytime and anywhere there is this amount of assets, you can bet the ranch that the sharpies and the frauds are on the scene, standing ready to fleece the unwary sheep—and that might be you.

Three elements of credit card fraud that directly affect you: the use of counterfeit credit cards, the use of stolen cards, and the fraudulent use of valid credit card numbers without the physical presence of the card.

Much of the impact of counterfeit cards has been countered by technological advances. Those birds and monogrammed globes you find on credit cards are not there to amuse your children. They are laser-generated holograms, which are incredibly complicated and relatively expensive to produce, but the card companies realize that the costs of unrestricted counterfeiting would be many times greater. While the credit card frauds may be stymied at present, you may be certain that these cheats are working hard to produce look-alikes designed to separate you and your money one way or another.

A less expensive way for a credit thief to rip you off is the tactic used against my friend by the pickpocket, to wit, stealing his cards. For the high-volume thief desiring a larger take, vendors sell lists of valid credit card numbers. These are obtained in a number of ways—pickpockets, robbers, burglars, prostitutes, addicts, light-fingered juvenile delinquents, and dishonest bank employees (who may have access to the account numbers of every one of the bank's credit card holders).

Most of the activity on a fraudulently obtained credit card occurs during the first three days of a thief's possession. After this time, the card will be sold to another, or switched, perhaps by an accomplice, for a valid card. From this point, the whole operation repeats.

As you might expect, Fridays are big days for credit card frauds. Not only is the legitimate cardholder filled with the "thank God it's Friday" spirit, but the card abuser has two extra weekend days of grace to cheat and steal before Monday's "business as usual" stems the tide of weekend theft.

Another group that, at the very least, abets the frauds is the merchants. Their contribution is primarily apathy and carelessness rather than duplicity. Ask yourself this question: When was the last time that your signature on the credit card was compared with that on the credit voucher you just signed? Merchants also fail to check the list of canceled cards or the card pickup bulletins that the credit firms issue.

Others are cheats, though. They print extra billing sets using your card. They also cheat by violating no-authorization limits imposed on certain transactions. Still other merchants are outright crooks. They will buy stolen cards, borrow or steal lists of valid card numbers, and run them through as legitimate transactions, often splitting the take with the list vendor.

Con artists may attempt to steal from you through the abuse of your credit cards. They may represent themselves as "security officers" checking into illegal use of credit cards. They will ask you for your card number in order to "verify" it. *Do not give your card number to anyone.* Call the issuing company immediately.

Many cardholders themselves are credit card criminals. They have only fifty dollars to lose, so they might think they can get away with simply reporting the loss of their card, and then they go on a spending spree. If they report the loss early enough, they will probably not be charged the fifty-dollar fee. Of course, it may be their bad luck to attempt a charge through one of the so-called point-of-sale terminals. These are tied into a central computer that updates customer's balances as transactions occur. These smart "real-time" systems, which are increasingly replacing the slower manual systems, make things tougher for the credit card sharpie, as any such charge would not be honored.

Protection of Your Credit Cards
To protect yourself, you need to compile the following information for each credit card in your possession:

- Card name (American Express, Visa, MasterCard, etc.).
- Issuing organization (such as a bank or other financial institution).
- Your account number. (This is usually the longest number on the card. There may also be a four-digit number elsewhere on the face of the card; include this number, too.)
- Telephone number for reporting lost or stolen cards. (The number may be displayed on the card.)
- Street address for sending confirming telegram of card loss. (The operator responding to your telephone call may advise you that this is an unnecessary expense; on the other hand, your copy of the confirming telegrams could be worth a great deal of money. Should you decide not to confirm in writing, at least get the name of the person to whom you made your loss report.)

You will probably be issued a new card by your credit card company. In many instances, you will find that you haven't lost your card at all, but merely misplaced it. In this event, you need only destroy the old one and begin using the new one. You may be contacted by the security department of the issuer, particularly if a number of bogus charges are made to your card. Of course, you should cooperate.

Finally, when you get your bill, it may include some bogus charges. You should call these to the company's attention, but at the same time pay only the charges you legally owe. Federal law allows you to challenge charges for which you are not responsible, but will not exempt you from paying your just debts.

If You Lose a Credit Card
Report the loss of a credit card as soon as you realize the loss has occurred. Follow religiously the instructions you receive from the issuing firm. File a report with the police within twenty-four hours of the loss or theft.

Credit Card User's Responsibilities
You have probably been screened by the issuing company, and they have determined that you are a responsible person. As a responsible person, you are morally, if not strictly legally, required to do certain things.

Examine all charge tickets before you sign them. In this way, you can prevent errors or frauds before they become a fact. Retain your copies of billing sets and compare them with charges on your statements. There is a time lag, and there may be a considerable passage of time from the charge until it finally appears on your statement. Hang on to your billing copy until you pay it. Don't make the mistake of feeling that you have met all your financial obligations merely because you have paid your statement in full. In this manner, you can protect yourself from charges that appear on your statement but that aren't yours. Don't leave your credit cards lying around the home, office, or especially, your auto. Don't carry your cards in your billfold along with your cash and driver's license. In this way, you won't risk losing everything at once.

An essential safety precaution is to destroy any unneeded duplicate cards. You are liable for the first $50 of illegal charges made before you report the theft or loss of a card. Insurance is available for reimbursing losses stemming from credit card theft or loss.

Services that will register all your credit cards are available. Should your cards be stolen, you call a twenty-four-hour toll-free number, and the service will immediately notify all issuers of your credit cards. All liability is ended as soon as you report the loss, including the $50 of illegal charges. Related services—including emergency cash and prepaid airline tickets for a stranded traveler, requests for replacement of stolen cards, and warning labels to affix to each credit card—are also available. There is no limit on the number of credit cards covered by these services, so the more cards you carry, the more advantageous the service is to you.

BANK SERVICES

Never carry a lot of cash with you or keep cash around the house. Pay by check, or use charge accounts. If you have to carry "mad money" or emergency funds, use traveler's checks—you don't have to be traveling to cash them. Also, never leave checks lying around. Lock up or hide your checkbook in the home.

One particularly valuable service offered by banks is a safe-deposit box. There are also specially secured twenty-four-hour-a-day nonbank depositories. Such locations are often better secured than bank boxes— many have around-the-clock armed guards—and they have the convenience of being accessible at any time, day or night. Some nonbank depositories have the added advantage of being owned outright, rather than leased. Virtually all these services are insured for the protection of clients, and when you arrange for this type of service, it would be an excellent tactic to investigate the extent of any insurance coverage.

Both kinds of deposit boxes are recommended for storing valuable jewelry, stock or bond certificates, and all other valuable or important documents.

One document that should *not* be placed in a safe-deposit bank box is the letter of last instruction, commonly known as your will. The law in many states requires that a safe-deposit box be sealed upon the owner's death in order to safeguard its contents. It may take several days to obtain the necessary court authorization to open the box, so your family would not have immediate access to your will.

The best strategy may be to leave it with your lawyer. Attorneys have special safes that can easily accommodate and secure these documents, and they can make your will available when necessary. It is a good idea to keep a copy of your will at home in a strongbox or in another relatively secure place, perhaps a nonbank depository.

Securities and Valuable Documents

It is sometimes difficult to determine which items should be protected by off-premises secure storage, whether a nonbank depository, a bank safe-deposit box, or your attorney's custody. Your attorney should be consulted in this regard. However, there are a few basic rules.

Do not assume that stock certificates are not negotiable simply because they are issued in your name. Stolen stock certificates are frequently used as collateral for loans, which are then, of course, defaulted. Obtaining reissuance of a stock certificate to replace one that has been lost or stolen is a laborious and time-consuming process, for the issuee is generally required to post a bond to indemnify the transfer agent for any possible loss resulting from the sale of the stolen certificate. There is also the distinct possibility that you might suffer a loss from being unable to sell a security while it is tied up for months in a reissuing process.

The best means of protecting certificates is to leave them in your safe-deposit box, in a nonbank depository, or in the custody of your broker. A federally sponsored insurance program protects investors from loss, within specified limits, of securities held by brokers for their clients. This arrangement certainly is preferable to keeping certificates around the house, even though recovering on the federal insurance can embroil you in an administrative nightmare during which your assets may not be liquid.

Bearer bonds and other freely negotiable securities should be avoided in favor of registered equivalents. If, however, there is no alternative to your owning bearer instruments, they should be kept in a bank safe-deposit box or specially secured twenty-four-hour nonbank depository.

HANDGUNS

At least 200 million firearms are to be found in the homes of Americans. Perhaps 60 million of these are handguns. There is one thing upon which all parties to the handgun controversy agree. Guns are deadly. About thirty thousand Americans die each year from gunshots due to suicide, homicide, or accidents. One side of the controversy feels that it is important to preserve the constitutional right of citizens to keep and bear arms, and that the ultimate protection of the people of this country may rest in the protections available within the family unit. The other side insists that the loss of lives that this nation experiences as the result of handgun use and abuse is too dear a price to pay. They also point out that other constitutional rights have been modified to accommodate changing conditions. Maryland recently passed legislation outlawing the manufacture and sale of cheap handguns known as Saturday night specials.

Regardless of our handgun biases, we all realize the awesome potential that these weapons have for taking human life. One study charted the use of handguns in the commission of three serious crimes—rapes, robberies, and assaults—over a ten-year period. Of more than sixty-five million of these attacks, handguns were involved in more than eight million. A gunshot victim will spend more than twice as long recuperating in a hospital as the average patient—sixteen days as opposed to seven or eight.

The overwhelming reason for having a handgun in the home is protection. Unfortunately, far more persons in the home are injured by firearms than are intruders. Half of all firearms fatalities occur at, or very near, the victim's home. Tragically, 40 percent of the lives lost are those of children, many of whom found where "Daddy kept his pistol."

The NRA, the organization that is most celebrated for its defense of our rights to keep and bear firearms in a legal manner, offers a number of commonsense suggestions for safeguarding a weapon kept in the home. This group suggests that firearms be kept out of the reach of children, the immature, and the irresponsible. Unloaded firearms should be kept under locked protection in the home. Under most circumstances, it is preferable that the weapons be out of sight, providing less temptation to a thief who may be in or see into your home. Similarly, the ammunition for your weapons should be locked and out of sight.

There is but one reason for keeping a loaded gun in your house—protection of lives, and maybe protection of assets. If it is assets you feel the need to protect, consider securing them in a bank or, more conveniently, a nonbank depository. Some authorities suggest that the safest way to keep a weapon in the home is to store the weapon and the ammunition apart from one another. Without question, this will provide a safer home environment most of the time. The exception, of course, is when you really need the weapon for the protection for which it is intended. This is a difficult decision. Several companies manufacture steel-sided combination- or key-locking handgun and shoulder-fired weapon containers that can be bolted to the wall or to a closet shelf so that a weapon will be difficult for an intruder or a child to get his or her hands on. Ask yourself this question: What do I fear more than the possibility of my child's having access to a loaded firearm? Your answer to this question, based upon your knowledge of your family, will dictate your course of action.

If you have a weapon in your home, you have the responsibility of assuring that it is available to you when you need it but, at the same time, denying it to anyone for whom you wish otherwise. Toward this end, you should take these precautions:

- Keep it unloaded until you're ready to use it.
- Keep all ammunition in boxes that are clearly and accurately marked to describe the contents.
- Keep your finger out of the trigger guard unless you are ready to fire.
- Provide childproof storage.
- Check your weapon before you use it or store it.
- Open the action immediately upon removing the gun from its case or rack.
- Ensure that your weapon is free of rust.
- Be able to say, with absolute certainty, whether or not your weapon is loaded.
- Treat all weapons you touch as if they were loaded.
- Carry your weapon with the muzzle under control at all times.
- Ensure that the bore is unobstructed.

- Make certain that all metal parts are free from accumulations of heavy grease.
- Be certain that the action works freely.
- Be certain that the trigger works freely.
- Be certain that the safety works properly.
- Be certain that you carry *only* the ammunition for the weapon that you are carrying.
- Ensure that your weapon is cased, or its action opened, whenever entering or leaving an automobile.

However comforting a gun might be to you, it is important that you realize that it also increases the chances of an accident or homicide. Unless you and every member of your household know exactly how to keep and use a firearm safely, it is probably more hazardous to you than to any intruder.

At the very least, all firearms in the home, including hunting rifles and shotguns, should be equipped with lockable trigger guards. You should remove the firing pins of guns that are part of a collection or are used for decorative purposes. A firearm capable of and intended for firing should be maintained in good condition—it may be needed on short notice.

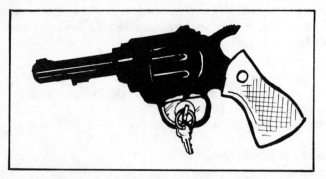

A trigger lock will prevent accidental discharge of a firearm.

Similarly, firing a defective weapon could cause injury or death to the user. Any firearm should be stored in a safe place, away from children's prying eyes and where an intruder would be unlikely to find it.

ENTERING AN EMPTY HOUSE

A woman of our acquaintance who lives alone has a rather active social life. When she leaves the house, she invariably leaves a fifty-dollar bill on a lamp table near the front door. She reasons that an intruder would be satisfied with this take, which is sufficient to purchase a round or two of most popular drugs. She believes that the thief will be deterred from carrying off the other valuables in the house. More importantly, she earnestly desires to avoid confrontation with an unwelcome visitor.

Another tactic she uses is based upon most burglars' wish to avoid confrontation as earnestly as their unwilling hosts. When she arrives home, she presses her own doorbell. This should cause any intruder to vacate promptly. She was once asked what she would do if an intruder answered her ring. She had learned the name of an individual who lived on the next street, with a house number the same as her own. Her intention is to tell the intruder—if he or she answered the door—that she was seeking that person. She reasoned the intruder just might check the address in a telephone book, and satisfied that her story was plausible, remain to continue the theft. Perhaps he or she would remain long enough for the arrival of the police, which she would have called.

There are two lessons to be learned from this extraordinary woman. First, through proper planning, it is possible to react correctly to virtually any problem one might face. The second lesson is that you may encounter an intruder in your own home, and if you do, you are in substantial danger.

If You Encounter an Intruder

Even if you have done a good job of securing your home, it is entirely possible that you may return and see someone inside. Your first impulse will almost certainly be fright, plus a desire to protect your possessions, leading to the temptation to yell or otherwise bring on a confrontation. This is not a particularly good idea, if only because you very well might be directly between the intruder and his or her only certain avenue of escape, in which case you become an obstacle to the intruder's survival—a very dangerous situation if the intruder is armed or of a desperate or violent disposition.

A far better way of handling the situation is to go as quickly and as quietly as possible to a neighbor's house and call the police. Then call a neighbor on the other side, and enlist his or her assistance in watching your house while you await the police.

LIVING ALONE

The person living alone, especially a woman, should always have a telephone in the bedroom and a strong lock on the bedroom door. The bedroom door lock should be key-operated, and a duplicate key should be left with a friend or a trusted neighbor in case of sudden illness or other event necessitating quick assistance. (For additional information, see Chapter 10.)

WOULD YOU BE ABLE TO RECOGNIZE A BURGLAR

It is doubtful that you would be able to recognize a burglar if you saw one. First of all, you would probably be expecting a hardened criminal, not the fuzzy-cheeked teenager who came around last week to see if you wanted your lawn mowed. You would not believe that the Swiss Army knife your nephew carried could be used to remove a small pane of glass from a front door, providing access to the night latch (as opposed to the dead bolt lock, which would provide more reliable protection). You might even think that the nice kid who dates your daughter really did buy the stereo he gave her for her birthday.

REPORTS TO POLICE

There may be a time when you will find it necessary to report a burglar or other type of criminal to the police. These are the things they will be interested in hearing from you:

- "I wish to report a crime."
- Where—the address or the street intersection.
- What—the type of crime, injury, shots, fight, etc.
- Who—the persons involved, including how many, descriptions.
- How escaping—if in an auto, license number, make, and model.
- Where to—the direction headed, whether the car turned around, toward what nearby intersections, etc.

Interior Security: A Checklist

1. Don't admit anyone into your home unless you know the person or the person has properly identified him- or herself and the reasons for calling on you.
2. Use a chain lock and a rubber doorstop while identifying a stranger at your door.
3. Check and double-check the identification offered by strangers.
4. Do not assume that a stranger in uniform is legitimate. Verify the stranger's status with his or her employer.
5. Before you admit a stranger who has phoned ahead and made an appointment to see you at home, verify that the stranger is employed by the organization that he or she claims to represent.

6. Be particularly wary of people claiming to be building or fire inspectors or door-to-door salespersons. Check with their place of employment before admitting them.

7. Beware of people attempting to get you away from your home.

8. Turn on at least one radio when you leave your abode so that an aspiring thief will think someone is at home.

9. Make an inventory of all your belongings, and keep your list up-to-date. Protect the list carefully.

10. Use the nonbank depository type of safe-deposit boxes for the convenience of around-the-clock access to your valuables.

11. Identify appropriate items of property with an etcher or similar device.

12. Consider installing a security closet in your home.

13. Plan your course of action in the event that your credit cards are lost or stolen. Destroy unneeded duplicate cards.

14. Always examine your monthly credit card billings for fraudulent charges or errors, and then follow all proper notification procedures.

15. Never keep a lot of cash in your home or on your person.

16. Never leave checks lying around, and lock up or hide your checkbook in the home.

17. Use a safe-deposit box or specially secured nonbank depository for storage of valuables and valuable documents.

18. Equip any firearms you own with lockable trigger guards.

19. If you surprise a burglar or robber in your home, cooperate—don't try to be a hero.

20. Install locks on your bedroom door, and have a telephone in the room.

INVENTORY SHEET

Be certain to include cars and items such as lawn mowers that are not normally kept inside the home. Cover attics, basements, garages, and so on. Prepare supplemental lists for contents of lockboxes.

Room: _____   Date: _____

Item	Serial Number	Date Purchased	Cost	Approximate Value	Amount of Insurance Coverage	Comments

3
Alarm Systems

"I was sound asleep, and all of a sudden this clanging sound woke me up," Don said to the fire marshal. "I didn't know what it was at first, but then it occurred to me that it must be the alarm. The alarm had just been installed that day! We lost a lot, but thank God, no one was hurt."

An alarm system does two things: it detects, and it communicates. The alarm system that might be installed in your home would probably function both as a fire alarm and as an intrusion alarm. So-called panic buttons would add a third function, that of manually communicating the need for some sort of assistance. The system could also have other functions; it could monitor a vital piece of equipment, such as a boiler or wine-cellar temperature control.

A chronic problem with alarm systems, especially home alarm systems, has been a very high false alarm rate. In most of these cases, however, the false alarms have been due to misapplication of sensors or to user error.

FIRE DETECTION

You're more likely to have a fire than an intruder, so this chapter covers that function of the alarm system first.

Fires develop in four stages: the incipient stage, the smoldering stage, the flame stage, and the heat stage. There are a number of sensors on the market designed to detect the fire in one of these stages. Naturally, the earlier in its development that a fire can be detected, the better are chances to limit the damage it will cause. No sensor, however, is the proper one for all applications.

In its incipient stage, a fire doesn't produce any smoke or flame. It does, however, generate products of combustion. These are microscopic particles that rise on air currents.

Ceiling-mounted products of combustion or ionization detectors have an inner chamber that contains a small amount of radioactive material. An outer chamber is open to the air. Air passing through the outer chamber becomes ionized or electrically charged. When particles of combustion enter the chamber, the electrical charge between the two chambers is altered, setting off an alarm. This is the most expensive of the sensors available. Due to its method of detection, it may false alarm in a dusty atmosphere.

The photoelectric detector will alarm during the fire's smoldering stage. Smoke or visible products of combustion enter the detector's sensing chamber and interrupt a light beam, causing an alarm. This type of detector, however, is not good for areas that may normally have smoke, such as a kitchen or near a fireplace, since it will cause a false alarm if excessive but nonthreatening smoke is produced. These units are relatively inexpensive.

A rate-of-rise or temperature-change detector senses the rapid temperature increase that occurs as the fire progresses from the smoldering to the flame stage and then to the heat stage. A heat or fixed-temperature detector, which activates when the air around it reaches a designated temperature, may be incorporated with the rate-of-rise detector into a single unit. The fusible link on the sprinkler heads of an automatic sprinkler system also operates on the heat-detector principle.

Generally, no single type of detector is used exclusively in a home. For example, you wouldn't use a smoke detector in a kitchen, where burning toast would set it off. The heat detector is usually used in conjunction with a sprinkler system and is inappropriate for most home uses. But one or another of these systems provides a relatively inexpensive means of fire protection. Many insurance companies discount premiums for customers who install them.

INTRUDER DETECTION

There are two broad categories of devices to detect intruders: point protection, and space or volumetric protection. Point-protection devices detect an intrusion through a specific location, such as a door or window, or even through a wall. Space-protection devices detect movement within a particular area.

The magnetic contact switch uses a magnet to hold one of the contacts of a switch away from the other. Contact-switch sets can be either surface-mounted or concealed. When the magnet is attached to a door or window and the switch is attached to the door jamb or window frame, the magnet keeps the two switch points apart. When the door or window is opened, the magnet can no longer hold the spring-loaded contact to prevent the switch from engaging, and the alarm sounds.

One problem with this type of device, however, is that it can be defeated by using another magnet to hold the switch contact, even though the door is opened. Using a balanced switch set or a concealed contact set can overcome this vulnerability.

Virtually everyone has seen foil tape, the silver-colored strips attached to store windows. A low-voltage electrical current flows through the tape. If the window is shattered, the broken tape interrupts the flow of electricity and causes an alarm to sound. This type of protection, while relatively inexpensive, is far from foolproof. Given sufficient time, an intruder can cut the glass without breaking the foil, and thus gain entry into the building without alarming anyone.

There are shock or seismic detectors, which provide protection for the specific objects upon which they are mounted, such as walls, safes, file cabinets, and closets. They also guard window frames, glass panes, and patio or French doors. Any vibrations resulting from pushing, knocking, banging, touching, or kicking will upset the equilibrium of the device and sound the alarm.

A fourth type of device, the pressure detector, uses something like a doormat that is installed under the carpet inside the doorway, in a hallway, or on stairs. An individual's weight on the mat brings electrical contacts together and activates the alarm. Some self-opening doors at supermarkets and discount stores employ the same principle.

A fifth type of detector uses a beam of light shining across the inside of a door or window to a photoelectric sensor, like those that prevent some elevator doors from closing on passengers. The alarm is activated by the interruption of the beam. In the past, however, an intruder could circumvent a photoelectric sensor merely by stepping over or sliding under the beam or by shining a light beam at the sensor. To overcome this vulnerability, many photoelectric sensors use infrared light, which is invisible to the human eye, moving at a given number of bursts of light per second between the transmitter and receiver, marking an advance over "visible spectrum" light sources. In either case, a transmitter sends a ray of light (visible or invisible) to a receiver and sounds the alarm when the light's passage is interrupted or changes rhythm. This technology can also be used for space protection by placing the transmitter at one end of a room and the receiver at the other.

The ultrasonic sensor generates high-frequency sound waves. Such a device can protect a three-dimensional teardrop-shaped area approximately twenty-five feet out from the sensor. These waves are too high in pitch to be heard by the human ear, so any intruder is unaware of their existence. When the waves bounce off him or her, their pattern is altered, activating the alarm.

Unfortunately some individuals—and many pets—are irritated by these ultrasonic "noises," and these sensors are also subject to false alarms caused by the flapping of a curtain, a ringing telephone, or even a rush of air from a heater starting up. Loud noises in adjacent spaces might also activate such a system. Two sensors, tuned to different frequencies, may cause false alarms if installed too near one another.

A similar system uses electromagnetic microwaves rather than sound waves. While this eliminates the irritation to sensitive ears, if not installed correctly these waves will penetrate walls, rather than bounce off them like the ultrasonic waves. This means that movement in the next room or outside the building can activate such a detector.

A passive infrared sensor detects an intruder's presence by sensing his or her body heat. There are numerous detection patterns available with passive infrared sensors. These range from a ceiling-mounted, 360-degree-radius sensitive unit; to a long narrow zone; to a curtain to protect a wall.

When an intruder enters a protected space, the passive system can detect the alien presence immediately. A person's body temperature will be roughly twenty-five degrees hotter than the ambient room temperature. As with all intrusion detection devices, there are drawbacks with a system such as this. Obviously, such a system would be impractical for protecting an area often frequented by people. Animals, heating ducts, electric motors cycling on and off, and even a television receiver would be capable of emitting sufficient heat to affect the operation of a passive infrared detection device. Similarly, these devices become less reliable at temperatures approaching normal body temperature, because at such levels the body's temperature would be masked by that of the surrounding air.

Audio detectors are used to protect entire rooms. These consist of wall- or ceiling-mounted microphones. The detectors are set at a certain noise level, and if that level is exceeded, a signal is sent to a central station. One problem with this system is that central station personnel can eavesdrop on the installation at any time the system is activated.

In an effort to overcome the problem of false alarms, which affect the reliability of space detection sensors, manufacturers now combine them into single units, known as dual technology sensors. In these, a passive infrared sensor is paired with an ultrasonic or a microwave sensor. Both sensor types must trip before an alarm is sent. In effect each half of the unit questions the other half, compensating for the weaknesses in each technology that result in a false alarm.

In most cases the sensors are connected by wires to the alarm control unit, which houses the alarm's off-on switch and the part of the system that sends the alarm signal to an on-site sounder or out to a response center. In more and more cases, systems are now using wireless technology, in which each sensor has a small battery-powered transmitter that sends the signal to the control unit. An internal alarm in the system will tell the control unit if the sensor's battery is running down or if the sensor is being tampered with.

No single sensor technology can be considered effective on its own, thus the concept of concentric rings of security. A free-standing residence may have magnetic contact switches on all exterior doors and windows, space protection in hallways or areas where there is a large amount of peripheral glass, and a magnetic contact on the door to a silver cupboard. A good system uses a mix of techniques so that if an intruder defeats one layer of protection, he or she will be caught by the next one.

Again, a qualified professional can help determine which mixture of sensing devices is best for you.

COMMUNICATING THE ALARM

Once a detector has sensed a fire or intruder, the system must be able to communicate that fact. The detectors can be set to activate a bell or siren on the premises or to activate a radio that transmits an emergency message. Many installations use a telephone line to transmit a signal to a contract central station where personnel on duty telephone the police or fire department to respond.

As stated at the beginning of this chapter, false alarms—as high as 90 to 95 percent of all alarm signals transmitted—have traditionally been a major problem. The alarm industry has made a determined effort, through improving the products and through dealer, installer, and user education, to reduce this rate.

In many communities, police and fire departments no longer will accept alarm signals directly from residential or most commercial alarm-control units. Instead the signal must travel from the protected premises to a contract central station, where personnel then telephone the appropriate public agency. Even with this, in many communities the police allow a given number of false alarms per year and then assess a fine for each alarm call exceeding the limit.

Also, some radio-operated devices violate Federal Communications Commission (FCC) regulations. Bells or sirens that go off repeatedly can cause neighbors to ignore the alarm—perhaps at the time of a true emergency. This is unfortunate, because most alarm systems signal in the immediate area, rather than transmit to a remote location.

An earlier edition of *How to Protect Yourself from Crime* said that the opening up of many communities to cable TV puts an exciting possibility for alarm systems on the horizon. Cable TV can connect homes to the system on a two-way basis, bringing TV into the home and transmitting emergency information from the home to a central station on the same cable. Signals transmitting through cable TV are less expensive than those sent over telephone lines. Not only fire and intrusion detectors but respirators, boiler-level monitors, or virtually any type of sensor could be made part of such a system. This promise remains; reality, however, is still some time away.

ARMING AN ALARM

Unfortunately, regardless of how well planned and sophisticated your alarm system may be, there is always one problem: you. You are in and out of the home all day. Whatever the alarm system, it must be told when it's you "turning it on" and especially "off" and when it's someone or something else. This is called arming an alarm.

Obviously you don't want your alarm to "cry wolf" every time you enter the house, so you must be able to turn it on and off and enter your home without triggering the alarm or compromising its effectiveness at detecting an intruder. Following are the three arming (or disarming) mechanisms generally used with an alarm system.

The key-armed system, as the name implies, uses a key to arm and disarm the system so that you can enter the house without creating an uproar. This can be inconvenient if your arms are full, and moreover, if your keys fall into the hands of a burglar, your entire alarm system becomes valueless.

Push-button keypad arm/disarm systems are more convenient and secure than key-operated systems, but if the combination of your push-button system is discovered, perhaps by a person with some long-range optical device or a repairperson who, while working in your house, discovers the system's control panel in a closet with the arm/disarm code taped to it, then the security of your system is compromised.

A time-delay feature is commonly available in intrusion alarm systems. Time delay enables a person to set the system from inside the residence and then have a predetermined amount of time to exit through an exterior door before the system actually is armed. On reentering the premises, the time delay gives a person a similar length of time to shut off the system before an alarm is activated. In these cases the system will sound a prealarm tone within the premises to remind the authorized person to disarm the systems and to let an intruder know that the building has an alarm system.

The greatest false alarm hazard lies in your failure, on reentering your protected premises, to properly identify yourself to the alarm control unit either with a key or your code number within the allotted time.

HOW TO BUY AN ALARM SYSTEM

When you set out to purchase an alarm system, begin by seeking objective advice. Many police crime-prevention units and fire departments have alarm-system specialists. Your casualty insurance carrier probably has a specialist who will be able to not only recommend special equipment but also tell you how to lower your insurance premiums by installing it. If you aren't satisfied, contact a master locksmith. He or she may be an impartial source of information for you and may steer you away from some of the fly-by-night firms. While you have his or her attention, get the locksmith to replace all your night latches with dual-keyway dead-bolt locks equipped with one-inch-long throw bolts. Of course, alarm manufacturers and installers will be more than happy to offer advice. It may not be totally objective, but if it is the only advice available, it is better than nothing.

Some alarm systems are worse than none at all. You obviously cannot afford a system that delivers only false security. In selecting a source for your alarm system, remember that the equipment is complex and that you must have good service available for it. Generally, this would rule out buying a system by mail, from a distant supplier, or from any firm other than one that specializes in the sale, installation, and service of such systems.

As a rule, the longer the warranty, the better the system. But if the system is issued by a "here today and gone tomorrow" firm, the warranty, regardless of terms, is suspect.

Check parts inventories. If a critical part is available only from a single manufacturer located in Yokohama (or Yonkers, if you live on the West Coast), you may be asking for trouble. If your dealer doesn't have the parts on hand, your system may well be useless to you.

Certain features should be a part of your alarm installation. Among these is the system's self-check capability. This enables you to check the "health" of your alarm system and be certain it is in proper operating condition. Of course, you must remember to make these capability checks. Even if you should forget, an alarm with a low-battery warning signal will probably jog your memory.

One feature that is most important is provision for emergency power for your system if normal power supplies are interrupted. In the event of a fire, which may have interrupted your power, your auxiliary power could save your life. If an intruder deliberately interrupts your power, you could prevent loss of property, injury, or death at the hands of the thief.

Some auxiliary power systems employ nonrechargeable batteries. If yours is such a system, it is absolutely essential that you follow the manufacturer's recommendations for periodic testing to assure the viability of the auxiliary power system. Rechargeable batteries can malfunction, too; if your system has this type of backup, you should determine proper testing procedures. It may be necessary to write to the manufacturer of the batteries to obtain the information, since the equipment installer may not have it or may represent that the batteries never need replacement.

Make certain that your alarm's signal horn sounds loud enough to be effective. Ideally, the horn should be mounted in the attic and sound through a vent to the outside.

Before you sign any contract, try to arrange to see an actual installation performed by your chosen contractor. Check for appearance and workmanship and customer satisfaction.

Finally, check with your tax accountant. Certain types of installations may affect the tax treatment you receive when you sell your home. A through-the-wall installation, for example, although more expensive initially, might be the least expensive choice in the long run.

CAVEAT EMPTOR

Let the buyer beware! The proliferation of crime is perhaps matched only by the proliferation of opportunists preying on the near-paranoid reactions of some sectors of the public to their safety. The use of scare tactics to sell alarm systems is deplorable. Be especially cautious about such an approach, particularly from unsolicited direct-mail advertising or door-to-door salespeople. Don't allow yourself to be stampeded into immediate action. The best response to a now-or-never sales approach is "Never!"

Beware of installation charges. If at all possible, contract a firm price, installed. Many unscrupulous operators will quote absurdly low prices (for, as a general rule, absurdly inferior equipment) plus a "nominal installation fee." Your definition of *nominal* may be a lot different from theirs.

Many buyers will have to finance an alarm system. The dealer may offer to arrange financing for you and hint that he or she will carry your note. In most instances, the dealer will carry it no further than the discount window of the nearest bank or finance company, where it will be sold to the bank or finance company, which becomes its holder in due course. The dealer is then responsible for carrying out the contract, but the holder in due course is entitled to payment. If the dealer defaults on the contract or even skips town, you will probably still be liable to pay the holder in due course. You could very well get fleeced under such an agreement, especially if there is collusion between an unethical contractor and an equally unethical holder. Thus, it is absolutely necessary to deal with a completely reliable, ethical contractor.

Take care, too, in selecting the communication phase of an alarm's operation. Find out how the alarm signal will be carried from the protected premises to a response point. If you buy a system that the installer programs to dial the police or fire department with an emergency message, make sure your town's departments will respond to such calls. Be certain that radio-transmitted messages don't violate FCC regulations. Check out every angle before you sign anything.

One last word of warning: Beware of service contracts. While good service from a reliable contractor is the main consideration when you purchase an alarm system, contractual prepayment for this service may be unnecessarily expensive. Be certain to investigate total costs before making your commitment.

KEEP YOUR SECURITY SECRET

Several paragraphs earlier, this chapter advised that you examine an alarm installation put in by your selected contractor. However, once your alarm is operating, you should not return the favor. The less that people know about the steps you take to secure your property, the more secure you will be.

Do not advertise everything you do to make your home secure, because virtually every defensive action you might reasonably take can be countered, subverted, or bypassed when a would-be intruder knows exactly what to expect. This may seem a little contradictory when viewed in light of the earlier suggestion that decals be used. But the fact is that many houses display alarm decals when, in reality, they are not protected by an intrusion alarm. Unfortunately the professional burglar generally knows this—and, furthermore, knows how to determine for sure whether such a system has been installed. Should there actually be a system, he or she possibly can circumvent it if he or she has the time and absence of disturbance required. On the other hand, the amateur burglar is generally not as well schooled in the mechanics of theft as the professional and thus is more easily deterred by exterior warnings.

Your interest is obviously to avoid a rip-off, be it administered by the old pro or the tyro. You thus need to strike a balance between deterrence and total disclosure—revealing enough to discourage the random burglar, but not so much that you make it easy for the skilled and determined pro who singles you out.

It is important that you be guarded in what you tell people. Suppose a neighbor has a valuable collection of cut glass, which is stolen while she is out of town. Later, when the police crack the burglary ring, it is discovered that one of its members is a young man who lives in the neighborhood. It is hardly coincidental that the neighbor remarked that the thieves "seemed to know exactly what they were looking for."

Alarm Systems: A Checklist

1. Give serious consideration to installing alarm systems or panic buttons and to providing auxiliary power sources for them.
2. Use exterior deterrent signs, but do not reveal anything about your security system.

3. Avoid disclosures that indicate you own items of special value.
4. In considering alarm systems, investigate multipurpose systems that detect both fire and intrusion incidents.
5. Some equipment may be adaptable to other detection and communication functions, for example, monitoring items of equipment such as boilers, wine-cellar coolers, and heaters.
6. The ionization type of fire detector is probably the one best suited for most home uses; however, it is also the most expensive.
7. An intrusion system might employ several types of detectors, depending on your requirements. Explore these possibilities with a qualified professional before settling on an alarm system.
8. Alarms are communicated locally (for example, a bell rings) or remotely (for example, transmitted via phone lines to the fire department, police, or commercial alarm central station). Be diligent in determining which is most cost-effective for you.
9. Seek objective advice in determining your alarm needs. Fire departments, police, or insurance carriers often have specialists who can advise you. You may also find that installation of certain equipment can reduce insurance premiums.
10. A warranty is only as valuable as the person or entity guaranteeing its performance. Beware of the "here today, gone tomorrow" installer. Beware, also, of high-pressure sales tactics. Beware of unspecified installation charges. Beware of service contracts—some are good, while others add considerably to the total cost of a system.

4
Your Telephone

Every day for the past six years in a Miami suburb, Barney, eighty-five, has dialed the same telephone number just before 9:00 A.M.

"Good morning, Dorothy," he says to police complaint clerk Dorothy.

"Good morning, Barney. Have a nice day," says Dorothy.

This daily conversation is part of a police service originally named Reassurance Program and later called Operation Good Morning. Police say the program, started in 1968, has saved the lives of elderly people living alone. The more than fifty people on the other end of the line say it helps save them from loneliness.

The telephone is a marvelous invention that has been adapted to many uses, most of them benign like the one in the opening example. But the telephone is also an instrument of crime—in fact, possibly the most widely used criminal instrument. The cardinal rule is that you should always use your telephone on your terms, not those of the caller. Moreover, never talk on the phone unless you do so willingly.

GUARD WHAT YOU SAY

A very important lesson of telephone security is never to tell anyone anything that you don't wish him or her to know. For example, a caller who asks for the man of the home should never be told that there is not one or that he is out of town. Far better to tell the caller that your father or husband "is asleep right now and will return the call when he awakes."

43

It is vitally important that this lesson be taught to children, as well as ingrained as a habit in adults.

Every caller who hangs up when the phone is answered is not a burglar attempting to find out if there is anyone at home. Telephone equipment can malfunction; calls can be disconnected; callers can become flustered when an unfamiliar voice answers the phone and hang up as a reflex action. However, there is always the possibility that the caller is a would-be burglar, and it is a good idea to assume just that and to check immediately to see that all doors and windows are properly secured.

SUMMONING EMERGENCY ASSISTANCE

Emergency numbers for police and fire departments should be available at every phone in the home; however, under the stress of emergency, people sometimes lose their composure to a point where they forget how to take otherwise routine actions. Thus, as a further precaution, place a small note (using a label maker is ideal) on the phone saying, "Dial 0," or, "Dial 911," if your local police department has adopted this special emergency number. And if you or yours are highly excitable, it isn't a bad idea to include your own address as well!

TELEPHONE-ANSWERING MACHINES AND SERVICES

A telephone-answering service is a valuable security measure, especially if there is no one at home for considerable periods of time. Under no circumstances should the service tell callers that the user is out of town or away from home or give a time when he or she is expected to return. Likewise, the service should be instructed not to reveal that the operator is, in fact, an answering service, but rather to give the impression that the operator is a houseguest, a visitor, or a domestic employee.

Telephone-answering equipment that delivers a prerecorded message and records a caller's message can be used advantageously as a security device if you always indicate in your messages to callers that you expect to return home shortly. For a strictly residential phone, it is usually a good idea to use first names only to avoid revealing your surname to a caller who doesn't already know it. Similarly, it isn't necessary to repeat the phone number the caller has reached.

If you travel extensively, consider buying an answering device that enables you to receive your messages from another telephone. In this way, you can return your calls, even from far away, and still avoid revealing that you are out of town.

Incidentally, don't be alarmed if you get a lot of calls in which no messages are left. Many people simply object to talking to a machine and hang up as a result.

TELEPHONE SECURITY WHILE AWAY

The telephone is one service that you should never have discontinued while you are away from home. A temporary disconnection message delivered by a special operator is a clear indication of one of two things: you haven't paid your bill, or you are out of town. You don't wish to leave either impression on callers.

NUISANCE AND OBSCENE CALLS

It is a crime, under federal and most state laws, to make harassing or obscene telephone calls. For these offenses, penalties of up to a year in prison or fines of up to $1,000 are prescribed. Typically a state law might provide, "It shall be unlawful for any person or persons . . . to telephone another person repeatedly, if such calls are not for a lawful business purpose, but are made with intent to abuse, torment, threaten, harass, or embarrass one or more persons." Similarly, the statute generally prohibits obscene phone calls, described as any "lewd, obscene, or lascivious remarks, suggestions, or proposals, manifestly intended to embarrass, disturb, annoy the person to whom the said remarks, suggestions, or proposals are made."

If you do receive an obscene call, hang up and forget it! Most obscene calls are isolated, one-time occurrences, possibly placed by someone dialing numbers at random. Often the callers are adolescents, putting forth a display of bravado for their friends, although annoyance callers can also include neighbors, acquaintances, or fellow employees. Should the calls continue, do not broadcast your displeasure, but do maintain a log of the calls, and notify your telephone company immediately. The methods the telephone company will use to bring an end to this nuisance can vary widely depending on the particular equipment serving your home. Thus, you shouldn't feel shortchanged if your nuisance-call problem is handled differently from your neighbor's.

Under no circumstances should you attempt to debate or get into a shouting or cursing match with your caller—unless, of course, you should be requested to do so by telephone security personnel to assist in their investigation. But be certain who is requesting your assistance, since some obscene callers get someone to call first and pretend to be from the phone company. To excite or inflame anyone, especially one demonstrating such antisocial behavior, is a certain invitation for a repeat performance. The most effective means of avoiding a series of obscene or nuisance calls is to get an unlisted number. However, this is a most inconvenient tactic.

Like making obscene calls, taping or otherwise deliberately gaining access to a telephone call without permission from one of the parties to the call is a crime. Law officers, of course, may do so, but only when they have a court order covering a specific telephone for a specified time.

TELEPHONE SURVEYS

The use of the telephone for sales purposes, often through the gimmick of a so-called survey, can be very annoying to some people, but unless there are serious misrepresentations, it is not illegal. There are, however, other types of "surveyors" who are gathering intelligence information for illegal purposes, and thus it pays never to give confidential information over the phone unless you are certain about the person to whom you are speaking. Do not, for example, spontaneously answer questions concerning where you work, what you look like, your income, any items of value you may have in the home, your sexual habits, or anything else of a personal nature. You may wish to respond to legitimate surveys, but do so only after you have determined that their objectives are worthwhile and beneficial.

KNOW YOUR CALLER

Occasionally you may get a call from a person claiming to be a peace officer or government agent making an inquiry. Unless you are subpoenaed by a court of law, you are not required to give information. Generally, as law-abiding citizens, we do have an obligation to cooperate with law officers, but that obligation does not extend to cooperating unquestioningly with people who merely represent themselves as such.

When you get a suspicious call of this nature, insist that your caller visit you in person so that you can properly examine his or her identification. Say something like, "May I call you back? It isn't convenient for me to talk right now." Then return the call at his or her office, having first checked the number against the telephone directory to assure that the caller is actually who he or she claims to be. If you are unable to verify the telephone number in the directory, call the directory number of the agency that the caller claimed to represent. If the agency cannot identify your caller, report the incident to the police, and give them the number that your caller gave you.

A final warning: Beware of the caller who claims that your name has been given as a reference. You have an obligation to your friends and neighbors not to reveal information about them indiscriminately. You should always arrange to return a call requesting such information so that you can first verify that the call is legitimate. Alternatively, you might check with the acquaintance who submitted your name as a reference, or you might agree to respond only to a written request for such information.

It is, incidentally, a good idea to advise anyone whose name you give as a reference that you have done so, so that time will not be taken up unnecessarily in double-checking a call received on your behalf.

CELLULAR TELEPHONES

Cellular telephones generally have a great deal of security built in, much of it resulting from the nature of the system's "cells." Cities are divided into hexagonal areas, which provide a number of frequencies to vehicles and pedestrians traveling through them. As phone users leave one cell, powerful computers switch their calls to the neighboring one without interruption.

Stealing a cellular phone would be relatively easy, but using it would not. Built into the system are theft-prevention protocols, including user-entered code, without which the system will not operate. If, however, a careless owner leaves the code on a scrap of paper behind the sun visor, the thief can make all the free calls he or she wishes.

Even in this instance, there would be some protection for the owner. When the cellular service provider was notified of the theft, the service could be deactivated.

Portable cellular systems are a convenience, but are harder to protect. Batteries are expensive (roughly four times the monthly base charges), and AC chargers cost as much as a bestselling novel or a moderately priced dinner.

Although the cellular phones are designed with security in mind, be aware that today's state of the art is tomorrow's garage sale. In protecting this convenience, you must be aware that someone will devise a method or piece of equipment to defeat your safeguards. You must continually upgrade the safety, sanctity, and security of your loved ones and your possessions.

UNWANTED PHONE CALLS

Many of us are bothered by unsolicited telephone calls from telemarketing firms. While some people find this a satisfactory way of shopping, others find it highly intrusive. People who wish to have their names removed from telemarketing lists should send their names to:

> Telephone Preference Service
> Direct Marketing Association
> 6 East 43 St.
> New York, NY 10017

There may be a time lapse before your name is removed, however, since their lists are updated only four times a year.

Your Telephone: A Checklist

1. Do not reveal personal information to strangers who phone you—especially information about when you will be away from home.
2. Impress upon children the importance of not revealing personal information to callers.
3. A caller who hangs up without speaking may be attempting to determine whether or not the house is occupied. Use such a call as a reminder to check your security measures.
4. Keep emergency numbers available at all telephones. If you are easily excited, have your address available as well.
5. Consider a telephone-answering service or a telephone-answering device.
6. Never record precise information about when you will be away from home, or when you anticipate returning, on an answering device or relay such information to an answering service.
7. Never cancel your telephone service when on vacation or an extended trip.
8. Report repeated nuisance or obscene telephone calls to the telephone company.
9. Do not talk to or debate with an obscene or nuisance caller.
10. Beware of people who contact you by telephone, seeking information about you, your associates, your friends, or your neighbors. Call back to verify that you are talking to a person having a legitimate reason for requiring such information.

11. Cellular phones have a number of built-in protections. Your failure to utilize them will often result in losses.
12. Be aware that emerging technology, particularly that designed for the illicit market, may require you to upgrade your security system from time to time, in order to maintain your security.

5
Your Dog

Police Dog Patrol Officer Block today reported the fourth burglary suspect catch in a week by her dog, Max. Officer Block said she was cruising in the area of a burglary at the Southside Liquor Store, about two-thirty this morning, when she saw two suspects running, arms loaded with bottles. She said that when she shouted for them to halt, one stopped, but the other continued running. She sent Max after the man. Max quickly overtook the suspect and brought him down.

Along with the boulder rolled across the mouth of the cave, the dog was high on the list of people's first security measures. The dog became an ideal pet, subservient to its owner but inherently possessed of an urge to protect its owner's property.

If you don't already have a dog, you should give serious consideration to owning one. Dogs have considerably better-developed senses of hearing and smell than do people, enabling them to detect the presence of would-be intruders well ahead of humans. By giving warning of the presence of an intruder, a dog allows you time to take some sort of protective or defensive measures—while at the same time letting the intruder know that his or her presence has been detected, which will usually be enough to make him or her move rapidly elsewhere. When an intruder does not move along, most dogs rarely hesitate to attack, whatever the odds, in defense of their owner's and their own territory.

YARD DOG OR HOUSE DOG?

The question of whether a yard dog or a house dog is better from a security standpoint is moot. A yard dog is likely to be a better deterrent, but a house dog is likely to be a better defense if an intruder actually gains entry to your home. Consider also that yard dogs are more susceptible to being poisoned or to being set loose by would-be intruders.

What breed of dog you select is largely a matter of personal preference. In general, a large dog is better than a small one. Perhaps even more important than size, however, is the dog's "voice"—the louder and more persistent its bark, the better.

Like the wolves and foxes from which they descended, dogs are nocturnal animals by nature, but they often adapt to the rest patterns of their masters. Nevertheless, their innate sense of nighttime hunting makes them particularly valuable protectors while the rest of the household is asleep.

For this and other reasons, dogs have been used in police work for almost forty years. In the 1960s, as the nation's "drug culture" developed, dogs were used to detect drugs. So effective are they for this purpose that the U.S. Customs Service considers them to be the very best means of locating drugs. "Dope dogs" are a select group, with senses of smell half again as great as that of the typical pet dog. These dogs are recruited not from fancy kennels, but from urban animal shelters, for the customs officials prefer the streetwise city dogs.

SPECIALLY TRAINED SECURITY DOGS

This discussion has purposely avoided referring to specially trained security or attack dogs, because—except in extraordinary circumstances—these animals are not suitable for the average household. They are expensive, they require periodic retraining, and they must have constant practice and handling in order to retain their specialized skills.

A security-trained dog who gets loose and roams the neighborhood can become a menace, especially if it becomes confused in unfamiliar territory. Lack of regular training and handling can cause such a dog to totally or partially lose some of its "fail-safe" restraints. Thus, only people who are subject to extortion or kidnapping or other very serious crimes, or those who keep extremely valuable items around the house, should consider these animals. Even then, owners should be aware of the risks involved, including the very heavy liability they face if the dog attacks under the wrong circumstances.

If you consider this type of animal, for whatever reason, be sure to investigate thoroughly before buying. The recent increase in crime—especially burglaries, rapes, and robberies—has given rise to a spate of charlatans who pass off ill-trained or untrained animals as trained security dogs. These dogs can be real hazards, both to their owners and to other people, especially to young children. So enlist the aid of a veterinarian, the head of the police dog squad, and other qualified individuals in selecting the source of an attack dog.

Undoubtedly, a large dog is a formidable foe and can, under certain circumstances, be excellent security. It can, however, be a neighborhood menace if not properly tended. If you must, risk alienating a neighbor who owns such a dog, but do not allow any dog to imperil you and yours. Humane shelters will pick up not only neglected pets but also nuisance animals, and may also subject the owners of offending animals to sanctions.

At the risk of offending the millions of cat owners in the world, we must state that cats do not offer much security protection, both because of their small size and because of their lack of bark. The dog's primary weapon is definitely its bark—and it's probably just as well if that bark is worse than the dog's bite.

Your Dog: A Checklist

1. A dog can be a very effective security weapon, and you should seriously consider owning one if you do not already.
2. The dog's principal use is to serve as a warning device and as a deterrent.
3. A specially trained security dog, especially an attack dog, is not a good idea except in the most extraordinary circumstances. Always investigate very thoroughly before buying such a dog.
4. Training of the owner/handler of a security dog is as important as training of the dog.
5. Specially trained security dogs must be regularly schooled to maintain their skills.
6. The best-trained dog will not be effective if its handler cannot interpret its actions.
7. Dogs that have been improperly trained may often be more vicious and uncontrollable than totally untrained dogs.
8. Unscrupulous kennels may sell you an overqualified dog, knowing you lack the ability to handle the animal. When you try to return the dog, an inferior animal may be offered as a substitute at the same price.
9. Large dogs provide excellent security when carefully trained and monitored.

6
Domestic Employees and Invited Strangers

Detective Sergeant Ernest LaFay today announced the arrest of four persons, including a former newspaper carrier, in connection with a series of daylight burglaries in Newport.

This chapter might seem at first something of an anachronism in that the use of employees in the home isn't as widespread as it was even a few years ago. But don't pass it over simply on the grounds that you don't have home help, because the fact is you do—in the form of newspaper carriers, milk deliverers, dry cleaners, baby-sitters, repairpeople, pest control personnel, decorators, carpenters, remodelers, meter readers, mail carriers—the list goes on and on.

All these people who call on you have one thing in common: they have the opportunity to pick up a key ring or leave one of your doors or windows unlatched. Many of them may know where items of value are kept in your home. And at least one of them, the domestic employee—whether full- or part-time—knows practically as much about all of your household habits, idiosyncrasies, income, savings, and just about all other aspects of your and your family's lives as you yourself do. And there is one more important thing that all these people have in common: the ability to develop a real or imagined grievance against you, which frequently offers an even greater motive than greed for placing your person or property in jeopardy—that of revenge.

How do you protect yourself against such risks? Let's break the problem down into categories, dealing first with people who will be in your home regularly, sometimes when you yourself are not there. This group includes domestic employees such as cleaning staff, maids, children's nurses or governesses, chauffeurs, gardeners, and baby-sitters.

CHECK REFERENCES

Remember this primary rule of thumb: do not let anyone into your home unless you know who he or she is, and always check references completely. If a prospective employee can't provide references, then do not hire that person under any circumstances. If it is warranted, have a background investigation conducted by a reputable investigative agency, plus a retail credit check if this was not a part of the agency's investigation.

If you still are left with even the slightest doubts, it is worth going to the trouble of requesting a records check from the police departments of areas where the applicant has previously lived. You may encounter some difficulty here because right-of-privacy legislation can prohibit police from releasing information about people from their files. Do your best, however, because the truth of the matter is that an alarming number of applicants for domestic positions are actually subjects of outstanding arrest warrants!

Wherever possible, your investigations should extend also to immediate members of the applicant's family. A maid whose spouse has had a number of convictions for breaking and entering is hardly an ideal employment prospect.

BONDING

The bonding of domestic employees is not cheap, but the benefits should outweigh all other considerations if you are really concerned about security. In simple terms, this fidelity bond is a contract in which a bonding company will protect you against dishonest acts by an employee. A bond differs from insurance in that it covers acts that the principal (the person bonded) has control over, while insurance covers uncontrolled events such as accidents and acts of God. Your insurance carrier can provide you with information or bonding employees. Bonding also presents a valuable by-product in that it requires yet another investigation into the background of the employee, one independent of your own.

EMPLOYMENT AGENCIES

One word of caution about domestic employment agencies: some are very good, and some are not. So, if you deal with an agency, investigate it as thoroughly as you do the individual it recommends. A relative or friend who has had a satisfactory experience with an employment agency is certainly be the first person you should contact when checking out an agency. Consult the Better Business Bureau for complaints. Check past editions of the Yellow Pages (at the phone company or at the library) to determine which firms have stood the test of time.

BABY-SITTERS

Typically baby-sitters are either neighborhood teenagers or mature women, quite often widows whose own families have already been reared. Nice and trustworthy as they may seem to be, either type of baby-sitter can present genuine security problems.

You may have known the teenager down the street all your life, and you may be a friend of the family. What you may not know, however, is that the teenager's boyfriend or girlfriend happens to have a drug problem and that, despite any objections on your part, as soon as the children are asleep, this person may pay a visit to your house and remain until just before you are expected home.

The mature woman, on the other hand, might pose quite different problems. Just suppose, for instance, that she finds her Social Security benefits or the small pension she receives totally inadequate to meet her living requirements. It is common sense to recognize that she will have the same survival instincts that we all do.

This discussion is not going to try to assess which type of baby-sitter offers the lesser risk, because in the long run that always depends on the individuals involved. But there is no doubt at all that the best baby-sitter is the indulgent grandparent or the favorite aunt. Beyond that, in the selection of a baby-sitter, your best defenses are thorough investigation of whomever you choose and trusting your own instincts.

A clear understanding with the teenager's parents, and perhaps an occasional check by them, can be a valuable measure, as is a request to a neighbor to keep an eye open on your behalf. These simple steps might prevent someone from backing a truck up to your door and stripping the place.

Regardless of the age or experience of the baby-sitter, you must leave clear, complete, and written instructions, including such things as where you will be and the phone number; the name and phone number of a neighbor to contact in an emergency; the name of your physician and directions to the nearest hospital emergency room; fire, police, poison information hot line, and other emergency phone numbers; medications that should be administered and instructions on administering them;

location of aspirin, bandages, or similar supplies; any callers who might be expected to drop by; or other pertinent information. Ask the sitter for help in compiling your list of information.

WHEN AN EMPLOYEE LEAVES

When a domestic employee leaves your employ, the first thing you should do is check your home inventory, and the second is change your locks. Even if you do not have a spare door key somewhere around the house—even if you've never left a key lying around the house that might have been duplicated—change the locks.

Although you may keep most of your valuables in a safe-deposit box or nonbank depository, over the years you will have developed special hiding places at home for valuable items you use on a day-to-day basis. Your one-day-a-week maid will have found these caches. Fearing apprehension, he or she probably hasn't taken anything while working for you, but now that he or she is leaving, he or she may feel the time is right. Periodically changing your hiding places will minimize this risk. Don't simply trade places—change them. Move the good silver from the dining room to a spot in the kitchen or to an upstairs bedroom; transfer the diamond ring from the powder box in the bathroom to the toe of an evening shoe in the closet. And make absolutely certain that you change the entry on your home inventory list; otherwise, there's a chance that you yourself will forget the new location. Also, find a new and secure spot for the inventory list itself, unless you want to present a burglar with a nice, neat shopping list.

REPAIRPEOPLE AND THE LIKE

Irregular or semiregular visitors to your home—such as in-home salespeople, movers, carpenters, painters, decorators, and repairpeople—offer the greatest security hazard of all. Almost without exception, they are in the employ of others who are providing services to you under some form of contractual arrangement, which means that you have virtually no control over the selection or investigation of the people who will actually be entering your home. The work they will be doing usually involves some degree of confusion and probably a lot of inward and outward traffic of people and commodities. Unless you can be everywhere at once, with eyes in the back of your head, you are vulnerable.

Consequently, well before the first worker shows up, you need to do some careful planning. Move jewelry, furs, art objects, valuable documents, and any other portable valuable items to your safe-deposit box, security closet, or some other secure place, such as a neighbor's home. Do the same also with liquor, wine, medication, firearms, and small appliances.

Deal only with reputable companies or individuals that can furnish ample references, and check those references. Make certain that someone you trust is present to check up on things and generally to look after your interests. If you plan to do it yourself, do not do the job alone—it is more than a one-person task, at best, and there is much truth in the old saying about safety in numbers.

Consider engaging a security guard or patrol service in the evening hours, especially if there are ladders lying around the yard or windows that must remain open to allow paint to dry. If you move out until the work is completed, hire a house-sitter or security guard to protect your residence.

Once things get back to normal, make an inventory check. Someone may have had the opportunity to duplicate a key that might have been found in your home. Consider changing your lock cylinders—including window locks, if you neglected to remove the emergency keys from their places near those locks. Indeed, these are ideal occasions for making a thorough check of all your safety and security procedures.

Domestic Employees and Invited Strangers: A Checklist

1. Remember that domestic employees have a great opportunity to case your home and thus offer valuable information to burglars.
2. All domestic employees—including baby-sitters—should be thoroughly investigated before being hired.
3. If you use domestic employment agencies, investigate them thoroughly.
4. Consider fidelity bonding for domestic help and all employees, including baby-sitters.
5. Do not permit baby-sitters to entertain visitors in your home.
6. Ask a neighbor to keep an eye on your house when it is entrusted to a baby-sitter.
7. Leave clear and concise instructions for baby-sitters; be sure you include appropriate phone numbers.
8. When a domestic employee leaves your employ, inventory your valuables, change your locks, and change hiding places of valuables.

9. Do not provide route people and service personnel with information about your comings and goings.
10. Workers in your home pose a particular hazard. Deal with only the most reputable contractors and service organizations. Arrange for someone to check on the progress and activities of the workers in your absence.
11. If workers will be in your home for more than one day, or if more than two or three will be present, remove or lock away all easily movable items of value, including not only jewelry and cash but liquor, drugs, firearms, and important documents.
12. If work done in your home seriously impairs your security measures, consider hiring a guard or a security patrol during the hours of darkness.
13. When work in your home is completed, make an inventory check, change locks, and reevaluate all of your security and emergency measures.

7
Lighting Your Home

*"My front porch light had burned out about a week ago," said
John D. Sloan, of 1828 Iroquois, "and I never got around to
changing the bulb. When I came in, that sucker was waiting
for me, and he really rang my bell. I must have been out for
forty-five minutes. I guess I was lucky, though; I only had
about ten bucks on me, and a lot of that was in change. He
took every nickel of that, though, he sure did."*

The first chapter of this book conceded that, given enough time and
determination, an intruder could break into your home regardless of any
security measures you might take. By not lighting your house and
grounds adequately, you give a would-be burglar one of his or her two
basic requirements: time. Theoretically, at least, a burglar has all night to
break into a dark house in a darkened setting.

The first principle of lighting for security is that it should be sufficient
at all wall openings (doors, windows, exhaust ducts, crawl space ac-
cesses, and so on) to deny an intruder the cover of darkness. The second
principle is that all other hazardous areas should be adequately lighted.

BUILDING EXTERIORS

In a few instances, two lighting elements on opposite corners of a house
can be sufficient to illuminate all openings in the walls of a structure.
Generally, however, some degree of lighting on all four sides of a house is
necessary to light it adequately. In all cases, the lighting should be
intense enough that your neighbors could see someone trying to break in,
but not so strong that it disturbs their peace and privacy.

Properly positioned spotlights will illuminate the sides of a house.

If your street is adequately lighted, so much the better. If it is not, consider lighting your entranceway in such a manner that you can be certain not to encounter any unpleasant surprises when you arrive late at night. Lighting as much of the front part of your property as possible at night is an excellent idea, and you should encourage your neighbors to do the same. Report any burned-out streetlights, and ask your neighbors to do this, too.

Shadowed Areas
Trees, heavy shrubbery, bay windows, cul-de-sacs, enclosed porches, and many other natural or constructed features of a house create shadowed areas, and these should be illuminated. In many cases, adequate light can be provided by burning a lamp inside the house close to a window. In most instances, however, one or more windows or doors will be so situated that they are effectively screened from the street and from neighbors as well, irrespective of interior lighting. These are principal areas of vulnerability, which definitely should be specially illuminated.

Alleys
Alleys servicing the rears of homes are invariably hazardous areas. They are usually dark, not particularly well kept, and seldom traveled at night, and they often harbor large numbers of trash containers, which can afford shelter to the would-be intruder. Typically such alleys are separated from houses by solid fences to hide their unsightliness, but fences also prevent residents from seeing what's going on. Adequate illumination of the entire area between the fence and your house is thus essential for maximum security.

The placement of trash receptacles should be considered, especially by the homeowner who has an adjacent alley. They offer excellent hiding places from which a would-be intruder—or even a passerby acting on impulse—could well surprise and overpower you, especially at night. Few people bother to lock the house door behind them on short trips to the garbage can, so if you are at home alone, you might put off taking out trash until morning or, alternatively, call a neighbor and ask that he or she watch you on your errand.

Adequate lighting is essential not only in alleys but also adjacent to the gates of all fences around your property.

How Much Lighting Is "Adequate"?

If you can see well enough to read a wristwatch by the light around any of your house's high-hazard exterior areas, then the lighting is satisfactory from a security viewpoint. If you can't easily read your watch, or if you have any doubts, add lighting.

INTERIOR LIGHTING

Many people are in the habit of leaving a light burning in the front part of the house or in a front porch at all times during hours of darkness. There are both advantages and disadvantages to such practices. Certainly the front door should always be adequately lighted. On the other hand, a porch light left burning periodically, rather than all the time, indicates to anyone who may have been casing your house that you are out but that you expect to return soon; that might well cause a potential intruder to pass you by. Probably the best technique is to alternate lighting sources to confuse the would-be intruder.

Front-room lights raise similar problems. Without qualification, we recommend that lights be left on in apartments where only the light from under the door shows in the hallway. In a freestanding house, however, one look through the window into a well-lighted interior can show the potential intruder that the coast is clear. Drawing heavy drapes helps somewhat, and it is always a good idea to draw the drapes when you are home at night. The experienced burglar, however, knows that if the room were occupied, he could expect to see an occasional shadow when a person passed between the light source and the drape.

Here again it is six of one and half a dozen of the other. A burglar who has singled you out and spent time casing your house isn't likely to be deterred by a living-room light, whereas the random burglar merely looking for someplace—any place—to hit probably would be. So once more a general rule of thumb must apply: if in doubt, light the light.

During your normal movements about the house, turning lights on and off as you go, you give plenty of evidence that you are at home. Burglars are shy people, with absolutely no desire to meet their unwilling benefactors face-to-face. You can generally be assured that if you're at home and awake and moving around, a burglar is going to skip you. When you move about the house at night, use your lights for more reasons than to avoid falling over your furniture.

Night Lights

When you retire for the evening, do not turn off all the lights—lighting, remember, is a major enemy of the burglar. But do not leave the same lights on every night, because if your house is being cased, you do not want to give your adversary the aid and comfort of your being predictable.

When you have to get up during the night, make some noise and turn on some lights. It is unlikely that a burglar will attempt to enter your home while you are in it, especially if he or she isn't reasonably sure that you are asleep. When he or she is so assured, you in turn can be assured that the burglar has a very quick escape route firmly in mind, no matter where he or she may be in your home, and that the burglar will use it the moment he or she knows that you are awake and moving around. So give him or her all the encouragement to leave that you can by lighting lights and banging doors.

An outdoor light switch in your bedroom and perhaps in some other room in which you spend considerable time after dark is a good idea, as is a second switch to turn on all (or many) inside lights simultaneously. A sneak thief cannot sneak very well when bathed in light.

When your house is unoccupied during the hours of darkness, always leave some lights on—not the same lights every time, but enough to ensure your safety in returning. If you're going to be gone for more than a few hours, consider getting timers that will periodically turn lamps on and off. (Chapter 9, on home security while on vacation or an extended trip, discusses some of the dangers of timers. This discussion refers to your being absent for only a few hours.)

LIGHTING FOR PARKING AREAS

When you come home at night, be sure that you park in a well-lighted area. This is especially important if your routine is such that you return at the same time or at a predictable time each night. If the lights illuminating your garage or parking place aren't burning—and you know you left them on—keep right on going, and find a police officer or a neighbor to accompany you back to your home.

Good protective lighting is available today, and at such inexpensive prices that it is well within the reach of every homeowner. Timers capable of handling four or more separate instructions cost less than a pullover shirt. Several of these, distributed throughout the home, should be capable of completely confusing a nighttime prowler. Typically, these timers are equipped with a dry-cell battery, which will keep the memory intact in a power outage. The instructions of the timer will continue once line power is restored.

Another, even less expensive, item is readily available and can be a godsend when the lights go out. These are emergency lights that can be plugged into home outlets. If there is an interruption in utility power, these lights will provide sufficient light to leave the building. Most of them can also be used as flashlights when power in the home is normal.

Lighting Your Home: A Checklist

1. Provide sufficient lighting at all doors, windows, and other openings in the walls of your house to deny the cover of darkness to an intruder. Lighting is generally sufficient when you can read a wristwatch by it at night.
2. Light the front of your property, and encourage your neighbors to do the same with theirs.
3. Report nonworking streetlights immediately.
4. Illuminate all shadowed areas caused by trees, shrubbery, or construction features of your house, being particularly attentive to any doors or windows that can't normally be seen from the street or from neighboring homes.
5. If an alley serves your home, illuminate the entire area between the alley and your house.
6. Provide additional illumination for areas where trash containers are located, especially if they are adjacent to an alley.
7. Light all gates in fences surrounding your property.
8. Use lights when you move from room to room at night.
9. Leave some lights burning all night.
10. Draw your drapes at night.

11. When you get up during the night, turn on lights and make a bit of noise.
12. Return to a well-lighted house.
13. Use timers to turn lights on and off during brief absences.
14. If you believe someone is in your house when you return, go to a neighbor and call the police. Do not attempt to be a hero.
15. Park only in well-lighted places.
16. Prepare emergency lights in the event of an interruption in utility power.

8
Outside Security

. . . high walls, dead-end driveways, and heavy shrubs or foliage provide protective cover for night intruders. Such barriers should be lighted, shrubs trimmed, and areas generally opened to maximum visibility consistent with usefulness and aesthetics.
—The President's Commission on Law Enforcement and Administration of Justice, Katzenbach et al., Task Force Report: The Police *(Washington, DC: U.S. Government Printing Office, 1967)*

Security is certainly not the prime consideration in your home's outside appearance. A house surrounded by an eight- or nine-foot fence, brilliantly illuminated with high-intensity lighting, with closed-circuit television scanning a remote-controlled gate and with large, vicious dogs roaming the yard, looks more like a prison or a top-secret missile base than a home. Nevertheless, there are various ways to maintain good security without sacrificing aesthetics.

The U.S. Department of Justice estimates that 2.8 million violent crimes occurred during the course of burglaries over the ten years from 1973 to 1982. Burglars are extremely dangerous, because they are responsible for three-fifths of all rapes and robberies in the home and a third of all household assaults.

PERIMETER FENCING

If you'd like a decorative hedge or a neat fence surrounding your property, by all means have it. In fact, clearly delineating your property line could easily establish trespassing if a would-be intruder were apprehended on your property, though not at that time attempting to break into your house. On the other hand, you don't want a hedge or fence so high that someone on the street couldn't see an intruder attempting a break-in.

It is common sense to do whatever you reasonably can to limit access to your property. For one thing, an injury to a child taking a shortcut through your property could involve you in lengthy litigation. So install, and use, latches with self-closing mechanisms on all gates.

Whether gates should be locked or not is debatable. If the lot is very large, they probably should be, at least after dark. But locking the gates whenever you leave the house is a giveaway to criminals. One compromise might be always to lock all gates except those in front, which would be locked only at night.

DON'T FLAUNT VALUABLES

If you have valuable art objects, collections, antiques, or similar treasures, place them on inside walls where you and your guests can enjoy them, but don't place them where they can be admired, and perhaps coveted, from the street. Don't place them near windows through which they can be removed. At night, draw your drapes.

NO NAMES, PLEASE

A random thief, walking down the street, sees your liquor cabinet through an undraped window. The thief gets your name and address from your mailbox and calls from a nearby telephone booth. If you aren't home to answer the phone, you're likely to experience a break-in then and there. Your name on the mailbox is all too often an invitation to a confidence man or a would-be intruder to fabricate a plausible enough story to persuade you to open your door, so don't give him or her ideas. Of course, if you're not home, the thief will just barge in, and probably start with the liquor cabinet.

STRANGERS AT YOUR DOOR

A stranger knocking at your door may be practically anyone. He or she may have some sad tale designed to separate you from your money voluntarily. He or she may need only seven dollars, which together with his or her own cash will be enough to get the airplane ticket that will rush him or her to the sick mother's deathbed. A door knocker may offer to perform chores around the house.

But you cannot know in advance whether the stranger at your door is one of these. Your best answer to any door knocker's plea is "No, thank you," delivered, preferably, through a locked door. Of course, many door knockers are honest and trustworthy and are sincere in everything they tell you. You may live to regret your faith in humanity—or you may not be so lucky.

OTHER STRUCTURES

Toolsheds, garage back doors, storm cellars, greenhouses, and other appurtenant structures should be equipped with strong padlocks as well as top-quality hasps and hinges. If the hinges are exposed, weld them in place, or insert set screws through the hinges at an unexposed point.

SWIMMING POOLS

A swimming pool presents several security problems. A high, sturdy fence is essential to prevent children from falling into the pool. Even when it is fenced off, however, a pool poses some lighting problems.

All-night lighting around the pool might discourage nocturnal swims by strangers, but it is also a signal to a thief that your home is one of some affluence, especially if your neighborhood has few pools.

If your house is secure, considerable pool lighting might be advantageous. A yard dog or a neighborhood patrol service, or even an organized Neighborhood Watch group might, however, be able to deter visitors enough to enable you to bypass the use of attention-drawing lighting.

STRANGERS IN THE NEIGHBORHOOD

One aspect of being a good neighbor is getting to know your neighbors—and knowing who isn't your neighbor. A stranger going through the neighborhood, perhaps driving around and around the block, could well be cause for concern. If in doubt, take down the car's license number.

Don't demand every stranger's reasons for being on your street, and don't phone the police every time you encounter an unfamiliar face. But do take notice of any stranger, and make it clear that you are taking notice. If he or she doesn't have a legitimate reason for being around, he or she will probably keep moving—away.

One group of thieves achieved spectacular success by staging fights in residential neighborhoods. Spectators would get so carried away by the mock hostility that they wouldn't notice one or two members of the crowd stealing away to nearby open-doored houses and coming back out, loot in hand, in less than fifteen seconds.

Many thieves also market their hauls. Usually, the goods are not hawked in the same neighborhood that they came from originally. Rather, they gravitate to poorer neighborhoods, where people tend to ignore their neighbors, particularly those who may be involved in criminal activities. Such buyers are also less likely to question the origins of bargain-price goods.

If you notice strangers in your neighborhood taking undue interest in an automobile that you know to be the property of a neighbor, be on your guard. You may have to notify the police. The same is true if you should hear breaking glass or an explosive noise that you can't account for.

And if you do have to phone the police, take a few seconds to compose yourself and plan what you intend telling them. First of all, *where:* "1235 Fifth Street, between Maple and Sycamore." Second, you will want to tell the police *what:* "a burglary, I think. I heard breaking glass, and their alarm went off." *Who involved:* "two men, Caucasian, both average height, both wearing jeans and T-shirts." *Autos:* "They left with two pillowcases full of lumpy objects, drove away in a 1977 brown Pinto, Minnesota plates, first three numbers are 2G7." *Where headed:* "They turned south on Sycamore, probably heading for the interstate ramp."

In actual practice, it is unlikely you would be reciting a litany such as this one. The police officer answering your call will, perhaps, switch you to the proper bureau, to be handled by the individual answering the telephone. In any event, the police will be interested in the types of information outlined (where, what, who, autos, and where headed), and they will probably ask you the questions, rather than allowing you to go through your spiel. But you should be prepared, just in case.

TRESPASSERS IN THE NEIGHBORHOOD

If you see a prowler or a trespasser in your yard or a neighbor's, turn on lights—the more, the better. Should the prowler take off running, activate an alarm if you have one, and phone the police. Don't attempt to chase down a fleeing suspect even if you do have all the help you need. It is better—and safer—to try to keep a suspect in sight than to try to apprehend him or her. Leave the chasing to the law enforcement officers, who know what they are doing.

SECURITY PATROL SERVICES

This book periodically refers to neighborhood security patrol services. A good one is a valuable addition to your security arsenal, but it is only a supplement. A capable burglar will see to it that he or she is working behind the patrol officer. Also, your dog is as likely to sound its canine alarm at the patrol officer's approach as at the burglar's. A patrol officr should vary the starting point of his or her route and occasionally double back so that the times of his or her appearances at your place aren't predictable.

The costs of patrol services vary according to frequency and quality of work. But all things considered, a good security patrol is a worthwhile investment. Be sure to investigate the company thoroughly, check references, and determine if the patrol officers are licensed or commissioned by the police.

It's not neighborly to piggyback or free-ride on a neighbor who has a security patrol service, although a patrol officer showing up next door would no doubt help deter a burglar from your place as well. Why not return the favor and engage a different patrol service, doubling the exposure of officers around your property and your neighbor's?

GOOD HOUSEKEEPING IS GOOD SECURITY

If you let the shrubs outside your house grow high enough to conceal an intruder, you are asking for trouble. The same holds for large accumulations of limbs cut from trees or other piles of rubbish. Another safety precaution is to knock down and flatten large shipping cartons or other containers before you put them out with the trash.

Many of us enjoy wood-burning fireplaces, but we should learn not to store firewood at a point adjoining the house, where it might serve as a good hiding place for an intruder or as a stepladder up to our windows. It is far better to store the firewood some distance from the house.

An open garage and nobody home, or bicycles or expensive toys lying around the yard are an open invitation to a thief as well as an indication of a careless homeowner—the thief's delight. A lawn in need of cutting or a sidewalk of unshoveled snow is also likely to catch the burglar's eye, giving the impression that the house is unoccupied. The family may just be at work, but the daylight burglar won't care. He or she is as capable of entering your home and removing its valuables while you are out for a few hours as when you are gone for a few days.

Outside Security: A Checklist
1. Delineate your property line with fences or hedges.
2. Keep hedges or fences low enough for a passerby to see an intruder attempting a break-in.
3. Use latches on all gates.
4. Don't display valuable possessions so that they can be seen by passersby.
5. Don't display valuable possessions where they might be accessible to and removed through a window, without a burglar's even being inside.
6. Keep garage doors locked; key-operated automatic devices are especially recommended.
7. Remove your name from the mailbox.
8. Secure toolsheds, greenhouses, and other appurtenant structures adequately.
9. Protect swimming pools from unauthorized use.
10. Don't call unnecessary attention to a pool, especially if it is the only one in the neighborhood.
11. Be aware of—but not foolhardy with—strangers in the neighborhood.
12. While you are out, never leave your door unlocked even for a few seconds. Criminals can loot your home in less than fifteen seconds.
13. Do not attempt to apprehend a trespasser or prowler.
14. Augment other security measures with a neighborhood security patrol if it is called for. Vary security patrol check times, and investigate security patrol services thoroughly. Use a different patrol service from your neighbor's to maximize the number of patrol visits to the neighborhood.
15. Keep your grounds in good order: lawn mowed, walks shoveled clear of snow, and so on.
16. Don't store firewood against the house.

9
Home Security During Vacation

Henry Smith, twenty, of Los Lotos was arrested in connection with a burglary from the home of Thomas Washington last month. Mr. Washington reported that he had returned from a business trip and found a number of items missing, including a TV, a microwave oven, and a .38-caliber pistol.

Your home is most vulnerable to an intruder when there is no one home, and a family vacation increases that risk. Don't make it obvious that you are away.

DELIVERIES

Most advisory services, such as travel agencies, tell us that if we will be away from home for more than a day or two, we should be sure to cancel the newspaper and milk deliveries and even ask the post office to hold mail because accumulations of all these items are dead giveaways to potential intruders. Is this good advice? Well, if you follow it, you will have told five or six people your plans, including how long you will be

An accumulation of newspapers or other deliveries is a vacation giveaway.

away, and they all are likely to be people who know considerably more about you than you know about them. It is thus far better to let the deliveries continue and to arrange with a friend or neighbor to have them brought into the home. If there is no one of whom you can ask this favor, then definitely cancel all deliveries, notifying the delivery people and the offices supervising them.

DON'T KENNEL YOUR DOG

When you are away from home on vacation, try, if at all possible, to have a friend or neighbor feed your dog (and walk it, if it is a house dog) rather than lodge it at a boarding kennel. The dog can be extremely valuable as a deterrent around an otherwise unoccupied house.

AVOID THE SECOND-CAR GIVEAWAY

If you're a one-car family and you take that car with you on vacation, there's really not much you can do to prevent someone from noticing that there is no car in the driveway. You're in better shape, of course, if you customarily keep your car in a closed garage. If you are a two-car family on a motor vacation, your second car, parked in the same spot day after day, gives further evidence that you are away from home. Ask your neighbor to move it every day or so.

LAWN CARE AND SNOW REMOVAL

Keeping your lawn cut or the snow shoveled is essential when you're away from home for a long period and you want everything to appear normal. However, unless you usually use a professional cutting service, entrust vacation mowing or snow shoveling to a neighborhood child. Pristine snow is a certain giveaway that you're not at home, so at the very least, have someone put footprints in the snow on your walk and driveway.

LOCKING GATES

While a locked gate will deter a burglar, one locked at noon will assure him or her you're not at home. Ideally, your neighbor—who by this time is surely overworked in your behalf—would lock your gate in the evening and unlock it in the morning while you're away. If this can't be arranged, you probably will just have to play the odds and lock the gate, hoping a burglar will think twice about lifting the loot over the fence, particularly in broad daylight.

TAKE OUT THE TRASH

It is rare for an occupied home to have no trash for two weeks. Ask your neighbor to put out some trash on pickup days. If your pickup is not regularly scheduled, try to arrange for a neighbor to share his or her garbage service with you.

Don't shut down air-conditioning or heating equipment. A still compressor on a muggy night would be proof positive to a skilled thief that the house was unoccupied.

OTHER GOING-AWAY MEASURES

Use your safe-deposit box or nonbank depository for valuables, or entrust them with a friend or relative while you're away.

Pay your bills before you leave, or else leave checks with a friend or associate to pay them as they arrive in the mail.

If your home is equipped with an intrusion/fire alarm, have it checked before you leave, remembering that there is no need to tell the service representative why you want it checked. Check auxiliary power supplies, too.

Always leave an itinerary with a friend, neighbor, or relative who can reach you in the event of an emergency.

A few toys or garden tools in the yard will make it appear that the house is occupied. However, in order to perpetuate your sham, it will be necessary that your bait be changed and rearranged. Otherwise an experienced thief will see through your ruse. Encourage neighborhood children to play in your yard while you're away.

If you normally leave your drapes open, don't draw them just because you are going to be away. If, on the other hand, you habitually open them during the day and close them at night, ask your neighbor to do the same for you. If you can't arrange this, leave at least the ground-floor drapes open the entire time. You won't fool the experienced burglar, but perhaps you can introduce some element of the unknown.

LIGHTS AND TIMERS

Almost every recommendation made so far in this chapter involves the assistance of a friend or neighbor as the best means for protecting your property while you're away. Unfortunately, in many cases this becomes just too much of an imposition. Here are some other ways to make your house look lived-in.

If the lights go on and off at precisely the same time every night, the experienced burglar will notice it. There are inexpensive timers that vary the on-off times continuously, including a timer that activates a lamp (or any electric appliance) each time the compression motor of a refrigerator activates.

If a timer isn't practical, at least leave some lights on when you go. They will probably go unnoticed during the daytime, but the total absence of lights would certainly be apparent at night. Turn down the volume control of your telephone so a passerby won't hear the continued ringing of an unanswered phone.

Since most vacations take place in summer, air-conditioners also should have thermostats or timers. To conserve energy, you can cut back on the cooling level, but at least arrange to have the fan motor running. Make certain that timers and associated wiring are of sufficient capacity and voltage to handle the power requirements of your air-conditioning equipment.

HOUSE-SITTERS

Consider engaging a house-sitter, who will actually live in your house while you're away. A friend, relative, or domestic employee in whom you have complete trust is ideal. A professional or semiprofessional house-sitter can often be engaged through college placement offices. Mature students or even faculty members often make themselves available for house-sitting duties. Other trustworthy house-sitters might be a person with whom you work or worship or people referred by neighbors.

AVOID PRETRIP PUBLICITY

If you are prominent in your community and news of your trip might be included in the social or business sections of your newspaper, make certain these items aren't run in the paper until after you return. If for some reason you can't delay this news, arrange for the protection of your home. If you can't find a trustworthy house-sitter, arrange for an on-premises security guard.

Professional thieves and burglars read newspapers, and if they know you will be in New York for the opening of your new play or in San Francisco for your daughter's wedding, they may well come calling. Even if you avoid publicity, professional thieves sometimes befriend deliverymen—who may even be paid accomplices—for information, so be prepared to outmaneuver a thorough and professional adversary.

NOTIFY POLICE

Notify the police that you will be away, so that they can provide some additional attention to your property while you're gone. If you've arranged for a house-sitter or the assistance of that friendly neighbor, give his or her name to the police to avoid any unpleasant incident. Also provide the police with the names of any other friends or relatives who have keys to your house.

DON'T PACK THE CAR THE NIGHT BEFORE

Don't try to get a few minutes' early start on your vacation by packing the car the night before. It's not worth it when you consider the risk of awakening to find everything, car included, gone from your driveway or garage. And even if all is intact, there may be a burglar watching you pull away, waiting to get at all the goodies you didn't take along.

Finally, while you're en route, your out-of-state license plates distinguish you as a "mark." A thief can capitalize on this information through any number of methods designed to separate you from your assets. The thief derives comfort from the belief that, even if caught red-handed, he or she would probably go free, because you would be reluctant to return in order to testify against him or her. You should park in a manner that would shield your license plate from the thief's prying eyes, perhaps backing into a space against a building wall or parking between two cars.

Home Security During Vacation: A Checklist

1. Arrange for a friend or neighbor to bring in mail, milk, and newspapers. If this isn't possible, cancel deliveries.
2. Arrange to have your dog fed, watered, and walked at home rather than kept at a kennel.
3. If you have a second car, arrange to have it moved occasionally in your absence.
4. Arrange to have your lawn cut or snow shoveled as required during your absence.
5. Have fence gates locked, preferably at nighttime only, during your absence.
6. Arrange for garbage and trash to be put out for pickup as usual.
7. Arrange for secure storage of furs, jewelry, and other valuables outside the house while you are away.

8. Pay bills that will be due in your absence, and arrange for the payment of others that may arrive while you're away.

9. Have your alarm system checked before your departure.

10. Leave shades and drapes in the positions that they would normally be in if you were home, arranging, if possible, to have them raised and lowered or opened and closed routinely.

11. Set thermostats, or utilize timers, for air-conditioner operation that fits the weather conditions. Turn down volume control on telephones.

12. If you don't have a generous neighbor, use a qualified and trustworthy house-sitter in your absence.

13. Avoid publicity about your impending trip.

14. Leave an itinerary with someone, so that you can be notified in case of an emergency.

15. Consider use of a neighborhood patrol service during your absence.

16. Notify police of your absence, providing them with the names of house-sitters or neighbors who will be assisting and others who have possession of keys to your house.

17. Don't pack your car the night before departure; load it quickly in the morning.

18. Last thing before departure, check to see that all doors and windows are locked and that you have taken all necessary keys.

19. Toys or tools in the yard will indicate that the house is occupied, provided that they are replaced and relocated periodically.

20. Encourage neighborhood children to play in your yard while you are away.

10
Special Tips for Apartment Dwellers

A Housing Authority police officer shot and slightly wounded a twenty-seven-year-old man he found lurking on the roof of the Polo Grounds Towers project at 2955 Eighth Avenue. The wounded man, identified as Leonard Brown of 311 West 42nd, was said to have had a knife in his pocket. Brown had advanced toward the patrol officers with his hand in his pocket when he was ordered to halt.

While many of the home-security suggestions made so far apply to all dwelling units, some pertain solely to a freestanding house. Other special considerations are the more or less exclusive province of the occupant of an apartment, co-op, or condominium.

An apartment's limited access may make it more secure, but it also creates some specific problems. For example, the front door has to be better secured, since it is unlikely an intruder will be disturbed by a passerby, although an inquisitive neighbor may suddenly appear. On the other hand, assistance in an apartment can be only a few steps away, rather than many yards.

APARTMENT SECURITY FEATURES

The following is a shopping list of features you will want to consider before renting an apartment—or a list of services you may want to pressure your landlord into providing. A secure apartment building should have these features:

- A round-the-clock doorman or security guard who announces all guests and requires proper identification of all visitors and callers

- Attended elevators
- Fire stairs equipped with one-way doors, which should operate only from inside the fire stairwell on the ground floor and roof and only from outside the fire stairwell on all other floors
- Garages equipped with self-closing outside doors or a guard, or both

Few apartment complexes have the resources to supply maximum security. But even a small, limited-budget building can follow good security measures, which must include the following:

- Door-opening systems, equipped with an intercom system or closed-circuit television, with every tenant trained to use the system properly
- Self-service elevators with small mirrors permitting a view of the entire interior of the car before boarding
- Entrance into attached or basement garages controlled by key or magnetic card, and automatic closure of these doors
- Fire stairs equipped with one-way doors
- Adequate lighting throughout the common spaces of the building
- Lighting fixtures located or protected so that an intruder can't get at them
- Roof doors operable only from the inside
- Alcoves or other blind spots in corridors, well lighted, with mirrors to prevent them from being used as hiding places

SECURITY OF KEYS

When you move into an apartment, change the locks. Your building superintendent may insist on having a key to your apartment, in which case point out that a burglar breaking into his or her apartment would then have access to every apartment in the building. If fire codes require the superintendent to have a key, give it to him or her in a sealed envelope with your name signed across the flap. It would be much better, if possible, to leave the key with a friend and notify the superintendent where the key can be found. Don't hide your key near the door.

Once your keys are protected, your apartment is probably more secure than the typical freestanding house. But there are other things you should do to increase your protection.

There is one fact that should motivate you to assess the effectiveness of your locking devices. In apartment buildings, most crimes result from the failure to use existing locks, or from their inadequacy.

You should consider adding a lock of your own to your apartment door. You would be protected if a passkey fell into the wrong hands. It is not unprecedented for a building super to misuse the keys entrusted to his or her custody. Your landlord will almost certainly object if he or she knows of your protective addition, but after all, it is your property, even your life, that might be on the line. The reverse side of this particular bit of advice should be considered. In the event of an emergency, the police or fire personnel would be unable to protect your belongings without forcibly opening your apartment. Once they leave, you are at even greater risk.

DOORS AND WINDOWS

Review Chapter 1 for basic precautions concerning doors and windows. Be sure to install outside doors with chain locks and peepholes. Outside doors should be locked at all times, whether you're in or not.

Doorplates and mailboxes should not indicate the gender of the occupant. "M. Jones," for example, is much preferable to "Ms. Mary Jones."

Don't leave notes on doors indicating when you'll return to your apartment or that you'll be returning alone. "We will return soon" is much better than "I will be back at 6:00 P.M."

If a fire escape adjoins one of your windows, try using a folding screen on the inside. It will prevent entry through the window but will also allow exit from it. If this violates building codes, shatterproof glass would serve the same purpose.

BUILDING SECURITY PRACTICES

The most important security measure for any apartment is a sense of neighborliness and cooperation on the part of all the tenants—a keen desire to make the communal home more secure. Know your neighbors, and involve yourself with them. Report anything not operating properly: door closers, burned-out lights, inoperative locks, rotted fire hoses, and so forth. Report any unusual or apparently illegal incidents to the landlord or superintendent and to the police. Don't open the exterior door to anyone unless you either recognize the person or can positively determine the purpose of the visit.

Apartment lobbies can be scenes of serious crime. Picture this scenario. A wrongdoer of some sort rings for admittance. No answer. He or she makes a mental note that the apartment is unoccupied and moves to the next buzzer. Again no answer, again a mental note. The next buzzer is answered, "What do you want?" A mumbled reply about "special delivery" or "package from (the local department store)" will usually persuade someone in the building to open the door. Once inside, the wrongdoer can loot with relative safety from detection, especially having discovered which apartments are unoccupied.

Draperies on lobby windows denote, to many, an air of privacy. But privacy in the lobby is not to be desired. The sight of a doorman, on the other hand, will usually send the criminal elsewhere. Neat and orderly premises speak of residents who care about their surroundings and probably have taken steps to ensure the sanctity of their homes. Draperies also can be a more menacing accessory. An intruder who in some manner gains entry into the building needs only to hide behind the protective drapes and to prey on residents who enter.

Intruders often position themselves near the mailboxes. Practically every tenant will visit the mailboxes daily, and will be much more attentive to the mail than to almost anything else. It's likely that the tenant will have left the apartment door open for the short trip downstairs, providing the thief yet another opportunity to do wrong. Traffic around the mailboxes may be especially heavy on days when Social Security or public assistance checks are delivered. Any person who receives checks in the mail on a regular and predictable basis must—*must*—use direct bank-deposit services for protection against the thief.

In consideration for taking your rent (or your condo maintenance) payments, your landlord (or management) owes you adequate lighting inside and out. As described earlier, adequate lighting is that sufficient to read a wristwatch by. A landlord or building manager may ignore, delay, or otherwise attempt to dissuade you from receiving your due. If you aren't able to get satisfaction from those managing your place, perhaps the local building inspector will prove helpful.

TENANTS' ASSOCIATIONS

The organizations known as tenants' associations assume all levels of formality. A simple arrangement may be nothing more than telling your neighbor that you will be away for a few days, and asking him to look after your interests. Or one tenant may tell another whom she is going to dinner with that evening, just in case. Some neighbors install buzzers between their apartments for quick response in the event of an emergency.

A slightly larger, but equally informal association would involve your taking the time to meet every person on your floor (or some part of a large floor). In this way, you would be able to identify someone who is not a resident of your floor. This might warn you of a potential danger. If your suspicions persist, call the manager, or else wait a few minutes before leaving the building. This little warning could possibly save you from injury, or worse.

A group of tenants could check with local police to determine the availability of a crime prevention squad. These units have proved highly successful in mobilizing a group of individuals into a cohesive protective element, merely by teaching the group members to better protect themselves. Sometimes tenant groups will band together and form patrols to provide security for their environs. Generally, these units operate only in larger housing complexes, often in problem housing developments.

ELEVATORS AND OTHER SPECIAL HAZARDS

Elevators can be a potential hazard to the apartment dweller. Don't ride an elevator with a stranger. If a suspicious-looking character gets on an elevator, press the alarm button. Always try to position yourself with your back against one of the elevator walls so that you minimize your exposure to the mugger and pickpocket. Don't ride an elevator if the roof escape hatch is ajar.

When you arrive at your destination floor, check the corridor before you leave the car. If there is a stranger in the hallway, don't leave the elevator. As a general rule, the basement is the most hazardous location in an apartment building, whether or not there is provision for parking in the basement. Obviously, basement parking increases the possibility of someone's entering the building by sneaking in along with a car legitimately there to park. Once there, the intruder is free to enter every floor in the building (unless, of course, tenants have keys to the elevator on the basement level or there is a TV monitor visible to the doorman in the lobby).

Basement laundry rooms are, perhaps, equally hazardous, in large measure because they are used less frequently than most other areas of the building. For this reason, they are favorite areas for attacks. To the criminal, especially the sexual offender, the lack of activity is beneficial. He can bide his time, awaiting the right moment and the right victim, and once he zeros in, he will likely have the time he needs to rape and perhaps murder.

Most of us, at one time or another, have boarded an elevator car headed in the direction opposite to that desired. Usually, this minor inconvenience costs us nothing but a few minutes. If, however, you find yourself on an elevator headed to the basement at the behest of a criminal looking for a victim, you could find yourself facing a serious problem. To avoid this danger, punch the "door open" button on the elevator, and then get off before the door closes. Then you have only to stand and wait in order to catch a car that you know is headed in your direction.

The first chapter of this book stressed the importance of proper security for the doors and windows that protect us. In an apartment, this is an equally necessary precaution, but some of the items are arranged differently. You almost certainly will have fewer windows to protect, and it is quite likely that only one or two walls will have any windows at all. Some of these windows, though, will open onto fire escapes, which offer access from your apartment to the ground and vice versa. These windows must be protected by lockable metal coverings to keep intruders out. In addition, the keys to these grills must be close enough to enable you to get out if the fire threat is genuine. A word of caution: don't situate the emergency keys close enough that they could be reached from outside the building. The ideal key storage location would be someplace where they would be out of sight from the fire escape.

Indoor emergency exits (fire stairs) should generally not be used except for emergencies. Realistically, few people will wait five minutes for an elevator just to visit a friend two floors below. But remember, these stairs are built to withstand an engaged fire, and their fireproof doors deaden all sounds on the stairs. Your cries for help could be inaudible outside the staircase, so that they would be ignored.

One authority lists the three most desirable security features in an apartment to be a twenty-four-hour doorman, closed-circuit TV, and an abundance of lighting, both inside and outside the building. And don't forget the axiom from the first chapter: dollar for dollar, the dead-bolt lock is the best means of defense that you can enlist in securing your home.

Basement laundries and apartment vestibules or mailbox areas are also vulnerable locations for assaults. Remember, there is some safety in numbers. It is far safer, and much more sociable as well, to go to the mailbox area or the basement laundry room with a neighbor. If you must go alone, keep moving if you don't like what you see.

HEALTH CLUBS AND SOLARIUMS

To attract the sociable and exercise-conscious yuppies as well as the down-to-earth, expanding middle-class, more and more new apartment houses, especially co-ops and condominiums, include health clubs and solariums. Many of these feature indoor or outdoor swimming pools, saunas, steam rooms, heated whirlpools, rest rooms, showers, lockers, rooms for physical fitness, expensive state-of-the-art exercise equipment, areas for aerobics, and even a play area stocked with toys for children. The solarium, often situated on or near the roof, may be equipped with expensive chaises, chairs, and tables. All this paraphernalia may provide constructive relaxation for hardworking residents, but it also presents a security nightmare.

For protection in these areas, the first rule is to follow all the basic security principles described in this chapter. For example, be sure that all doors to all rooms, storerooms, and utility closets are locked when not in use—with a dead bolt, of course. Rooms with expensive equipment should also be alarmed to signal the doorman or the concierge of unauthorized entry. For the club and swimming pool, the best security consists of an attendant and a lifeguard during scheduled hours. Closed-circuit television should monitor strategic points in each room, plus all hallways and corridors. In all rooms, panic buttons should be available to patrons who are threatened by any intruder who gets by the health club attendant. The solarium should be equally equipped, especially if it is situated far from the rest of the club. Take nothing of value with you to the health club; leave valuables securely locked in your apartment. While you exercise or swim, your purse, pocketbook, or wallet should be secured in a locker with your own combination lock. All your other personal belongings should also be secured in the locker.

TERRACES

A terrace, serving as a surrogate suburban patio in the middle of the city, may offer relaxation and privacy. But it may also attract burglars, who perceive it as a convenient access to your apartment. Even a terrace far from the street on a high floor is vulnerable to burglars, who may access it from an unsecured hallway door leading to the outside, or through a neighbor's apartment that was forcibly entered. Not finding anything of value in your neighbor's apartment, the disappointed burglar designates your apartment as the next primary target.

The most important preventive measure is that all windows and doors leading to your terrace be adequately secured. For sliding glass doors, probably the most vulnerable doors in your apartment, follow the procedures provided in Chapter 1. These include installing shatterproof glass or other impact-resistant glazing, inserting a broom handle (cut to size) in the track on which the doors slide, and attaching locks with vertical barrel bolts to fit into holes in the top and bottom tracks.

RENTING OUT YOUR APARTMENT

Mainly for your own protection, all security equipment such as locks, bolts, and alarms should be in working condition, but if you rent your condo or co-op, you must also be concerned for your tenant's safety. In California, a female condo renter was abducted from the condo's parking lot, robbed, and assaulted. Citing fraud and negligence, she sued the condo association for her injuries. She argued that the owner of the apartment had assured her that the private parking lot was protected by a modern key-entry-only security gate. Yet the criminals who attacked her were able to enter through a defective gate. The court found in her favor because condominium owners are required to take reasonable measures to safeguard tenants, and defective gates abrogated this responsibility. In many states besides California, the condo owner is liable for crimes against their tenants if the obligation of protecting them is assumed but not fulfilled.

DIFFERENT LEVELS OF SECURITY

Before you accept varying levels of security at different times of the day, consider possible consequences. If your tenants' association wants to hire a second doorman for only part of the day, when expectations of danger are greatest, check your local laws. A court, questioning why certain shifts are covered by two persons and others by only one, might attribute negligence to the building management during the other hours. For help in determining high-risk hours, call in a crime expert or even your local police department. The police are often willing to provide this expert advice without charge. Taking such reasonable measures could constitute a strong defense in a lawsuit.

Special Tips for Apartment Dwellers: A Checklist
  1. When moving into an apartment, look for these security-oriented features:
     a. Doormen or security guards who screen visitors

    b. Attended elevators

    c. Properly secured interior fire stairwells

    d. Properly secured garages

    e. Remotely operated door-opening systems, with intercom systems or closed-circuit television

    f. Interior-view mirrors in self-service elevators

    g. Adequate lighting

    h. Protection against alcoves or other blind spots being used as hiding places

    i. Roof doors operable only from inside

  2. On moving into an apartment, change locks.

  3. Protect spare or emergency keys.

  4. Equip outside doors with chain locks and peepholes.

  5. If female, do not indicate gender on mailbox or doorplates.

  6. Don't leave notes on doors indicating anticipated time of return or using "I" instead of "we."

  7. Protect windows, remembering that those adjoining fire escapes should prevent illegal entry but not prohibit emergency exit.

  8. Know your neighbors, and work together for your mutual security.

  9. Report anything peculiar—faulty equipment or an unusual incident.

10. The three most essential security features for an apartment include a twenty-four-hour doorman, closed-circuit TV, and sufficient lighting inside and outside the structure.

11. If your building has a health club, follow all the basic security measures described for securing your apartment.

12. Do not take anything of value to the health club, and secure all personal belongings in a locker.

13. Make sure to secure all windows and doors leading to your terrace.

14. When renting your condo or co-op, be certain that all security equipment is in working order.

PART TWO

SECURITY AWAY FROM HOME

11
Vehicle Security

On-the-job survey: More than 4,000 Chicago taxi drivers, tailors, and dry cleaners began polling customers' opinions on handgun restrictions. The hack drivers alone hoped to question 600,000 customers. One driver started badly; the same day the survey was announced, he was robbed at gunpoint, and his taxi stolen.

Motor vehicle theft is a wide-ranging crime that, according to the Bureau of Justice Statistics, has for the last several years touched about 2 percent of the nation's households. The bureau also estimated that losses due to car theft reached $28 billion over a thirteen-year period. Over 1.2 million motor vehicles, valued at $5.5 billion, are stolen each year. One out of every 700 registered vehicles is taken by a criminal. The situation is worsening. According to the FBI, the number of stolen motor vehicles—about three-quarters of them cars—rose 11 percent in 1986 and 5 percent more in 1987.

A motor vehicle is probably the second largest investment most of us make, and there are a number of things we can do to protect this investment. There are obvious strategies: Don't leave keys in the ignition, lock car doors, and park in a safe location. As basic as these precautions are, most car thefts would be eliminated if the tips were faithfully practiced. Four of five cars stolen were left unlocked, and nearly 20 percent had keys in the ignition. Chapter 13, under "Parking While Shopping," provides additional information about safeguarding your auto against theft—not only the entire vehicle but also the piece-by-piece theft by car strippers. This type of piecemeal theft has an advantage to a thief, as most parts are not identified by serial number. One hubcap is much like another. Also, a thief can get as much as five times the value of a car by selling parts to "chop shops"—garages that dismantle stolen vehicles.

A particularly vulnerable type of car is that which has an outside hood-release mechanism. Thieves can open the hood, cut battery cables with a bolt cutter, and be away within a matter of seconds. Key-operated hood locks are available at auto accessory stores, and heavy chains and padlocks can sometimes be used to prevent a hood from being raised. This method, while inexpensive and effective, is of course inconvenient when you attempt to open the hood for routine maintenance.

ACCESSORIES

Your car is not nearly as safe and secure as your home. No automobile— with the possible exception of a specially modified, specially equipped car—is completely protected against breaking and entering. Thus, a car is not satisfactory for protection of valuables, and it may hold attractions of its own for a thief.

If you have a tape player or a citizens band (CB) radio installed in your car, you are displaying desirable goods to a thief. If you've ever changed a car tire, you know how easy it would be for a thief to steal tires and rims with no equipment other than a jack and a tire iron.

Your driver's license and automobile registration should never be stored in your car. The glove compartment and the area above the sun visor are among the first places searched by a thief. Carry these papers on your person, and handle them as you would any valuable papers. If keeping registrations on one's person should prove totally impractical, as would be the case if a number of drivers used the same car frequently, the trunk would provide more secure storage for these documents.

Another accessory in your car that thieves look for is your radar detector. Do not tempt a thief by leaving such a device in plain view.

BEFORE ENTERING YOUR CAR

Before you get into your car, make it a habit to check it on all sides for flat tires and obstructions near the wheels. Also check for illegal entry. If you think your car has been broken into, don't disturb fingerprints or any other evidence that can assist the police.

Next, look in the window and check inside your car. Do this even if the car has been in an attended garage or if it has been delivered to you by a parking attendant. Again, you may discover evidence that you won't wish to disturb. You might also discover someone crouching on the floor. Carrying a small penlight in a pocket or handbag is an excellent security protection. You should use it during darkness hours to examine the interior of the vehicle thoroughly before entering. If all appears in order, unlock the door. If the door isn't locked and you're reasonably certain that you locked it when you left, be cautious. Before you get into the car, check to see if your radio and tape player are still there and if the glove compartment is in order.

A citizens band radio or a cellular telephone is an excellent item for the well-equipped auto, from a security standpoint. As a matter of fact, there is a good argument for having both devices. There are gaps in the coverage of cellular phones when you leave populated areas. In this circumstance, your CB might help you through an emergency. CB channel 9 is monitored continuously for emergency radio traffic throughout virtually all of the United States.

AFTER ENTERING YOUR CAR

Once you are in the car, lock all doors, fasten your seat belt or shoulder harness, and start the car. But what if it won't start?

If it is daylight and the car is parked in your driveway or in front of the house, the problem is almost certainly a mechanical malfunction. If it is late at night and you are parked in an unfamiliar or high-crime neighborhood, the car's disability might have been caused deliberately. Look around, and if you see nothing suspicious, get out of the car, lock the door, and get assistance. The best place to go is probably the place you just left. Even if you're qualified to make repairs yourself, you would be well advised to have someone you know with you.

If, on the other hand, you think that robbery or assault looks likely, and if you are not on a brightly lighted or heavily traveled thoroughfare, you have two choices. You can lock the car and go away, then return for your car in the light of day with assistance of your own choosing. Or you can lock the car and stay inside, being prepared to blow the horn if you are threatened.

Whatever you do, do not accept a stranger's offer of assistance. He or she may be the person who disabled your car. If he or she seems interested in helping you, ask him or her to call a friend, a relative, or the police. Don't let him or her call a service station for you; an accomplice may be standing by. If you're inside your car and he or she insists on helping you and attempts to get you to unlock the door, then blow the horn and keep blowing it until your "friend" leaves or until someone in the neighborhood gets disturbed enough to call the police.

SECURITY WHILE DRIVING

It is important to realize that the car you are driving can leave you stranded somewhere you'd rather not be. Every driver should be able to take care of the minimum auto maintenance and repair needs, and failure to acquire these skills could leave you in an untenable situation. Anyone can learn to check fluid levels in cooling systems, crankcase oil, and fuel. A tire pressure gauge is inexpensive and easy to use, and one should be in every car. If you frequently travel by automobile, it would be an excellent idea to carry a container of water, a few quarts of motor oil, a spare fan belt and other belts, spare fuses, and a couple of canisters of aerosol flat-tire "fix."

This last is not to be considered a substitute for a properly inflated spare tire, but for many flat tires, this product will seal the hole and provide sufficient pressure for you to drive safely to a service station for more permanent repairs. It also has the very real advantage of minimizing the time required to effect repairs, and the double advantage of being out of the vehicle for the least possible time and thus limiting your exposure to harm, either accidental or deliberate.

Don't stop your car merely because someone asks you to, especially in a remote location. If someone appears to need assistance, don't be reckless or foolhardy. You might stop, roll down the window slightly, and ask if you can send help. Don't allow yourself to be talked into giving assistance. Go for help.

If someone other than a uniformed or plainclothes police officer in a squad car or in another clearly identifiable department vehicle attempts to force you to the curb, don't do it, even if it means a collision. Sound the horn, and drive to a service station, a lighted house, or anywhere else you might reasonably expect to find assistance, and from there report the matter to the police.

If someone attempts to enter your car at a stop sign or a stoplight, drive away. Run the light. Risk a collision if you must, but drive on. If you turn to the right, you probably will be heading with the closest oncoming traffic, which will minimize the damage of any resulting collision. Since someone attempting to force his or her way into your car will most likely approach you from the curb side, the movement of your car to the right will also tend to force the intruder away from you. Sound your horn, and attract as much attention as possible. To report the accident, if there is one, drive to a service station or to any open public business. You aren't leaving the scene, but merely going to the nearest phone to report an accident.

Several years ago, in a major city, there was a rapist with an unusual modus operandi. He would deliberately involve a lone female driver in an accident. When she got out of the car to survey the damage, she was assaulted. The lesson here is to stay in your car at all costs when in isolated areas and strange neighborhoods.

To whatever extent possible, avoid traveling alone. If you must travel alone, consider the two rules below. One lady we know has a department store mannequin's head and upper torso, which she keeps in her automobile. This presents the impression that she is not a woman traveling alone. Two unmarried sisters carry a man's hat in their car. When they travel together, one of them wears the hat to convey the impression that a protective male is aboard.

Learn the location of all police stations, precinct houses, or other locations that police tend to frequent. All-night restaurants, especially those near the station house, may be favored spots for coffee breaks.

Travel familiar streets, and make it a point to find out as much as possible about the areas through which you pass. Shopping occasionally in these places would enable merchants to recognize you as a customer, and they would be much more likely to go out of the way to be of assistance at a time when you really need it.

BEING FOLLOWED?

Do you think someone is following you by car? Ask yourself if you have given anyone a reason to do so. Did you flash a roll of money in a store? Did you just cash a check? If you think it is likely that someone is following you, take evasive action, and drive in the center lane. If your follower persists, stop at a service business, and make a call. While it is true that a service station can be a haven, it is equally true that you might be followed there. Stations, particularly at night, are often staffed by only one person, and it is quite possible that this individual may not wish to be involved. Therefore, you would be better off looking for a service station adjacent to a diner.

If you cannot locate exactly the safe haven you seek, and you still feel threatened by someone following you, drive to the busiest intersection you can find, activate your flashers, double-check that your doors are locked, and honk your horn until suitable assistance arrives. As a general rule, assistance is defined as a uniformed police officer.

At some time, you may be driving in an area that makes you feel uneasy when a flat tire or other problem requires you to leave the road. If your car's engine is inoperative, you have little choice but to attempt to coast to the side of the road; putting the car in neutral will allow you to coast a maximum distance. Once there, lock up and await the proper assistance. If, on the other hand, your distress is mere tire trouble, you should maneuver to the slow lane and then drive slowly to assistance. If in an isolated area, you might be better off to continue driving until you reach the type of assistance you require. Ruining a tire or a wheel rim is little enough price to pay for avoiding becoming a crime statistic.

PARKING YOUR CAR

Park where the passersby, either walking or driving, will serve as a deterrent to someone who might steal, or steal from, your car. If it's daylight, ask yourself if it will still be light when you return. Try to park near a storefront that will be brightly lighted, on a main thoroughfare, under a streetlamp, or somewhere you anticipate heavy traffic (either vehicle or pedestrian). Avoid remote, unlighted areas.

Once you are parked, roll up your windows, and always lock your car, even if you will be away for only a few minutes. Remember, more cars are stolen through the use of a key left in the ignition of an unlocked car than from any other cause. Always take your key with you when you exit your automobile, and always double-check to be sure that all car doors are locked and that all windows are closed.

ALARMS AND OTHER SECURITY DEVICES

If you must carry items of value in your car, an alarm device would likely be a good investment. However, any such system is subject to false alarms, and the system can be circumvented. Only extraordinary circumstances call for car alarms, and even then, you may be just letting the thief know that there are valuables to be found inside. Despite these limitations, an auto alarm is useful for security. It is unlikely that any passerby would act to protect your property, should the alarm be activated. However, research has revealed that most cars (two-thirds) are stolen at night and that half of car thefts occur in residential areas. The combination of nighttime and a residential neighborhood makes it likely that you, or any other alarmed auto owner, would act to protect a car threatened with theft.

Fiscal restraints are causing many municipalities to limit or drop insurance coverage on parking lots and other community property. Some schools are recommending that teachers' private cars parked on campuses have alarms installed.

In addressing interior security, Chapter 2 discussed the use of decals on homes as a deterrent to theft. While most of these decals advertise that the premises are protected by alarm systems, not all of them are. The same thing may be said of stickers announcing vehicle alarms. Not all of them are backed up by hardware. Thus, as with home alarms, auto alarm decals won't hurt anything, and they may even help, particularly if the person attempting to steal the auto isn't very sophisticated. The practiced thief, however, will be able to sort the grain from the chaff, and will act accordingly, probably against your best interests.

ASKING FOR TROUBLE

If you're in your car at a time when the motor isn't running—while at a drive-in movie, for example—lock yourself in. Roll the windows up, leaving only a slight crack for fresh air. In a drive-in restaurant, if you are at all isolated, place the food in the car; don't leave the window open for a tray table.

If you are parked in a completely isolated area, head your car outward, and keep the doors locked and the windows up. And keep your eyes open. Lovers' lanes are favorite haunts not only for young lovers but also for robbers, rapists, and sexual deviates.

CAR KEY SECURITY

Those little magnetic holders with spare ignition keys, attached to the car's frame, are an open invitation to a thief to steal your car.

At an attended garage, leave only your ignition key. One enterprising parking attendant had considerable success as part of a burglary ring. When parking a car, particularly an expensive one, he would search for the identification of the driver. A phone call to the house would determine if anyone was home. If not, an accomplice in a truck nearby would duplicate the house key on a portable key cutter and be quickly on his way to strip the place. Even when the victim returned for his or her car and left the garage, the attendant had ample time to telephone the victim's home and warn the accomplice that it was time to leave.

MOTOR HOMES, RECREATIONAL VEHICLES, AND VANS

Motor homes and recreational vehicles (RVs) generally can be protected by employing the same measures as for automobiles. There are, however, a few areas of particular concern. Motor homes are especially vulnerable at times of season change, when they might be taken for sale to vacationers or for transportation to another climate. Frankly, the likelihood of theft of an RV is less now than previously, when operating costs, especially fuel, were not as great.

Elaborately styled and personalized vans are another consideration. The individualized nature of many of them makes them less attractive to the local thief but more attractive to the organized career criminal, who has the resources to transport them to another part of the country and who has a suitable sales outlet there to move the vehicle quickly. Such an operator will have little difficulty, if any, in obtaining titles or other documents to transfer to these stolen vehicles. Often totally wrecked autos are purchased just to acquire the ownership documents, which are then altered to transfer to a stolen car.

MOTORCYCLES AND MOPEDS

Motorcycles and mopeds are increasingly popular, offering economy and fun while traveling. This has led to an increase in thefts of these vehicles. No lock is 100 percent theftproof, but there are devices that discourage or delay a thief considerably. Invest in a lock that allows you to link your motorcycle when not in use to a pole or street sign. Among the locks available today are krypton U-shaped bars, braided and plastic-covered steel cables, and the old-fashioned chains and padlocks. A beeper that sounds when someone tampers with your motorcycle is also available; it is audible for up to a half-mile. Don't rely on the automatic steering lock built into a motorcycle. This will prevent the wheels from turning but will not keep the motorcycle from being lifted onto a truck and spirited away.

Ride safely. Wear protective clothing; familiarize yourself with the safety laws in your state; test your brakes, automatic signals, gears, and throttle before you start up. Don't be surprised by faulty controls in traffic.

BICYCLE PROTECTION

A bicycle is easily stolen and extremely difficult to trace. This condition demands your vigilance. Bicycles have grown up, in the sense that they are no longer transportation exclusively for kids. You can spend as much today for a good bike as you would have paid for a good used car ten years ago. Bicycles are "in" as an exercise tool for young professionals. Because they are trendy, they are desirable items. Wherever items are desired, you may be certain that criminals will try to fill the demand by stealing.

One way to discourage bicycle thieves is to buy a secondhand machine. There is a legal market for used bikes, which usually represent great buys, as bike riders trade up to more powerful ones. Since your "like new" transportation will not have the resale potential of the pace-setting models, you're less likely to be ripped off.

Regardless of whether your bike is state-of-the-art or more sedate, you need to protect it from theft. A good padlock is the most important security protection for your bicycle.

Many bicycle locks are available—heavy shackle locks, chain and key padlocks, horseshoe-shaped clamps, and cable combination locks. The oversize shackle lock is considered best by many authorities, including police theft squads and *Consumer Reports*, but perhaps more important is the way the bike is secured and the item to which it is secured. Secure the bike through the frame or both the frame and tire rather than just the tire. Secure it to a lamppost, tree, or other item that is large enough to prevent it from being removed along with the bike. The item should be tall enough that the whole assembly—bike, chain, lock, and all—cannot be slipped off the top.

A further safeguard against bicycle theft is recording your bike's serial number and registering it with your local police department. When you are not riding the bicycle, put it in a locked room, basement, or garage, not in your backyard or driveway, where it can be seen from the street. And remember to lock the bike, even if it's in the locked garage. A thief could get in the garage, but your bike would still be out of harm's way if you remembered to take the five or so seconds required to further lock it.

Know the precepts of bicycle safety. Obey all traffic signals, and walk your bicycle through busy traffic crossings. Ride with the flow of traffic, on the right-hand side of the road. If you ride at night, make sure your bike has reflectors, a headlight, and a taillight. Wear light-colored clothing for increased visibility. Know and use hand signals. Always be alert for suddenly opened car doors, and watch for pedestrians and joggers.

PROTECTING BOATS

Protecting boats is, in many ways, similar to protecting your home.

Often, your boat *is* your home away from home. You would be well advised to reread the protective principles in Chapter 1. You will require good dead-bolt locks, quality protective lighting, and alarm systems to protect yourself and your property. You will need to maintain up-to-date inventory lists (see Chapter 2), and you should etch or otherwise identify items that are part of your maritime home. Compasses, sextants, depth-sounding gear, radar, radios, and life-preserving equipment should all bear your identification marks. You should cooperate with your neighbors at marinas or anchorages for common security. Ideally, you should make use of continuously staffed mooring facilities.

When you leave your craft, employ the maximum available protections. Secure outboard motors with excellent padlocks and excellent chain (Chapter 1). Installing a secret ignition cutoff switch might easily prevent your craft from being stolen. Removing the screw or hiding the distributor rotor could foil thieves. Most importantly, when you leave ship, make absolutely certain that you don't leave the registration papers behind. You certainly wouldn't want your deck sold out from under you.

You may be required to display craft registration numbers on your hull. Though not required, you should also place this identifier on structural members of the boat in remote locations on the vessel. Certain boats are exempt from craft registration requirements. If you are permitted to register your boat, even if not required to do so, by all means, add this protection.

Vehicle Security: A Checklist

1. Automobiles with exterior hood releases require additional precautions.
2. Check your car on all sides before approaching the door.
3. Check inside the car before unlocking it.
4. Don't display accessories such as tape players, CB radios, or radar detectors where they will attract a thief's attention.
5. If your car won't start, either get assistance or get away. Your car may have been disabled deliberately.
6. Do not accept unsolicited offers of assistance.
7. Do not unlock the door to admit a stranger.
8. Sound your horn and continue to do so if a stranger remains around your locked car and appears to be a menace.
9. Acquire minimum auto maintenance and repair skills. This knowledge will minimize auto breakdowns, and it will prove invaluable should one occur.

10. Lock your car if you must abandon it to go for assistance, and exercise prudence when walking.

11. If someone appears to need assistance, drive to a phone and send assistance; do not stop.

12. If someone attempts to force you to stop, do not do so—even if it means a collision. Sound the horn, and drive toward lights or wherever you may find assistance.

13. Take evasive action if you are being followed, and drive in the center lane. If your follower persists, drive to some occupied location, and phone for assistance.

14. If someone attempts to enter your car at a stoplight or a stop sign, drive away, sounding your horn, even if it means running a red light. In general, turn to the right when driving away.

15. Don't get out of your car in a dark, remote location, even if you've been involved in an accident. Drive to an open service station or business, and report the accident to the police.

16. Learn the location of police stations, precinct houses, and other places where police tend to gather. This knowledge may save your life in an emergency.

17. Park only in lighted, populous locations.

18. Exercise caution when parked in areas like drive-ins or lovers' lanes. Be ready to leave on short notice.

19. If parked at an attended lot, leave only your ignition key behind.

20. Motorcycles, mopeds, and bicycles should be secured to lampposts or street signs when left on the street.

21. Motorcycle steering locks do not offer protection against the vehicle's being lifted onto a truck and stolen.

22. Bicycle serial numbers should be recorded with the police department.

23. The oversize shackle lock is considered best for security bicycles, motorcycles, and mopeds.

24. Apply to boat security all principles for protection of your home.

12
Security in the Streets

"I was just standing there," said William Redd, "minding my own business and waiting for the bus. This great big dude walked up, and pow, *he knocked me right over. I still don't know what I ever did to that guy, but the next time I'm in the Tenderloin at that time of night, I'm taking a taxi home!"*

More crimes against people are committed on the streets than in any other place. Recently, a New York City woman was attacked and killed in broad daylight as she and her son were going to church, by a stranger wielding a two-by-four. The police said the assault was "totally unexpected and appeared to be totally unprovoked." A few precautions will greatly reduce your chances of being victimized.

DON'T CARRY A GREAT DEAL OF MONEY

The first rule is to limit your losses. Don't carry more than you can easily afford to lose. A famous woman was once quoted as saying that she never carried more than $25 with her at any time. She said she carried that amount because she knew it was the going rate for a heroin fix at that time. Many street robberies are committed solely to finance narcotic addictions. If you carry little cash, the robber's take won't break you, but it should be big enough to satisfy him or her. Otherwise, the robber may give vent to his or her rage by a physical assault, especially if he or she is strung out on drugs.

Sometimes, though, it may be necessary to carry more cash than you feel comfortable with. In that event, carry the money in a stamped self-addressed envelope, and if you feel the least bit threatened, drop it in the corner mailbox. If, however, you have reason to fear that the person who is threatening you knows who you are and, thus, where you live, you should use the address of a trusted friend or relative. Obviously, for this tactic to be effective, you must know the exact location of the nearest mail drop. As Chapter 11 advised, make stops in businesses that lie along frequently traveled routes. In time, you will become recognized by the merchants, a fact that might stand you in good stead if you are attacked on the street.

Vary the route you travel in making these trips. Vary the time of day, too. You might even wear a disguise of some sort—anything to confuse the crook who is lying in ambush.

When you pick up the cash you are to transport to a destination, ask that someone accompany you to your auto or taxi. Women shouldn't carry cash in their handbags. Purses are too easily stolen. A coat pocket (particularly an inside one) is more secure.

SURRENDER YOUR VALUABLES

The second rule is simple. Remain calm and obey all commands. Surrender your valuables, and do so quickly. A friend was robbed on the streets of a large city he was visiting. He surrendered his cash but claimed that he was unable to remove a ring from his finger. His assailant offered to remove it, finger and all, with the switchblade knife he was carrying.

Try to avoid letting your attacker move you into an alley, doorway, or other secluded place. Assure him or her that there's no need to do that, that you are perfectly willing to cooperate. But don't let your eagerness to cooperate lead you into making any sudden moves. Tell your assailant that you're reaching for your wallet, then do it very slowly. You may be risking a fair amount of money (the average street robbery yield is about $600), but the robber is risking a minimum of ten years. He or she will be as nervous as you are.

Regardless of how accommodating you are, there is still the distinct possibility that you will be attacked. A robber may have emotional needs that can be served only by inflicting a sadistic beating on someone— meaning that all the money in the world won't be satisfactory. In this case, you have little choice but to defend yourself. Your best defenses are screaming for help and running away, not fighting. Chances are the robber is better equipped for combat than you are—that's one criterion in the selection of victims. Moreover, he or she is likely to be armed with a gun or knife.

WALK SECURELY

A third protective rule is this: walk facing oncoming traffic. This eliminates the possibility of someone's sneaking up behind you in an auto. If you should be accosted, an oncoming motorist might witness this and send assistance.

PURSE SNATCHING

The most frequent type of street robbery is probably the snatching of a briefcase or a purse. Your best defense against the purse snatcher is to walk some distance from the curb, with your purse or briefcase in the hand away from the street.

A purse should be carried with the strap over one shoulder and with the bag suspended between your arm and body. If your handbag strap is too short to carry this way, push your arm through the strap, and cradle the purse in your arm like a halfback carrying a football. A strapless bag also should be carried like a football.

Many women carry bags with the shoulder straps crossed over their bodies. This can increase the chances of serious injury, since the purse snatcher's usual method of attack is to yank a purse hard enough to break the strap, while at the same time shoving the victim the other way.

Another defensive tactic you might try is to flatten yourself against the side of a building when you hear rapidly approaching footsteps behind you. If you are the intended victim, this might prevent your purse from being taken. If you aren't, it may keep you from being trampled. But try to avoid flattening yourself against a plate-glass window because if it is the older type of plate glass, you could suffer severe cuts should the assailant give you the customary shove.

BEWARE OF PICKPOCKETS

A pickpocket works best in a crowd. A subway at rush hour is the milieu of the dip (another term for pickpocket). An extremely light touch is the stock in trade of these thieves. Your only awareness of anything out of the ordinary will be the slightest pressure on you. When exerting that pressure, the pickpocket is removing your billfold from your purse or your inside coat pocket.

One method of dealing with the dip is to speak up loudly. "Somebody's pushing on me, and I don't like it," is a phrase that should affect the thief's concentration and warn all others within earshot. If someone does say that, be sure to resist the impulse to check the pockets or purses where valuable are kept. This could tell the pickpocket exactly where to look.

A purse snatching, on the average, nets the thief about $100. Pickpockets do slightly better: about $125 for each theft.

BEING FOLLOWED?

If you are being followed on a well-traveled street, slow down, speed up, reverse directions—in other words, indicate to your pursuer that you are aware you are being followed. Then go straight for help. If you are being followed on a deserted street, don't play games. Walk as fast as you can to the nearest police officer or telephone, and report it. Look ahead for other people or a mailbox. The presence of other people will deter a purse snatcher. A mailbox is a relatively safe place to deposit your purse or wallet to avoid its theft. Technically you are in violation of the law by placing something other than mail in a postal box, but this is something that postal authorities are accustomed to handling.

If you're being followed, don't run straight for home, especially if no one is there to assist you. You are safer on the street than you would be inside your home or in an elevator alone with your assailant. If your "shadow" is after you, rather than your property, running straight home reveals where you can be found later, at the assailant's convenience.

DEFENSIVE WEAPONS AND PROCEDURES

Many so-called weapons—small handguns, tear gas guns, Mace devices—aren't much help. They may be grabbed and used against you or, more likely, will still be in your purse as it is removed from you.

One good weapon is a whistle with a piercing sound, like a traffic officer's, worn strapped to the wrist not used to carry the purse. The whistle on a bracelet slipped over the fingers, such as that which football officials carry, is also useful if it is worn rather than carried in the purse. But never wear a whistle on a chain around your neck; in an effort to discourage you from sounding it, the robber may well strangle you with your chain.

You can cut your losses by spreading the wealth. For years women who have had to carry money have been hiding it in their lingerie, and old-fashioned money belts are also recommended.

If at all possible, don't carry keys in your purse along with identification. You might lose your purse and then find that your home has been stripped before you have even finished filing the police report.

Carry only credit cards that you think you are likely to need. (See Chapter 2 for more information on credit card security.)

If you have to make frequent bank deposits in connection with your work, don't carry them in your own bag along with your personal valuables. Use a deposit bag that can be slipped loosely over the wrist. The use of armored car services is recommended for large deposits.

WALKING AT NIGHT

If you must walk at night, avoid the curb, whether vehicles are parked on the street or not. Someone could hide between two parked cars and ambush you. Or someone driving by could reach through the car window and snatch your purse or briefcase.

Don't walk too far from the curb either. Be especially guarded about doorways or shrubbery abutting the sidewalk, either of which can afford an excellent ambush point.

If the route to your destination is filled both with parked cars and with doorways or shrubbery adjacent to the sidewalk, then walk in the street (obviously keeping a sharp eye out for traffic).

If your late-night walks are regular and predictable, vary your route, particularly on paydays, Social Security check days, or other times when you might be suspected of carrying more than your usual amount of cash.

OUTSIDE PHONE BOOTHS

You are especially vulnerable when using an outside public phone booth. Engrossed in conversation, you become a prime target for pickpockets, muggers, and rapists. Be certain that the telephone booth is adequately illuminated, and if it is not, find one that is. Never stand with your back to the street and facing the phone. Hold the receiver in your hand and face the street or sidewalk with your back to the dialing mechanism. This way you can observe any suspicious-looking characters who may approach you.

When using a pay telephone, especially an older one, you may experience the exasperation of your coins not being returned to you when they should be. This may be an equipment malfunction or a rip-off. Your loss might be the result of a thief's blocking the coin return chute in order to capture the coins and hold them for recovery later. If this happens to you, notify the operator. Not only will the operator see to it that your loss is reimbursed, but more important, your call will set in motion the restoration of the phone to proper working order and perhaps the apprehension of the thief. Newer telephone instruments have built-in guards, which thwart this type of nuisance theft.

MASS TRANSPORTATION

Public transportation can be an economical and quick way of getting around in some parts of the world. However, transit crimes—robbery, rape, purse snatching, pickpocketing, indecent exposure, assault, and even homicide—have made public transportation risky. The New York City Transit Police recently reported a rise of 9 percent in felonies during the first three months of 1988 over 1987. It attributed the increase to drug-related crime. Yet, according to a recent study, a person using public transportation has substantially lower exposure to crime than he or she would have on the street.

It is a good idea to have a companion when using mass transportation in one of the more dangerous locales. Naturally this isn't always possible. Have your fare or token in your hand when you leave your home. This way you won't be required to open your handbag or produce your billfold. This will go a long way toward thwarting a pickpocket.

Don't sit near an exit. A purse snatcher could grab your belongings and be gone before you could get out of your seat. Similarly, if you are seated next to an open window, consider the possibility of someone's reaching through the window to steal your purse. The best way to protect your belongings is to place them on the seat between you and the wall of the bus or car, or protect them by holding them in your lap. Carry your purse like a football, but hold it in the arm up against the wall of the vehicle. You may wish to loop your arm *loosely* through the bag's strap, but be prepared to let it go.

Keep your wallet in an inside coat pocket, not in a back pocket, where it presents a temptation for pickpockets. Be alert to anyone who bumps into you for no reason. It's a good idea to look around and take note of who is beside and in back of you. If there is no place to sit, try to stand where you are not crowded by other people. Keep your arms close to your body. Thieves can snatch a wristwatch, particularly one held by an expansion band, right off your arm.

Never stand near the edge of a train platform. Commuters have been pushed off platforms into the paths of oncoming trains. Many robberies take place on isolated platforms. Try to stand near the token booth attendant while waiting for a subway train.

During summer months, chain snatchings reach epidemic proportions in urban areas. The best way to protect yourself from this crime is to avoid wearing a chain at all. Turn your rings around so that the stones don't show. Needless to say, don't take out your wallet or display money.

If you suspect you're being followed, don't get off at a deserted stop. Ride on to a busy one, and take a taxi or call for help. Remember, subways and buses are equipped with two-way radios. In an emergency situation, go to the driver, motorman, or conductor or to a police officer.

"Don't Sleep in the Subway, Darling" is more than the title of a once-popular song—it's excellent security advice. The alternative could be a literal "rude awakening."

EXCITEMENT IN THE STREETS

Another possible—if uncommon—street hazard is being an innocent victim of an incident not directed at you, such as a riot, fire, brawl, demonstration, or some similar chance mishap. More than one innocent bystander has been killed while a desperado shot it out with the law; more than one bystander has been run in by police along with demonstrators. If you find yourself at such a scene, seek a vantage point as far away as possible from the action, one that offers maximum cover between you and the activity.

Bear in mind that some of these exciting events might be staged. When the audience is caught up in the unfolding drama, their pockets may be in the process of being picked.

If you're a witness to a crime on the streets, don't help by getting immediately involved personally. Send help by calling the police or an ambulance. Only then should you offer your personal assistance, and even then, do so only if you're positive that there is no danger to you personally.

Security in the Streets: A Checklist
1. Don't carry more money or valuables than you can afford to lose.
2. If approached by a robber, cooperate, remain calm—surrender your valuables.
3. Try to avoid being taken to an alley or other remote location, but if your assailant insists, don't fight back.
4. Don't make any sudden moves—your attacker is probably as nervous as you are.
5. If you are physically attacked, try to get away.

6. Walk on the side of the street facing oncoming traffic.
7. On a busy street, carry your purse or briefcase on the side of you farthest from the curb, and stay close to buildings.
8. Carry a shoulder-strap purse so that it hangs straight down from your shoulder, suspended between your arm and body. The strap should not cross over your body.
9. Carry handbags with short straps as you would a football, with your arm placed through the strap.
10. Flatten yourself against a building if you hear rapidly approaching footsteps behind you.
11. If you are being followed on a well-traveled street, slow down, speed up, reverse directions—in other words, indicate to your pursuer that you are aware you are being followed. Then go straight for help.
12. Don't play games if you are followed on a deserted street. Walk briskly either to other people or to a mailbox, preparing to drop your billfold inside to prevent it from being stolen.
13. If followed, don't run straight for home unless help is available.
14. Running, screaming, and use of a loud whistle are recommended defensive weapons. Whistles, however, should not be kept in a purse or around the neck.
15. If you must carry large amounts of money, don't keep it all in one place. Money belts or certain items of women's lingerie are good alternative places for carrying cash.
16. Don't carry keys in the same place as identification that would tell a robber where to find the door that the key fits.
17. Carry credit cards only if there is some likelihood that you will be using them.
18. If you make frequent bank deposits in conjunction with your work, don't carry them with your own valuables. Use armored car services for large deposits.
19. Avoid walking the streets alone after dark. Use taxicabs whenever practical.
20. If you must walk alone at night, do not walk near cars parked at the curb or close to doorways or shrubbery, which could conceal an ambush.
21. If necessary, do not hesitate to walk in the street.
22. If you must walk streets at night regularly, vary your route to minimize the possibility of someone's lying in wait to assault you.

23. When using public transportation, sit near a companion, the motorman, or a conductor. However, take care to avoid the seat nearest an exit door.

24. If seated near an open window, protect your purse or other belongings from being stolen through the window.

25. Prepare your fare or token before you leave home, in order to avoid opening your handbag or producing your wallet.

26. Should you be walking the street and encounter an arrest, riot, fire, brawl, or other incident, resist the impulse to be a spectator, and shield yourself from the action.

27. If you witness a crime or accident while walking, send for help, don't be of help. Only if qualified help is on the way and you are positive there is no personal danger to you should you attempt to be of assistance personally.

13
Security While Shopping

Marilyn Bradkowski of Brook River is in guarded condition at Saint Diane's Hospital following an attack which occurred at the Tid-E-Time Washeteria on Locust Street last night. Her assailants, described by passersby as two teenagers, have not been apprehended. No purse was recovered near Mrs. Bradkowski, and police theorize that robbery was the motive for the attack.

Many of the suggestions in the two preceding chapters will enable you to be more secure while shopping, but there are also other factors to keep in mind. During the everyday activity of shopping, you are an especially attractive target because you're likely to be carrying more money than usual.

When you shop, you obviously have to pay for your purchases. The most secure method of doing so is to charge them, not by use of credit card but through the use of an old-fashioned charge account. The next most secure method of payment is by check, followed by credit card payment. Payment with cash, except for very small purchases, should be avoided.

Don't wear your best jewelry when shopping, and don't wear extravagant clothing—for example, your mink coat. And if, for some reason, you do have to carry a large amount of cash, take care to dress in a modest, inexpensive outfit that will call minimum attention to you.

PROTECTION OF YOUR PURCHASES

If at all possible, arrange to have your parcels delivered. That will prevent your being assaulted on the streets by someone trying to snatch your shopping bag. It will also keep a small package from being pilfered out of your shopping bag while you walk down the street or ride on an elevator or subway.

When you do carry packages home, have a small table right inside the door on which you place your parcels. Then close and lock the door. This may help prevent someone from following you right into the house—and even doing so undetected while you're carrying your purchases into another room.

If your shopping jaunt will take you to more than one store and you must carry your parcels home yourself, store them in the trunk of your car, not on the back seat. Remember, though, that while the trunk of your car is considerably more secure than the passenger section, it is by no means impregnable, and arrange your shopping itinerary so that you acquire the most expensive items last.

It is certainly more pleasant to shop with a friend than by yourself. It is also more secure. In any event, it is a tiring chore, and most dedicated shoppers occasionally take a little break. We've all enjoyed a cup of coffee or a soft drink, perhaps kicking off our shoes and stretching. But what if your packages disappeared while you were enjoying a little leisure? It's almost a certainty that you'd never see them again. You would find, if you reported the incident to the police or to security personnel, that there was little chance of recovering your newly acquired and newly lost property. You might be advised that you were a victim of larceny/theft, the most common of the eight crimes that the FBI includes of its list of serious crimes. A larceny/theft occurs every four seconds—fifteen times a minute, nine hundred times an hour. The odds are that every man, woman, and child in the country will be victimized by this crime at least once during his or her lifetime.

PARKING WHILE SHOPPING

There is little chance of being assaulted physically in a busy store or shop, but there is sometimes danger if you are parked in an out-of-the-way location. According to the National Crime Survey, over 400,000 violent crimes took place in parking lots in 1985.

Most lots are huge, have inadequate lighting, and lack reliable security. They are perfect places to commit a crime. They are usually set off from main buildings. It is easy to be accosted in a wide-open area where there are few people and help is far away. Many parkers are confused about their car's location, loaded down with packages, and concentrating on the search for their car keys. They are perfect crime victims. Many hidden spots between and underneath vehicles provide excellent hiding places for criminals.

Choose your parking place with care. In a downtown area, for example, try to use an attended parking garage, but remember to remove any personal identification materials from the car and to leave only your ignition key with the attendant. If you're parking in a shopping center lot, select a spot near the main stream of traffic—the end of the row is ideal. If your shopping excursion is likely to extend through sundown, be sure to park near a source of light. Avoid parking near extensive shrubbery, as it provides perfect cover for a criminal. Do not park next to an occupied car or near suspicious-looking individuals.

Never expose cash or valuables in a lot (or for that matter, at any time while shopping), and never leave valuables visible inside your car. Put packages in the trunk rather than on the back seat, but since many criminals are skilled at opening trunks, do not store packages at all while shopping, unless absolutely necessary. Do not leave any personal identification inside your car. Never leave an animal, and especially not a child, inside your car, no matter how short the time you expect to be away from the vehicle. Maintain your awareness as you walk through the parking lot, and walk confidently to communicate that message.

Upon reentering the parking area, do not weigh yourself down with many packages. Prepare your car keys before entering the lot. Do not walk through a lot by yourself, especially after dark. If you feel uncomfortable or see suspicious persons, ask a security guard to accompany you to your vehicle. If you think you are being followed, go quickly to a populated area, and find a security guard or police officer. Report any crime or suspicious incident in the lot. When you reach your car, glance in the back seat before getting in, and lock your doors immediately upon entry.

Be wary of strangers who approach you in a lot, and never accept their help should your vehicle fail. If anyone informs you that there is something wrong with your car, go to the closest building, preferably a populated area, and find a phone or a security guard. Call the police if you are suspicious.

Follow the regular locking and checking procedures when you park your car and when you return to it. One particularly vicious rapist in a large city preyed exclusively on women at shopping centers. His method of operation was exceedingly simple. He would follow a potential victim, inevitably a lone woman, to her car. Once she was in the car, he would enter through the unlocked passenger door, threaten her with a knife, and direct her to a lonely spot.

If all shoppers took the split second required to lock all doors when leaving and after entering cars, a great deal of crime could be avoided.

MALL SECURITY

According to the International Council of Shopping Centers, there are 28,500 shopping centers in the United States serving 163 million customers. Malls have obviously become the preferred place to shop.

Attractive as they are, however, malls also distract the shopper and can be extremely dangerous. Recently, two women were sitting in a car in midafternoon in a Memphis mall when an intruder poked the barrel of a gun through a small opening in the window of the car. He fired twice, killing one of the women and wounding the friend. In one mall parking lot in California, several women have been abducted by criminals posing as helpful passersby. In New York City, the body of a woman who had been stabbed to death was found in the back of her car at a shopping center.

In addition to the shoppers' state of unawareness, the wide variety of potential victims and the larger-than-usual amount of cash carried by shoppers attract criminals to shopping malls. Pretending to assist with packages or the car, they pull a weapon and drive away with a hostage. About 95 percent of mall crime is directed against women, the most frequent mall patrons.

While most crimes at malls, like auto theft, abduction, and rape, occur in parking areas, shoppers should also beware of swindlers and pickpockets. They should avoid wearing their best clothes and keep their jewelry to a minimum. The more affluent they appear, the more sought after they will be by criminals.

Always be aware of your purse or bag. Straps are easily cut, and you may not feel your purse being stolen. Keep your bag or purse tucked under your arm. When paying for a purchase, do not place your purse or other purchases on a counter. Knowing this is a moment of distraction, thieves take advantage of this opportunity. In the dressing rooms of a store or in a public rest room, try not to place purchases or bags on the floor, especially near a door, where they may be easily snatched.

Never place your wallet where it is visible or easily accessible in your purse or pockets. The pickpocket often bumps into a shopper, seemingly by accident, while deftly lifting a wallet. If anyone brushes against you, check for your purse and wallet immediately. Try to see whoever it was that bumped you. The criminal may not always be conspicuous, least of all in a crowded mall. Pickpockets usually pass a wallet to a confederate, so you will have to move quickly to catch one.

Always check your purchases before leaving a store to be certain that you got what you paid for. Beware of any "deal" that seems too good to be true. Criminals posing as store employees can offer you a break on a stereo or a VCR. When you get home, you may find that your fantastic purchase is a piece of wood in a box.

Crimes at malls are also perpetrated by teenagers and younger children at arcades and restaurants. Groups of teens often menace shoppers, or are disruptive or are drinking or selling drugs. Report immediately to a guard or police officer any teen causing trouble or engaging in illegal activities. Do not allow your own youngsters to spend excessive time "hanging out." They may be influenced by the negative environment and participate in the menacing done by the group.

Malls are the perfect place to abduct a child. Crowds of people ensure cover for the kidnapper, who often targets and accosts children who have strayed from their parents. Know where your children are at all times, and do not leave them unattended in stores, arcades, theaters, or rest rooms. Many child molesters wait in public rest rooms for children who enter alone. It takes only a second for someone to grab your child.

THE SUPERMARKET

Supermarkets, the most frequent shopping destinations, are often high-crime locations. For example, women have had purses stolen in supermarkets—or, more frequently, have had wallets stolen from inside purses.

Never set your purse on a shopping cart. Keep it on your arm. Many a shopper has had his or her wallet "pinched" while he or she was engrossed in pinching tomatoes. Many another has had a purse snatched by a juvenile running past the cart and right out through an open door or emergency exit.

If you do lose a purse or wallet in a supermarket, report it at once, and demand that store personnel help you try to find it. A supermarket robber, to avoid keeping incriminating evidence on his person, will remove the cash and perhaps the credit cards and then discard the wallet, so it is worth looking for.

If your purse is nabbed and it contains keys to your home and identification, change the locks on your home and car.

Many supermarkets will cash checks for the amount of purchase only. The checks must be cashed at a special cashier's window, with the customer returning to the checkout station to exchange the cash for the groceries. If you shop and pay by check at such a store, don't depend on checkout personnel to guard your groceries while you cash your check. Examine exposed items in your bag before you go to cash your check. If any are missing on your return, insist on a recheck before you pay for them. Also, be sure to protect your money while transporting it from the cashier's station to the checkout station, by wadding it up in your clenched fist. This will prevent someone from snatching it from your fingers.

REST ROOM RIP-OFFS

Several years ago, a pair of robbers devised an unusual method for committing their crimes. They simply stationed themselves inside a public rest room and robbed each person who entered. When the crowd was nearing unmanageable proportions, they forced their victims at gunpoint to undress and lie on the floor. Then they left. By the time the victims recovered their composure and their clothes, the robbers were long gone.

It is difficult to see how anyone could have guarded against this bizarre rip-off, but if any of these victims had been shopping with a friend, it is at least possible that the friend, concerned that it was taking too long for the co-shopper to return, might have sounded an alarm.

A much more frequent rest room theft involves women's purses. A thief will wait until she sees a purse on the floor inside a cubicle, then reach underneath the partial wall, snatch the purse, and flee. This can be avoided simply by keeping your purse off the floor of the cubicle. Do not hang it on the clothes hook mounted on the cubicle door. Brazen thieves have been known to lift coats, jackets, and pocketbooks off the hooks of toilet and dressing room doors. Looping your handbag over your arm would provide a great deal of protection and a minimum of inconvenience. If you are in need of a washbasin, do not select the one nearest the door. A thief could easily snatch the bag and be out the door before you could react effectively.

CREDIT CARD SECURITY

Make sure that the clerk validates only your charges with your card. It isn't uncommon for a salesclerk to validate with your card two or more charge tickets, trace your signature through one of the very thin copies of the document set, and fill in some additional items later. This is a particular hazard in a service station, where you might remain in your car while the attendant takes your card inside to complete the paperwork. Try always to stay with your card, and thereby avoid the effort of having to prove forgery later.

Organized-crime rings steal and sell credit cards. There is usually a time lag of several weeks before the numbers of stolen credit cards are distributed widely, giving the credit card criminal considerable time to use a stolen card.

When the card gets listed as missing, however, a thief may try to switch cards with you, exchanging his hot card for your clean one. Get into the habit of checking the name on your card each time it is returned to you. If you are victimized by a switch, and you discover it immediately, take it up with the manager, not with the salesperson or waiter involved. The clerk or waiter would simply claim an error and hurry to retrieve your card.

Make certain that the clerk returns *all* the carbons to you along with your receipt. The numbers on the carbon may be easily read, and this information in the hands of a card "booster" could result in an expensive experience for you.

NIGHTTIME SHOPPING

Today nearly half the work force is female, and for many the most convenient time for shopping is after work, at night. All elements of concern during daytime shopping are also present at night, when there are a few additional causes for alarm. Darkness is the ally of the thief because visibility is impaired at night. You must be more alert. If you are on foot, you will be less able to discern someone approaching you at night than you would be during the day. An intruder crouched in the back seat of your car would be more difficult to spot, and a thief who took your belongings would find it easier to disappear under the cover of darkness. Moreover, the composition of nighttime crowds is different— more muggers, pickpockets, and robbers are cruising the streets at night. Most retail establishments have fewer personnel on the job at night, so you will be less protected in the places where you do shop. At night there also tend to be more intoxicated shoppers, who are subject to irrational behavior that might be directed at you.

Self-service laundries—or, for that matter, self-service anythings—are especially dangerous at night, so dangerous that you should never go to such places alone at night. If you can't arrange to have someone accompany you, don't go.

TWENTY-FOUR-HOUR BANKING

The computer-operated twenty-four-hour banking establishments that have proliferated throughout the country are very hazardous. According to the U.S. Department of Justice, in 1983 about $262 billion was processed through 2.7 billion automatic teller machine transactions. If you feel you are being menaced while operating this banking device, you can protect yourself somewhat by entering an incorrect number three times in succession. If you do this, many machines not only will fail to deliver money to you but will also keep your card; that might avert a robbery. However, not all computerized banking devices work this way. Still better protection is to do your banking during daylight hours.

If, however, you must go to the bank at night and cannot arrange for someone to accompany you, be cautious. Look around for suspicious-looking people outside the bank or waiting nearby in a car. Check for loiterers inside the bank. Wait until questionable people leave or until others enter the bank. Have your card ready so you don't have to fumble for it, and don't waste time. Complete your transaction, and leave as quickly as possible. (Follow the same guidelines for terminals located outside a building.) Put the money and your bank card into your pocket or handbag quickly; take the time to arrange everything later. Check to see if anyone is following you; if so, go directly to the police station or any public place to ask for assistance.

Treat your bank card like cash. If it is lost or stolen, report it immediately. Never lend it to anyone or use it to help someone else with a transaction. Do not accept assistance from anyone on the use of your card. Never disclose your personal identification number. If you must record it, store the record securely. Better still, memorize the number. In selecting an identification number, do not use a sequence of numbers from your phone number, date of birth, Social Security number, street address, or any other numbers found among identification papers you carry. If a dishonest person should come into possession of your bank card, you want to deny him or her an easy guess of your identification number. If you carry several such cards, select different ID numbers for each. Thus, if someone guesses (or observes) one number, you may limit your losses to assets available through the use of that one compromised card.

Security While Shopping: A Checklist

1. Don't carry cash while shopping if it can be avoided.
2. Use a charge account, followed by—in order of preference— check, credit card, or cash.
3. Do not overdress while shopping, and avoid wearing jewelry.
4. Arrange for delivery of parcels if possible.
5. Locate a small table near the front door of your home on which to place parcels while you lock the door.
6. Use the car trunk, not the passenger compartment, for storing parcels.
7. Arrange to purchase expensive items last, to minimize the time you will be required to safeguard them.
8. Shop with a friend whenever possible.
9. Select a secure parking spot, especially if your shopping is likely to extend through sundown.
10. Deliberately park close to the building you will be entering, or park near the main flow of traffic; avoid the edges of a lot.
11. Park in a well-lit area or under a light at night. Avoid bushes that provide cover for a criminal.
12. When choosing a spot, avoid suspicious-looking persons, and do not park next to occupied vehicles.
13. Lock all doors when exiting your vehicle. If in an attended garage, leave only your ignition key with the attendant.
14. Never expose valuables or cash in the parking lot, and do not leave valuables or personal identification in the car. Place packages in the trunk only if you cannot have them delivered to your home.
15. Never leave a pet or, especially, a child unattended in a vehicle.
16. Walk purposefully through the lot to communicate confidence.
17. Avoid overloading yourself with bags when returning to your vehicle, and have your keys ready before entering the lot.
18. Do not walk alone in a lot, especially at night. If you are alone or feel uncomfortable, ask a guard to escort you to your vehicle.
19. If you suspect someone is following you, go to the nearest populated area, and find a security guard or law enforcement officer.
20. Report any crime in the parking lot.
21. Check your back seat before getting in your vehicle, and then lock all doors.

22. If you have car trouble, never accept a stranger's help. Return to a populated area, and find a phone or security guard.

23. Keep an eye on your purse, bag, and other packages. Hold purses under your arm, and never put them on a store counter or in a dressing area or rest room.

24. Do not place your wallet on top of your bag or in a pocket where it is visible and accessible. Be extra alert if someone brushes against you, and identify who it was in case you have been pickpocketed.

25. Be wary of "bargains" offered by "store employees" who may be criminals attempting to swindle you.

26. Do not permit your children to spend extended time at malls, and report any disruptive or illegal teenage behavior that you experience or witness.

27. Never leave young children unattended in a mall, especially in crowded areas or rest rooms.

28. Nighttime shopping introduces perils of its own. There are more muggers, pickpockets, robbers, and drunks, and fewer store clerks, all of which works to the shopper's disadvantage.

29. Do not leave a purse unattended in a supermarket cart.

30. Search for a purse or billfold that has been lost in a store. Thieves usually discard all but money and, in some instances, credit cards.

31. If your stolen purse contains keys and I.D.s, change your locks.

32. If you must transport money from a supermarket cashier's cage to a checkout station, protect it.

33. Keep your purse off the floor when using a public rest room.

34. Be sure that only your own credit card charge has been validated.

35. Beware the switch of a stolen credit card for your own.

36. Take extra precautions when shopping after dark.

37. Do not go to self-service or unattended merchandise or service outlets alone at night.

38. Be cautious when using twenty-four-hour banking equipment. If you notice suspicious-looking people hanging out, wait until they leave, or visit another branch.

39. Select random, difficult-to-guess identification numbers for use with bank cards.

40. If you utilize several different bank cards, select different ID numbers for each.

14
Security in the Office

. . . the average company thief is a married man, has two or three children, lives in a fairly good community, plays bridge with his neighbors, goes to church regularly, is well thought of by his boss. He is highly trusted and a good worker, one of the best in the plant. That's why he can steal so much over such long periods and why it's so hard to discover his identity.
—Mark Lipman, Stealing *(New York: Harper's Magazine Press, 1973), 160*

Most of us spend about one-third of our time on the job—not counting the time it takes us to get there and back—so it's worth taking some steps to protect yourself during what is really the bulk of your waking hours.

Every company—ranging from the one-person shop with a special hiding place for accumulations of cash to the giant defense contractor with a security department numbering thousands of employees—has some sort of security program.

YOUR COMPANY'S SECURITY PRACTICES

Don't view company security policies as an expression of your firm's lack of trust in you, but rather as a protective shield for you and your job. It has been estimated by the Chamber of Commerce of the United States that about half of all business failures may be directly attributable to employee dishonesty. So company security really can mean protection of your job as well as your person.

The Chamber of Commerce statistics also reveal that half of all the nation's workers steal from their employers. About one-sixth steal in economically significant quantities and use the products or supplies for their own benefit or give them to friends and relatives. About one-twentieth steal, again in economically significant quantities, and then resell the stolen items for gain and profit.

Statistically speaking, two houses on your block will be burglarized this year. (This figure assumes there are twenty houses on your block, ten on each side of the street, and that there are seventy-eight persons living on your block. This example is based on per capita figures of reported crimes.) Well, *thirteen* of the working people on your block will steal significantly from their employers, and four of them will resell the stolen merchandise. So you are more likely to live next to a thief than to be victimized by one.

SECURITY ON THE JOB

Don't leave billfolds or keys in your jacket or coat at work. Place your purse in a desk drawer, and lock it. Take nothing for granted. One friend, a third-grade teacher, had her purse stolen from a desk drawer in her classroom. The thief was never caught. She had only a few dollars and no credit cards with her that day, and a relative was able to bring her a spare set of keys, so she was inconvenienced very little. Because she was cautious, she had limited the size of her loss. Still, after she had changed the locks in her home and car and replaced her lost purse, wallet, glasses, driver's license, and other documents, the theft cost her well over $200. She never recovered her loss from her insurance carrier, nor was she able to establish it with the Internal Revenue Service, simply because the desk drawer was not locked. One excellent rule for protecting a handbag is this: If you are not in physical contact with your bag—actually *touching* it—then it must be locked away.

A purse is not all you might lose at the office. Other favorite targets are cash, small calculators, typewriters, clothing, pen and pencil sets, cameras, radios, and color television sets. If you work in a building with many tenants who are strangers to each other, you are much more likely to suffer a loss than if you work in a place where everyone knows everyone else, at least by sight.

When leaving your office, put calculators or other small valuable items in your desk, and lock it. Few desks have adequate locks, but you might at least prevent random pilferage this way.

You can secure large equipment such as typewriters, slide projectors, and adding machines with special desktop equipment locks, using bolts or adhesive pads. Some adhesive pads resist a pull of three tons, yet do not require the drilling of any holes in the desk.

If you encounter strangers passing through your office, a friendly "May I help you, please?" is an excellent deterrent. If the stranger is in need of assistance, he or she will be grateful. If not, he or she will probably go away. Of course, this could backfire. We know of one instance when a buyer in a major Midwestern department store asked that question of a man in coveralls holding an appliance dolly. "Yes, sir, I'm supposed to pick up that television set for the window display at the so-and-so suburban store," came the reply. The buyer not only let him take the set but even helped him load it into a truck. No one saw the driver or the TV set again.

The protection of a company's information is often more critical than the security of a company's property. If a switchboard operator should say, "I'm sorry, Mr. Smith is out of the country and won't return until the twenty-seventh," he or she might be responsible for a burglary at the Smith residence, maybe even the kidnapping of the Smith children or an assault on a member of the family, without ever realizing it.

An engineer might make a remark like, "If we don't get that boron in, we'll never have the new condensers ready for the 1990 models" and thereby place millions of dollars' worth of research and development expenditures at the disposal of a competitor. A secretary might be careless in disposing of an unnecessary carbon or photocopy (or sheet of carbon paper, for that matter) used on a highly confidential memo and cost the company millions. A casual remark by a lawyer's or physician's clerk-typist could cause a large loss in an invasion-of-privacy suit.

The list of things that can go wrong through the inadvertent release of confidential or personal information is endless. So lock up all important reports and memos when you leave the office, even if only for a few minutes. And don't be in such a hurry at quitting time that you fail to lock filing cabinets. In short, leave a clean, orderly desk when you're away from it. This way, you are doing all you can to guard against the use of confidential information against your company and thus indirectly against you.

PROTECTION AGAINST COMMON BUSINESS CRIMES

Here are just a few of the things that you, as an employee, can do to protect yourself and your company against the most common types of crimes committed against business.

Bad checks probably account for between 10 and 15 percent of crime-related business losses. If your work involves handling checks, you must guard against this type of loss. Follow your company's full procedures, and insist on adequate identification before you cash a check for anyone. If there is any doubt in your mind, or if the person offering the check cannot provide satisfactory identification, don't cash it.

If you handle cash on the job, you may come into contact with *counterfeit money*. The government will not reimburse a businessperson who accepts a counterfeit bill. If he or she accepts a counterfeit bill and attempts to pass it on, knowing it to be a bogus bill, this might well be in violation of federal laws. The easiest way to spot a counterfeit is to look at it and feel it. The paper on which legitimate bills are printed is of a special manufacture, available only to the government. It has a distinctive enough feel that a side-by-side touch comparison will enable you to determine the difference. The authentic paper is made from fibers, and its red and blue fibers are visible even to the naked eye. The engraving reproduction quality of a bogus bill will be noticeably inferior to that of an authentic bill. The background behind the pictures on genuine bills is composed of many small dots or finely etched lines. Even if the counterfeiters use a photographic process in their reproduction, counterfeit backgrounds will tend to "close in" and be considerably darker than those on legitimate bills. The same is true of the fine weblike filigree work around the borders of genuine bills.

The differences between most counterfeit bills and the genuine article are so striking that there is really no excuse for accepting a fake. When in doubt, make a side-by-side comparison, and refuse to accept a questionable bill. The person offering it will be outraged, but by holding your ground, you can avoid loss to your company.

Forgeries, especially forged checks, are another problem you may encounter. If you can't adequately identify an endorser, and the endorser can't adequately identify him- or herself, don't cash the check. Satisfactory identification consists of at least two items that bear the person's signature—for example, a driver's license and a credit card. Strictly enforced limits on the amount for which a check may be cashed are especially recommended.

Don't assume that a check is good just because it is drawn on the federal, state, or local government. If you cash such a check, and the signature of the rightful recipient has been forged by someone who stole it from a mailbox, you and your firm will suffer the loss. This is especially hazardous in the late spring or early summer, when income tax refund checks are so abundant, and also at those times when welfare, Social Security, or other assistance checks are in the mails.

SHOPLIFTING

If you work in a place that may be victimized by a shoplifter, keep your eyes open, and don't forget to ask, "May I help you?" The last thing a shoplifter wants is a lot of attention. Usually he or she will try to distract you by requesting additional merchandise or by dropping items on the floor. Keep an eye out for people wearing bulky coats or carrying large shopping bags, partially opened umbrellas, folded newspapers, or schoolbooks.

Shoplifters often work in teams. One person may take a position to block your view of the other's theft. An accomplice may create a distraction while the partner steals. Small children, accompanied by their parents, may have been trained to steal.

Pay attention to people who try on merchandise in open view of store personnel. Professional shoplifters may don sweaters, gloves, hats, and scarves and walk casually out of the store as if the merchandise were theirs.

Follow your company's policies for the apprehension and detention of shoplifters. Be alert and concerned, but play it by the book. No matter how well intentioned it may be, an overzealous reaction on your part could result in losses to you personally, and to your company, in the event of false arrest.

A number of actions can minimize shoplifting losses, which can be staggering—an average of 10 percent of gross, according to one authority. But these potential losses can be reduced significantly. Practically no one steals when store personnel are looking. Therefore, lowering the tops of shelves to four or five feet in height will enable store workers to see much more of the store. Wider aisles and open spaces, adding to the visibility, make theft more difficult. This economy is achieved, however, at the expense of space that otherwise could contain merchandise. Some trade-offs obviously will be necessary to achieve optimum use of space.

You can also extend your employees' range of vision by judiciously placing mirrors (especially the parabolic type with a wide field of vision) throughout the store.

Some of your merchandise is more expensive than the rest. The most expensive items should be afforded the protection of locked showcases.

Another protection for your better goods is to locate them as far from the exit doors as is practical. Doing so will require the thief to negotiate a longer escape route.

Spread the word that you're tough on shoplifters. Post signs in the store: "Shoplifters Will Be Prosecuted." And mean it.

SECURING THE INSIDE

Installing your cash register as near to the front of the store as possible will allow passersby to note an in-progress robbery or an after-hours burglary.

Cooperate with neighborhood merchants for your mutual self-protection. In one of the toughest areas of South Bronx, a group of merchants banded together. They installed buzzers that sounded in the buildings next to their own. It was thus relatively easy for an in-progress crime to be reported to the police, without a confrontation with the thieves. These "Buddy Buzzers" proved an excellent security weapon, at the total cost of a few dollars.

SECURING THE OUTSIDE

A determined thief will exploit every weakness that you fail to remedy adequately. Your place of business should be secured as well as your home, if not better. The typical losses of a small business are, according to one source, twenty-five times greater than those of large businesses.

Obviously, your protection must begin outside the structure, for that's where you want to contain an intruder. You should avoid leaving ladders or stacks of pallets outside the building. Either of these could provide above-ground-level entry into your business. Parking up against the building should be discouraged, because an auto not only could be used as a stepladder to the second story, but also as a convenient method of removing the loot.

EMPLOYEE THEFT

Employee theft is a more serious threat to business than shoplifting, burglary, or bookkeeping errors combined. Despite the millions spent on security devices, employee theft continues. According to the National Retail Merchants Association, large retailers (those selling more than $100 million of merchandise per year) lose a national total of $20 million a day through *internal* theft.

Thefts often occur after business hours. Employees put merchandise into their cars or hide it in garbage cans or empty boxes for later removal. Other common methods of employee theft include underadding merchandise at cash registers and changing inventory counts and accounting books.

The best way that you as an employee can help fight theft is to abide by and respect company rules. The most dedicated scofflaw might well be stealing—while attempting to make you an unwitting accomplice by undermining employee respect for antitheft rules. Such rules are necessary because some of your co-workers are undeserving of trust, and it is your obligation to do whatever you can to get rid of them.

Discovering that a co-worker is stealing is a tough problem, leading to the question of how many pencils one must steal before it becomes serious. Knowledge of an obviously serious theft might place you in actual physical danger. Yet failure to do anything about it would make you a morally, if not legally, culpable accessory. Your obligation to your employer should outweigh any loyalty that you might have to a thief who also happens to be a friend.

Extent of Employee Theft

In addition to the $7 billion annual take of employee thieves, there are other losses that are impossible to quantify. How much, for example, does it cost the basically honest employee, in terms of lost self-respect, when he or she takes things "because everybody else does"? What does it cost a harried manager to receive a financial statement that shows sudden and unexplainable losses? How much time is lost pondering these imponderable questions?

SEXUAL HARASSMENT

Many employers are codifying sexual harassment regulations. While it is in the interest of employers to issue such workplace regulations, the regulations sometimes may lack enforcement. Anyone subjected to this type of abuse has the right of redress. Harassing actions are prohibited by Section 703, Title VII of the Civil Rights Act of 1963, and depending on the nature of your employment, other legislation also may apply to you.

Sexual harassment is defined as unwelcome sexual advances, requests for sexual favors, and other verbal or physical conduct of a sexual nature where:

• Submission to such conduct is made explicitly or implicitly a term or condition of an individual's employment; or

- Submission to or rejection of such conduct by an individual is used as the basis for employment or decisions affecting the status of the individual; or
- Such conduct has the purpose or effect of unreasonably interfering with an individual's work performance, or creating an intimidating, hostile, or offensive working environment.

Your employer should have clear and specific guidelines for reporting and investigating complaints. If you feel that your employer is not providing adequate procedures for handling your complaint, you may seek satisfaction from higher-ups in the organization, or you may contact the Resource Management Division, Equal Employment Opportunity Commission, Washington, DC 20507.

OCCUPATIONAL SAFETY AND HEALTH ADMINISTRATION (OSHA)

The Occupational Safety and Health Administration (OSHA), a part of the Department of Labor, has the mission of developing and promulgating on-the-job safety and health standards. It investigates, inspects, and enforces compliance with safety and health directives. Furthermore, it issues citations and proposes suitable penalties for noncompliance.

To fulfill its responsibility to the nation's workers, this organization also has considerable powers of enforcement. The main thrust of OSHA seems directed against on-the-job accidents and protection against hazardous chemicals. For information or assistance, you may contact OSHA, Department of Labor, Washington, DC 20210.

PROTECT YOUR PROPERTY

It is unfortunate that the specter of crime threatens us in our offices, as well as in our homes and on the streets. Merchants and cab drivers are used to on-the-job assault, and secretaries, executives, and the steno pool are rapidly rising on the risk scale.

Today's office is much more sophisticated than in days past, and the equipment used is much more expensive. A generation ago, a steno pad and a typewriter were the tools of the trade for word processors. Today's equipment can command much higher prices. The wonder computers of the 1960s, which revolutionized our banking industry, had less computing power than the PC sitting on today's secretarial desk.

Among many truisms that describe and define crime is this: if you have something both valuable and small, someone will try to steal it. That is why security guards have replaced the elevator operators in most office buildings. Even if your office has no easily portable and valuable equipment, a thief may steal your telephone in a second or two.

An intruder in your building may have been looking for physicians' offices and drugs and, on the way out, take your purse. At lunchtime, most office personnel are taking a break, leaving one person to take care of the office. If safeguards are ignored, much mischief can be done.

Excellent protection is a building guard, who will be a substantial deterrent to the criminal. Another protection lies in locking spaces for valuable items, including the personal property of those working in the building.

The very best protection, however, is to be found in an alert and caring employee group. Employees should be reminded regularly that they devote about 30 percent of their lives to their jobs, and with that sort of commitment, they need to do everything they can to protect the environment in which they spend so much of their time. Much of what is stolen is their property. And what is stolen from the employer affects them as well, since their job security and prosperity depend on the employer's continued survival.

Security in the Office: A Checklist

1. Comply with and support your company's safety and security program and regulations, and insist that others do the same.
2. Protect billfolds, keys, purses, and other personal valuables on the job.
3. Challenge strangers in restricted areas.
4. Do not discuss company affairs off the job.
5. When leaving the office, even for a short period of time, clean up and secure your work space, with special attention to confidential documents, and also provide for the protection of company equipment assigned to you.
6. If you handle money as part of your job, insist on positive identification before you cash any checks, and refuse obviously counterfeit or questionable currency.
7. If you work in a retail establishment or any other business, guard against shoplifting and employee theft within the framework of the law.
8. To deter shoplifting, speak to all customers in your area. Be wary

of bulky coats, large shopping bags, partially opened umbrellas, and folded newspapers.

9. Know your company's policy on dealing with shoplifters, and adhere to it.
10. Make certain your employer has clear and adequate guidelines for handling complaints of sexual harassment.
11. Retain security guards, because they provide substantial deterrent to the criminal.

15
Vacations, Business Trips, and Traveling

It was a routine business trip for Marshall D. Illing and, up until the third night, an uneventful one. On the advice of a person he met at the Purple Onion Lounge, he went to the Cascade Grill for a frog leg dinner. He found on arrival that the Cascade did not serve frogs' legs and never had. While awaiting a taxi to return to his hotel, he was robbed of $475 by a lone gunman.

Travel usually imposes an entirely different regimen on a person. The traveler may suffer from jet lag. He or she almost certainly dines differently, does different things, perhaps keeps different hours, may drink more, and in general attempts to cram as much of the new and different as is possible into a limited space of time.

The traveler also is probably carrying more money than usual, feels less self-confident, has fewer places to turn to for assistance (and is less able to find the assistance that is available), and, because of his or her dress or speech, is easily identifiable as being out of his or her element. In other words, the traveler is a "mark," and everybody knows it— unless, of course, he or she takes the trouble to dress to blend into the surroundings, to behave in a manner that doesn't attract attention, to avoid overindulgence in drink, to confine his or her activities to the wholesome, and to leave dens of iniquity to the more daring.

Travel experts estimate that over 6.1 million Americans venture abroad each year. *Your Trip Abroad*, published by the State Department, contains very useful information for travelers including information on passports, medicines, currency, safety, and what consultants are able to do if you get into trouble in a foreign country. This booklet may be obtained from:

R. Woods
Consumer Information Center
Pueblo, CO 81009
(Item 162T)

The remainder of this chapter discusses many of the pitfalls that await the unwary traveler.

CURRENCY PROBLEMS

Away from home, you must first deal with the matter of money. Far removed from the neighborhood drugstore where you customarily cash checks, you are faced with the prospect of carrying more cash than you feel comfortable with. The obvious and best solution is not to do it. Stick within a reasonable cash limit. Traveler's checks are considerably more secure than cash and are accepted as legal tender throughout the world. Certain bank credit cards, such as Visa or MasterCard, can be used for cash advances through any bank sponsoring these services throughout the world. Other credit cards often have similar arrangements.

GETTING HELP

Language problems can come up even if you never cross a national border. The farther you go from home, the more pronounced language differences can become. It thus pays to learn at least enough of any local language to report a crime or to ask for assistance.

One problem you might encounter in an unfamiliar place is being unable to recognize a law enforcement officer when you see one. Uniforms vary widely, even within a single community.

Going to a hotel doorman for help—which happens every day all over the world—can be a waste of valuable time in an emergency.

THE STRANGER

You are considerably more likely to encounter crimes against your person, especially assault and robbery, when you're away from home. Particularly on the increase are thefts, which the robber is reasonably certain will never be reported. A classic example of this involves the big-spending visitor who utilizes a taxi driver or bellhop to find him an after-hours bottle of bourbon or a supply of marijuana. Even if he receives colored water or a small packet of oregano, he will, in all likelihood, take no action. To do so would be to implicate himself in a crime.

A variation on this theme involves a prostitute and her accomplice. She lures her victim to a hotel room, where he is rewarded not with rapture, but with robbery at the hands of the accomplice. Rarely will the visiting "john" report the crime, even if he has no wife or family at home, simply because he does not wish to return to the city to testify at a trial. He may chalk it up to experience, even though he will probably have suffered a greater than average loss.

SECURITY IN YOUR HOTEL ROOM

Perhaps you have concluded that the best way to avoid being victimized in the big, strange city is to avoid the hostile environment outside by retreating to the safety and security of your hotel room. But the key you are given when you check in isn't, unfortunately, the only one that will open your door. Even if it were, many hotel room doors can be easily opened by slipping a plastic card or flexible metal spatula into the crack between the door and its frame. Most hotel rooms provide some backup device such as a door chain or a dead bolt that is operated by a turn knob, by the additional turn of a key, or by a button that, when pushed, "excludes all keys."

Because there is a way that these added features may be defeated, you should consider improvising certain protective measures of your own. For example, a chair back wedged under a doorknob can be an effective additional "lock," as can a furniture barricade. Placing an empty dresser

A portable travel lock adds peace of mind away from home.

drawer on the molding at the top of the door so that it will fall if the door is opened can be an effective intrusion alarm. Inserting a simple rubber wedge in the crack between the door and floor will always prevent the door from being opened. And as a last resort, you might even want to consider carrying your own portable travel lock; when this lock is attached, it is very difficult to open the door without breaking it down.

Windows or balconies accessible from outside should be locked, and don't open your room door unless you determine the identity of the caller. Call the front desk if you are in doubt about room service, a bellhop, a housekeeper, or other hotel personnel.

A HOTEL FIRE

There are more than ten thousand hotel fires in the United States each year. In 1979, hotel fires caused 140 deaths and 1,225 injuries. Review carefully all fire instructions provided by the hotel. These are usually posted on your room door; if not, request a set of instructions from the front desk. Determine whether the fire signal is a bell or other audible signal, and ascertain what to do if the alarm is activated.

Before retiring for the night, you should perform this life-saving exercise. Step into the corridor outside your room, and locate the nearest fire exit. Usually, it will be easy to find, because it will probably be illuminated and should bear the word *EXIT.* Next, count the number of doors between your room and the emergency exit. If smoke should engulf the floor on which you are staying, you would be able to locate the fire exit even if your vision were completely obscured. Counting the doors would lead you to safety.

In the event of fire, try to leave as soon as you see or smell smoke. First, however, carefully touch your room door. Only if it is not hot should you carefully open it, just a little, and while holding your breath, examine the passageway. If all appears in order, return to your room, get your key and a wet towel, and fill your lungs with air. Make for the emergency exit, either upright or on all fours, depending upon air quality. The wet towel can, literally, be a life saver. It may be used for many things. Use it to wipe your face and eyes, to cool and filter the air you breathe, and to cool and protect exposed skin surfaces. If you encounter smoke outside your room, drop to your knees, since the air near the floor is less likely to be filled with volatile, toxic substances. Do not use the elevator; elevator shafts usually fill with smoke during a fire. Proceed to the nearest fire exit, and determine the location of the fire. If it is above you, descend the stairs; if it is below, ascend the stairs toward the roof.

It is possible that you will not be able to escape a fire that has spread to a number of floors of a structure. You may be forced to return to your room to ride out the fire. In this event, close the door. It can offer protection against the spread of the fire into your room. Fill the tub with water—immersing yourself may save you from serious burns. Put dampened towels around the door to help prevent the spread of noxious gases into the room. Try to maintain an attitude of optimism. Most occupants survive hotel fires, and the responding fire-fighting units will muster every available resource to combat such fires.

Above all, do not panic. Your chances of surviving are greater if you maintain your composure.

MOTOR VACATION PROBLEMS

If you are traveling by automobile, make special efforts to travel securely. The trunk of your car is more secure than the passenger compartment but is still no formidable obstacle to a burglar. If you are stopping for the night, take all your bags and packages into your room with you. They are much more likely to be there when you look for them the next morning.

Consult a service such as the American Automobile Association (AAA) or a travel agency for travel advice about such things as speed traps or other hazards, things to do, things not to do, recommended motels, and so forth. Remember, your out-of-state (or country) license plates brand you as a stranger and hence as a potential easy victim.

Take time to learn the local traffic rules and regulations, and be certain that you are adequately covered by your insurance company. Personnel managing border-crossing points are often excellent sources of information concerning legal and insurance requirements and road conditions as well. Travel clubs and motoring associations are often even better sources.

SOUVENIR SHOPPING

Shopping is almost invariably a part of any travel. It is unlikely that you will be shopping in a place where you have a charge account, and little more likely that you would be able to pay by check. However, traveler's checks are almost always a suitable substitute for cash, and many stores worldwide accept credit cards. When souvenir shopping, you can anticipate walking the streets with your packages. Carry your purse or

briefcase in the same hand as your parcels, with the purse or briefcase—
and your most valuable purchase—close to your body.

PUBLIC TRANSPORTATION

If you're traveling by air or other public carrier, don't pack your luggage
too full, and be sure to lock it. An overpacked bag will often pop open if
dropped. Dishonest baggage handlers may drop bags deliberately and
rifle their contents or may open unlocked bags. Of course, even a locked
bag can be broken into with little effort, so cash, jewelry, and other
expensive items should always be packed in carry-on luggage. Be careful,
though. A new breed of thief haunts security screening checkpoints,
looking for purses or briefcases to steal. Keep yours in sight.

Be careful about safeguarding your airline ticket. Not only are unused
tickets redeemable for cash, but organized rings of thieves are in business
to steal and resell valid tickets. Some particularly brazen thieves have
even been known to approach passengers seated in waiting areas and ask
to see their tickets, whereupon they take the valid tickets from the
passengers' flight coupon books and then hand them boarding passes
picked out of a trash container.

If you have a number of packages or pieces of luggage, and if you have
a long layover in an air terminal, use one of the coin-operated lockers,
preferably near your departure gate, to store your belongings. Once
you've retrieved all your packages, be extremely careful about accepting
offers of assistance from anyone other than air carrier station personnel
or skycaps.

Try to establish taxi fares from the airport to your destination in
advance. Unscrupulous drivers will often try to overcharge an unwitting
visitor.

CAMPING OR WILDERNESS VACATIONING

If you are taking a vacation trip using a camper or motor home, be sure
all the doors and windows are locked while you're on the road. It is
relatively easy for you to avoid a hitchhiker, and it is also in your best
interest to avoid a stowaway.

Maybe your vacation is going to involve a return to nature. You're
going to backpack through the high country and commune with the
earth and sky. Fine—but watch yourself. A bear rummaging through
your food isn't the only hazard you might encounter. A far more serious
threat to your safety and security is your fellow camper. Every year there

are many reports of rapes, assaults, robberies, and other crimes in isolated camping areas. You can best protect yourself by checking in with ranger stations or park police and by camping at sites they suggest. At least let them know where you plan to be. Take the time to find out how to reach help on foot, just in the unlikely event that you might need to. And introduce yourself to any campers near you; you *could* need their assistance.

If you are threatened and your car is nearby, your horn will carry a long distance in still mountain air.

RESORT AREAS

Your tastes in vacation spots may run more to the bright lights and activity of the resort than the isolation of the campsite. Marauding bears may be a rarity on the beach, but human wolves and jackals are not. Pimps, hustlers, deviates, robbers, strong-arms, organized criminals, con artists, addicts, shakedown artists, pickpockets, and all types of plain and fancy hoodlums haunt these areas. Always ask yourself why any stranger is going out of his or her way to be friendly and accommodating. If you can't come up with a good answer, beware.

If you are going to devote an evening to a round of nightclubbing or a day to shopping, take the suggestions of the hotel manager or desk clerk, rather than those of a taxi driver or the cocktail waitress in a bar. If at all possible, go places with a crowd of your choosing. It is usually the lone, lost sheep that falls victim to the wolf pack. Stay on the beaten path, especially at night. See the quaint out-of-the-way places during the day, when the light is better, preferably in the company of a reliable guide.

Vacations, Business Trips, and Traveling: A Checklist
1. Utilize traveler's checks or credit cards, rather than carrying large amounts of cash.
2. Plan for any language barriers. Try to know some of the language commonly spoken wherever you're traveling.
3. Learn to recognize the uniforms of local law enforcement officers.
4. Attempt to dress inconspicuously.
5. Avoid meeting strangers in unknown, isolated places.
6. Don't depend on the door of your hotel room to protect you and your valuables, whether you're in the room or not. For extra protection use a chair, a drawer, a rubber wedge, or a portable travel lock.

7. In a hotel, lock balcony doors or any windows accessible from outside.
8. Locate fire exits; be able to recognize the fire alarm signal, and plan your actions in the event of a hotel fire.
9. If escape during a fire is not possible, fill the tub with water, and be prepared to ride out the fire in the bathroom.
10. In an auto, use your trunk for carrying luggage.
11. Bring all your luggage into the hotel room with you at night.
12. Use the AAA, travel agencies, or other reliable sources for information about where you're going and what you should do, or avoid, while there.
13. Exercise caution when shopping, because you probably won't have the conveniences of charge accounts, check cashing, or package delivery that you have at home. Carry the most valuable package nearest your body.
14. Lock your baggage, and don't overpack when using public transportation.
15. Guard your transportation tickets.
16. Store luggage in a coin-operated locker during a layover.
17. Use only skycaps or other authorized baggage-handling personnel for assistance with your luggage.
18. Determine taxi fares before you use taxi service.
19. Lock camper or motor home doors, even while driving.
20. Notify rangers, park police, or nearby campers of your camping location.
21. Use your auto horn as an emergency alarm.
22. Be especially dubious of unwarranted attention or offers of friendship from strangers in resort areas.
23. Take precautions against pickpockets in a crowd.
24. Go sightseeing with a group of your own choosing, and be cautious of suggestions for places to see and things to do.

PART THREE
FAMILY AND COMMUNITY SECURITY

16
Drug and Alcohol Abuse

A twenty-five-year-old security guard at the Center City Community Center was slashed forty-one times when he was surprised by four apparent cocaine users. When he asked one of them for identification, he was jumped by all four. Three of them wielded knives.

The history of drug abuse is long and checkered. Stone Age people used hallucinogenic mushrooms to alter moods. Socrates, allegedly a corrupter of Athenian young people, died of a self-induced dose of poison hemlock.

And like our ancestors, we take drugs that we don't need—painkillers when our only pain is mental, amphetamines to keep us awake when our biological clocks tell us that we should be sleeping, and barbiturates to bring us down from the frenzy of our diet pills. We may accelerate the actions of these drugs with a liberal addition of alcohol (the most widely used drug in the world), sometimes with fatal results.

Our children not only abuse the same drugs that we do, but sniff a few of their own—glue, typewriter correction fluid, and some aerosol propellants.

We are outraged when our children mirror our own behavior, and querulously damn our children for learning too well the lessons we teach.

Approximately twenty-three million Americans illegally use controlled substances every month. One in five people twenty to forty years of age use drugs regularly. One in six workers is on drugs, costing American business $60 billion a year mostly in decreased productivity. About 824,000 persons are arrested each year for drug-related offenses.

139

Heroin, cocaine, and marijuana account for 3,600 deaths a year.

Drugs are a major factor in crime, and some authorities believe that drugs are the principal cause of crime. A magazine article on violent crime noted that criminologists estimate that half of all street crime is drug-related. Perhaps the most significant of the drug-related street criminals are cocaine users, who finance their addiction through theft, selling drugs, and a host of other crimes, including con games, forgery, gambling, and pimping. One study found that 243 opiate addicts were responsible for 500,000 crimes during an eleven-year period. Two-thirds of this group had from 100 to 365 crime-days per year during the time they were taking drugs. During periods of abstinence, the crime-days decreased to 40.8 each year.

Obviously the drug problem is serious. If you have a teenager with a drug problem, he or she needs help, and so do you. Your family physician, even the child's pediatrician, can provide guidance once it is determined that a problem exists.

RECOGNIZING A TEENAGER WITH A DRUG PROBLEM

Because the parent is the most effective person to intervene in a child's drug abuse, parents must be aware of the symptoms of drug abuse. First of all, drug use usually produces noticeable physical changes in a user—sleeplessness, diarrhea, dilated pupils, vomiting, involuntary muscular movements (twitching), runny eyes or nose, loss of appetite, lethargy or torpor not unlike intoxication, yellow stains on fingers (caused by the high tar element in marijuana joints), sudden weight loss, craving for sweets, excessive thirst, sweating, shakiness, itching, and, of course, the telltale needle tracks not only on the arms but on the legs, abdomen, and other parts of the body. The user may be inconsistent in actions—for example, sitting for long periods in a trancelike state and then suddenly becoming hyperactive.

Drug use may also manifest itself in emotional or personality changes. A volatility of temperament, ranging from extreme happiness to blackest depression, may signal drug use; so, too, may uncharacteristic anger, radical changes in activity patterns or choice of associates, a sudden deterioration in physical appearance, sloppiness in dress, or inattention to personal hygiene. School grades may drop, and the drug user may lose interest in things that once held importance, such as school, athletics, and dating. The drug user may seem to be always tired, coming home only to fall asleep. A drug-troubled child may spend considerable time in the house, especially in a locked bathroom. A previously friendly and outgoing child may suddenly become secretive. A formerly easygoing child may become irritable and overly sensitive. The young user may be argumentative and have angry outbursts for no apparent reason.

There may be other evidence of drug use—the presence of the burned ends of marijuana joints (often referred to as roaches) or more serious drug paraphernalia, such as a "work kit" with syringes, cotton, needles, a "cooker" (a metal bottle cap used for converting heroin into a liquid so it can be injected), or small glassine envelopes tucked into a dresser drawer.

A number of steps describe those who abuse drugs. The beginning stage of an abuser is characterized by an ability to take it or leave it alone. If the use of drugs becomes more frequent, with periodic or chronic states of insensibility or limited perception, that person is described as a chronic user. Beyond that point, a person who develops a compelling need, as opposed to desire, to continually obtain drugs, at whatever cost in money or action, is addicted.

FREQUENTLY ABUSED DRUGS

Alcohol

Alcohol is the most widely used of the drugs of abuse. One recent study estimated that 113 million Americans drink alcohol at least once a month and that alcohol abuse costs society over $100 billion a year. A study by the House of Representatives' research group, the Office of Technology Assessment, pegged the national cost of alcohol abuse at $120 billion. The National Safety Council estimates that 13,000 lives annually could be saved with mandatory seat belt regulations; alcohol is responsible for about 100,000 deaths a year.

Use of alcohol causes impairment of muscle coordination and of judgment. Prolonged use can cause heart and liver damage. Alcohol contributes to many fatal automobile accidents. In overdose quantities, it may also cause death. Withdrawal may cause anxiety, insomnia, tremors, delirium, and convulsions.

Alcohol, particularly in combination with other drugs, is the most deadly of commonly used drugs. It is extremely likely to cause physical dependence, tissue damage, and changes in behavior; its user is also moderately likely to develop tolerances, requiring increasingly larger doses to produce its effect.

Practically every one of us has had the experience of ingesting alcohol. More than 90 percent of high school students have consumed alcohol at least once; two-thirds will have had an alcoholic beverage in any given month; one-fourth don't drink at all; one in twenty drink so much that therapy is required, and one of every forty-three of these young people will leave school because of alcohol.

Teenagers drink alcohol for two main reasons: peer pressure and parental attitude toward drinking. As with virtually every aspect of adolescent behavior, peer pressure is primary in determining how young people will react to different situations.

Abuse of alcohol, even by grammar school children, is fast becoming a nagging national problem. Of American children in grades four, five, and six, 42 percent have sampled wine-based carbonated beverages. Only 17 percent, one in six, thought that daily use of these products would prove harmful.

Alcohol is significantly present in 90 percent of child abuse cases; it plays a role in incest and neglect. Children of alcoholics have compulsions to control their environment and to deny their feelings, and they have low self-esteem, guilt, and a restricted ability to enter into satisfactory relationships. They also tend toward learning disabilities, anxieties, suicidal tendencies, and compulsive achieving.

One issue not much discussed a few years ago concerns children of alcoholic parents. Whether weaknesses concerning alcohol are inherent or acquired, the fact remains that more than half of all alcoholics, some twenty-eight million, have an alcoholic parent; one-third of American families contain at least one alcohol abuser. The child of an alcoholic home, in addition to the likelihood of having alcohol-related problems, has the further high risk of becoming alcoholic or marrying someone who becomes alcoholic. It is almost as if alcoholism is a contagious disease.

Problems of alcoholics' children are quite difficult for others to determine, for these children are usually adept at engaging in socially acceptable behavior, and tend toward social acceptability. Nevertheless, when such children are committed to the juvenile justice system, its courts, prisons, and other facilities, their numbers are disproportionately larger than their counterparts without family histories of alcohol.

Too often, youngsters drink excessively at parties or other social functions and then attempt to drive home. The deaths of thousands have resulted from this frivolous behavior. Many accidents could have been avoided by having a designated driver, a friend who had agreed not to indulge on that occasion. Or you might have made a "contract" with your teenagers stipulating that they call you for the drive home should they have decided to drink with their friends.

Depressants

Drugs that depress the central nervous system are used medically to treat tension and some neuroses, to control pain and severe diarrhea, to minimize the effects of cough and cold symptoms, and to treat insomnia. Included among the depressants are barbiturates, narcotics, heroin, morphine, codeine, hypnotics, and methaqualone. These drugs are either injected into the veins or swallowed as liquid or pills. Drowsiness, confusion, impaired judgment, pupil constriction, lethargy, and needle marks may be valid evidence of the use of depressants.

The lesser hazards of using these drugs include infection, appetite loss, and nausea; more severe hazards are addiction, withdrawal symptoms, and death from overdoses, drug-induced accidents, and/or severe interactions with alcohol. Withdrawal from these drugs may lead to anxiety, insomnia, tremors, delirium, convulsions, and death.

Hallucinogens

Hallucinogenic drugs alter one's perceptions of reality. There is little, if any, medical application for them. There are, however, some experimental uses. Among these drugs are PCP (angel dust), LSD, mescaline, and psilocybin. The latter two occur naturally, mescaline being a type of cactus, and psilocybin a mushroom native to South America. PCP is often smoked; the others usually swallowed or injected.   The cactus and mushroom configurations are ingested in their natural state.

PCP and LSD are, perhaps, the two most behaviorally damaging drugs. It is little wonder that one of PCP's street names is "killer." In addition to aggressive behavior, users of hallucinogens exhibit slurred speech, blurred vision, confusion, incoordination, agitation, hallucinations, illusions, and broad mood swings. These chemicals are particularly hazardous, for they can be stored in the body's tissues and, months after the last use, be released from tissue imprisonment to profoundly affect behavior. Other hazards are anxiety, depression, breaks from reality, and emotional collapse. Strangely, there is no apparent symptom of withdrawal associated with these drugs.

Inhalants

Inhalants, as their name signifies, are abused by inhaling or sniffing. Among these substances are gasoline, airplane glue, paint thinner, dry-cleaning solution, laughing gas, and amyl nitrate. Abuse of these drugs has these symptoms: poor motor coordination; impaired vision, memory, and thought processes; abusive, violent behavior; and light-headedness.

The hazards of using these substances include a high risk of sudden death; drastic weight loss; and substantial damage to blood, liver, and bone marrow. Among the causes of death resulting from abuse are anoxia, neuropathy, muscle weakness, and anemia.

Cannabis

Cannabis includes marijuana and hashish. In many parts of this country, these particularly popular drugs are the largest cash crop. Cannabis is usually smoked, although sometimes it is swallowed in solid form.

A sweetish, burnt odor is present when cannabis is used. Some symptoms of abuse are loss of interest in what goes on around a person, lack of motivation, paranoia, mood shifts, infertility, and sometimes weight loss. Hazards of using this drug include damage to lungs, heart, and the body's immune system. Although not physically addicting, these drugs can engender a strong psychological dependence. Withdrawal from cannabis may result in insomnia, hyperactivity, and decreased appetite.

Stimulants

Amphetamines and cocaine are both deadly, addictive drugs. Amphetamines are usually taken in pill form, and cocaine is commonly inhaled as a powder. Their availability in liquid form tends to intensify their harmfulness.

Both drugs tend to cause excesses of activity and irritability, and often are accompanied by mood swings—an intense high followed by dysphoria. Even in average doses, they are often fatal, capable of producing loss of appetite, hallucinations, paranoia, convulsions, coma, and brain damage. In addition, there is the distinct possibility of intense psychological dependence. Among withdrawal symptoms are apathy, long periods of sleep, irritability, disorientation, and depression, sometimes leading to suicide.

The Cocaine Generation

Twenty million Americans have used cocaine in their lives. Of this group, as many as eight million are regular users. Between 15 and 20 percent of the high school graduating class of 1985 had used cocaine at least once. The number of *regular* users increased dramatically between 1982 and 1985, from 4.2 million to 5.8 million. So serious is the cocaine problem that, for the first time in ten years, Americans consider drugs the principal problem among students.

Many high schools around the nation have found it necessary to prohibit students from bringing electronic pagers ("beepers") on campus. There is a tendency among drug dealers to utilize minor children for the delivery of controlled substances. One student was called into the principal's office to investigate possession of a beeper. He was asked to empty his pockets, and five packets of cocaine were found. He was a thirteen-year-old eighth-grader.

More and more children are being recruited for selling drugs. One thirteen-year-old gang member from East Los Angeles rakes in $200 a week selling cocaine. He uses the drug money to rent a Nissan Z, even though at four feet, ten inches, he has a problem seeing over the dashboard.

The incidence of drug gangs is growing rapidly in most major cities. Los Angeles has the most extensive problem, with an estimated 600 gangs and 75,000 members. Chicago has an estimated 100 gangs with 13,000 members; New York City has 50 gangs and 5,000 members. Many smaller cities have been reporting increases in the activity of drug gangs. These gangs are armed with Uzis, AK-47 assault rifles, M-16 rifles, nine-millimeter semiautomatic pistols, and AR-15 semiautomatics. More than seventy police officers have been killed over the last decade investigating and arresting drug dealers.

Cocaine is tricky. It leads you down a primrose path, only to abandon you in the briars and brambles. Initially, it gives you what you believe to be increased confidence and sociability, even control of your environment. You don't realize that your euphoria is mere illusion, at least not until it's too late. But for the rosy early stages, you're on top; you're in total control.

Continued use, though, takes the edge off of the feelings of well-being, to be replaced by stress and depression. You also find it takes increasingly greater doses of cocaine to elevate you to the "good" feeling you once enjoyed. You find yourself edgy, confused, and depressed. Your only return avenue to the heights you once reached is more and more cocaine, which produces less and less of the drug's early promise. You find that you require stronger and stronger doses just to maintain not a high, but mere functional capability. You will, by now, have lost your job and your self-respect; you've abandoned your friends in your undeviating search for the lost euphoria of coke. In time, the hallucinations take hold of you, and finally you mix large numbers of different drugs, and you die.

What is even more disquieting is the large number of cocaine users who are freebasing, using "crack," or otherwise intensifying the potency of the cocaine they use. Crack, a highly concentrated, extremely addictive form of cocaine, claimed the life of an All-American basketball player the day after he was drafted to play in the professional league. A poll by the University of Michigan showed that 6 percent of American high school seniors had used crack.

Users claim euphoria, increases in alertness, greater sociability, feelings of increased strength, a decrease in appetite, and a decreased need for sleep.

On the other hand, physicians report that the use of these stronger drugs can induce the most severe of psychological dependencies, which continues and intensifies long after the early exhilaration ceases. As the euphoria abates, it is replaced by aggression, suspicion, even complete psychotic outbursts. Cardiac arrest, sometimes preceded by coma, is the frequent result of cocaine overdoses.

A perplexing question is whether these substances are satisfying natural appetites. Experiments with other primates (monkeys, for example) have produced conflicting evidence. In one experiment, rhesus monkeys refused to smoke tobacco or marijuana. All monkeys, however, will smoke cocaine, preferring it to either sex or food. One monkey, the subject of a cocaine experiment, sat patiently pressing a button almost thirteen thousand times, to receive a single dose of cocaine.

The countries in South America and Asia that supply cocaine have sometimes seen their entire economies shift to a dependence on these crops, and the consequent rise in power of those who buy, process, and distribute them.

Ecstasy

Ecstasy is, perhaps, the heir-apparent to the "in drug" mantle. Reports from a trend-setting West Coast university indicate that about one-third of students have experimented with the drug. While research has shown that the drug produces brain damage in animals, there is no clear evidence that it is either toxic or safe for human use. The drug has been listed as a Schedule I substance, meaning that possession is illegal unless government-agency approval is obtained, even for researchers.

The substance, a mild amphetamine (often mentholated), first appeared in 1914, intended as an appetite suppressant, but it is possible that it was never used for this purpose. As recently as 1986, it was considered a "small-time" drug by federal authorities. Scant research is available, but there is some evidence that indicates that the drug reduces fear but increases anxiety and defensiveness. This combination could likely produce combativeness and antisocial behavior in users.

WHERE TO FIND HELP

The best place for immediate help is a hospital with a staff specifically trained to treat addicts. If your hospital does not have such a treatment facility, it will be able to refer you to one that does.

An effective chemical dependency program is structured to treat the patient's physical and psychological needs by providing expert medical and psychiatric care. A typical program includes a staff of physicians (including psychiatrists), clinical social workers, family therapists, registered nurses, and substance abuse counselors. Many programs are divided into five phases, which focus on individual, group, and family therapy. These treatment levels include:

1. Medically supervised evaluation
2. Medically supervised detoxification
3. Rehabilitation
4. Intensive family program
5. Aftercare

The initial four phases of the typical treatment program often last twenty-eight days and emphasize individual and group therapy. Moreover, the patient's family is encouraged to participate in the rehabilitative process. Family members also receive individual and group therapy and attend educational lectures on substance abuse.

An aftercare program is essential because it recognizes the previous and special problems encountered when a recovering addict/alcoholic reenters the community. Therefore, the recovering addict/alcoholic is required, for at least two years, to attend regular "growth group" sessions and to participate in self-help groups, such as Narcotics Anonymous and Alcoholics Anonymous. An effective aftercare program also provides counseling and support for family members.

In the early 1970s there was a surge in treatment programs, but the growth failed to keep pace with the rising number of addicts. Unfortunately, many abusers who seek help must wait months to enter a treatment program. You can help by joining advocates who lobby for more and better treatment programs.

Another possible source of help is a drug rehabilitation center, such as Phoenix House in New York and California, where the drug abuser can be treated as an outpatient or can live on the premises. These centers operate group sessions at which ex-addicts and professional staff members work together to teach people how to live drug-free lives. Through open and honest discussion, members of the sessions try to determine the root causes of their drug involvement and how they must change so that they no longer need drugs as crutches.

Other users may benefit to a greater extent from one-to-one sessions with a psychotherapist. Here the drug abuser with the help of a trained therapist can perhaps find the road to rehabilitation—possibly more quickly than in group encounters.

PREVENTING DRUG AND ALCOHOL ABUSE

Here are some helpful preventive guidelines:

Curb your own substance use. Children are great imitators. If they see you using drugs, they are likely to follow your example. If you smoke marijuana or drink excessively, you are only asking for trouble. Children may not have the ability to know their limits or to use drugs such as liquor in moderation.

Know your children's friends. Perhaps you can view them more objectively than you can your own child. Be sure you meet your child's dates.

Do not keep outdated medications around the house. This is particularly applicable to diet drugs or painkillers. In addition to the obvious opportunity for abuse, there exists the possibility of accidental overdose and even death.

Help your teenager find benign activities. The active child—one involved with school clubs, special projects, hobbies, and sports—may not feel a need to use drugs out of frustration and boredom.

Read up on drug abuse. Share current literature about drug abuse with your child.

Know your child. This is the most important measure you can take. Make time available for you and your child to talk about problems, worries, dreams, and goals. Teach your child through example that facing and coping with problems are much better than escaping from them. Escape through the use of drugs is only temporary and creates, in turn, still more problems. If your child knows that you care, there will be no question for which he or she may have to look to drugs as an answer.

Over the long term, we must realistically admit that this nation is fast reaching the point of being caught in a cocaine stranglehold. How can we reasonably expect to fight against a pleasure that monkeys (and perhaps humans) prefer to sex and food?

One observer suggests a unique measure to stem the nation's tide of drug abuse. He notes that there are already on our statute books regulations that permit the seizure of automobiles used to transport illegal drugs. His suggestion is simple: enforce those laws. How many Wall Street abusers would have to lose their Mercedes or BMWs before demand for coke and crack and rock would dry up? That particular solution to our drug problem may be a bit extreme, but we are fast nearing the point where exceptional measures may be called for.

Drug and Alcohol Abuse: A Checklist

1. Beware of the physical signs of drug use, which may include watery eyes, dilated pupils, loss of appetite, insomnia, heavy perspiration, and even needle tracks on any part of the body.

2. Watch for sudden changes in personality. A normally happy person may abruptly become hypersensitive and suffer tearful episodes for no apparent reason.

3. If you discover a drug abuser, urge that person to seek professional help. Drug rehabilitation programs are especially useful.

4. Set a good example for your children. Remember, if they see you using drugs, they are likely to copy your behavior.

5. Make sure that your child is not part of a teenager group that uses drugs for kicks.

6. Do not keep old prescription drugs in the medicine cabinet, where they can be found and swallowed by young children.

7. Help your child develop an interest in pastimes such as recreational clubs and team sports. Do not let your child use drugs for "entertainment."

8. Be familiar with the recent literature on drug abuse. Share this with your child.

9. Encourage your child to come to you with problems when life is going smoothly. If you keep communication lines open, your child may seek your advice on important matters that otherwise could precipitate the use of drugs.

10. Urge your local police department to enforce all laws against drugs.

17
Family Violence

A warrant was issued yesterday for the arrest of Henry and Gladys Lane for removing their infant daughter from Charity Hospital in violation of a Family Court order. The child was being held pending the investigation of child abuse charges. When she was admitted to the hospital last Thursday, she had an inflamed right eye, several cuts and bruises, and a burn mark on one arm.

CHILD ABUSE

Perhaps the most despicable crimes are the personal crimes against children by adults. The saddest of all may be child abuse, because it is so often inflicted by parents, whom the child loves the most and whom the child is most dependent upon for very life.

The law describes a child as a person under age eighteen. The abused child is one who is assaulted with weapons, most frequently the hands; sexually assaulted; held in close confinement, as when locked in a closet or tied up; or otherwise mistreated. Another useful term is *neglected*, to define a person who is not receiving necessary care, lacking adequate supervision or medical assistance, being truant, and most of all receiving inadequate nurturing or affection.

As a crime, child abuse, according to several studies, is more frequent than auto theft. Twenty-five percent of all girls and 10 percent of all boys will be sexually molested before attaining age eighteen. The older children are, the more likely they are to suffer sexual abuse. Adolescents are attacked twice as often as elementary school children, and they, in turn, are victimized twice as often as preschoolers.

The most frequent attacker is a male relative. An estimated five million American females have suffered at least once in their lives a sexual attack at the hands of a relative.

Extent of Child Abuse

Each year, between 4,000 and 5,000 children are killed, roughly 100,000 are severely beaten, and an estimated 100,000 children are sexually abused by their parents or guardians. Thousands upon thousands of other children are neglected emotionally, medically, and educationally. Those under the age of five account for more than half of these seemingly forgotten children. Child abuse occurs in people of all races, ethnic backgrounds, religions, age brackets, and income levels. It is just as likely to happen to the child of the wealthy as to the child of the poor.

More than four of every five abused children are victims of people they see often—parents, brothers and sisters, neighbors, baby-sitters, day-care personnel, teachers, coaches, ministers, and others whose lives frequently touch those of children. Between 20 and 30 percent of abused children's attacks are incestuous.

Often the reason given for abuse is vague and irrational. A nineteen-year-old mother punished her daughters, aged three and five, by putting them into a tub of steaming water. They had taken soda from the refrigerator without asking permission. The three-year-old died, and the five-year-old was rushed to the hospital in critical condition.

A twenty-four-year-old mother threw her seven-month-old infant from a twelfth-floor apartment window, believing her baby was possessed by demons. The baby survived the fall.

Causes of Child Abuse

Child abusers are sick and require medical and/or psychological help. This sickness is the primary cause of child abuse. Stress is the number one trigger in child abuse. The parent may be facing job pressures, unemployment, too many bills, or too many mouths to feed. Under these circumstances, a mild spanking can turn into a severe beating.

Furthermore, most child abusers themselves were battered children. They are only repeating the violence that they experienced while growing up.

Parents, typically young ones, may never have learned child-rearing techniques, and may lash out because they know no other way to deal with their children.

How to Recognize an Abused Child

A seriously abused child will show signs of battering and neglect—for example, frequent, unexplained injuries, such as bruises, welts, cuts, and burn marks, on the body. A neglected child may be left alone for many hours or be outside during winter without a coat. You may see the child roaming the streets after dark. The child may seem excessively fearful of contact, shying away from a hug or a pat on the head.

You may hear constant screaming at the child. Verbal berating can often be more emotionally damaging than physical assault. These nonphysical, emotional attacks are much more frequent than physical assaults and beatings.

Assistance to an Abused Child

Neighbors often know of abuse but are reluctant to report the parents to a child protection agency. This fear of involvement is unfounded. If a child needs immediate medical attention, you can safely phone the police. You do not have to give your name. You can also place a call (anonymously if you wish) to your local child welfare bureau. Do not inform the parents that you have taken such action. Abusive parents have been known to coach a child so that when an investigator shows up, everything seems normal.

If *you* have an abuse problem, get help. Call your local division of youth and family services. A child will not be removed from the home' unless all else has failed. It may be helpful to contact Parents Anonymous, a nationwide group of adults with abuse problems who meet to give mutual support and to learn ways of dealing with their children without resorting to physical violence. Parents Anonymous also staffs a twenty-four-hour hot line, which can be used when things get rough.

In the mid-1980s, the newspapers were filled with accounts of organized attacks on children by adult groups. Among those accused were entrepreneurs and employees of a respected day-care center in a Western state. After intensive probes, investigators believed that child abuse had been practiced there for years. According to one of the witnesses, a staff member at this institution mutilated the dead body of a cat in the presence of the children, threatening that disclosure of incidents at the school would result in similar mutilation of the children's parents. Protection from this horrific form of child abuse is provided in Chapter 19.

Punishment or Child Abuse?

At what point is punishment abuse? Since all children require discipline, and punishment often seems to be the only way to achieve it, many parents fall back on physical or emotional pain as an instrument of control. In a 1987 study, three of five parents admitted using physical means of enforcing discipline. Most agreed that they were themselves subjected to corporal punishment much more often when they were young. Almost half felt they were more lenient than their parents, one-eighth thought themselves stricter, and the rest felt that they were about the same as their parents.

Parents who did not use physical means for punishing were able to enforce discipline by withdrawing privileges, restricting children to quarters, or using similar tactics.

These commonsense rules may assist you in keeping punishment of young children from becoming abuse:

- Only a parent, or someone delegated by the parent, should administer punishment. At present, roughly one-third of the states allow teachers to do so with or without such consent.
- In general, children should be punished for acts that they have committed, rather than for their failure to act.
- Regardless of what a child may have done, the punishment meted out may not be so severe that it would cause serious harm, extreme pain, disfigurement, or severe mental duress.

Sometimes, the courts will act to terminate a parent's rights to raise children. Typically, a private hearing will be held in a judge's chambers in an effort to minimize the damaging emotionalism of proceedings of this type. Usually, an attorney tries to protect the interests of the child, which may be quite different from those of the parents. Finally, the state must show "clear and convincing" evidence that the parents' right to raise their children must be terminated.

Protecting Children from Abuse
First of all, to protect children from abuse, an abuser in the home must seek help. This is the number one priority. Beyond that, here are some tactics that should help protect your child from abuse:

- Teach safety at home.
- Find out what the school can do to help, not only with programs to teach children about abuse, but through specialists on campus who may be able to recognize the signs of child abuse.
- Make certain that you are among the parents who warn children to be cautious of strangers.

- Make certain that your children tell you (or, if at school, a teacher) about any incidents of improper touching by adults, and by older children as well.
- As soon as your children are able, teach them to use the telephone. Make sure they know how to reach you at home or at work.
- Teach your children when to scream for help and run away.
- Determine the screening procedures under which teachers are hired in your community.
- If your child tells a story of abuse, don't dismiss it offhand. It may be genuine. Psychologists tell us that it is very difficult for small children to lie. Furthermore, it is unlikely that a child would, at least without assistance, create a fantasy involving sexual abuse.

What to Tell Children

First of all, what you *don't* want to tell children is a detailed, scary list of do's and don'ts designed to frighten. Furthermore, you don't want to weigh the child down with an endless list of things to do and things to avoid. Use this list, short and to the point:

- Police officers are your friends; they will help you.
- Go to school with your friends; come home with your friends.
- Whenever you leave home, tell your parents where you're going.
- If you're not at home or at school, and you have to use the rest room, ask a friend to go with you.
- Play where other kids play—friends' houses, playgrounds, or at home.
- Never play in empty buildings.
- Never get in an automobile with anyone you don't know.
- Never talk to people you don't know.
- When a grown-up does something bad to you, tell your parents, your teacher, or your friend, the police officer.

One final word about child abuse is in order. Every week, a dozen children, on the average, are *thrown away* and left to die. This is not the case of a foundling left on a doorstep, which you might find in a Victorian novel. Rather it is an outrageous act of willful abandonment, perpetrated by someone too selfish or too irresponsible to face the consequence of his or her acts.

SPOUSE ABUSE

If spouses hit one another, that is a violation of law known as spouse (or spousal) abuse. Certain circumstances in certain jurisdictions may preclude an arrest, but it is nevertheless a criminal assault.

Under other circumstances or in other jurisdictions, these assaults may be diligently prosecuted—if they are reported to the police. However, like child abuse, spousal abuse is a most underreported crime.

Spouse battering is so widespread that the chances are that you know a battered spouse. The National Institute of Justice disclosed that each year nearly four million Americans experience severe beatings by a spouse or are threatened or injured by a spouse wielding a knife or gun. Another study reported that in one year, 28 percent of all American families experienced physical violence between spouses, such as slapping, punching, kicking, pushing down a flight of stairs, twisting and breaking arms, scaldings with hot liquids and irons, stabbings, and shootings. According to some authorities, if you are a woman, you have a 50 percent chance of being the victim of a spouse-battering incident at some time in your life.

Husband beating can be equally serious. Although it occurs less frequently than wife beating, it is even more concealed because of the embarrassment the husband feels. One study found that almost as many wives kill husbands as husbands kill wives.

Often, the pattern of abuse continues for a considerable period, because the victimized spouse (usually the wife) lacks the skills and resources to abandon the unhappy marriage and still be able to care for herself and the children. All too often, these victims are subjected to attack over and over again. Many times, the only way out of this Catch-22 of a marriage is through the death of one of the spouses at the hand of the other. Either the abusing partner will go too far and slay the other, or the victim will strike out to bring this misery to an end.

Spouse battering tends to occur more often during vacations or holiday seasons. In addition to the emotional stress that holidays bring, spouses are together more frequently during these times of year, bringing on attacks of "cabin fever."

Spouse battering, like child beating, is not limited to any age bracket, race, religious background, or educational or income level.

Characteristics of the Batterer
Spouse batterers tend to be insecure, frustrated, possessive, and extremely jealous people who do not know how to handle their anger in a nonviolent way. It has been estimated that more than 80 percent of the batterers were exposed to abuse as children, either having been beaten

themselves or having seen one of their parents constantly beaten. Alcohol, drugs, and stress often trigger violent behavior. On the other hand, beatings can also occur for no apparent reason.

In many other respects, spousal abusers appear different from other groups. For example, persons with only a junior high school diploma are most likely to be spousal abusers. The next most frequent abusers, however, are those with postbaccalaureate educational achievement. As for age, if husband and wife are both younger than fifty, the husband is more likely than the wife to be the abuser. If both are over fifty, it is the wife who is more abusive. In either case, however, it is the husband who is responsible for the bulk of *physical* assaults.

A government-funded study several years ago examined spouse abuse. The police, when answering misdemeanor abuse cases, would randomly select one of three courses for action. Some abusers would be arrested, another group would be removed from the home in order to "cool off," and the third group was counseled and advised. Among the group arrested, 19 percent had subsequent spousal abuse arrests within a six-month period. Of those who were spared arrest, 35 percent, almost double, committed an additional spousal abuse within the six-month period. The effect of arrest (at least in the short term) seems adequately demonstrated. This effect is all the more impressive when we learn that of all of those arrested for spousal abuse during this study, only 2.2 percent were convicted.

The Battered-Wife Syndrome

Many wives charged with the murder of their abusing spouses will plead self-defense. So common is this occurrence that psychologists have been able to identify a set of symptoms shared by many of these abuse victims. These symptoms are referred to as constituting the "battered-wife syndrome."

However, many, perhaps most, courts do not recognize this syndrome or the scientific basis that its proponents claim. Nevertheless, it is a recorded fact that about four thousand women will be beaten to death by their husbands in the United States during the next twelve months.

Assistance to a Battered Spouse

If you believe your neighbor is being hurt, do not hesitate to call the police. The battered spouse may be unable to get to the phone. In a nonemergency situation, try to open the lines of communication with the battered spouse. For instance, give the battered wife the phone number of a women's shelter or make the call for her.

The target of a beating should have color photographs taken of cuts and bruises. If the beating results in hospitalization, the names of the doctors, nurses, police officers, and witnesses should be obtained, as should copies of x-rays and medical reports. These can be used as evidence if the incident results in a court appearance.

If *you* are a battered spouse, don't keep it a secret. You are protecting the batterer, who may consider it a license to continue these assaults. In an emergency situation, call the police and sign a complaint.

You, as a battered wife, may find it helpful to contact a women's shelter. Such shelters often provide a place to stay, food, clothing, financial and legal advice, emotional support, and counseling for you and your children. Staff members will also accompany you to court if you wish to press charges and will help you with job interviews, apartment hunts, and welfare benefits if you need financial aid.

Domestic violence shelters typically offer both medical and legal assistance. If you need such assistance but don't know how to find it, call the police, family court, or juvenile court (if minor children are involved). Many jurisdictions have victim/witness assistance units, which will lead you through the sometimes complicated maze of a community's assistance offices.

Funds for assistance to abused spouses, like those of all assistance programs, seem to be perpetually in short supply. However, some very preliminary evidence indicates that for this purpose, at least, a little money goes a long way. One study, involving more than 100 abusers, had a success rate of 100 percent. A number of other similar projects also achieved excellent results.

ELDERLY ABUSE

Less is known about abuse of the elderly than about either child abuse or spousal abuse. While hard statistics are few, one study does provide a clue. This research indicates that slightly more than one-fourth of wives are abused by their husbands, while slightly fewer than one-fourth of children are abused. Approximately one-sixth of the elderly are victimized.

A similar study asked people their opinions of the seriousness of certain actions. Almost two-thirds of the sample considered child abuse very serious, while about two-fifths thought spouse abuse to be serious. Almost as many thought that elder abuse was just as serious (see Chapter 21).

We can only guess the seriousness of all of these family violence components, for each of them is a highly underreported crime. But remember, no one deserves to be beaten. Once physical violence occurs, it is more than likely to recur unless measures are taken to stop it. Do not wait for a serious injury to occur before you seek help.

Family Violence: A Checklist

1. Know the physical signs of child beating, such as frequent bruises, burns, cuts, and welts.
2. Be aware of children who act unusually fearful of adults.
3. If a child is seriously injured and is being ignored by the parents, call the police.
4. Report cases of child abuse to your local child welfare agency. Do not tell the parents that you are calling the agency.
5. Only a parent or someone delegated by the parent should punish the child.
6. Never administer severe punishment that will harm your child.
7. Instruct your children to follow specific safety measures when they are alone.
8. Battered spouses can be recognized by frequent screaming and sobbing you hear coming from their homes. In addition, you may notice cuts and bruises on a neighbor's face.
9. If you yourself are being beaten or threatened, call the police. Arrest and subsequent counseling are the most effective remedies for spousal abuse.
10. If you have been previously slapped around by your spouse, chances are it will happen again. Seek help for the problem.
11. Collect evidence after a beating incident, such as pictures of your injuries, hospital reports, and names and addresses of people you have had contact with.
12. Do not, for the sake of your children, stay with someone who beats you. A violent home is not a happy place for anyone.

18
Teen Suicide

Joey's parents are executives in two major corporations, and he is the only son of three children. While Joey is not antisocial, he is a study-bug, spending much of his time at home. His father often comments, "Joey is going to go places."

Diane has been complaining of headaches. Her teacher noticed she often daydreams. When asked if anything is troubling her, she replies, "Oh, nothing; I'm OK."

Brad has been going through rough times at school, but he is beginning to make progress. During this time, he has made some references to killing himself but has not acted on them. He is participating in activities once again, and has resumed an interest in his friends.

All three of these adolescents committed suicide. Each of us has painful memories of adolescence, and most of us remember incidents that, at the time, we felt we were incapable of surviving. It was a stressful period, but somehow we coped. Too often, however, there are young people who find it impossible to keep going. The triggering for this self-destructive behavior may be internal, perhaps a secret too horrible to discuss, or it could be external, such as that of the young girl whose mother became the only parent ever criminally charged in a child's suicide. The girl, under pressure from her mother, performed as a topless dancer. Despite the youngster's objections, her mother insisted she continue dancing, which, on occasion, netted as much as $1,000 per week. After three months, the girl took her mother's .357 Magnum and killed herself.

Unfortunately, teenage suicide has become a common occurrence in our society, and the figures continue to rise. Although suicide is generally the nation's eighth major cause of death, it ranks second (after accidents) among adolescents and young adults. About two thousand young people, mostly boys between the ages of fifteen and nineteen (nine adolescents per one million population), take their own lives each year. Although they are hard to believe, statistics tell us that every twenty-four hours, more than one thousand youths attempt suicide. These figures are alarming, not only for America's parents, but for educators and communities as well.

Many parents, and often educators as well, react unsympathetically to the tribulations of adolescence, but this is precisely the period when teens most need understanding and love.

VITAL INFORMATION

Unfortunately, the problems that your adolescents are facing cannot all be specified and put onto one master list. Physicians treating suicidal teenagers tell us that the preliminary signs of suicide often are vague. Many of these symptoms also signal normal adolescent development. Frequent confusion, moodiness, and depression do not imply that an adolescent is contemplating suicide. Your youngster is going through a time of separation, the beginnings of independence, and still needs your support, understanding, and love.

An array of warning signals may nevertheless indicate a potentially dangerous situation. It is also important to realize that certain unavoidable events, like divorce, frequent moving, or the death of a loved one, while usually not the primary causes of suicide, certainly increase the pressure on adolescents. These occurrences may be present among many who kill themselves (or try to), but they also occur in the lives of millions of teenagers who never even consider suicide. Most teens simply deal with these stressful events. Most importantly, parents and friends can do a lot to help their teens through the crisis by opening up meaningful channels of communication, by sharing feelings, and by accepting.

Warning Signs

The clues or warning signs of danger include changes in behavior, actual statements by your teen, and situational factors beyond a youngster's control. The shifts in behavior are usually sudden and may be observed at home or in school. Specifically be alerted by a decline in the quality of homework; a general lack of consistency; preoccupation with death;

uncharacteristic disregard for appearance; withdrawal from family, peers, activities; marked differences in eating and/or sleeping habits; substantial changes in personality; noticeable boredom; unexplained crying; giving away valued possessions; restlessness, defiance, recklessness, violent behavior, or rebellion; running away from home; and, above all, abuse of drugs and alcohol.

Any reference your teenager makes to dying must be taken seriously. Statements that preceded actual cases of suicide include "What would you do if I killed myself?"; "Everyone would be better off without me around"; and "You won't have me to worry about much longer." Be especially attentive if the foregoing danger signals are accompanied by disappointing experiences, including death, divorce, breakup of a close or intimate relationship, frequent moving, failure to achieve an important goal, serious physical illness, and, above all, the suicide of a peer or loved one.

These danger signals will give you something to go by in determining whether or not the adolescent in your life is battling with suicidal thoughts or depression. Research has found that three or more of these symptoms usually persist over time in those who attempt or commit suicide. Such statistical clues along with other signs are a good cause for action. Remember that these signs may not be clear or very evident. Look closely, but avoid being paranoid.

Making the Final Determination
If you observe the danger signals, there are concrete things you should do. First, ask your teen questions. Don't be afraid to come out and say, "Are you thinking of suicide?" if that is what you suspect. Be prepared to drop everything to talk to this person, but, more importantly, be prepared for your teen to say, "Yes, I am thinking of it." Continue to ask specific questions, and try to assess the real risk. The more thoroughly your child has thought about suicide, the more likely it is that an attempt will be made.

Try to put yourself in the youngster's place, and imagine the pain that drives a person to such a dreadful decision. Your empathy is needed, but just feeling sorry and doing nothing may only hasten the undesirable end.

Be attentive and loving, honest, and sharing. You should engage in "active listening," where you paraphrase what your child is saying. For example, suppose your son, in a quivering voice, says he is unhappy because "all my friends except me have a brand-new ten-speed bicycle."

You might say, "So you are upset because you don't have a new bike." Let your youngster lead the conversation. This technique assures your teen that you are paying attention and are concerned about the problem. It encourages a continuous stream of communication rather than suppressing feelings through parental domination.

The last thing your youngster needs is constant rejection. Be particularly careful not to humiliate or degrade your child during this crisis. Make yourself emotionally and physically available, by getting rid of your own anger and preoccupations before entering a dialogue. Don't expect your child to make you feel better. If your child is not receptive, at least be physically present, even begin a conversation, but don't press to talk. You do not want to be part of the problem. Be persistent, but not pushy. Whatever you decide to talk about, make sure that your conversation is directed toward helping your teen, not toward serving to vent your frustration.

Here are some simple rules: Don't use the word *why* very much, because it makes people feel as though they are under scrutiny and may only encourage defensiveness. Don't defend your feelings, but try to avoid barriers to communication and keep an open mind. Don't offer any suggestions for solutions until you know that the young person feels that you have heard and that you understand the feelings expressed.

Don't make promises that you cannot keep, since you can't make everything better. Be honest with yourself, too. Don't criticize, ridicule, or imply that the person is crazy. Above all, never interrupt or offer advice while your youngster is talking. Children automatically shut down when parents try to offer them advice.

Statements that may minimize your youngster's feelings are counterproductive and should be avoided. Examples are, "You'll get over it. It will all look better tomorrow." "You have your whole life ahead of you." "If you think you have it tough now, wait till you grow up and have to work for a living and pay bills."

If you sense a strong intention to commit suicide, or even if you are suspicious, remain with your child until you can contact someone else to help you, especially if your attempts at communication are failing. Whatever you do, never handle the situation alone; be sure to enlist the help of someone you trust. You will surely regret having not found help should anything happen. Call a suicide hot line; you don't have to be the one contemplating suicide to call and get help. You can also contact hospitals, suicide prevention centers, and school suicide intervention programs. For professional help, contact a psychologist, therapist, or psychiatrist who specializes in suicide prevention and treatment. You may even need to turn to close friends, relatives, or other adults whom your teen respects.

COPYCAT OR CLUSTER SUICIDE

More and more cases are reported of young people's imitating the suicide of others or simply of a group who make a pact to die together If your teen's friend threatens suicide or actually carries out the threat, your own loved one may therefore be in danger. Although these "copycat" or "cluster" suicides seem to be an expression of the times, there is, unfortunately, no evidence that they will automatically stop over the next few years. In one case, four teens, two boys and two girls, between sixteen and nineteen, entered a car in a closed garage, wrote suicide notes on a brown paper bag, left the car running, and died together. Only one day after the bodies of these four teens were found, two girls, one seventeen and the other nineteen, died in the same manner in a Chicago suburb.

We don't know much about the dynamics of copycat or cluster suicide. What we do know is that youngsters most similar to victims in age, sex, and social activities are at a higher risk than others. If your child is exposed in some way to a suicide or a cluster suicide, review the warning signs and suggestions mentioned previously for preventing a lone suicide.

You can also make sure that your youngster's school develops a program to prevent imitation suicides. The key points of this program should include group discussions that provide all peers an opportunity to share openly their feelings, thoughts, fears, and concerns regarding the suicide. Self-esteem and personal confidence should also be addressed. School professionals should be available and accessible to the students, especially those reluctant to talk to a teacher or a group. And if a friend or someone students know is suicidal, it is imperative that they tell another person.

Teen Suicide: A Checklist
1. Know the warning signals of teen suicide, including sudden changes in behavior and comments regarding suicide.
2. Be aware that many signs of normal adolescent development may resemble symptoms of suicidal behavior.

3. Offer the troubled adolescent support, understanding, and love.
4. Be extra sensitive to the teen who is experiencing a situational crisis, such as divorce in the family or the death of a loved one.
5. A potential suicide may be recognized by three or more symptoms, such as depression, withdrawal from friends and family, changes in eating habits, violent behavior, drug and alcohol abuse, or suicidal comments.
6. Question the potentially suicidal person and determine how developed are the thoughts regarding suicide.
7. Active listening is one of the best ways to communicate with your children and to demonstrate concern for their problems.
8. Maintain honesty, sharing, and attentiveness with children, especially the suicidal teen. Do not dominate conversations, and interrupt only to clarify a feeling or thought expressed to you.
9. Never ridicule or chastise your children, especially if they are suicidal. Work through your own anger, hurt, and frustration before talking with them. Reassure them that you are always available if they need to talk, and see to it that you are.
10. Follow simple conversation rules when attempting communication: stay honest, avoid defensiveness, keep an open mind, and do not make promises that you cannot keep.
11. If you suspect that a teen has decided to attempt suicide, confide in someone you trust. Never try to handle all this on your own. Contact a suicide hot line, a hospital or school intervention program, or a professional, such as a psychologist who counsels suicidal individuals.
12. Should your child be exposed to suicide or cluster suicide, provide support, especially if your child shares similar characteristics with the victim. Review the warning signs for an individual potential suicide.
13. Help establish a suicide intervention program at your child's school. Stress the importance of openly sharing feelings and thoughts about suicide.
14. Impress upon your children the importance of telling an adult if one of their friends or acquaintances is contemplating suicide.

19
Abuse at Day-Care Centers

On the first day the four-year-old boy entered the day-care center, his caregiver held him on her lap repeatedly and stroked his body. The boy returned home and told his mother that the teacher liked him very much but he was afraid of her.

No doubt your most precious possession is not your pearl necklace, gold watch, diamond ring, fur coat, VCR, sports car, or even your own house or condo. It is your children, especially your infants and toddlers, who are so vulnerable and defenseless.

We must protect our little ones at any cost, and that is why it is so important for working parents to find the finest and safest day care for their child.

Only 16 percent of American families fit the classical configuration of Father, who goes to work each weekday, and Mother, who stays home to care for the two children. More typical is the family of the late twentieth century—a family where both parents work, and the children are tended by relatives, baby-sitters, or, outside the home, day-care centers. These centers have been affected in recent years by a great deal of negative publicity.

REAL CASES

One's expectations that day care is safe and secure are destroyed by the shocking cases of child abuse and sexual molestation reported in day-care facilities across the nation. From east to west, border to border, these reports have been surfacing with alarming frequency. Don't be surprised if you experience disgust, revulsion, repugnance, and rage when you learn the truth about this horrendous form of abuse. It is essential for you to grasp the problem so that you will be convinced of your child's potential danger. This is one area where careful preliminary screening and homework may prevent your child from becoming a victim of this heinous crime.

In Newark, New Jersey, a day-care center teacher was recently convicted of sexually assaulting nineteen youngsters ages three, four, and five. She was found guilty of 115 counts, ranging from first-degree aggravated sexual assault to third-degree endangering the welfare of the child. The charges stated that the twenty-six-year-old caregiver undressed in front of the children, organized licking games, had them pile on top of each other naked, played piano for the children in the nude, smeared peanut butter and jelly on the youngsters' bodies, and invaded the children's body cavities.

An equally revolting case involved a sixty-one-year-old mother and twenty-nine-year-old son charged with some one hundred molestations over a five-year period at a suburban day-care center in California. The allegations not only covered typical forms of child abuse like fondling and oral copulation but also included Satan worship, animal mutilation, and secret trips to remote places.

In one bizarre case in Texas, a day-care worker who poisoned and suffocated her wards caused choking, seizure, and cardiac arrest. Experts suggest the woman did this because she wished to create a medical emergency and then act as a heroine by summoning help.

One of the most frightening aspects of abuse in day-care centers is the large number of children involved, the substantial period over which the abuse occurs, and the extraordinarily long time it takes to detect the incidents.

A BOOMING INDUSTRY

The need for day-care centers is growing at a rapid pace. As of 1987, there were an estimated 18.3 million children aged five and under, up from 18 million in 1985. During that same year, 1987, more than 50 percent of new mothers were in the job market, marking the first time a majority of women actively sought employment within a year of giving birth. Senator Edward Kennedy, concerned about the safety of children with working parents, has proposed legislation that would provide carefully supervised day care to all of the nation's four-year-olds. Senators Orin Hatch and Christopher Dodd have also sponsored bills that would authorize substantial funds for child care. Currently, about 4,000 companies nationwide have some form of day-care programs.

According to the National Association for the Education of Young Children in Washington, more than 60,000 licensed day-care centers have been established in the country. Additionally, there are over 161,000 certified family day-care homes that supervise groups of up to about a dozen children. The majority of youngsters, however, spend their time in unlicensed day-care facilities or are supervised by a relative. It is estimated that more then eight million children under six years of age are in some form of day care. The need for this type of service will increase in the 1990s, when 80 percent of mothers will be working, compared to about 60 percent during the 1980s.

Of course, some facilities will be better than others, and you will wish to utilize only the best available for your children. If you aren't familiar with the care units in your area, ask the principal of your school, your physician, neighbors, or your priest, rabbi, or minister.

TYPES OF DAY CARE

It is easy to become confused when attempting to classify the varieties of day care. There are public nonprofit centers that charge on a sliding scale depending on income. Private day care usually is more expensive but may also offer "scholarships" (discounts) based upon need. There is highly structured care outside the home, as well as more intimate family-type programs in private homes; there are all-day and half-day programs. Many day-care programs have extended hours for latchkey children who return from school while their parents are still at work (see Chapter 34).

Some programs with many children afford little ones satisfying social contacts. On the other hand, colds, infections, diarrhea, and other illnesses spread more easily among large groups of children. Only you can judge which form of program is most suitable for you, your child, and your budget. But whatever combination of day care you choose, be sure it is effective, safe, and wholesome.

HOW TO RECOGNIZE SAFE DAY CARE

Signs of child abuse at day care are not recognized easily by how play activities, toys, games, and equipment are organized. Nor will you detect any indication of child molestation from the quality of food or snacks or the safety precautions against accidents. But several basic signals will alert you to the possibility of danger.

By contacting your local government organization that monitors day-care centers, you can determine if the day-care center is properly licensed or registered to carry out its activities. Examine the background checks carried out by the center to determine the fitness of personnel, including the custodial and kitchen staff. Were their references checked carefully? Are the caregivers qualified for the work? How long have they been in child care? What procedures are in place if someone other than the parent or designated person comes to pick up the child? Determine whether an adequate staff-to-child ratio exists; experts have recommended about one to four for children three years and younger and about one to seven for children four years and older.

Find out as much as you can about disciplinary procedures, how misconduct is managed. See if the administration is comfortable discussing the subject of child abuse. And don't hesitate to ask the day-care center administrator questions about strategies for preventing sexual molestation or physical abuse.

Make sure the children are never the object of physical punishment, especially beatings. Remember that caretakers who hit children also have the potential to physically abuse them. Don't feel strange or embarrassed to visit the center at any time unannounced. By observing the children in their routine activities, you will sense what life is really like at the center. No area should be off-limits. You will be able to determine whether the children are happy or if there is an air of tension, anxiety, and intimidation.

Be sure that caretakers always receive your written permission to take your child on a trip away from the day-care center. Instruct your children in no uncertain terms that they are prohibited from leaving the day-care center without your permission.

CARE YOU DON'T NEED

Once you find the best care suitable for your child, you still have to assume an active role to make sure that the care does not deteriorate because of staff turnover, changing policies, shifting organizational structure, or general loss of enthusiasm.

Never allow your child to continue in a program that is poorly evaluated by neighbors, friends, or parents familiar with it. The old adage "where there is smoke, there is fire" certainly is applicable to day-care centers, because infants, toddlers, and preschoolers are virtually defenseless against abuse. Remove your child from a program that does not welcome unannounced visits while the center is open. Be especially on your guard if you are required to call before each visit and then are confined to the office or other administrative areas but not allowed into places where the children are at play or engaged in other activities. Be suspicious if, after a reasonable period of adjustment, your little one is afraid of the caregivers or resists returning to the center.

Should you notice a major staff turnover and strange people caring for your child, find out immediately what's going on. Be aware if your child comes home with suspicious injuries or body marks. These are not always signs of abuse, but at least they indicate deteriorating, negligent, and eroding care. Sure signs of impending problems are your child's complaints about long periods of playing alone or waiting. If these occur, you will probably begin to notice poor supervision, indifference, and a lax attitude on part of the caregivers.

Fewer organized activities and outdated or broken toys often signify a diminution in the level of supervision. Another danger signal is harsh, rude, and irrational behavior by the caregivers toward the children and toward you. They may, for example, become defensive and even angry when you express your concerns. You will know the program is not for you when you begin to worry about your child, lose confidence in the caregivers, and generally feel uncomfortable with the level of care and organization.

PREEMPTING SEXUAL ABUSE

Several steps can be taken by you and your little one to prevent sexual abuse in day care before it occurs. At home, instruct you children on the body's private parts and rehearse alternatives for reacting to an unusual situation. Teach your children in advance to say no to adults who threaten them or touch them in places where they feel uncomfortable. Convince them that it's not their fault if an adult touches them in a sensitive area. Instruct them that their body belongs to them and they have the right to tell adults not to touch it. Tell your children to report to you anyone who touches them where they shouldn't. Small children should be taught to tell you about any pain or punishment or any other dangerous situation they experienced in day care. Explain to your child that you can always provide protection. A child will confide in you if convinced that you have the power to help.

Should your child report to you any form of physical abuse, follow through with your promises and contact the police or a social service agency. For your child's sake, don't procrastinate, since circumstances are likely to deteriorate further. Remember, the abuser is likely to repeat the behavior either with your child or with another youngster. Also, your child is likely to require medical or psychological assistance, which ought to be sought without delay.

Remember, the safety, security, and health of your child depends on you and on the time and energy you spend investigating the best day care and being alert for danger signals. Don't disappoint your child by failing to take the necessary steps to ensure protection.

Abuse at Day-Care Centers: A Checklist

1. The day-care facility of your choice must be fully licensed or accredited.
2. The day-care facility must have an effective system for checking the qualifications and references of its staff.
3. The staff-child ratio must be adequate, about one to four for children three years and younger and one to seven for youngsters four and above.
4. The day-care staff must never administer physical or abusive punishment to discipline the children.
5. The children should be observed in their usual routine so that you fully grasp the level of care.
6. Unannounced visits to the day-care center should be permitted at all times.
7. All areas of the day-care center should be accessible to parents.
8. The staff should be prohibited from taking children away from the day-care center without written permission from parents.
9. Your children should be instructed never to leave the day-care center without your permission.
10. The day-care center's policies for preventing child abuse by the staff should be discussed openly.
11. An active interest in the day-care center will allow you to learn about deteriorating care.
12. Negative reports by friends, neighbors, or parents familiar with a specific day-care center should not be ignored.
13. Children who are afraid of returning to a day-care center after a reasonable period of adjustment should be removed from the program.
14. Note any major shifts in the staff of the day-care center.
15. Immediately investigate injuries or bruises of unknown origin.

16. Investigate any complaints by your child of long periods of playing alone.
17. Investigate any rude, harsh, or otherwise discourteous behavior by caregivers.
18. Instruct children at home on the signs of child abuse.
19. Rehearse children at home on alternatives for reacting to an uncomfortable situation.
20. Teach children to say no to adults who threaten them or touch them in sensitive places.
21. Alert your children to report to you anyone who touches them in sensitive areas.
22. Your children should tell you about all punishment received at the child-care center.
23. Any incident of child abuse should be reported to the proper authorities.

20
School and Campus Security

One morning, Jenny's mom gave in to her pleas to be treated
more like a "young lady" and let her walk to the school bus
alone. At the bus stop, Jenny was asked by a "nice" man in a
big car if she would like to take a ride with him to school.
Luckily, at that point, the bus came and the man drove off.

Incidents such as this should come as no surprise to any parent. Crime
threatens all members of our society, but as this book repeatedly shows,
children, who are less able to defend themselves, are often faced with
greater danger. Even more shocking than Jenny's scenario are the stories
of violence in our schools.

Your children are threatened there not only by strangers, but sometimes by their peers as well. The National Crime Survey of twenty-six
big cities found that during one year, 212,244 students and 58,053
teachers were victimized by crime in schools. On the local level for
1987, the New York City Board of Education counted in its school
system 1,495 incidents involving weapons such as knives, razor blades,
and guns. Obviously, there is cause for alarm and for action.

Since knowledge is often power, it is up to parents to teach their
children how to defend themselves early on. Unfortunately, many parents
believe that protection for their children means allowing them to carry
weapons. This strategy serves only to escalate tension, fears, and the
violent attacks. Instead, school children should be taught to follow
certain safety rules and to practice caution. They should cooperate,
because their well-being is at stake. This training will make them more
resistant to crime when they attend school.

172

BEGINNING SCHOOL

By the time children are old enough to attend school, they spend more time away from the security of the home. More time spent in the outside world means an increased need for protection. They should already have been educated in the basics of personal safety. Still, until you are sure they can travel alone and know their way, drive or walk with them to and from school.

If they travel on their own, be aware of how much time it takes to go to and return from school, and do not allow them to take shortcuts that may be dangerous. Check immediately on any delay in their trip to or from school. Forbid them to hitchhike or to accept rides from anyone other than persons you have designated beforehand. They must learn to inform you and their teachers or principal of any strangers who approach them.

THE OLDER STUDENT

For the older child, additional precautions are necessary. Remind your children not to take large sums of money to school and to keep as few valuables with them as possible. Encourage them to place all personal possessions in school lockers and never to give out the combination. Leaving the combination undone or on the last number so that only one spin will open it may be less of a hassle when in a hurry, but it is also a convenience for the thief.

Incidents of crime or situations involving drugs or alcohol in or around the school must be reported to the school's main office, or at least to you, the parent. Then it is up to you to alert the school.

Take an objective look at the liberty you allow your children, and be sure that these freedoms are not dangerous or inappropriate for their level of development. Do not base your children's level of maturity only on their age or on comparisons with other children. Every child has a unique rate of development, and as a parent you are responsible for identifying it.

No matter what their ages, your children need to be warned of the dangers involved in walking alone in deserted hallways, corridors, or stairwells. Not only strangers and peers, but often other school personnel, are a threat. Children may benefit from learning jujitsu, karate, or another form of self-defense, especially if they express an interest in these martial arts. Martial arts encourage self-confidence and discipline and may assist your child if faced with a confrontation.

These precautions do not imply that your children need be completely isolated during their school years, nor mistrustful of everyone they meet. The key is not to be constantly suspicious, but always cautious.

Encourage your children to tell you everything, and keep open the lines of communication. They and their friends may even be contributors to unsafe conditions in school, not the victims; with communication, love, and understanding, plus the help of the school, other parents, and professionals, you can work through such a situation. Above all, if your children or their friends are suffering from drug or alcohol abuse or any other emotional problems, seek advice and support from their teachers or school counselors.

Know your children's playmates, friends, teachers, and school officials, and communicate with them. By knowing your children's peers, you are better able to exclude bullies and thugs. Within the school as a whole, parental support for security and discipline is vital to proper protection of students and teachers. Demand proper security measures in the schools, especially in high-crime areas. Suggest self-defense instruction. Become involved in the school board even if only by voicing your dissatisfaction and insisting upon safe conditions in the schools. A safe and pleasant environment for learning is not too much to ask.

The learning environment is also jeopardized by violence and vandalism against the school. A number of programs have been designed to reduce or minimize this likelihood. One includes a neighborhood watch that enlists the school neighbors' help in watching the school and reporting suspicious incidents to authorities. Other programs focus on student involvement in deterring and repairing vandalism. Besides becoming part of an effort to prevent or reduce vandalism, you must stress the undesirable effects of destructive behavior and encourage your children to report vandals to school authorities or to you. It is vital to involve students in this effort. Promote the idea that it is their school, and encourage them to work with teachers and school personnel to improve awareness, protection, and prevention.

CAMPUS SECURITY

Recently, a young student at a Pennsylvania university was raped, tortured, and murdered during a robbery of her dormitory room. The murderer was a student and employee of the college. In another incident, a student with a sawed-off shotgun murdered two other students on a Michigan campus. A new fad known as "sharking," in which a man approaches a woman he does not know and bites her breast, has begun to take root on America's campuses. FBI data show that the average campus experiences seven violent crimes a year. Although many young adults between eighteen and twenty-two feel they are immune to crime, stories and statistics such as these prove otherwise. The perpetrators of crimes on college campuses are usually outsiders who engage in theft and sexual assault, or students, who commit mainly sexual assaults.

The college campus is something like a small city. Student dorms are, in fact, apartment buildings, and the security measures the student takes must be no less serious than for an apartment. There are also special considerations for students, who are in much closer contact with dormmates. Many more people are likely to be in and out of one's room than in a regular apartment situation.

As a college student, you should protect your residence by following a few simple "no-hassle" security rules. First, note the conditions of the door and window locks, as well as the lighting both outside and inside your room, and demand improvements if necessary. Become familiar with your roommate(s), and encourage their use of crime prevention. If you can't agree, request a room change.

Keep a complete and up-to-date inventory of your valuables. Determine whether the campus security office has an organized tagging or labeling system for stereos, TVs, and the like to deter thieves and aid in recovering stolen items. Always lock your bike or vehicle securely, and be cautious in parking areas.

In addition, follow these rules. Maintain a record of anyone with a key to your room, and be sure to request a rekeying if a key falls into the wrong hands or even if it is lost. Do not allow your room to be left unlocked, and do not leave visitors in your room when you are away. Never let a stranger into the room, especially if you are alone.

Exercise caution when giving out your phone number, and set up a rule with all roommates to check with the others before giving out the number. Near the phone, keep a complete listing of emergency numbers, including campus security. Always provide an updated list of emergency and next-of-kin information to the college's registration office. Do not give your student ID number (Social Security number) to anyone other than college faculty, administration, or staff. Never leave lying around any papers that have your ID number on them, especially in registration areas.

Secure your personal belongings in class, the rest room, library, cafeteria, and computer facilities. Never leave your pocketbook or backpack out of your sight. Either carry them with you, or secure them with a trustworthy friend or classmate. Many students have experienced thefts while leaving their pocketbooks or backpacks hanging from a chair for only a few minutes.

Never travel alone after dark, and always be on guard. Even your college campus has deserted and isolated areas that may pose dangers. Be careful, and follow safety rules when walking alone off campus. Be especially alert if the surrounding area is a high-crime neighborhood. Check with the security office for an escort or shuttle service across campus at night, or form your own. Do not use unlighted or unfamiliar shortcuts across campus, and never hitchhike. Avoid exercising or jogging outside at night or early in the morning, unless with a group.

Finally, ask your security office for further crime prevention tips, and be aware of security problems on campus. If the security office is unresponsive to your complaints or concerns, bring them, and the unresponsiveness, to the attention of college administrators and the student government. Above all, make an effort to determine the level of crime at the college of your choice before you make your final decision.

DATE RAPE

An extremely important concern on the campus is rape, but especially date or acquaintance rape, which is widespread but not always obvious. A 1985 survey of 7,000 American students on thirty-two campuses found that one in eight women were victims of rape, including date rape. Moreover, one in twelve male students admitted that they had forced women into having sexual intercourse with them. However, very few of these violent sexual attacks were reported to the authorities.

Do not perceive dating as a casual experience that does not require your full awareness. You must be alert on every date, but if it is your first meeting, be especially careful. Blind dates should always involve two or more couples. Be sure to report any incident of sexual assault. Chapter 25 provides detailed advice for your protection. Read it carefully.

SPECIAL CONSIDERATIONS FOR TEACHERS

Communication is a basic necessity for effective teacher-pupil relationships, but in some cases it may not be enough. Increased levels of drug and alcohol abuse in the schools are presenting teachers with growing vulnerability to violence and abuse. To protect themselves and at the same time fulfill their professional obligation, teachers need to develop an appropriate strategy and work it out in detailed tactics.

Establish good communication with your students, and involve them in setting up classroom rules, but be sure they understand that you are still in control. When trying to control students, never use sarcasm, shouting, or embarrassment, and do not threaten punishments unless you are willing to carry them out. Know the problem students, and consult with other school personnel to determine how to handle them.

You can improve your personal safety by immediately reporting any threats by students to administrators and the police. Never walk in secluded areas alone or stay late at school without company. Most of all, try to be a friend to your students, support their successes, and guide them through their failures. Most students still look up to their teachers; your advice and friendship may be just what they need.

School and Campus Security: A Checklist

1. If you are a parent, teach your children from an early age about crime and how to protect and defend themselves.
2. Don't allow your children to carry weapons or firearms.
3. Accompany children to and from school until they know their way, and set up strict rules regarding routes and contact with strangers. Never allow hitchhiking.
4. Encourage your youngsters to report strangers who approach them.
5. Remind your children not to carry extra money or valuables to school.
6. Teach your children to secure their personal belongings in school lockers and not to give out combinations.
7. Warn your youngsters about dark corridors and lonely staircases in schools.
8. Encourage your children to learn martial arts, especially if they express an interest.
9. Open the lines of communication with your children, their peers, friends, teachers, and school officials.
10. Be aware of bullies and troubled youth, and do not tolerate their presence.
11. If you or your friends have a drug- or alcohol-related problem, seek counseling.
12. Voice your concerns to other parents and to your school board and its officials.

13. Forbid your children to engage in vandalism, and encourage them to protect their school.
14. In selecting a college and dormitory, be aware of high crime rates and security effectiveness.
15. If you are a dormitory resident, examine door and window locks for their dependability, and insist on adequate lighting in your room and around your room.
16. Encourage crime prevention among your roommates.
17. Keep a record of valuables, and participate in any equipment-labeling system.
18. Secure all personal belongings at all times.
19. Keep a record of everyone with a key to your room. Should the key be lost or stolen, rekey the room.
20. Restrict the distribution of your phone number. Keep emergency numbers posted by the phone.
21. Provide the registration office with updated emergency-contact information.
22. Be cautious with your student ID number.
23. Never travel alone, take shortcuts, or hitchhike. Avoid being alone outside at night. Be especially alert in the neighborhood surrounding the campus.
24. Lock up any vehicle properly, and be cautious in parking areas.
25. Never leave your room unlocked, don't allow guests to remain alone in your room, and never let a stranger in your room.
26. Protect yourself against sexual assault, including date rape.
27. Voice your concerns and problems to security, administration, and student government.
28. If you are a teacher, establish effective communication with students, and invite their input, but be sure they know you are the teacher.
29. Never ridicule, chastise, or harass students, especially in front of others.
30. Be aware of problematic students, and prepare ways to handle them.
31. Report any threats to the proper authorities, and increase your self-protection.

21
Abuse of the Elderly

An elderly man died after being pushed down the stairs by his children. Another aged man was treated for a fractured skull inflicted by family members.

Several incidents of abuse of senior citizens were reported recently by the mass media. An elderly woman was assaulted by her unemployed son and daughter-in-law, who lived together in her cramped apartment. Her "dear ones," just to be mean, also prohibited her from using the stove or refrigerator, so she had to eat meals with a neighbor. The night before Thanksgiving, her son had locked her out of the apartment until a neighbor found her sitting outside crying. The aged mother exposed a two-inch scar in the center of her forehead from a blow with an iron skillet, and an injury between her eye and the bridge of her nose inflicted by a kick to the face with a steel-toed shoe. In spite of repeated beatings, she was afraid and embarrassed to notify the police.

A sixty-five-year-old woman was a virtual prisoner in her own apartment. When she tried to leave, her daughter threw her to the floor. Her daughter physically and verbally abused her for five years before the woman finally notified the police and had her daughter arrested.

A woman of seventy-eight arrived at a hospital emergency room suffering from bruises to her stomach, bite marks around her neck, and blood clots on her brain. The wounds had been inflicted by her son.

A woman eighty years old was tied to her bed by her son in ninety-degree heat with just saltines and a canister of water to sustain her. She suffered from crippling arthritis and relied on her son for care.

INCIDENCE OF MALTREATMENT

These repugnant cases of mistreatment of the elderly by family members, often children, unfortunately are not rare events. A 1986 study of persons sixty-five years and above by the Family Research Laboratory at the University of New Hampshire estimated that about 1.1 million senior citizens, or one of every twenty-five older Americans, are abused each year. A psychologist and human services planner with the Texas Department of Human Services recently conducted a statewide survey of 4,300 nurses, physicians, law-enforcement officers, and other professionals likely to come in contact with senior citizens. Nearly 47 percent of those who responded to the questionnaire reported instances of abuse or neglect that had occurred over the past twelve to sixteen months. But those who actually had worked with abused persons had each experienced at least five cases of maltreatment.

FEW CASES OF ABUSE ARE REPORTED

The extent of this problem is even greater than may appear from official statistics, because citizens as well as the victims themselves are reluctant to report abuse. One recent study concluded that only one in fourteen such cases are reported to authorities. Although more than forty states have laws requiring people to come forward if they know about elderly abuse, people often are reluctant to get involved or to mix into private family matters.

Victims themselves are often incapable, physically or psychologically, of reporting incidents. Some fear further punishment or, even worse, abandonment. Others are embarrassed, ashamed, or guilty about coming forward. Like battered wives, elder victims often have a poor self-image and believe they deserve the brutal punishment, thinking, "If I behave myself, nobody will hurt me." Many elderly citizens do not know where or how to find assistance.

ABUSE WILL GROW

The number of older persons abused is likely to increase, because over the next decade the elderly population will grow dramatically. The group eighty-five and above will grow by about 60 percent. In a pattern that is likely to continue over the next several decades, reported cases of elderly abuse have increased by about 100,000 new cases every year since 1981.

Also likely to contribute to abuse of the elderly are recent changes in tax laws that make supporting elderly parents more complicated and more costly. The old technique of renting a home to parents may not pay anymore because of fewer tax credits. Instead, children and parents forming one household will experience increasing tension and the risk of abuse.

ABUSED AND ABUSERS

Many men in their seventies, eighties, and even nineties are victims of maltreatment by their "loved ones." But the typical victims of abuse are women about seventy-five years old. Often ill or weak, they are unable to care for themselves, and they make easy targets for the degenerate adult child.

If you think that most abusers are strangers or acquaintances, you are dead wrong. Surveys tell us that six out of seven, or 86 percent, of the abused elderly are mistreated by members of their own families. One study noted that 65 percent of the abused were mistreated by their spouses but over 20 percent by their children. Physical abuse is most often inflicted by sons, while psychological mistreatment appears to be the forte of daughters.

Many abusers are initially well intentioned but eventually succumb to the stress, anxiety, and difficulty of caring for someone perhaps chronically ill or mentally disturbed. Mistreatment usually follows.

FORMS OF ABUSE

Like torture, elderly abuse has many different faces. Perhaps the most horrible is *physical*. This includes beating, punching, slapping, bruising, burning, bone breaking, raping, or even killing. Physical abuse may comprise more than one form of violence. For example, a seventy-four-year-old New Jersey woman, beaten and raped by her son-in-law, maintained silence because her daughter threatened her with eviction if she told anyone about the incident.

Psychological abuse often can be as severe. This mind abuse frequently includes humiliation, subjugation, denigration, degradation, subordination, domination, and control. Verbal abuse is part of this formula. The vulnerable, sometimes entirely defenseless, victims are told they are evil, insane, unstable. They are handcuffed to their beds, locked in their rooms, and forced to eat out of the dog's dish. In one bizarre case, a woman was forced to stay in an unheated chicken coop. In another case, an undernourished eighty-year-old man from New York was afraid to eat because he believed his daughter's threats to poison his food.

Yet another form of brutality is *financial/material*, in which money or some object, such as a bed, is withheld from the victim. In one instance, a successful businessman controlled the $500,000 estate of his aged sister by withholding much of the income, and then forced her to live a Spartan life in a house lacking water or adequate electricity. Another case involved a woman who over an eleven-year period embezzled $173,000 from thirty-two elderly former servicemen residing at the United States Soldiers' and Airmen's Home in Washington. Most instances of financial/material abuse involve taking the victim's money and using it for the caretaker's personal needs.

Neglect is another form of abuse where, for example, food or medication is withheld, or where the helpless victim suffers bedsores from long periods of confinement to bed. Often the victims remain in the same filthy clothes for long periods without being washed or cleaned. A typical case of neglect involved a daughter who consistently refused to shop or conduct household chores for her eighty-four-year-old father, who was terminally ill. The man was kept alive only by the meager items brought by the milkman.

CAUSES

Care of the elderly is extremely difficult. One home-care worker spent eighty-four hours a week caring for a ninety-year-old who was wheelchair-bound and suffered from many medical problems. Another care giver had spent every night in a small apartment with his elderly ward. He bathed, dressed, and fed the older man. He had to lift his patient from bed to wheelchair without mechanical aid. Often they went out to shop or to a movie.

Stress, pressure, persistent responsibilities, and vulnerability of the victims are only partial reasons that caregivers abuse the ones they care for. Adult children who are alcoholics or drug addicts are likely to abuse their parents, especially physically. Troubled, unstable, or mentally ill adult children who are economically and emotionally dependent on their parents are also likely to be abusive. Patterns or cycles of domestic violence from generation to generation, including spouse and child abuse, frequently evolve into patterns of mistreatment by an adult child who "pays back" the parents for childhood suffering and pain. Absence of meaningful communication during childhood and adolescence, likely to continue into adulthood, provides the setting for violence.

SOLUTIONS

Elderly abuse, the shame of our nation, can be prevented, or at least controlled, by following a few simple procedures. First, you should be alert for signs of abuse in others and, on discovery, immediately intervene by notifying the proper authorities. Learn to recognize injuries, bruises, welts, scratches, or bite marks whose origins are unknown. Long periods of isolation, frequent screams and yells for help, self-reports describing abuse, signs of malnutrition, filth in the home, and unwashed clothes and bodies are equally significant danger signs. However, remember that all families argue, complain, and have problems, and that not every disagreement or temper tantrum signals elderly abuse. Many children manage their parents' finances or attend to their personal needs honestly and intelligently.

For the elderly, a certain method for reducing maltreatment is to maintain contact with other senior citizens in one's family and community, especially those who are isolated and housebound. As a parent, you should do everything to open communication channels with your adult children. You should get together and talk about the increasing requirements for care as you age. The discussions should include sharing responsibilities, budget management, and available community help. You should suggest that your adult children take courses on care for the elderly, their unique needs, what to expect, what to do if the tasks become intolerable, and how to reach out for help.

Remember, not only are you an individual but you also are a member of the community. You can contribute to the diminution of mistreatment by joining a community group that educates on where and how to get assistance and, even more important, that it is not shameful or a sign of weakness to seek help. You should have ready access to a hot line for emergencies and any other situations requiring assistance.

Find out about any adult protective services in your community where reports of abuse are immediately investigated and where, if necessary, appropriate action can be taken to resolve unbearable situations. Learn about home-care services that will send a companion, practical nurse, or home health aide to look after an aged citizen part-time or at least once a day. If your community has an adult day-care center, visit it and introduce yourself to the people in charge. Don't hesitate to contact professionals who are concerned with elderly abuse, including social workers, nurses, physicians, health-care workers, members of the clergy, and police officers. If you can, join a Neighborhood Watch program and suggest that it expand its responsibilities to daily checks on individuals who are housebound, infirm, or otherwise vulnerable to abuse and neglect.

PROTECT YOURSELF FINANCIALLY

There are many steps that you can take now to put your finances in order. One of the most important is to prepare a will. Review it annually, but think hard before revising it. Be suspicious of suggestions to deed your house, personal property, or other assets to anyone in exchange for care or other assurances that you will not have to enter a nursing home. Sign nothing before you check with someone you absolutely trust and whose interests are not being served.

Thoroughly familiarize yourself with your financial situation, know how to manage your assets, and determine who will take over for you in an emergency. This is particularly essential for older women, who may not have experience in financial management.

Always have your Social Security checks and other regular payments deposited directly to your bank account. Be sure to cultivate new friends and maintain old ones of all ages, so that you do not rely only on your family for social activities and for health care. Be very careful about allowing an adult child to return home to live with you, especially one who is troubled or who might have a history of drug addiction, alcoholism, compulsive gambling, violence, mental illness, or criminality. As an alternative, helping to support the adult child in a separate residence is an excellent way of preserving everyone's dignity and at the same time protecting yourself.

Now is the time to make peace with alienated friends or family, not only because it is the "right" thing to do, but because it provides a pool of caring people to assist you in time of need. Plan for later periods of vulnerability by having your attorney advise you about powers of attorney, conservatorships or guardianships, "living wills," and natural death acts. Appointing several individuals to serve as co-guardians or co-conservators assures that, in case of an emergency, there is always someone responsible and available to manage your affairs.

Abuse of the Elderly: A Checklist

1. Learn to recognize the signs of elderly abuse, including unusual injuries, bruises, welts, scratches, bite marks, long periods of isolation, malnutrition, and other signs of neglect.
2. If you are abused or are aware of someone else in similar unfortunate circumstances, notify the authorities immediately.
3. Maintain contact with other senior citizens in your community by telephone or home visits.

4. Open lines of communication between yourself and your children.
5. Discuss with your children the requirement for care when you will be unable to care for yourself.
6. Familiarize yourself with all community support services, including visiting nurse care, home health aides, household help, senior day-care centers, and adult protective services.
7. Have ready access to an abuse hot line for the aged.
8. Join a Neighborhood Watch program that checks on the housebound, infirm, and other individuals vulnerable to maltreatment.
9. Put your finances in order now before it is too late.
10. Prepare a will.
11. Don't sign anything unless it is reviewed by someone you have good reason to trust.
12. Assign someone you have trusted for a long time to take over your financial matters in an emergency.
13. Learn about powers of attorney, conservatorships or guardianships, "living wills," and natural death acts.
14. Have all regular payments and Social Security checks deposited directly to your bank account.
15. Widen your circle of friends.
16. If your adult child has a history of substance abuse, compulsive gambling, violence, mental illness, or criminality, be certain of total recovery before extending an invitation to come live with you.

22
Crime and the Elderly

Seventy-five-year-old Ida James was attacked and beaten two weeks ago in the storage room of the house for the elderly in which she lives at 2807 Jackson Boulevard. That same week, Mary Lane, seventy-five, a tenant in the same building, was beaten in the recreation room and received a head wound that required forty stitches.

Unfortunately, elderly citizens are frequently targets of crime. The elderly have a particular physical, psychological, and financial vulnerability. Fear of crime often makes a senior citizen a virtual prisoner. A recent poll revealed that the elderly are more concerned about crime than about either their health or economic security. For a younger person, who often can earn or borrow money without undue difficulty, the theft of $500 may be upsetting, but it probably would not spell economic disaster. The same amount of money may represent the monthly expenses for food and shelter for an elderly person, who usually has no way of replacing it. A robbery is a frightening experience for anyone, but for the senior citizen, it is frequently accompanied by injury or even death.

As time passes, the elderly will become an even greater attraction for the robber and thief, because our senior citizens are becoming increasingly better off financially. In 1984, according to Social Security Administration figures, the elderly person's income was approximately 84 percent of that of the under-sixty-five group. By way of comparison, in 1967, the elderly person's income, on the average, was only 69 percent of that of the under-sixty-five group. The elderly have benefited from Social Security increases and higher interest rates on their investments.

Despite being better off financially, there is little that the older person can do to reverse the ravages of time. The senior citizen is less able to flee from danger, or defend against attack, or recover from injury, or afford the loss of assets, or resist the lure of the confidence game. And because of a feeling that the assets on hand must make do for the balance of their lives, senior citizens sometimes fall prey to the frauds who promise the moon but can deliver only privation.

THE ENEMY OF THE ELDERLY

Most of the crimes against the elderly are street crimes and, as a general rule, are committed by males under age twenty. They are, for the most part, unplanned, spur-of-the-moment efforts. Many crimes against the elderly can be considered crimes of opportunity—some lapse in the victim's defenses signals to a criminal that there are easy pickings available.

Easy Pickings

The elderly person's worst enemy, as far as crime is concerned, is often him- or herself. Three-quarters of the burglaries victimizing older people involve unlocked doors or windows. And strange as it may seem, half of these burglaries are never reported to anyone.

The burglar is not the senior citizen's only threat, though. Twelve percent of all crimes against the elderly are purse snatchings and street robberies. The typical purse theft involves grabbing the purse with one hand, shoving the victim with the other, and running away. Broken bones are common in this type of crime—often a more serious situation than the loss of the contents of the purse.

Payday for the robber, mugger, purse snatcher, or burglar often coincides with delivery day for government checks. It is so easy to avoid losing money to thugs by using direct deposit, in which funds are transferred directly to the bank for deposit. Most communities have at least one bank that provides free checking accounts to seniors. Yet many older citizens continue to make the regular "payday" trip to cash a check and all too often provide a payday for someone else.

Incidences of three of the leading crimes committed against the elderly could be drastically reduced by three simple steps:

1. Lock doors and windows.
2. Don't carry more money than you can afford to lose.
3. Don't carry a purse.

Instead of a purse, use pockets in slacks, jackets, or coats. If necessary, sew pockets in your clothing. You may still be stopped on the street and robbed at gunpoint, but you're less likely to get the broken leg that could result from being knocked to the ground.

THINGS FOR SENIOR CITIZENS TO DO

Senior citizens should establish daily telephone contact with their children, encourage frequent visits, and check with neighbors on a regular basis. It is a good idea for an elderly person to join others for mutual self-protection in a group such as a citizen crime prevention group, a property identification program, or similar activity.

Establish a light-up, lock-up routine on retiring for the night. Be sure to close drapes at that time, too.

If you're returning home, have your key ready, and don't delay at the door. If shopping, keep lunch money and bus or cab fare separate from other funds. This serves two purposes: you won't expose the entire bankroll needlessly, and even if one of the caches is taken or lost, you will still be able to get home.

Check references of anyone who wants money from you for any reason. Seek trusted advice before signing any contract or making any major expenditures—especially insurance purchases. Mail offers that seem too good to be true usually are just that. Before undertaking any medical treatment suggested by someone who approaches you, check it with your own physician or community health clinic. Entrust home repairs only to qualified workers. Get a receipt for any significant expenditure you make.

THINGS FOR SENIOR CITIZENS TO AVOID

Don't let strangers stop you for conversation, and avoid parked cars with running motors. Don't be conspicuous wherever you may be; dress simply, and avoid displays of cash or valuable jewelry. Avoid large groups of adolescents. Avoid isolated, sparsely traveled streets or roads. Avoid carrying a purse if at all possible, and, if you must, never let it out of your sight or grasp. Don't be a hero—surrender valuables if you're robbed. When possible, don't ride elevators with strangers. The elderly are particularly vulnerable to con artists and con games.

Under no circumstances should you take any of these risky actions:

- Don't give "good-faith money" for any investment that hasn't been thoroughly checked by someone you have known and trusted for many years.

- Don't pay in advance for any significant purchase, unless you are buying from a reputable merchant with whom you have traded for years.
- Don't sign any contract whatsoever without first checking with your children, a trusted friend, your attorney, or the Better Business Bureau. To be even more protective of your assets, place a call to the police department's fraud or bunco squad. Even if you have signed a contract, you have three days in which to change your mind. Just make certain that the correct date appears on anything you sign.

Even if you have done everything suggested in this chapter, it is possible that something has been overlooked. Perhaps you made a mistake and entered the wrong date on the order form, or maybe the salesperson took your copy of the contract, and you were left holding the bag. Call the police anyway, or the district attorney or the local consumer protection office. More than likely, a crook who victimizes you will also have victimized others, and your identification could be the piece of evidence that would bring an end to this particular fraud.

WHERE TO FIND HELP WHEN NEEDED

First of all, in finding help, don't be afraid of "being a burden" to your children. You were there when they needed you!

Know emergency phone numbers—in most communities help is available by dialing 911 or the operator (0). Help is always available at a police station or precinct house, a fire station, sometimes even at a business that you patronize.

One word of advice: if you need help, ask for it. Don't wait for someone to come to your aid. If you wait, you may attract the wrong person—a scavenger after easy prey.

Other sources of help are community health clinics or hospital emergency rooms, various senior citizens' anticrime groups, emergency hot lines of all types, witness aid bureaus, and victim assistance bureaus. Call national, state, county, and local information lines for information on old-age assistance, free-lunch programs, food stamps, and the location of senior citizen centers.

SOUND OFF

For goodness' sake, if you are the victim of a crime, report it! Half the crimes against seniors are never reported.

Here is what failure to report a crime can mean to you. First of all, there is no way the criminal can be arrested unless the police know that a crime has been committed. Second, money is tight, and police departments, like you and almost everybody else, must allocate their resources as wisely as possible. Your failure to report a crime can mean you're not getting your fair share of police protection. Third, unless a crime is reported, you usually cannot obtain reimbursement for losses from insurance carriers. Fourth, even if no reimbursement is forthcoming, you may be eligible for an income tax deduction if the crime is reported. Fifth, many jurisdictions have victim compensation programs, but of course, this requires a police report. Last of all, it is your duty. Perhaps you are physically unable to take part in a citizens' patrol, police auxiliary units, or other citizen-oriented anticrime activities, but you still have an obligation to do what you can to protect not only yourself but all of us from crime.

Crime and the Elderly: A Checklist

1. Establish daily telephone contacts with relatives, arrange frequent visits, and check with neighbors on a regular basis.
2. Be on guard at all times for criminals who will take advantage of your weaknesses.
3. Many crimes against the elderly will be eliminated if you lock doors and windows, limit the amounts of money or valuables you carry, and keep the carrying of handbags at an absolute minimum.
4. Use checking accounts and direct deposit of regularly received checks.
5. Do:
   a. Establish nighttime routines.
   b. Have your key ready for use when coming home.
   c. Keep shopping money separate from lunch and transportation funds.
   d. Check references and seek advice that is competent and trusted before making any significant expenditure—especially medical, insurance, or home repair—and obtain a receipt.
6. Avoid the following risks:
   a. Unsolicited conversations with strangers
   b. Conspicuous dress or actions
   c. Congregations of adolescents
   d. Isolated, sparsely traveled streets

 e. Carrying valuables

 f. Doing business with a stranger whose reputation is unknown

7. Learn where to find help in your community, but seek help, don't wait for help to find you. Your ostensible helper may actually be looking for your valuables.

8. For many good reasons, report any crime that befalls you.

23
Security in Hospitals and Nursing Homes

A seventy-two-year-old man, waiting in City General Hospital for routine surgery to repair a hernia, decided to take a short walk around his hospital floor. When he returned to his room, all his personal valuables had disappeared, including his wallet, credit cards, watch, gold ring, keys, and even dentures. He immediately reported the theft to the nurse, who summoned hospital security.

SECURITY IN THE HOSPITAL

Hospitals present unique security problems because, unlike many offices, they operate twenty-four hours a day to admit the sick and injured. They also allow visits from family and other visitors at all hours. All day and night, large numbers of staff members, including physicians, nurses, health aides, pharmacists, cashiers, clerks, and repair and maintenance people, constantly enter and leave through the many entrances and doors. The patients, on the other hand, are unable to provide even minimum defense against crime, because they are often too ill to walk, move, talk, or listen.

As the demand for hospital care keeps going up, more and more crime is likely to occur in this environment. In over seven thousand hospitals (including their outpatient and emergency services) and many more medical clinics, two million individuals are treated daily. Additionally, more than six million visitors, vendors, and delivery persons enter hospital facilities during an average twenty-four-hour period. Also, an ever-growing number of employees representing more than 160 different job skills or classifications work in hospitals.

As hospitals and nursing homes become more crowded because of increasing demand, in part due to the projected increase in the elderly population, the need for security and safety will increase. You can, therefore, realize how important it is to be aware of your personal safety and property while in one of these facilities. You will have to exercise special care to protect yourself from becoming a patient-victim.

Not only patients, but hospital personnel also are at risk. More criminals, while probably not aware of the precise statistics, must have a good idea that over 70 percent of hospital employees are women and that during late-night hours more than 95 percent of the work force is female. Where the lure of patients' property is enhanced by the prospects for rape and perhaps stealing drugs, hospitals can be seen as very attractive targets for criminals.

In such circumstances, staff, patients, family, and other visitors must take special precautions. Patients should not have to experience robbery while suffering from a serious illness. The patients themselves need to contribute to their own protection. Many simple and specific actions can reduce the hazards of becoming victims of crimes in hospitals.

One preventive measure, for example, is checking valuables in the hospital vault or, better yet, leaving them at home. Some hospitals require waivers absolving them of responsibility for valuables not secured in their vaults. Patients who are too ill at the time of admission to secure their personal belongings can request a nurse to bring a safe-deposit envelope to store their valuables. The envelope should be sealed in the patient's presence, signed on the outside, and signed as well by the hospital representative. Then someone specific will be held accountable if the patient's property is lost, stolen, or damaged. The receipt should be stored safely in the table drawer until it can be given to a family member for safekeeping.

Other rules for protection against hospital crime are simple and obvious. Do not wear expensive jewelry. Keep only small change and a few small bills in a drawer next to your bed, and don't leave clothing or drugs lying around. In addition to your wallet, check your credit cards, keys, rings, watches, and other valuables. In many cases, pocketbooks or purses with house keys have been stolen by thieves who were able to determine the patient's address. Then the thief had all the time in the world to ransack patients' homes, knowing full well the victim was lying helpless in the hospital.

Do not place dentures, hearing aids, eyeglasses, radios, or similar objects in the safe-deposit, because they are likely to be damaged during handling and storage. Many hospitals require patients to remove their dentures, because precious metal in them attracts thieves. Remember if there is a theft, notify hospital security at once.

Emergency Room

The emergency room is a particularly risky area, because that is where victims of drug overdoses, shootings, stabbings, and other crime-related injuries are treated. Intoxicated individuals, people high on drugs, criminals, and disoriented persons filled with rage, resentment, and violence arrive regularly at the emergency rooms. Many of them have been brought there against their will by friends or family members, who may also be under the influence. Some patients or visitors may still be carrying concealed weapons, including guns, knives, brass knuckles, or blunt instruments. These angry and hostile individuals often provoke verbal attacks, physical attacks, and other forms of disruptive behavior. They may destroy property.

Recently in a West Los Angeles hospital, a physician was stabbed in the back by an emergency room patient. The hospital then installed walk-through metal detectors, similar to those used at airports. The illegal weapons detected numbered 243, including guns and knives. Also discovered were over 8,000 potential weapons, including razors, scissors, ice picks, and small knives. Other hospitals that have installed these devices have had similar experiences.

Often the long waiting periods before treatment irritate emergency room patients, making them tense, nervous, and anxious. Other patients should be alert to these overwrought individuals and under no circumstances attempt to calm them down or provide assistance to resolve a dispute. They should stay calm and not mix in. It is the job of hospital personnel, especially the security department, to handle these highly volatile and sensitive situations. Hospital personnel are trained for these difficult and dangerous tasks. If someone nearby is disruptive or abusive, a patient can change seats immediately as far as possible from the area of disturbance. The new seat should be near the nursing station, or at least within sight of the emergency room security guard or other hospital personnel.

Be particularly careful if no security guard is on duty, as on the late-night shift or at small hospitals. Do not wander around hospital corridors or hallways while waiting for treatment, especially at night, when many areas are deserted. Also, people accompanying you should be instructed regarding this potential danger. Although emergency rooms and adjacent areas are critical for delivering essential medical care rapidly, they can also be places of grave danger.

The Maternity Ward

The safest place in a hospital ought to be the maternity ward, where mothers can peacefully recover from the travails of childbirth and rest assured that their newborns are safe and sound. Unfortunately, maternity wards have become the most dangerous areas in the hospital because of infant kidnappings.

Often dressed as hospital personnel, as nurses and physicians, kidnappers gain entry to the newborn section or nursery and abduct infants. One horrible incident occurred at the 940-bed Johns Hopkins Hospital in Baltimore. A two-day-old infant was abducted from his mother's room in the nursery unit and still hasn't been found. After the incident, Johns Hopkins and other area hospitals increased security to prevent copycat incidents. In addition to increasing patrols, the hospitals are now requiring identification badges for visitors.

Once an abduction occurs, it is obviously too late to take precautions. Serious thought must be given in advance to every aspect of security for your child and its mother. Find out about your obstetrician's hospital affiliations before choosing a hospital. Then check the security procedures for the maternity ward and newborn nursery at that hospital. Most important, be assured that there is adequate control over access to these areas. Make certain that the entire maternity ward is a restricted area. At the very minimum, the newborn section should be locked at all times with carefully monitored visiting privileges.

Identification cards and card key systems, which have proven useful for access control, can be tested by a single visit to the maternity ward. Are you challenged when you walk past the entry point into the ward? Do all hospital personnel who care for the babies wear uniforms of the same type and color, bearing special employee identification badges? If not, anyone could don hospital garb, mix with the staff, and walk off with your newborn.

Stroll through the corridors, and get a sense of the level of safety and security. If you feel funny or dissatisfied, there probably is something wrong. Discuss your impressions with a hospital representative. If you are unhappy with the response, choose another hospital. Some hospitals use infants' footprints, a relatively simple procedure, to aid in identification. This not only provides some help with administrative problems, but may also prove useful in kidnappings. Ask whether this procedure is used at the hospital you are investigating.

Parking Areas

Parking lots at hospitals may be even more isolated and deserted than those at shopping centers or malls. Often they sprawl over large areas and are accessible to anyone twenty-four hours a day. After the stress and tension of visiting a sick loved one, the last thing you want is to return to your car and find that it has been vandalized or has disappeared. Even worse, on the way to your car you may be robbed and/or raped.

Many of the security procedures discussed for parking while shopping (see Chapter 13) should definitely be followed for hospital parking. As always, lock all doors and close all windows. Park in a space close to the hospital entrance, but be certain that it has adequate lighting. Try to make sure that you and your car are visible to any parking attendant. If this is not possible, at least be within earshot or in the line of vision of pedestrians going in and out of the hospital.

Be alert for suspicious persons loitering in or near the parking lot. Most people who visit patients or work at a hospital leave their cars immediately and return directly to them. Rarely do they just hang out in the parking lot. Above all, be alert to anyone who does.

Hospital Staff

If you work for a hospital, particularly as a physician, nurse, or aide, your schedule usually varies over twenty-four hours, and you frequently come and go at odd hours or during off periods. Be especially careful to follow the procedures outlined for safe access to your auto. All of us have heard many horror stories of assault, rape, even murder on the way to one's car. Remember, every addict craving a fix knows that hospitals store large quantities of drugs. These desperate individuals may force you to obtain some for them. If your hospital separates employee from visitor parking, take advantage of this safeguard. Allow security to protect you by spotting loiterers who can be easily identified between shift changes.

Always be aware of your responsibility to protect each patient's property. Be alert for suspicious persons in patient-care areas, particularly the maternity ward and, even more, the newborn nursery. A stranger should be asked, politely but firmly, what business he or she has in the area. A kidnapping may be perpetrated by an upset person. If you are suspicious or intimidated, act as if nothing is wrong but call for assistance and also notify security. Do not incite or anger the suspect. The security staff are trained to handle these situations. Let them do so.

Follow these same procedures in the emergency room, especially when confronted by disruptive, hostile individuals. Some hospitals have provided training for all employees through films and police instruction. Topics covered include managing intruders, recognizing the beginning stages of an altercation, and intervening without escalating the altercation. Finally, be alert as you walk around the maze of deserted and isolated hallways typical of most hospitals. Recently, in a Miami hospital, a husky patient (obviously intoxicated) cornered a nurse in a hallway and began tearing at her clothing. Her screams brought help, and the attacker was finally subdued with judo holds plus a sedative.

NURSING HOMES

Health United States 1987, issued by the Department of Health and Human Services, reports that in 1985 there were 1.3 million residents over sixty-five years of age in nursing homes, an increase of 200,000 from 1977. As the elderly population becomes larger, the number of nursing homes will increase, and they will differ according to cost, level of medical care, convenience of location, visiting rights, accreditation or licensing, quality of food, privacy, adequate lighting, proper staffing, sufficient number of personnel, and cheery atmosphere. Also important in your final choice should be security and safety. Highly publicized scandals and investigation into criminal misconduct by nursing home owners over the last fifteen years have highlighted the terrible dangers and conditions found in some nursing homes. Several even had connections to organized crime.

Because abuse by nursing home staff is not uncommon, you must exercise extreme caution in your selection. Recently, in an unlicensed Florida nursing home, elderly persons ranging in age from seventy-three to ninety-five were found strapped into urine-soaked chairs. One of them suffered deformities caused by lack of exercise. They all suffered injuries and bedsores from the abusive care, neglect, and filth.

Such horrible experiences can be avoided by visiting nursing homes with members of your family before making your final selection. During your visit, ask questions of the staff and residents. Find out whether the staff is caring, compassionate, understanding, and energetic. Determine what residents think about the nursing home. If they are unhappy, you are sure to be displeased as well. Avoid nursing homes that have had a record of abuse. Be sure to review the procedures in this book for preventing elderly abuse (see Chapter 21).

Nothing undermines the morale of a resident more than an unsafe nursing home. While theft is the most common crime in many nursing homes, there have also been many cases of physical and sexual assaults, robberies, and even homicides. Be sure, therefore, that the nursing home administration is truly concerned about the security of your family member, and that its plan of action ensures a safe environment. Review the guidelines offered in the previous sections concerning hospitals, which apply equally to nursing homes.

Since theft is the most common crime in nursing homes, both patient and family should sit down with the administrators and determine which valuables (if any) should be brought along. These should be put in a safe-deposit box maintained by the nursing home or placed in a locked, private patient property-storage container mounted on a wall, cabinet, door, or similar convenient location. An alternative—less convenient but safer—is to have the nursing administrator or the patient's family make arrangements with a local bank to store valuables. If the person is mobile, this arrangement also requires an occasional trip to town and affords a chance to see people not associated with the nursing home. A change of scenery is a great morale booster.

If your nursing home has a property identification program ("Operation ID") by which valuable personal property can be engraved with a unique identification number, it should be used. Then a special decal can be displayed to indicate that expensive belongings have a serial number and that the thief will have difficulty disposing of them.

Hallway Watch
At some nursing homes, residents on the same floor have gotten together and organized a hallway watch or floor watch. They meet periodically to discuss security and arrange to watch out for each others' safety the same way groups of neighbors do in the Neighborhood Watch program. It is highly recommended that such a watch be organized at every home. The hallway watch or floor watch is useful for preventing crime by both outsiders and employees. Members of the hallway watch should always be alert for strangers, suspicious persons, and people having no legitimate business in the nursing home. Missing property should be reported to the nursing staff as soon as possible. A thief who finds it easy to steal will try again at the same spot or nearby.

For more information on how to select a safe and secure nursing home suitable for your needs, check your local agency on aging or write to:

American Association of Retired Persons, Health Advocacy Services, 1909 K Street, NW, Washington, DC 20036

Security in Hospitals and Nursing Homes: A Checklist

1. Check the level of security at the hospital or nursing home of your choice.
2. Deposit your valuables in the vault provided by the hospital or nursing home, or, better yet, leave them at home.
3. Do not place dentures, hearing aids, eyeglasses, radios, or similar objects in the safe-deposit, because they are often damaged due to faulty storage facilities.
4. Notify the security office at your hospital or nursing home if you are aware of a theft.
5. Never mix into an altercation in the hospital, especially in the emergency room. Notify hospital staff.
6. Never wander aimlessly around hospital corridors or hallways.
7. To protect yourself when parking at the hospital or nursing home, review procedures in this book for parking while shopping.
8. Park your car within view or earshot of parking attendants or pedestrians and in an adequately lighted place.
9. Always be alert in parking lots, especially for suspicious persons.
10. Always lock your car.
11. If you work at a hospital or nursing home, be alert for suspicious individuals. Find out the purpose of their presence, and if you are not satisfied, notify security.
12. Avoid nursing homes with a history of scandals, corruption, or ties to organized crime.
13. To aid you in self-protection, review the guidelines in this book on abuse of the elderly.
14. Report all incidents of abuse to your family and the nursing home administrator.
15. To protect yourself and your valuables, take advantage of all programs offered by your nursing home, including Operation ID and a hallway watch.

24
Compulsive Gambling

On occasion, Mr. B and his wife take off for the casinos at Atlantic City. Mr. B plays blackjack exclusively. Each time, he allows himself $100 to play.

During the week, Mrs. R plays the lottery, allowing herself $5 a day for lottery tickets.

Mr. O, a businessman, goes to the track every night. He promises to limit himself to $20 on each race, but when the night ends, his entire paycheck has been wagered.

Legalized gambling is increasingly popular. Public acceptance and the desire of governments to generate revenues without raising taxes have stimulated the growth of opportunities to gamble. At present, forty-six states sanction some form of gaming such as lotteries, bingo, jai alai, horse racing, and dog racing.

A recent *Business Week* article noted that approximately 68 percent of all adults bet occasionally. Enthusiasm is so great that in 1986 Americans gambled $198.7 billion, more than fifteen times the amount they donated to churches. This figure rose to $241 billion in 1988.

While legitimate gambling may be increasingly acceptable to more and more people, illegal betting can be as serious a threat to personal security as robbery or rape. Because so many forms of gambling are either sanctioned by government or churches or actually sponsored by these respectable institutions, many people can see no harm in "trying their luck." Also, the hazards of losing unacceptable amounts of money and becoming addicted to this habit make it a major threat to individual safety.

Because in gambling the same person is both the culprit and at least one of the victims, we must ask, "Why do people gamble?" Many people do so for the obvious reason, to win. Few people have not thought, at one time or another, how nice it would be to win the fortune that would change their lives. Moreover, gambling is a social activity. Bingo at the church or the crowd at the track provides a sense of belonging, a feeling of fraternity. For others, gambling is simply an entertainment, an exciting diversion.

TYPES OF GAMBLERS

Gambling authorities Robert L. Custer and Harry Milt concur that gamblers may be classified, identified, and, if necessary, successfully treated. Gamblers are not all alike. They differ in how much time and money they spend on gambling, whether they gamble for the money they can win or for entertainment, and in how essential gambling becomes to their lives. Experts suggest several categories: casual social, serious social, illegitimate, and compulsive gamblers.

Casual Social Gamblers
Casual social gamblers indulge only occasionally and do so for entertainment, sociability, and a little excitement. Gambling is just one of the many things they do for pleasure, and it takes up only a small part of their leisure time.

Serious Social Gamblers
Serious social gamblers, according to experts, bet regularly rather than occasionally and do so with great concentration and energy. For them gambling is a major source of entertainment, excitement, and pleasure. However, it is controlled. The money that is allotted for and spent on gambling is well within their means and does not intrude into the rest of their lives. Their preoccupation is similar to that of the "football junkie" or "tennis nut."

Illegitimate Gamblers
Illegitimate gamblers are individuals who place illegal bets—with bookmakers, for example—or who are underage and are prohibited from gambling. While many states have set the minimum age for gambling at twenty-one years, many young people begin gambling in their midteens, often imitating their parents or older friends. A young woman who began betting in the casinos in Atlantic City at fifteen played not only the slots but blackjack as well, and for years remained undetected by

security, casino hosts, and pit bosses. Her chronic betting habit was finally discovered only when her father, an Atlantic City cop, distraught because she frequently returned home late from her job without adequate explanation, found her in a casino.

Compulsive Gamblers

Compulsive gambling is described by the National Council on Compulsive Gambling as a progressive behavior disorder in which an individual becomes dependent upon gambling to the exclusion of everything else in life. It is a disease with deep psychological and emotional roots. Like alcoholics, compulsive gamblers exhibit an emotional dependence on their activity, suffer loss of control, and fail to function normally in daily life. Gambling behavior tends to increase, in terms of both time and money. Although the intent of compulsive gamblers may be self-control and decreased involvement in their preoccupation, actual behavior moves in the opposite direction. Emotional and financial suffering afflict not only the compulsive individuals' families, but also their employers and the general community.

While research on the prevalence of compulsive gambling has been limited, it is nevertheless estimated that from one to ten million people are compulsive gamblers, and with the expansion of state-authorized gambling, their number is growing.

RECOGNIZING AN INDIVIDUAL WITH A GAMBLING PROBLEM

Recognizing compulsive gamblers in the early phases of their problem is not so easy. The obvious behavioral changes have not yet occurred. Yet a number of indicators, in combination with one another, suggest a gambling problem.

- *The amount of time spent gambling*—First you need to be aware of the time the individual spends gambling, in relation to the rest of his or her life. How does it compare with the behavior of others in the same social setting? Gambling that seems significantly out of line with the norm could very well signal a problem. Keep alert for any increase in the amount of time or energy spent gambling, especially if you notice a surge in activities away from home in other cities.
- *Growing size of bets*—You should recognize any sharp increase in

the amount of the bets, of course taking into account increases in income. If someone placed $5 to $20 bets over the last year or two and now has increased them to $50 or $100, you can be sure that compulsiveness is imminent.

- *An intensity of emphasis on gambling*—An individual who is moving in the direction of compulsive gambling finds it exciting to talk and boast endlessly about that activity. A high level of excitement and tension is evident each time a bet is placed. The compulsive gambler will also search out or "work up" special occasions for gambling, like sporting events, parties, and junkets.

- *Loss of interest in other activities*—Once gambling takes control, it becomes the most exciting and important event in the gambler's life. Activities that have been important in the past now seem dull and boring. You should be alert to a gambling spouse whose interest in you and the children begins to wane.

- *Suspicious absences from home and work*—When gambling becomes excessive, it is likely that the activity will be concealed. Strong indicators of compulsive gambling are absences from work and from home without explanation or with only suspicious explanations. Also, be aware of any increase in the use of the telephone, which usually means your loved one is contacting the bookmaker and placing an illegal wager.

- *Shifts in personality structure*—The stress associated with winning and losing often produces short-tempered and belligerent behavior. The constant pressure, even when winning, leads to an increase in criticism, impatience, and irritability.

- *Siphoning off family funds*—To obtain funds for gambling, the compulsive gambler is often compelled to secretly raid the family resources, by cashing in insurance policies, redeeming securities or savings bonds, draining the family savings account, or selling a spouse's jewelry. When this occurs, you can be sure that gambling has reached the addictive stage.

TWENTY QUESTIONS YOU SHOULD ASK

Since the compulsive gambler is the victim of the crime, the cure can begin only with that individual. The first step, obviously, is self-diagnosis and nullification of denial—convincing oneself there is a real problem. Gamblers Anonymous suggests that gamblers ask themselves the following twenty key questions. If they answer "yes" to seven or more, advise them that they have joined the ranks of compulsive gamblers. They had *better* seek help before it is too late.

1. Do you lose time from work due to gambling?
2. Is gambling making your home life unhappy?
3. Is gambling affecting your reputation?
4. Have you ever felt remorse after gambling?
5. Do you ever gamble to get money with which to pay debts or to otherwise solve financial difficulties?
6. Does gambling cause a decrease in your ambition or efficiency?
7. After losing, do you feel you must return as soon as possible and win back your losses?
8. After a win, do you have a strong urge to return and win more?
9. Do you often gamble until your last dollar is gone?
10. Do you ever borrow to finance your gambling?
11. Have you ever sold any real estate or personal property to finance gambling?
12. Are you reluctant to use "gambling money" for normal expenditures?
13. Does gambling make you careless of your family's welfare?
14. Do you ever gamble longer than you had planned?
15. Do you ever gamble to escape worry or trouble?
16. Have you ever committed, or considered committing, an illegal act to finance gambling?
17. Does gambling cause you to have difficulty sleeping?
18. Do arguments, disappointments, or frustrations create within you an urge to gamble?
19. Do you have an urge to celebrate any good fortune by a few hours of gambling?
20. Have you ever considered self-destruction as a result of your gambling?

GETTING HELP

Like many other addicts, compulsive gamblers usually resist treatment until there is no choice. When they finally accept help, there are basically two sources: Gamblers Anonymous and professional counseling.

Gamblers Anonymous (GA) is the only national voluntary organization for compulsive gamblers. Founded in 1957, it is structured along the lines of Alcoholics Anonymous. Compulsive gamblers who either have gained control over their addiction or are in the process of doing so gather for weekly or more frequent support meetings during which they confront their pathological gambling patterns.

Gam-Anon is the GA counterpart for family members of the compulsive gambler. These group meetings provide support and teach family members ways to cope with the gambling problem of their loved ones.

On the whole, treatment centers restricted to compulsive gamblers are in short supply. In the entire country there are no more than twenty places where compulsive gamblers can be treated specifically for that disorder. The next best treatment alternative is traditional psychotherapy, either with a professional in private practice or at a psychiatric clinic or community mental health center.

Remember, as soon as you spot the signs of compulsive gambling in yourself, go for help. Contact your local chapter of Gamblers Anonymous. Do not delay; you are unlikely to overcome this problem by yourself.

Compulsive Gambling: A Checklist

1. Know the behavioral signs of problem gambling. These include increased interest in and time spent gambling, increases in size of bets, boasting about winnings or exaggerated displays of money, and a drop-off in other activities and interests.
2. Watch for sudden changes in personality. The change from warmth to hostility may come long before the losing phase of compulsive gambling begins.
3. Avoid gambling with money you cannot afford to spend.
4. Avoid borrowing money or using credit to finance your gambling.
5. Allocate a limited amount of money for gambling. Avoid using money that has been set aside for other purposes.
6. Do not gamble to get money with which to pay debts or to otherwise solve financial problems.
7. Do not gamble illegally, as with a bookmaker.
8. Do not allow gambling to involve you in illegal activities.
9. Avoid using gambling as an escape from problems or personal troubles. Communicate your feelings and thoughts with your family and friends.
10. Answer honestly all twenty questions that reflect signs of compulsive gambling posed by Gamblers Anonymous. If you respond affirmatively to seven of them, you are already in trouble. Seek help immediately.
11. Learn where to find help in your community. Do not try to fight the battle alone. Call or go for help.

25
Defenses Against Rape

A Criminal Court jury last night found two men guilty of raping a woman inside the Unity Sanctuary Church and sentenced them to ninety-nine-year prison terms. The jury also convicted the defendants of robbing the woman of five dollars at the point of a long pair of scissors. The prosecutor, in his final argument, emphasized that the victim was raped on her wedding anniversary.

A twenty-eight-year-old investment banker jogging in Central Park was raped by a teenage wolfpack.

Each chapter in this book has special suggestions for women, but this chapter is devoted to a crime primarily against women: rape.

Rape is a crime greatly misunderstood by most people, men and women alike. More than any other type of crime, the physical and psychological effects of rape tend to be long-lasting. Rape carries with it the immediate physical dangers of being beaten, injured, or killed as well as the possibility of pregnancy or sexually transmitted diseases. The victim is also subjected to psychological stress and trauma that may last a lifetime. The rape victim often feels humiliated and ostracized. These consequences are compounded by prevailing community attitudes toward rape.

Attitudes toward rape vary greatly. Men have a considerably different view of rape than women. Typical comments—easily identifiable by gender—range from "A woman can run faster with her pants up than a man can with his down" to "Castration should be a mandatory penalty for any rape conviction."

Forcible rape is defined as "to carnally know and ravish a woman against her will." Statutory rape consists of a man's having sexual relations with a female under a legal age of consent (sixteen in most jurisdictions), even with her consent.

INCIDENCE OF RAPE

According to FBI statistics, there were 63,500 forcible rapes in 1976. Ten years later, preliminary figures approximated 92,500, an increase approaching 70 percent. Forcible rape has consistently led in rates of increase among crimes included in the FBI's *Uniform Crime Reports*. Over the last ten years, it has exhibited the largest single increase among serious crimes. In 1985, approximately 36 of 100,000 women were rape victims.

But because of fear, humiliation, guilt, and embarrassment, rape is among the most unreported of all crimes. In 1985, a national survey of crime victims revealed that 192,000 rapes had been committed. FBI statistics for that same year, however, showed only 76,400 attacks had been reported. In other words, more than two out of every three rapes were not recorded by the police and thus were not forwarded to the FBI for inclusion in that year's *Uniform Crime Reports*.

Geographically, this crime is spread throughout the nation. In all regions, rape volume increased during 1985, with the South registering a 7 percent increase. The increase in the Northeast amounted to 3 percent, contrasted with 2 percent in the Midwest. A 1 percent increase in the West was the nation's most enviable.

Forty-five percent of rapes were charged against males under age twenty-five, and 30 percent against males in the eighteen-to-twenty-two age group. Fifty-two percent of the rapists were white, 46 percent were black, and the remaining 2 percent were of other races.

MYTHS ABOUT RAPE

Perhaps it is necessary to clear up several misconceptions about rape.

Myth: Rape is an interracial crime.

Reality: In a study conducted in the District of Columbia, the victim and the assailant were of the same race in seven out of every eight assaults. A similar study in Philadelphia indicated that nine out of ten rapes involved two people of the same race. A report in Memphis revealed that five out of six rapes involved people of the same race.

Myth: The major motive for rape is sexual.

Reality: The major motive for rape is power, not sex. Rape is a crime of violence; sex is merely a weapon.

Myth: A healthy woman can avoid being raped.

Reality: Studies show that the rapist uses psychological tactics. Fear is a major weapon. Threat of injury or death easily immobilizes the woman, and she is terrorized into cooperation.

Myth: Rape will never happen to a decent woman.

Reality: A woman does not control whether or not she will be raped. The rapist does. Rape victims are of all ages, social strata, ethnic backgrounds, and appearances. Most rape victims have excellent reputations.

Myth: Most women actually enjoy being raped.

Reality: The problem here is a confusion of sex with sexual assault. Most women enjoy sex, but no one wants to be threatened, attacked, injured, or killed.

Myth: The majority of rape attacks are inflicted by strangers in back alleys.

Reality: Recent research has shown that about one-half of the rapists are friends, family members, acquaintances, or social companions of the victim and that about one-third of all rapes occur in the victim's home.

NOT ALL RAPISTS ARE STRANGERS

Selected FBI statistics on the relationship of the victim to the offender show broad discrepancies. Estimates range from a low of 20 percent in which the assailant was a stranger to a high of nearly 75 percent. Since rapes occur more often in the victim's home than anywhere else, it follows that the attacker must have been in the proximity of the home; the likelihood is that he is a neighbor. He may be known only by sight, or he may be an acquaintance or even a close friend. The disparity in the stranger-versus-nonstranger statistics may well be the result of the definition of a stranger. A more useful delineation would be "known, at least by sight, or not known, even by sight."

According to the FBI's *Uniform Crime Reports*, rape is most likely to occur on a Saturday, followed in order by Sunday, Monday, Thursday,

Tuesday, Wednesday, and Friday. Rapes occur more often in July than in any other month, followed by August, June, May, September, October, April, March, November, December, January, and February.

Rapes occur most frequently in the late evening or early morning hours. The afternoon hours are also times of frequent rape—especially in the summer months, when schools are not in session. Approximately half of all rapes are committed during the hours of 11:00 P.M. to 7:00 A.M., and approximately 40 percent during the late afternoon and early evening hours (3:00 P.M. to 11:00 P.M.). The balance of the day (7:00 A.M. to 3:00 P.M.) provides a relative respite from rape.

The most frequently attacked age group is women aged sixteen to nineteen. Those twenty to twenty-four are next. Others, in order, are those twenty-five to thirty-four, twelve to fifteen, thirty-five to forty-nine, sixty-five and older, and, finally, those aged fifty to sixty-four. Females of lower-income circumstances are five times more likely to be victimized than the wealthiest, according to the conclusions of one recent study. Along similar lines, black females are more likely than their white counterparts to be victims, but only slightly more (55 percent of rape victims are black).

Roughly two out of every five rapes take place in or near the victim's home, or in a school or other nonresidential structure, including public conveyances. A like number of attacks take place outdoors, and the balance in locations not determined. More than three of every four attackers did not use guns, knives, or other weapons, except for their hands and possibly feet. Of those who did use so-called deadly weapons, 11 percent used knives, and 5 percent used firearms. All other weapons (sticks, bricks) amounted to 7 percent usage.

More than half of rape victims were students; another fifth were unemployed. Waitresses and prostitutes were also attacked in significant numbers. Tragically, preschool children constituted the next most frequently attacked group, followed by nurses, homemakers, and salespersons. However, more than half of the victims in this study listed no occupation whatsoever.

Various studies indicate that from 13 percent to 43 percent of all rapes involve more than one assailant. These gang rapes were characterized by excessive brutality, humiliation, and repeated assault.

The most frequent rape is the assault of a school-age female, by a man of the same race, during the hours of 11:00 P.M. to 7:00 A.M., on a Saturday in July. The assailant is alone, has no weapon, and is probably known to the victim, at least by sight. Perhaps this tells us that the typical rape victim is a little too young, a little too trusting, and a little too inexperienced to take proper safeguards. Obviously, then, we should start our protection with the school-age females in your home.

PROTECTION FROM RAPE

Chapter 34 suggests that a parent should always know where the children are, what they're doing, and with whom. This could be very important in protecting a teenage girl from sexual assault. The following guidelines are also important:

- A teenage girl should never entertain her male friends at home without supervision, and early in life she should have learned the importance of not admitting strangers into the home.
- She must be taught that there is safety in numbers, but with the caveat that she is safest in the company of other girls. Remember, from 13 to 43 percent of all rapes are gang rapes.
- She should be home by the time that most people in the community are asleep. Once she is home, she should utilize all protective measures available.
- She should exercise particular caution when she might be at home alone during daylight hours, such as after school. She should take special care to see that after-school activities avoid one-to-one relationships or a situation in which she might be the only female in a group.
- She should exercise extreme caution in accepting dates. Getting picked up by a stranger is ill advised at the very best. Parents should *always* insist on meeting the dates of schoolgirls living at home.

If you are a woman living alone, you should not advertise the fact. If you live in an apartment, list only your first initial with your last name in the tenant roster, so a potential rapist cannot determine that a female resides in a particular apartment. Similar procedures are recommended for the telephone directory.

SOCIAL RAPE

Social rape, also known as date rape, occurs between social companions. What appears to be a friendly, innocent sexual overture suddenly turns into ugly rape. This type of "friendly" rape is just as horrible and demeaning as back-alley rape. Experts say early warning signals for social rape include intimidating stares, standing too close, enjoying your discomfort, acting as if he knows you better than he does, calling you names that make you uncomfortable, constantly blocking your way and following you, touching you in sensitive places by "accident," ignoring what you say, and becoming angry when you disagree with him.

Here are some suggestions on what you can do to prevent date rape:

- Be certain you know the name of every man you date and something of his occupation and where he lives.
- Be apprehensive if your date unexpectedly turns the conversation around to sex or dirty jokes or suddenly puts his hand on some part of your body.
- Always maintain a measure of reserve and distance on the first date. This does not mean that you should be cold, uncooperative, and impersonal. You can be dignified and at the same time warm, compassionate, and understanding.
- Never invite a person whom you met in the street, a bar, or any other public place to be alone with you in your residence.
- Should you decide to go somewhere alone with your date, be sure to tell someone, and be sure your date knows you have done so.
- Resist with all your strength as soon as an initial sexual gesture is made. Scream, yell, and be furious.
- Threaten to call the police if your date does not stop. At the same time, however, try to keep him calm. Otherwise, his sexual advances many turn into violent behavior.
- Assure him that the next time you date you will do everything he wants. Try to persuade him to wait one more day.
- Tell your date you need another hour or two to get to know each other better. Meanwhile, try to escape or attract assistance or talk him out of his impulsive desires.
- Do not allow the rapist an extra liberty with the hope that this will appease him and prevent further aggression. Acquaintance rape, like stranger rape, is partially an act of violence and aggression in which the assailant seeks to dominate and hold power over the victim. Sex is not all the assailant is after; thus, a token sexual gesture is unlikely to stop him.
- Do not feel guilty or blame yourself after a date rape.

In a 1985 study, 75 percent of female students in a coeducational Eastern university reported sexual harassment at least once in the preceding five years.

IF ATTACKED

To whatever extent she is temperamentally and emotionally capable, every woman should be prepared to defend herself physically. If she isn't serious or simply is not capable of inflicting pain or physical harm on her assailant, she shouldn't attempt it. If she is determined to defend herself, she should remember that her best defense is escape. Remember that legs are to run with and voices are to scream with. High-heeled shoes can be loosened and kicked at an assailant. His natural reaction will be to duck, and his being off-balance may give the victim the chance to run.

The best time to make a break for it is as early during the assault as possible. Authorities suggest that the optimum moment to react is during the first twenty seconds. The attacker won't expect an escape then. Also, the less time you are under the control of the rapist, the less likely you are to be hurt or intimidated. Moreover, your chances of escape are better before the rapist gains total control and before he has the chance to throw you to the ground or force you to a secluded spot. The longer you submit passively to his demands, the less likely you are to react later on. Fear of antagonizing your assailant will worsen, and overcoming inertia will become more difficult with time.

Scream as you run, and in case your voice fails you, keep a whistle strapped to your wrist. It will make noise when your voice might not. Some people have suggested that screaming "Fire!" rather than "Help!" might bring assistance more quickly.

If you are trapped and have little chance of escape, should you fight or not? A woman will tell you to fight; a man will tell you not to. Available statistics indicate that you *will* be attacked physically—from having an arm twisted up to suffering a brutal beating. The best policy is never to attack an assailant armed with a knife or gun, but if his only weapon is superior strength, the chance of avoiding being raped through resistance is worth taking.

In general, a rape victim *must* resist her attacker. Lacking this, there may be charges of consenting sexual intercourse. However, the resistance need not be physical. To say, "I don't want to do that. Please don't make me do that," clearly establishes resistance. There is, however, the distinct possibility that your attacker will contradict this in court. If, on the other hand, you physically attack your assailant, leaving cuts and contusions on him, you have gone far in establishing your resistance. Of course, this type of action risks retaliation in kind.

You may be able to change the rapist's intentions. He may be reluctant to have sexual contact with you if he believes you have a sexually transmitted disease. You may be able to persuade the rapist that you want to have a sexual relationship with him, but in a more comfortable setting. Pretend to invite him to your place, with the intention of escaping or summoning assistance. Try to make yourself unattractive by telling him you are at the peak of your menstrual period or you have stomach cramps. This may distract the assailant or perhaps cause him to loosen his grip. Some women have vomited or relieved themselves to ward off a persistent assailant, and others have been successful by feigning mental retardation.

Defensive Weapons and Tactics
If you have a weapon, you may even swing the odds in your favor. We have already suggested avoiding weapons such as handguns, knives, tear gas, or Mace. Concealing such a weapon could be a violation of the law, and it might also be taken from you and used against you.

There are other items that pose little chance of being classified as concealed weapons but that might be even more effective because they can be carried in a hand or in a coat pocket rather than in a handbag. These include hatpins, a pen or pencil, a corkscrew, pepper, lemon juice in a squeeze bottle, or even a key ring clenched in the fist with keys protruding between the fingers, all of which can be used against the attacker's eyes. An umbrella can be a good weapon if used like a spear or sword rather than a club.

An umbrella or car keys can double as defensive weapons.

However, you should be warned: many men have had some boxing or other self-defense training, and your assailant may be able to parry your thrust and block your swings. Even so, his reversal from offensive to defensive tactics may give you a chance to flee, and, if you're lucky, you'll at least discourage him from his initial objective. But remember, if you do attack, be prepared to keep it up.

Some authorities will tell you to attack the assailant in the groin area. While this is his most vulnerable spot, he is also likely to protect this area, both through instinct and from a lifetime of training. Instead, go for the pit of the stomach, the throat, the eyes, the temples, or even the kneecap. However, if he should make an embracing type of attack from the front, then a knee to the groin might be in order. If you are grabbed from the rear, an elbow to the stomach can be effective in securing your release. Stomping on the attacker's foot, especially with high-heeled shoes, can easily break his foot—try to hit about halfway between the ankle and the toes. The pain of this might well discourage any further attack. Even if it doesn't, it might make it easier for you to break free and run. Other aggressive actions include eye gouging, biting, scratching, and kicking.

The rapist usually will try to throw you to the ground. Once you are on the ground, your chances of defense are lessened *but not hopeless*. Suppose the rapist has succeeded in wrestling you to the ground and is on top of you, clutching your throat with both hands in a stranglehold. It is his intention to choke you until you are too weak and terrified to resist. Then he may tear off your clothing and sexually assault you. The assailant will sit on your abdomen with his legs straddling your body. He is bent forward slightly with both hands clasping your throat. There are two simple coordinated moves that can free you:

1. Place your hands just behind the elbows of the assailant, and strike his elbows with all your force, pushing him forward in the direction of your head. This will cause the rapist to loosen his grip on your throat.
2. At the same moment, bend one of your legs slightly so that it is now in an upright position, with your sole flat on the ground. This movement will give you support and leverage while you raise the other leg and strike the assailant's buttocks with your knee. *This move must be precisely coordinated with your double thrust on the assailant's elbows.* You should put your weight on your grounded leg and arch your back slightly to increase the impact of the blow. The force of these movements should throw the rapist over your head and allow you the few extra critical seconds for escape. Since this maneuver requires coordination of the hand and knee thrusts, it should be practiced.

If, however, you are trapped and so threatened that you cannot escape, you still may be able to avoid attack by doing nothing more than crying, which shouldn't be too difficult under the circumstances. Psychological studies show no particular variations in personality among rapists compared with nonrapists, so there is a chance you can sob your way out of an attack. You might also try to establish some sort of conversation.

Even if you can't talk your way out of rape, you may be able to lessen the physical, verbal, or emotional abuse that might be loosed upon you. One theory of a rapist's motivation is that he has not achieved as much in life as he thinks he should. By building up his ego—his feelings of self-importance—you may give him the gratification he seeks and might, just might, prevent him from taking further gratification at your expense.

Your assailant may force you to submit to perverse or humiliating acts, such as oral or anal intercourse. Even after achieving sexual climax, he may continue to force his will upon you. His intention is not the sensual pleasure of the sex act, but the emotional high of a seriously psychotic individual experiencing the total dominance and control over another person. Many rapists would not hesitate to beat, maim, or even murder. A rapist might welcome resistance as a challenge to his right of mastery and increase the fury of his attack. Perhaps the only thing that you may reasonably expect from a rapist's attack is humiliation.

There may be circumstances, however, under which you may not be able to resist. If, for example, he threatens not you but your child, you may feel that there is no alternative but to accede to his demands. No matter what we, or anyone, may advise you, the decisions you make when face to face with an attacker must be yours, and must be based on circumstances as you see them at the time. Your body will release chemicals in the bloodstream that will help you fight, run, or outsmart. Once the incident is over, and you meditate on what you did and how you might have otherwise done, remember your actions were dictated by your body as well as your mind, and if you had it to do all over again, it would probably have turned out the same way.

Feelings of Rape Victims
Unlike the victims of most other crimes, the rape victim will experience lingering fear, guilt, a feeling of loss of control over her own life, embarrassment, anger, and a sense of inferiority long after the incident. Here is how a study sponsored by the U.S. Department of Justice described these feelings:

- *Fear*—During a rape, the victim believes that, in addition to the sexual assault, she is going to be brutally beaten or even murdered. Often the rapist threatens to assault the victim again if she goes to the police or threatens to expose his identity.

- *Guilt*—Many women feel guilt after being raped because they somehow believe they are to blame for having been raped. This feeling of guilt often prevents a rape victim from reporting the crime to the police.
- *Loss of control*—The rape victim often feels loss of control over her own life because she was forced to submit to an act she considers abhorrent. She may reason that "just as the rapist overcame my resistance by force, anyone can persuade me to do anything." It becomes difficult for her to make decisions about simple matters.
- *Embarrassment*—The rape victim is often too embarrassed to discuss the physical and psychological details of the assault. She is taught from childhood that her body and sexuality are private matters. This prevents the rape victim from discussing the assault with medical or law enforcement personnel, and may actually aid her attacker.
- *Anger*—A healthier and more appropriate response is anger.The victim has been attacked, demeaned, and humiliated. She may express the anger by telling other women about the attack or pressing charges. She may also generalize and extend her anger and mistrust to all men.
- *Inferiority*—The victim may wonder why the rapist chose her. These feelings are related to the widespread, but false, belief that women who are raped "asked for it."

These feelings greatly intensify, according to some experts, when the victim is quite young, or elderly. The naive youngster may not know that rape exists, while the mature woman may have felt that, because of her age, she would not be a likely victim. In either event, the experience could easily prove emotionally disabling, even fatal.

Once any rape is over, report it! To fail to prosecute is to encourage the rapist to try again. There are many reasons why a woman would not wish to report a rape, most of which deal with her perception of the reactions of her loved ones and friends. One victim failed to report because she felt that her attacker, a member of a racial minority, would almost certainly be convicted on the basis of race. Many other victims decline to prosecute, preferring not to be forced to relive the incident throughout what could be a long and perhaps extremely visible trial. Nevertheless, cooperation with the police would probably unearth information that would be of assistance in solving other rapes.

If you are attacked, call the police. You have been the victim of a serious crime, and you have an obligation to do what you can to assure that your attacker is punished. The police will transport you to qualified medical assistance at a facility with experience in treating the types of physical and emotional trauma that you are suffering.

Should you choose to delay immediate treatment, perhaps to locate a friend, physician, or relative whose presence would be comforting, get assistance nevertheless. Call a hospital emergency facility or, ideally, a rape crisis counseling service.

At the hospital, a twofold procedure will be initiated. First, you will receive emergency medical treatment, and second, evidence that could assist in identifying your attacker will be gathered.

Afterward, you can have the bath and the rest you need. Then try to resume your normal routine as quickly as possible.

You will probably be spending some time with physicians after the ordeal. There is "morning-after" medication that is somewhat effective in preventing pregnancy. However, its side effects may put you to bed for several days, and the drug itself may be carcinogenic.

You should have an examination for sexually transmitted diseases. Gonorrhea will usually require two examinations, for it is not easily identified in a female, and additional examinations may be ordered by the physician. Also have a comprehensive urogenital examination and, if necessary, psychiatric counseling.

Rape victims often cannot clearly see the attacker, as dark, isolated locations tend to assure his freedom from interruption. If you can concentrate on his appearance and mannerisms, you may be able to identify him, even if he was masked at the time of the attack. The rape victim should try to remember everything that occurred and was said, and she should not destroy any physical evidence.

Rape must be reported. Even though it may cause you further emotional stress to discuss the details of the crime with officials, reporting the rape will assist the police to apprehend the assailant, and thus you will help protect other women from him.

Write down or tape-record everything you can remember about the incident while it is fresh in your mind. In time, your memory will, mercifully, blank out some of the more traumatic incidents, but don't wish for this memory lapse until after you've given your testimony.

Regardless of how soiled you might feel, don't bathe, douche, or change clothes right after the incident. You may be destroying the evidence necessary for conviction. Your garments, whether torn or not, will probably be required for evidence, so bring a change of clothes.

Throughout the ordeal following your attack, and perhaps beginning in the emergency room, you may expect contact with the police. Sometimes some police officers (particularly males) may express skepticism.

Perhaps this attitude is chauvinistic, perhaps it is an investigatory technique. Regardless of what triggers it, disbelief is something you may encounter. Don't be surprised if your friends (especially the fair-weather variety) derive smug satisfaction from your misfortune. It feeds their unwarranted feelings of superiority.

It may be that if you go to trial, you can find that the judge, prosecutor, and opposing attorney (and perhaps the jury as well) are predominantly male. This imbalance could work to your disadvantage, particularly if your appearance and demeanor are not those of the girl next door.

You may have submitted to the demands of the rapist. This does not mean that you secretly wanted sex—it only means that you didn't or couldn't actively resist the attack. Fear of injury to oneself or to another does not signify consent, nor is it any reason for qualms of guilt. You have committed no crime; your attacker did. Take comfort in the fact that one of four rape victims suffers no disorder from her ordeal.

On the other hand, the majority suffer depression and, to some extent, psychological problems (fear, anxiety, social censure, and sexual dysfunction). It is not unusual for these disorders to exist for a year or even longer. So severe is the emotional trauma of rape victims that they exhibit substantially greater than average rates of suicide.

Rape Crisis Centers

Many rape victims are eased through the labyrinth of their ordeals through the excellent assistance of a rape crisis center. If there is a rape crisis center hot line in your community, by all means utilize it. If you don't know about such a service, ask the police or the telephone operator. Typically these centers perform a variety of essential services. A twenty-four-hour hot line, with a trained counselor, is often available for advice.

You can expect to be referred to community agencies that provide rape victims with assistance. A trained escort-counselor will accompany you through the medical investigation and the various complicated stages of the criminal justice process, including the police investigation, the prosecutor's office, preparation for trial, and all the court proceedings. A taped interview with law enforcement officials will probably be prepared, and this can be replayed to spare you from having to repeat and relive your experience. The rape crisis center also provides in-service training for medical and criminal justice personnel who interact with the rape victim. It also provides classes, conferences, literature, audiovisual aids, and speakers to increase community awareness of sex crimes.

Each counselor is trained to understand your physical and mental state, and he or she can assist you in breaking the news to members of your family. Your counselor will offer you calm, reassuring, and unwavering support to help you maintain, or regain, your dignity, self-respect, and self-confidence. After all, the rape incident must not be allowed to dominate your life.

IF A FRIEND IS RAPED

If one of your friends is raped, here are some ways you can help:

- Listen attentively to what happened, and show compassion for the victim.
- Do not offer too much advice; the victim is hypersensitive and under tremendous pressure.
- Be on the alert if your friend says someone else, not she, was raped.
- Use considerable tact; the victim may be reticent and withdrawn.
- Explain to the victim that thousands of other women have been raped, and she was *not* singled out for the attack.
- Tell the victim that while the experience will disrupt her life for a short period, things will return to normal in time.
- Assure your friend that her decision not to fight was right in that particular situation, whether or not it actually was. Assure her that you will be available at all times if she needs you.
- If she hasn't already obtained it, get your friend professional help.

A DAY IN COURT

With any luck, a suspect will be apprehended. Identifying him will be the start of your postrape ordeal. You will be called upon to provide information to the prosecuting attorney's office and to testify against your assailant, perhaps before a jury. Whether the arrest of a rapist results in his being brought to trial depends on the quality of the evidence against him. With good evidence, a prosecutor could expect a guilty plea. Otherwise, he should be inclined to take the case to trial. Lesser-quality evidence would increase the probability of a plea-bargained sentence. Evidence that is still poorer would probably force the prosecutor to drop the case.

It is important to realize that the decision to drop a case against a suspect in no way reflects upon the rape victim or her veracity. It is merely the prosecutor's assessment of the available evidence. A reasonable evaluation of the facts surrounding a typical rape would lead to the conclusion that many rapes will lack the quality of evidence needed to assure indictment. After all, a rape is a craven and furtive act—not a public spectacle with onlookers who could corroborate testimony.

The defendant is protected by the law to the extent that past crimes for which he has been charged will not be admissible as evidence against him, except under unusual circumstances. You may not be as well protected, for you have committed no crime. The defendant does not have to reveal things that might incriminate him. You, on the other hand may be questioned in a few jurisdictions about your sexual activities. Fortunately, there is a trend toward enactment of laws that exclude the victim's private life from the trial record.

The defense attorney has three primary weapons available to gain freedom for his or her client: (1) there was not a sexual assault; (2) you have mistakenly identified the defendant; (3) there was no rape, but rather sexual relations occasioned by your free will and willing consent.

In some states, corroborative evidence is needed for conviction. This includes witnesses, bloodstains, dirty or torn clothing, and evidence of abrasions and scratches. New rape laws are making corroboration less necessary, but injuries may not always convict without some corroboration. Federal courts, and some other jurisdictions as well, require corroboration only in the case of statutory rape or for crimes reported long after being committed. Many times, however, the rape victim herself may provide corroborative testimony. The presence of semen might be considered corroboration, as might scratches, contusions, and other physical trauma.

The law stipulates that the accused is innocent until proved guilty of the particular crime for which he is standing trial. If the defense counsel can raise reasonable doubt in the mind of one juror that the defendant is not guilty on all of the particulars of the charges, he or she has an excellent chance of gaining acquittal.

Even after you have suffered through the assault and the ordeal of the judicial process, the criminal may be set free. The odds are about even that there will never be a trial, and if there are trials, half the defendants are either acquitted or their case dismissed.

If there are no witnesses to a rape, and if there are no visible injuries—and this is usually the case—there may be no way to prove your allegations. In this event, your day in court could turn into a personality contest. Justice might hinge upon one's appearance or demeanor, or on the preconceived notions of judges and jurors.

Of those who are convicted, two out of five will be convicted of a lesser offense. This low conviction rate among those brought to trial is often attributed to the fact that the penalties are so severe that judges or juries are reluctant to bring a conviction.

FALSE RAPE CHARGES

Women sometimes file false rape charges following consensual sex. This may be done to appease a male in her life, or a parent, or to account for the presence of a sexually transmitted disease. Petting or foreplay that transcends boundaries also accounts for false rape charges. Police are rarely fooled by such ploys (which are sometimes termed partial consent).

THE RAPE TRAUMA SYNDROME

Every rape victim suffers a clearly defined set of anomalies known as the rape trauma syndrome. The initial stage of the syndrome is characterized by disorganization, often accompanied by anxiety, depression, physical pain, nausea, insomnia, self-doubts, and feelings of guilt.

As this period of self-recrimination abates (usually in no more than a few months' time), it is replaced by what is termed a reorganization period. This is a longer-term disorder, frequently a year or more in duration. In this stage, a victim will undergo changes in habits. Usually these are the result of fear, stemming from the previous attack. Victims may change jobs, retire, or otherwise alter behavior patterns.

It is important that these changes of behavior be recognized for what they are—normal. A victim may, in time, completely overcome the disorder. Proper counseling, of course, is a valuable means for speeding this recovery.

Many courts, however, do not currently recognize this syndrome.

SELF-PROTECTION

Unfortunately, your chances of being a rape victim are increasing. The following suggestions are indended to decrease the likelihood of your being victimized.

To Protect Yourself at Home
At home, take the following precautions:

- All entrances should be well lighted.
- All windows should have locks and be undamaged.
- Bars should be put on first-floor or basement windows.
- Curtains on windows provide privacy.
- All outside doors should have strong one-inch dead-bolt locks.
- Familiarize yourself with your residence in the dark. Turn off the lights, and walk around until you become accustomed to moving about in the dark. This will be extremely helpful in escaping from an intruder who breaks into your residence at night.
- Be alert to—and if possible eliminate—any places an intruder might conceal himself, including trees, shrubbery, stairwells, alleys, hallways, and doors.
- Never open the door until the caller has clearly identified himself. If his identity is in doubt, ask the caller to wait a few minutes until you make a few phone calls.
- Call for help over the telephone when a stranger in need appears at your doorstep. Never let the person into your residence to make phone calls.

To Protect Yourself Outside
When you are outside, protect yourself with the following precautions:

- Be aware of who is near you and what is happening around you.
- Have your keys ready so that you can unlock your doors and enter your residence quickly.
- Walk upright with an air of confidence and at a steady pace. Make it appear you are in control. You will then exude a strong image, and potential criminals may avoid you.
- Never walk alone after dark. Be certain to avoid public parks; areas with excessive trees, bushes, and shrubbery; parking lots; alleys; and deserted areas.
- Cross the street if you see a group of males approaching you.
- Be attentive to voices, noises, or footsteps behind you. If you are suspicious of someone or think you are being followed, quicken or slow your pace, suddenly cross the street, stop in a store or public place, or begin screaming.

- If a person in a car follows you, change directions or run away.
- If a stranger stops to ask directions, remain a good distance from his car to prevent him from grabbing you or knocking you down by opening the door of his car.
- Never walk alone under the influence of drugs or alcohol.
- Try to travel in a group.
- When waiting for a bus, a traffic light, or a friend, be alert. Your stationary position makes you more vulnerable to attack.
- If a car pulls up next to you or drives by several times, change direction or run away.

To Protect Yourself in Your Car

If you are traveling by car, you can protect yourself in several ways:

- Have your keys ready to unlock your car doors. Hesitation and fumbling for your keys near your car may invite trouble.
- Always lock your car doors whether you are inside or out.
- Before entering the car, check the backseat for someone hiding there.
- If someone approaches your car while you are waiting for a traffic light, blow the horn and proceed through the light, provided the intersection is clear. A sharp turn to the right into a potential attacker will force him away.
- If someone is following you, sound your horn to attract the attention of the police or passersby, or drive to a police, fire, or service station where help may be available. Remember the license plate number and description of the car that is following you.
- If your car is disabled, lift the front hood, and tie a white cloth around the aerial. Then lock yourself in the car. Police and tow truck operators are alert for cars displaying these signs.

To Protect Yourself When Hitchhiking

The best policy is never to accept a ride from a stranger, but if you must, here are the minimum precautions you should take:

- Never hitchhike alone or at night.
- Before entering the car, check the backseat to assure that no one is hiding there. Remember the license plate number, the make, and the color of the car.
- Converse with the driver to determine whether he or she appears to be drunk or unstable.
- Make sure the door handle on the passenger's side is in working

condition. It may have been removed to prevent exit from the car.
- Never get into a car that has changed directions to pick you up.
- Roll down the window a little so that you can scream for help if need be.
- Be sure that one of those "natural weapons" (keys, hatpin, etc.) is accessible in case of an emergency.
- Do not hitchhike in provocative attire. Avoid dresses; instead, wear loose-fitting slacks.
- Know how to get to your destination, so that you will know when the driver deviates from the route. Get out of the car as soon as possible in such a situation.
- If the driver acts nervous or erratic, or somehow arouses your suspicion, get out of the car at the first opportunity.
- Never get into a car with two or more males.
- Try to hitch a ride with a woman driver.

SEXUALLY TRANSMITTED DISEASES

Any of the diseases that are transmitted through sexual intercourse may be spread by the act of rape. Herpes simplex, gonorrhea, syphilis, and acquired immune deficiency syndrome (AIDS) are all potentially fatal consequences of a rape. All of these diseases can lodge within the body of the victim, threatening her health and even her life.

Nor does the list of consequences stop there. Sexual partners of the assailed female are at risk, as are gynecologists, emergency room personnel, and others who may have offered assistance. If the beleaguered woman is pregnant (or becomes so as the result of being attacked), the fetus she carries is at risk from a variety of venereal disorders. Clearly, the direst of these threats is AIDS.

In some respects, AIDS is like rape. The victims, deserving or not, are stigmatized, experience profound changes in their lives, bear emotional, physical, and psychological trauma throughout the remainder of their lives, and, most of all, must continue to ask themselves the agonizing question—"Why me?"

In times past, rapists have tended to disbelieve potential victims who claimed that they were infected with social diseases. You might expect that today's attackers would be similarly dubious. However, there is nothing to lose by telling your assailant that you suffer from AIDS. Don't expect him to believe it. Nevertheless, you will have to put him on the defensive. Tell him to look in your billfold, that there is a photograph of your "doomed" partner. This will distract him further. If you should have a snapshot of a slender male, you will send him packing to be sure. Carry a condom if you feel particularly in danger of rape. This might make your tale of affliction more believable. It would certainly raise doubts in the mind of your adversary.

VICTIM COMPENSATION

Some consolation can be found for rape victims. More than half the states have enacted some form of victim compensation legislation. These programs might reimburse you for medical expenses and lost earnings. To qualify, however, you must meet several eligibility criteria, including financial need, residency requirements, and cooperation with criminal justice agencies.

RAPE VICTIMS' BILL OF RIGHTS

Rights of rape victims are divided into three principal categories: personal, legal, and medical. You have the personal right to question any of the people with whom you have dealings during your crisis. These include police, medical, and legal personnel and any public or private agencies. You should not feel shame or guilt, for you have not done wrong. To feel unemotional, unfeeling, or even hysterical is normal. So too are fear, anger, loneliness, and helplessness.

You have the legal right to report the attack upon you and to expect that the police will pursue your right to swift and speedy justice. You also have the right not to prosecute. You have the right of a third-party report that does not release your name. You also may do nothing, or even withdraw your testimony. If qualified, you have the right to restitution from the victim compensation funds, and you have the right to file suit against your attacker.

In any court appearance, you are entitled to be treated with respect and consideration. You are entitled to have a person of your choosing accompany you throughout your court appearances. Pending availability, you can require that the law enforcement officer who handles the investigatory phase be a woman.

At any step throughout your ordeal, you have the right to understand exactly what is happening to you and around you. Ask questions as often as you wish, and don't be sidetracked by any attempt to rush you through the process. With the passage of time, events surrounding your ordeal may come more clearly into focus. Thus, you have the right to change or amend the information you have previously given to medical and police investigators.

It is likely that you will have received medical attention following your attack. That is your right. You have other medical rights as well. You are entitled to a rape crisis counselor to accompany you; your personal physician may attend you; you are entitled to the comfort of family and friends at virtually every stop along the way.

You have humanitarian rights, too. You have the right to privacy, gentleness, sensitivity, and respect. You are entitled to explanations of every test, procedure, and medication prior to its administration. Similarly, you are entitled to a full and complete explanation of every document you are requested to sign. Someone whom you trust may assist you in this regard.

Defenses Against Rape: A Checklist

1. Practice all personal and home-security procedures mentioned throughout this book.
2. Teach school-age females—who are most often victimized— proper safeguards, particularly in regard to relationships with strangers and the value of locks and other physical security measures.
3. Know where your children are, what they're doing, and with whom.
4. Ensure caution and supervision in a school-age female's entertainment of male friends.
5. Urge your daughter to travel in a group.
6. Enforce reasonable times for children to be home.
7. Exercise care in after-school activities.
8. Learn some rudiments of self-defense.
9. Use your feet to run with and your voice to scream with.
10. Don't physically resist or attack an armed assailant. An unarmed assailant might be vulnerable to physical attack sufficient to allow a break for freedom.
11. Carry everyday items for use as defensive weapons: a pen or pencil, red pepper, lemon juice in a squeeze bottle, a key ring, or an umbrella.
12. Attack an assailant at his throat, stomach, temples, eyes, or kneecaps.

13. Use a knee to the groin if an assailant makes an embracing attack from the front.

14. Deliver a sharp blow to the stomach with an elbow if you are attacked from the rear.

15. Stomp on the foot, at the instep, as a defensive measure.

16. Try an emotional appeal if escape or resistance is impossible or impractical. Crying or a reasonable attempt at conversation may thwart an attack or lessen its severity.

17. Building up a rapist's ego may give him the emotional gratification he seeks, deterring him from seeking physical gratification.

18. Resistance is the lesser of evils but might not be practical in every instance. When it comes to perverse, sadistic, or humiliating acts, submission to these acts might prevent pregnancy or sexually transmitted diseases.

19. Be aware that a date could degenerate into a rape; maintain defenses at all times.

20. Once the incident is over, report it and prosecute.

21. Know the number of the rape crisis center hot line if one is available in your community.

22. Do not bathe, change clothes, douche, or otherwise clean up after an attack. You may be destroying evidence. Take a change of clothing with you when you go to file the report because the clothing you were wearing might be required for evidence.

23. Write down or tape-record all incidents while they are fresh in your mind.

24. Undergo the required physician's examination, and consider having another from your own gynecologist.

25. To resist or not, the decision is solely up to the victim. The decision must be based on circumstances existing at the time of attack.

26. A female must resist a rapist, but not necessarily physically. "Don't make me do it" is a plea that indicates duress.

27. Although 25 percent of victims experience no disorder from being raped, rape victims have higher than average suicide rates. Medical authorities have identified a rape trauma syndrome. Not all advise females of their likelihood of sexual harassment and of the real threat of rape.

28. Corroboration of evidence is less important than was previously the case. It is required routinely, however, in cases involving statutory rape and those which are reported after the passage of an unreasonable amount of time.

29. New rape shield laws protect the identity of the victims by providing anonymity. Many of these laws provide for pretrial hearings to determine whether proposed defense evidence is relevant.

30. A woman must know and demand her personal, legal, and medical rights if she is the victim of a sexual assault.

26
Multiple Murder

James Ruppert, 41, armed with a .357 Magnum, two .22-caliber handguns, and an 18-shot rifle, fired first at his brother Leonard. Before the shooting spree ended, the blood-splattered bodies of eleven of Ruppert's relatives, including his mother, were scattered throughout the kitchen and living room.

Over the last few years, corresponding to a surge in murders involving many victims, interest in multiple homicides has increased. Movie makers, news broadcasters, and talk-show hosts have turned their attention to this type of crime. A common misconception is that the multiple murderer is a raving, ranting, vicious-looking, glassy-eyed maniac who randomly selects victims and strikes without warning or mercy. Against this type of random psychotic killer, protection may seem nearly impossible.

Researchers have gathered enough data and knowledge to sort out realities from myths and misconceptions. From all this study has come hard evidence for developing a defense against what earlier appeared to be a totally unpredictable phenomenon.

PROFILE

Experts say the typical multiple murderer is a white male in his late twenties or thirties. He exhibits a spotty history of property crime but is not a hardened criminal. Usually he kills for money, jealousy, or lust. Sometimes he kills to cover other crimes. In background, personality, appearance, and demeanor, the multiple murderer is extraordinarily ordinary. Rarely is he or she mentally ill or psychotic. The multiple murderer is in control of what he or she is doing during the commission of the crime. This is one reason for his or her "success" in killing—no one ever suspects him or her.

The multiple murderer strikes when severe frustration boils over or when a particular event ignites explosive rage. Afterward, he or she rarely displays remorse, sorrow, or guilt, and is most likely even to deny responsibility for the spree of violence.

We also know that multiple killers are not all alike. There are serial killers and mass murderers, and within each category several different types.

SERIAL MURDER

Serial murder involves the killing of many individuals over a period of at least several weeks or a few months. Gerald Stano went on a killing rampage resulting in the deaths of at least forty-one women in three states—Florida, Pennsylvania, and New Jersey. His unsuspecting victims were shot, stabbed, and strangled. At age fifteen, Edward Kemper III murdered his grandparents, then killed six young women who were hitchhiking around Santa Cruz and the San Francisco Bay area. By twenty-four he had murdered his mother.

Sometimes this syndrome includes socially disapproved sexual orientation. John Wayne Gacy murdered more than thirty-three boys and young men after having sexual relations with them. Elmer Wayne Henry, Jr., raped, tortured, and murdered twenty-seven teenage boys. Other notorious serial murderers, including the Hillside Strangler, Son of Sam, the Stocking Strangler, the Night Stalker, and the Boston Strangler, also exhibited severe sexual problems.

Types of Serial Killers
Criminologists have discerned four types of serial murderers. Their motive often is the pursuit of a personal goal that they have failed to otherwise achieve. The visionary killer acts in response to "voices" or a vision. The hedonistic murderer, seeking a thrill, derives pleasure from torture and deaths. The attacker oriented toward power/control gets satisfaction from the life-and-death control over the victim. Finally, the mission-oriented homicidal maniac focuses on eliminating a group or category of people.

The typical victims of all serial killers are strangers who are killed by beating or strangulation.

How Many?
Police estimate that over 3,300 homicides a year involve serial killers. Seventeen of these killers have murdered at least ten people, and nine have killed twenty or more. It is estimated that a new one surfaces each month. According to a Justice Department official, there are probably one hundred serial killers operating at any one time in the United States.

The horror of this crime is so great that even the smallest probability of such an encounter sends chills up our spines. Nevertheless, the chance that you or your loved ones will actually meet a serial killer is very small.

Recognizing the Killer
One problem in protecting yourself and your loved ones is that it is unlikely that you will be able to recognize the serial murderer. The vast majority of such criminals function in the community as law-abiding citizens and kill only when impulse tells them to. Above average in appearance, they usually dress well, speak smoothly, and exhibit charm and intelligence. Externally, they appear normal, hiding their rage, frustration, sexual feelings, and intentions. They don't appear disheveled, dirty, or shabby, nor do they talk to themselves as so many homeless people do. They are very episodic and act on the moment. One psychiatrist characterized them as wearing a "mask of sanity," which is removed only when they strike.

Serial murderers get along well with co-workers and neighbors. Many try to find jobs working with children; John Wayne Gacy, for example, was employed as a clown entertaining children in hospitals. This ability to assimilate into socially respected occupations makes them particularly dangerous.

Victims of Child Abuse
Many serial killers have a childhood history of abuse and rejection by their parents. While still young, they often set fires for fun and torture animals. When they mature, they want to control, dominate, and humiliate their victims, particularly children and women whom they easily overpower. They become avid consumers of the most graphically violent pornographic pictures, material, and literature. Many of their killings are accompanied by sexual assaults.

Protection
Obviously, protection against these individuals is very difficult, because you are unlikely to recognize their evil designs until it is too late. You can

nevertheless increase your security by following the standard practice of being cautious with strangers. If someone you don't know approaches you for no apparent reason or initiates conversation, do not act friendly or personable. Walk away as rapidly as you can. If you cannot avoid a conversation, your response should be terse and to the point. Under no circumstances allow the stranger to extend the conversation and to manipulate you. Never give out your address or telephone number to persons whom you cannot trust. Do not allow anyone into your home whom you fail to recognize or who does not have a specific, legitimate reason for being there.

Avoid situations that place you at the mercy of strangers, like hitchhiking or walking alone in isolated areas at night. Above all, change your attitude, and don't be complacent. Convincing yourself that victimization by a serial killer happens to "other" people but not to you tends to make you vulnerable.

MASS MURDER

It is even more difficult to protect yourself from mass murderers. Like the serial killers, these individuals are also filled with rage and frustration. A single event creating stress in the family or the workplace, like losing a job or a lover, wife, mother, or other close family member, triggers a sudden explosion of multiple homicide. Most of these acts are carried out with a handgun or rifle.

Mass murderers, like serial killers, are "life-losers" whose converging problems at home and at work drive them to vent their rage and frustration on innocent victims. Many mass murderers have been fired from their jobs or separated from their partners. The murderers blame those closest to them for all these problems. The majority of victims are family members, co-workers, clients, or people who just happen to be in the wrong place at the wrong time.

Consider what happened in Edmond, California, where a postal worker facing dismissal opened fire on twenty people in the post office and killed fourteen of them. A former employee of a convenience store in Russellville, Arkansas, killed two of his former supervisors and injured four co-workers in a shooting spree. A few weeks earlier, a former supervisor was shot dead on a Pacific Southwest Airlines jet by a dismissed airline employee. The bullets apparently damaged the plane's controls, and forty-three people died when it crashed.

In one recent case in California, a man's obsession with a woman ended in the deaths of seven persons, but not including the intended victim, the woman who had spurned his love. She was only wounded. Armed with a shotgun, a high-power rifle, and two automatic pistols, the thirty-nine-year-old computer programmer returned to the company that had fired him to stalk and shoot the girl who had repeatedly turned him down for a date. In the shooting spree that followed, he killed seven other employees.

Be Alert

In situations of this type, there is little more to do than try to run away. Do not try to fight or reason with the killer. These tactics will only enrage the killer and ensure your demise. If you are unable to escape a building, lock yourself in a closet as soon as you hear gunshots or comprehend what is going on.

Be on guard for the warning signs that surface just before these explosive violent events. For example, a highly verbal worker may suddenly withdraw or become depressed; a cheerful, reliable employee may suddenly turn irritable or begin arriving late for work. Also, be particularly alert for co-workers or employees who suffer from chemical dependency, marital stress, or other exceptional pressures. They should be urged to visit your company's employee assistance program. (Over ten thousand businesses have established these.) If your company lacks one, suggest this important contribution to employee morale and effectiveness, which could avert a major tragedy. Most important is that your co-worker or subordinate seek professional counseling. Above all, remember to be courteous, fair, and nice to people. Do not antagonize, insult, or in any way put them down. This strategy will turn the odds away from you as the object of the mass murderer.

Multiple Murder: A Checklist
1. Be more cautious, especially of strangers.
2. Never engage in conversation with a person who approaches you for no apparent reason. Walk away as quickly as you are able.
3. Recognize when someone is trying to manipulate you, and resist.
4. Do not give out your telephone number or address to strangers.
5. Never allow strangers to enter your home.
6. Avoid situations, such as walking in isolated areas, hitchhiking, or going out alone at night, where you might be at the mercy of strangers.

7. If you hear gunshots, run from the scene or lock yourself in a closet.
8. Never challenge the killer's instructions or authority.
9. Learn the warning signs of potential mass murderers, including sudden changes in personality, demeanor, attitude, mental health, marital situation, work behavior, or chemical dependency.
10. Encourage troubled individuals to seek counseling, whether from your company's employee assistance program or from counselors or private therapists.
11. Suggest that your company establish an employee assistance program if it does not already have one.
12. Change your life attitude by realizing that realistically you could be a victim of multiple murder.

27
Arson and Vandalism

Paul Brindle, an employee of the Lexicon Hotel, was charged yesterday with first-degree arson in connection with two fires at the hotel. Metro Police said Brindle was dissatisfied with the hotel job he had held since September.

ARSON

Arson is the willful or malicious burning, or attempt to burn (with or without intent to defraud), a dwelling house, public building, motor vehicle or aircraft, or personal property of another. Only fires determined to be willfully or maliciously started are classified as arson. Fires of suspicious or unknown origin are specifically excluded. But while perpetrators of these crimes may intend merely to destroy property, all too often their crimes result in serious injury and death.

Why Arson Fires Are Set
People deliberately set fires for a number of reasons; personal gain, revenge, mental sickness, profit, concealing another crime, vandalism, intimidation, jealousy, and spite are but a few. Revenge is the principal reason that arsonists start fires.

Extent of Arson
Several years ago, a study commissioned by the Law Enforcement Assistance Administration estimated that in one year, 1,000 deaths (including those of forty-five fire fighters) and 10,000 injuries resulted from arson fires. In 1986, these deliberate fires claimed 705 victims. The National Fire Protection Association, in a several-year-old study, estimated almost a quarter of a million fires—directly the result of arson—

in one single year. Property losses amounted to more than $1.25 billion. The dollar loss of the average arson is $7,000.

That is just the beginning of the losses. The victims have no place to live, and they likely had not increased their insurance coverage to stay in line with replacement cost. They are usually forced to move to less satisfactory quarters. In the meantime, the burned-out house that they were forced to abandon will have degenerated into an eyesore, which will adversely affect the value of all nearby homes. Possibly, the victims may find future insurance exorbitant, if not totally unavailable to them.

If arson is widespread, involving blocks of a neighborhood, an entire community can be destroyed. The burned-out homes can diminish the values of sound buildings, perhaps to the point where they cannot be sold at any price. Homeowners can be wiped out, and tenants forced to seek a less troubled neighborhood. The remaining tenantable structures may then be leased to undesirables, placing further pressures on the value of neighborhood property.

The Arsonist
Only one in one hundred arsonists is ever convicted and sentenced to a prison term. One fact that contributes to this low incarceration rate may be that the necessary investigation to determine if a crime had been committed may occur too late to turn up evidence to support charges.

The typical arsonist is a male under the age of twenty-five (63 percent of all arsonists; 40 percent are below the age of eighteen). Arson is the favorite serious crime of juveniles. On a percentage basis, more of the under-eighteen group were involved in the crime of arson than in any of the other seven serious crimes on the FBI's *Uniform Crime Reports* list.

In addition to the bored juvenile looking for excitement or seeking redress of real or imagined wrongs, the arsonist may be a property owner defrauding an insurance carrier, or a homeless drifter looking for an abandoned building to sleep in; when it is cold, homeless people often burn the woodwork for warmth. Property owners, especially absentee ones, inadvertently invite the attentions of this last group. The trash-strewn property with hip-high weeds is an irresistible attraction for an arsonist.

Preventive Measures
Several things may be done to reduce the incidence of arson. Some community organizations gather property and insurance information and report suspicious-looking individuals, vehicles, and fires. One such

group in Boston, known as STOP, actually uncovered an arson-for-profit ring that had destroyed $6 million worth of property and had set some thirty-five fires. Thirty-three persons, including a fire chief, a police officer, insurance adjusters, attorneys, and real estate operators, were arrested.

Teach your children proper attitudes toward fires and fire setting and the horrible consequences of setting fires. Older kids might be taught to identify fire setters and to organize neighborhood youths to clean up refuse-strewn lots or deteriorated buildings. Encourage civic or business groups to offer rewards for information leading to the arrest of an arsonist.

Education and public awareness are key elements in preventing malicious fires. Fire setters may be deterred by a climate of negative public opinion and knowledge of the terrible consequences of arson. Do your best to support workshops and discussion groups for senior citizens, neighborhood groups, and schoolchildren; perhaps your civic or social club could distribute educational materials relating to fires. A very successful campaign in Seattle involved athletes, T-shirts, and a contest to name the "Arson Rat."

Arson is often committed in isolated and dark areas, so keep your house and surrounding property well lighted. If you have a garden, it might be wise to erect a fence around it. This may be a keep-away sign to mischievous youths and envious neighbors as well as to hungry animals.

Leave your dog out in your yard now and then, provided the yard is enclosed. People are instinctively afraid of large dogs, and dogs also serve to deter burglars. If possible, keep your car in the garage, in your driveway, or where it can be seen from inside your house.

If you own a business, make your buildings as secure as possible. Install alarms and unbreakable glass, hire a guard to patrol the premises at night, and post signs to inform intruders that they will be prosecuted for defacing property.

One of the best preventive measures is a citizen patrol that works in teams, on foot or by car, to watch your neighborhood. Children can also participate in these patrols. Members of such groups should not try to apprehend a vandal or arsonist but should concentrate on notifying the police.

Perhaps the best advice for better dealing with arson is this: install smoke detectors. They can be purchased for very little money, and they can provide the early warning that would easily save your life. Fires in the home will injure nearly 70,000 people this year, and kill more than 6,000. Remember, 25 percent of the nation's homes don't have smoke detectors, but such homes account for 60 percent of fire fatalities.

VANDALISM

Vandalism is a pesky crime, usually committed by bored, playful, or vengeful teenagers. The effects of vandalism cost more than $1 billion per year, a large portion of that money coming from taxpayers. Whether you live in an urban, suburban, or rural area, chances are that you have faced some form of vandalism.

Types of Vandalism

Types of vandalism include defacing statues and monuments, breaking windows, destroying public pay phones and parking meters, writing on subway cars and storefronts, tearing pages from school and library books, smashing school furniture, clogging school toilets, turning over tombstones, and ruining business property.

Vandalism also damages your personal property. Many people have awakened to find tire tracks embedded in their front lawns, garden and shrubbery maliciously torn up, or automobile antennas missing. Perhaps you have had the unpleasant experience of cleaning dried eggs off your car and house or removing smashed pumpkins from your porch after Halloween.

Perhaps the most disheartening type of vandalism is that which is done directly and deliberately to our houses of worship. Churches have been spray-painted with obscenities, and sacred scrolls have been stolen from synagogues. In one recent year there were 377 malicious acts against Jewish institutions and property, including swastika dubbings, anti-Jewish slogans, and fire bombings—an increase of 192 percent over the preceding year. This particularly violent form of vandalism threatens us personally and collectively.

A few years ago, a London publication reported an incident of vandalism. A motorist experienced a flat tire on the expressway. After jacking up the rear end, he was removing the wheel, when he noticed someone opening the hood and attempting to remove the battery. Outraged, the offended driver challenged the opportunistic battery seeker. "Look," replied the latter, "you take the tires if you want—all I need is the battery."

This incident provides considerable insight into the motivation of the vandal. In general, the vandal *does* respect the property of others, but only so long as the property is properly maintained. Allowing anything to lapse into misuse or abuse is an open invitation to the vandal.

You probably have seen vacant houses in your neighborhood that remain untouched for months on end. If, however, a single window is broken, almost overnight all of the windows often are shattered, and the structure has been broken open. Soon the building gives every indication of having been thoroughly vandalized.

Besides mere amusement, revenge is the second motivator of the vandal. Usually, this type of damage is directed against schools. Often, a school must enforce discipline, sometimes to the displeasure of the affected students. A young person may respond to this provocation by plugging a toilet with tissue and disabling the water shutoff mechanism, thus inundating the surrounding area.

Some vandalistic actions can become life-threatening. Disabled elevators in a college dormitory would be considered by most observers a mild inconvenience. The same thing in a high rise for the elderly could, under certain circumstances, be tragic. Broken street lighting could lead to rape, robbery, or worse. The offenders rarely consider the possible consequences of what they often consider harmless pranks.

Combating Vandalism

Since subway cars don't belong to anybody, they therefore should be spray-painted. While this is illogical, it is also a widely held belief. Interestingly, when transit officials invited people to decorate the cars, they suddenly became objects that could be appreciated. Subsequent damage was minimized. This change tends to reinforce the earlier hypothesis that the vandal *does* respect the property of others, so long as it is maintained in a fashion that indicates someone cares about it.

Common Targets of Vandalism

Besides schools, vacant structures, and public transportation, the targets of the vandal include abandoned vehicles. These should be hauled away to storage lots or sold through legal channels. Public transportation, like abandoned private vehicles, is most vulnerable when not in operation, but proper fencing or guards can be valuable protection against damage.

Following is a top-to-bottom examination of a structure, noting possible vandalism targets and suggesting possible protections against them:

• Roof flashings are often stolen and sold to dealers for their lead or copper content. The best means of avoiding this loss is to deny access to the roof.

- Skylights may be broken in an attempt to enter a building. Wired glass panes or polycarbonate glazing should discourage such attempts.
- Downspouts are commonly broken. The best protection is to replace PVCs, asbestos, or light metals with a heavier weight steel.
- Graffiti is a continuing problem. Pencil or permanent damage can be discouraged by using rough-surfaced materials that defy this type of marking, but this surface would create difficulty in removing spray paints. Perhaps the best way to cope is to use smooth, hard surfaces that can easily be cleaned with mineral spirits or other solvents. Another option would be to paint over the damage as necessary.
- Children swinging on doors can alter the fit of the door into its jamb. Heavier hinges may solve the problem, but if not, then a heavy-duty door assembly will be required.
- Interior doors, often hollow-core doors, are easily kicked in accidentally. Kick plates on these doors may remedy the problem. Otherwise, solid-core doors will be required.
- Glass door panels can cause injury if broken. Avoid low-level panes of glass, if at all possible. Cross rails on larger glass doors will minimize the number of sharp-edged pieces of glass in the event of breakage, since it is unlikely that all of the panes would shatter.
- If glass breakage is a serious and continuing problem, shatterproof or virtually unbreakable substitutes may be called for. However, these products are easily scratched, tend to discolor, and, in the event of a fire, would not perform as well as glass, and might even melt. Persistent breakage might indicate the need for solid doors.
- Internal walls may often be broken, dented, even kicked in. Double thickness of wallboard may solve the problem. Breakage may also stem from construction shortcuts such as an inadequate number of wall studs. In new construction, assure that strong, sound materials are used and construction practices followed. This is no place to skimp. In existing construction, renovate so that replacement of wall, in whole or part, may be easily accomplished with minimum disruption.
- Toilet cubicles are vulnerable to a variety of abuses. Graffiti is an omnipresent possibility, one covered earlier in this list. The usual

gaps between partitions and the main walls provide leverage for prying aside the partition entirely. Finally, young people find the rail above the door of the cubicle stall an irresistible trapeze for swinging. Here, high-quality fixtures, stalls, and other items (such as tissue holders and coat hooks) should be utilized throughout. They will be subjected to considerable abuse.

- A glass panel, even of frosted glass, in a rest room door provides a considerable deterrent to vandalism by suggesting that someone might witness illegal acts.
- Handrails on staircases may be called on to support the entire weight of several students at one time. Obviously, heavy-duty hardware can bear these loads. Water bombs and other objects are often dropped down stairwells on people below. If this becomes a recurring problem, netting can be installed to intercept these missiles.
- Toilet seats are sometimes stolen by pranksters. Replacing the standard wing nuts with lock nuts would make theft more difficult.
- Toilet tanks are broken from their fittings. Bolting them through the wall or locating them quite high on the wall will make sabotage of these fixtures difficult.
- Urinals are sometimes pulled away from the walls. The use of stainless-steel fixtures in stalls is the best protection against this type of abuse; if properly secured, they will be the most trouble-free.
- Water fountains, with the usual flow constricted by fingers, can eject a stream of water a considerable distance, causing disruption. These fountains may also be damaged or even pulled away from the wall, possibly resulting in flooding. Locating them in high-traffic areas subject to supervision will prevent some abuses. One-piece stainless-steel fixtures are a further defense against deliberate damage.
- Thermostats, fan switches, and appliance controls are often improperly used, particularly in schools. They should be protected by locks.
- Finally, if outdoor lighting fixtures are broken frequently, glass fixtures should be replaced with plastic or other sturdy diffusers.

Arson and Vandalism: A Checklist
1. Form community organizations to combat arson and vandalism.

2. Teach your children fire and safety practices and the consequences of malicious destruction of property.
3. Set up groups to distribute educational materials on fire safety and the value of property.
4. Try to prevent arson and vandalism by minimizing the vulnerabilities of your property. This includes installing alarms and smoke detectors, erecting fences, and, if your business is large, hiring private security guards.
5. Well-maintained and cared-for property is one of the best ways to minimize vandalism.

28
Robbery Prevention and Defense

Mary Clark, of Livonia, was robbed of twenty-three dollars by an unknown juvenile at the corner of Fourth and Wallaby yesterday afternoon. Ms. Clark said, "I was walking along Wallaby in broad daylight when this little guy—he couldn't have been twelve years old—ran out of a doorway and threw himself at my legs just like a football player and knocked me down. By the time I got up," she continued, "he was half a block down the street with my purse and twenty-three dollars."

Robbery, unlike other crimes, represents a threat to both your person and your property. Robbery is the taking of another's property by force or threat of violence. It is a crime in which there is always a confrontation between the victim and offender. Muggers (street robbers) generally try to frighten or intimidate their victims in order to gain physical and psychological control over them.

Robbers prey on small businesses, particularly retailers open at night. According to the Small Business Administration, small businesses lose to robbers an amount three times greater proportionately than their larger counterparts. A mom-and-pop store with 3 percent net profit, for example, must sell $17,000 worth of goods to compensate for one $500 robbery.

EXTENT OF ROBBERY

Extrapolations of victimization surveys indicate that, on the average, one out of every forty-eight of the nation's households was touched by a robbery. From 1982 to 1984, robbery rates fell, but over the next three years through 1987, the most recent year for which statistics are available, this crime increased by 5 percent. This turnaround probably reflects the emergence of the second generation of the post–World War II Baby Boom. This Baby Boom Echo probably will continue to adversely affect our crime rates for years to come, well into the twenty-first century.

December and January are the prime robbery months, followed none too closely by the midsummer months. These facts might lead to the speculation that robberies are related to schools' being closed. At the very least, vacations would allow students more time for many pursuits, crime among them.

ROBBERY AND VIOLENCE

Robbery accounts for 40 percent of all crimes of violence. Force is employed in about half the robberies, and firearms in 40 percent. In attacks on victims, 20 percent involve guns, and 36 percent involve knives. Robbery is a crime of violence.

Do not be a hero or resist the robbers physically or verbally; this will increase your chances of injury. It is true that robbers may use force even if you don't resist, but if you do attempt to thwart their goals, they will become frustrated and will be more likely to employ violence. Do not be deceived by unarmed robbers, because they use strong-arm force. The presence of an armed robber's weapon—a gun in particular—is threatening enough to control the victims. The unarmed robber uses force to minimize victim resistance.

Your chances are about one in three that you will be hurt in a robbery and one in five that your injury will be serious enough to require hospitalization. Elderly people are particularly vulnerable, because they are much more likely to be shoved, pushed, or knocked to the ground by robbers than are younger people, and they are more likely to receive injuries that require hospitalization. Robberies seldom involve people who are known to each other. Studies show that more than three-quarters of all robbers are strangers to their victims.

ROBBER PROFILE

The typical robber is an uneducated lower-class male under twenty-one years of age. Robbers are well represented among all races and ethnic groups. So are their victims. Only eight out of every one hundred persons arrested for robbery in 1986 were females.

DETERRING ROBBERY IN SMALL BUSINESSES

If you own a small business or store, keep the premises orderly and clean. A cluttered store gives the impression of carelessness. Be active, moving around the store. Maximize the amount of space inside that is visible from the outside by using adequate lighting. Avoid obstructions near the window that might block the ability of passersby and the police to observe what is happening inside the store. Robbers may be reluctant to enter a store with high visibility from outside.

Vigilance Is the Best Strategy

Always greet customers in a friendly manner. This will not only benefit your business but also let a potential robber know that he or she may be identified later. Robbers seek to remain anonymous and to avoid friendly contact with potential victims. Be alert for anyone appearing to loiter inside or outside the store, seemingly waiting for you to be alone.

Careful Planning

Planning for a robbery is always a wise measure. Every employee—especially those who handle the money—should be advised what to do in the event of a robbery. You should prepare signals so that once a robbery is in progress, you can alert employees who may be in a position to notify the police.

Handling and Safeguarding Money

Keep a minimum of working cash in your store, especially at night, when most robberies occur. Put larger bills in a drop safe as soon as you receive them. Never allow cash to accumulate in your register. Make bank deposits during the day, varying your route and timing.

Be serious about protecting your money. Display burglar alarm decals in a prominent place. If you belong to a special citizens' robbery prevention program, post signs to this effect inside and outside the store. Since many robberies occur when you open or close the store, try to have someone else present at these times. Robbers case their potential targets and know when only one person will be on hand.

Do not balance registers or count receipts in full view. This actually tempts robbers, customers, and even other store employees. Have cash drawers taken to a secure location to count the money.

It is best not to rely on firearms. A robber will have the "drop" on you and usually is ruthless and desperate. Alarm systems, electronic surveillance equipment, safes with time locks, and other robbery-resistant items may provide better protection and should be considered for your store.

VIOLENCE PREVENTION PROCEDURES

Obey the instructions of robbers as quickly as possible. Never argue with them. Robbers are less likely to injure you if you cooperate. The shorter the time it takes the robbers to do their work, the less chance there is for injury or even death. In a small business, remain calm, and reassure your employees and customers. Do not fight with the robbers or attempt to use weapons. By the time you are confronted by a robber, it is too late for such actions. Alert the robbers to any surprises, such as an employee working in the back room or a delivery person who may return to the store at any moment.

Take mental notes about the crime and the criminals. Pay attention to the number of robbers, their ages, sex, ethnic backgrounds, appearance, clothing, weapons, voices, nicknames, special characteristics, and unusual behavior or identifying marks.

One antirobbery technique that is sometimes recommended is the installation of a doorbell in your place of business. The bell should ring in an adjacent store, enabling your neighboring merchant to notify the police when you are unable to do so. For your neighbor's protection, you can reciprocate.

A word of caution: If the robbers observe your signaling, they will, characteristically, do harm to you. But they may also take only cash or valuables that are easily located and not waste too much time in vacating the premises.

Postrobbery Action

Note the make, color, and year of the vehicle used in the robbery and the license plate number and state of registration. Do not chase or follow the criminal under any circumstances. The robbers may try to kill you, and the police may even mistake you for the criminals.

Notify the police immediately. Stay on the phone until they get all the necessary information, then remain close to the telephone. Take inventory of exactly what was stolen, but do not give this information to the responding officers. Reveal this information only to the detectives assigned to your case—the police may talk to reporters, and publicity about a substantial loss may convince other robbers to attack your store, too.

Record the names and addresses of witnesses. Do not disturb any objects the robbers may have touched or held, and avoid discussing the robbery until the police say it is OK for you to do so.

MUGGING DEFENSE

Most muggings take place on the street. Thus, the best protection is to be alert and cautious at all times. Be suspicious of strangers, and never trust anyone you do not know. Avoid walking at nighttime, especially in dangerous or unfamiliar neighborhoods. If you must go out at night, walk on well-lighted main thoroughfares. It is useful to carry a small amount of money, say, $50, to appease the potential mugger, but large sums should be avoided. Walk next to the curb, and stay away from buildings, alleys, doorways, shrubbery, trees, and benches. Walk at a determined speed, and appear in a hurry to reach a destination. Cross the street if you spot someone suspicious walking toward you or following you. Be sure that you have adequate change to make a phone call in an emergency; always carry several quarters.

If confronted by a robber, use your common sense, and follow the suggestions in this chapter. If there is an opportunity to escape without subjecting yourself to violence, take advantage of it; otherwise, maintain your cool and follow the mugger's instructions precisely. After the robbery, call the police. Bear in mind that a robber or a mugger initially is after your valuables, but if he or she should feel threatened by you, it could cost you your life.

In the 1980s, particularly the earlier part, several major robberies provided continuing press coverage. In November 1983, the then largest robbery in British history occurred. Forty million dollars in gold and $175,000 in diamonds were taken. Two days prior to this, $6.5 million was taken from a Memphis armored-car location, ironically on Thanksgiving Day. Two months before that, a Connecticut armored firm lost $7 million to robbers. About one year before that, the largest robbery in U.S. history occurred in New York. Another armored-car firm suffered an $11 million loss. Shortly thereafter, it went out of business.

In August 1987, a security-box firm in London was attacked at gunpoint by two well-dressed men who entered the building, they said, in order to rent a strongbox. They took $48 million, and a police official indicated that the "real" figure could be as great as $64 million.

Each of these incidents, except possibly the August 1987 one, was accomplished with the assistance of an insider. Perhaps some, or all, of these crimes could have been prevented if more care had been taken in the selection of employees by the victimized firms.

You can learn from these great robberies. You need only recognize that if these large firms, with all the forms of protection available to them, can be robbed, then you are at risk at any time, day or night. Take the time to learn and practice the techniques of protecting yourself from crime. They are to be found throughout this book.

Robbery Prevention and Defense: A Checklist

1. Keep your business tidy and clean.
2. Walk around and keep busy even when no customers in the store.
3. Keep your store well lighted and visible from the street.
4. Constantly be on the lookout for suspicious-looking people standing inside or outside the store.
5. Before a crime occurs, set up careful antirobbery plans, including prearranged signals for employees.
6. Do not keep substantial amounts of money in your store, especially at night.
7. Do not allow cash to accumulate in your register.
8. Try to schedule your bank deposits in the daytime at different hours, using different routes.
9. Make it known to the public that you are very concerned about your cash by displaying antirobbery and antiburglary decals.
10. Always open and close the store in the presence of another employee or other trusted person.
11. Your cashiers should not balance or count receipts in public.
12. Firearms should be utilized only if you are an expert trained in their use and only when you have the "drop" on the robber. Think very carefully if there is more than one robber.
13. Always obey the orders of the robbers, and never hesitate to carry them out.
14. Always retain your composure, and try to calm your employees and customers.
15. Alert the criminals to surprises such as the sudden appearance of a returning employee.
16. Get a description of the criminals and their vehicle.
17. Call the police without delay after the robbers escape.
18. Determine the amount of your loss, but reveal this only to the detectives who have been assigned to your case.
19. Try to identify witnesses to the robbery, and take their names and addresses.

20. Do not tamper with any evidence.
21. Keep the details of the robbery secret.
22. Always be aware and cautious when walking alone in the street, especially at night.
23. Avoid walking at night in unfamiliar or dangerous areas except on well-lighted streets and in the presence of at least one companion.
24. Take all necessary precautions, such as walking near the curb and away from dark alleys, doorways, and overgrown shrubbery.
25. Install a doorbell in your place of business that rings in an adjacent store. Have your store neighbor act in kind.
26. Select store employees with great care. Many robberies are accomplished with the assistance of an insider.

29
Neighborhood Crime Prevention

"It was the first night of our walking tour," said James Green of Pontotoc, "and we were walking down Maple Street when we saw these people moving things from this house and into a rental truck." One of the patrol group—the newly formed Grant City Citizens Alert Group—suggested notifying the police. Chief of Police James Tobias was quoted as saying, "The patrol officers asked one workman where they were taking the furniture. The man broke out into a run." The property was owned by Henry Smalley, who, according to relatives, was on vacation.

The best way to avoid becoming a victim of crime is to prevent it in the first place. Police, courts, and the penal system do not provide the answer. According to a recent New York Police Department study, less than 1 percent of all suspects arrested and charged with a felony went to prison. Moreover, less than 2 percent of felons arrested were even prosecuted for their crimes. Unfortunately, similar patterns characterize most major cities.

CITIZEN CRIME PREVENTION

The crime issue provides us all with an opportunity to become personally involved. Citizen crime prevention exemplifies the main philosophy of this book—to deal with crime in a proactive rather than reactive manner.

Citizen crime prevention programs may be divided into programs involving cooperative citizen efforts; steps individual citizens can take to protect themselves, their families, and their homes; and environmental design.

COLLECTIVE CRIME PREVENTION INITIATIVES

A most productive way of protecting yourself from crime is through collective and cooperative citizen efforts. Some programs strengthen the crime prevention posture of your neighborhood, while others increase the efficiency of criminal justice agencies charged with combating crime. These programs are not difficult to develop, and they have been found to reduce the chances of victimization. At the very least, the programs will increase the cohesiveness, unity, and solidarity of your neighborhood; this alone will have an impact on crime.

Block Clubs
Some clubs consist of the residents of one block. Among the activities of these groups are systematic and organized efforts to educate neighbors and make them aware of crime and public safety. Many block programs also conduct street surveillance. Block club participants, including children, are encouraged to report crimes and suspicious-looking people to the police.

Neighborhood Watch
Neighborhood Watch programs are similar to the block club but cover a broader area. About 7 percent of American households participate in some form of Neighborhood Watch. Citizens are trained to report crime and suspicious events or persons in the neighborhood. Special telephone numbers to police headquarters often are provided in case of an emergency.

Interviews with criminals have revealed that the Neighborhood Watch program is a very effective deterrent against robbery. Most burglars claim that they would leave a neighborhood if they were observed or challenged by a resident. These programs have demonstrated that improving crime reporting reduces crime—and the fear of crime. Contact your police or sheriff's department for information on the national Neighborhood Watch program.

Citizen Patrols
The fear of crime has caused citizens to organize crime patrols. In some areas residents carry out the patrol activities, and in others they hire professionally trained security guards. Some patrols concentrate on

specific buildings or housing areas, while others cover entire neighborhoods. The patrols are usually equipped with citizens band radios. Thousands of such groups, comprising everyone from young adults to senior citizens, have been formed throughout the country.

Unlike building patrols, which may prevent unwanted visitors from entering buildings, neighborhood patrols cannot deny people access to their streets. Instead, they concentrate on uncovering suspicious and criminal behavior, which they report to the police. Some patrols also perform social service functions, such as escorting senior citizens and providing job opportunities for teenagers. Others monitor police activities. These patrols are often organized when police-community relations need improvement.

How effective can individual initiatives such as these be? A resident of a large Southern city who works nights is involved in protecting himself from crime. First of all, he and his wife formed a Neighborhood Watch unit. He thus became acquainted with many of his neighbors.

All of his efforts on behalf of his family and his neighbors paid off. He was working in his yard when he saw a man breaking into a neighbor's house. He called the police. He had made advance preparation for an occasion such as this. He had entered the police emergency telephone number on his automatic dialing equipment. With one eye on the window through which the intruder gained entry into his neighbor's home, he reported the break-in. The police arrived one minute later, according to the good neighbor's report. Not only was he able to assure the police that the intruder was still inside the structure, he was also able to advise them that there were several firearms in the house, a fact he had learned when organizing the Neighborhood Watch organization.

This action may have prevented a tragic attack on an unwary police officer. Rather than barging into the crime scene, the police radioed for a tactical (SWAT) squad.

Because the doors of the house were protected by double-cylinder dead-bolt locks (which can be opened only by a key), the intruder was unable to escape.

This incident is a "small" crime, but one that was almost certainly repeated many times on that day. It was also a very large crime, because it proved, beyond doubt, that we don't have to be held hostage to the thieves and other criminals who would prey upon us. In your hands lies the answer to protecting yourself from crime. It is you.

Crime-Reporting Programs

In selecting crime-reporting programs for your community to participate in, you may want to consider some of the following alternatives:

- *The Whistle-Stop Program*—Whistle-carrying citizens sound off when they are victimized or when they see a crime in progress. The whistles serve as a community signal system. Neighbors who hear the sound also blow their whistles to disrupt the crime and alert the police.
- *Radio watch projects*—Radio-equipped autos patrol neighborhood streets, looking for criminal activity or suspicious people. When they spot something amiss, they report it either to a dispatcher, who then notifies the police, or directly to the police on special emergency frequencies. It is estimated that there are forty-six citizens band radio patrols in Chicago alone. New York City has established a Civilian Radio Taxi Patrol, utilizing taxi drivers concerned about street crime.
- *Special telephone or secret witness programs*—These projects provide special telephone lines so that people may report suspicious behavior or can report criminal activity without revealing their identity. Rewards are frequently offered to citizens for their assistance. "Crimestoppers" is a successful example of this type of program.
- *Drug watch*—This recent but excellent program involves the community in combating drug dealing. One specific program in New York City known as Westside Crime Prevention provides drug-watch training sessions to its members. Participants are shown slides of drug arrests, drug selling locations, and visible signs of drug transactions. A retired police lieutenant with experience in narcotics enforcement teaches how to accurately report dealing to the police. Members are taught it is not sufficient for the police to hear that someone is selling drugs in their neighborhood or on the street. Participants of Westside Crime Prevention learn that descriptions must be specific enough to identify the perpetrator and to provide probable cause.

Community-Based Adolescent-Diversion Projects

In several university communities, the schools have joined forces with the local criminal justice system to help juveniles in trouble. These youths are referred to the project, rather than the prosecutor's office or juvenile court, and are assigned to student volunteers, who develop special programs for them. The students are trained and supervised by experienced psychologists, and they receive credit for their efforts. Project New Pride began in 1973 in Denver and today stands out as one of the most successful programs for redirecting "hard-core" youths back into the mainstream of their communities.

Other Community Programs

The following community programs may give you further ideas:

- *Anticrime campaigns*—These involve special citizen groups organized to combat crime and improve criminal justice agencies such as the police, courts, and corrections. The St. Louis Women's Crusade, the Philadelphia Crime Commission, and the Metropolitan Crime Commission in New Orleans are examples of organizations that have conducted successful anticrime campaigns.
- *Police community relations programs*—Thousands of programs in which police officers and citizens work together have sprung up throughout the nation. Their objectives are to improve formal and informal communications between local police and neighborhood residents, to prevent crime, and to combat juvenile delinquency. A successful illustration of this type of program is the 3,000-member Association of Chicago Beat Representatives. These volunteers periodically receive community crime information from the local police commander at special meetings. Acting on this information, they have assisted the police in solving homicides and robberies. Also, these representatives have helped the police rid neighborhoods of youth gangs.
- *Auxiliary police*—Many police departments, because of fiscal restraints and limited personnel, have helped organize auxiliary police organizations. Civilian volunteers are trained in police methods and procedures. They wear uniforms similar to those of police officers, and they often patrol on foot and in vehicles supplied by the police department. Their main function is crime prevention and deterrence. They report crimes to the police but will come to a person's aid if necessary. Auxiliary police officers are usually discouraged from making actual arrests. Instead, they are urged to summon police officers to do this. Auxiliary police officers often assist regular police officers in crowd and traffic control, at demonstrations, or at an accident scene.

Private-Sector Security

Private security elements play an increasingly important role in the battle against crime. Lacking most of the police powers of their public-sector counterparts, the private industry has long emphasized the prevention of crime. Private security is concerned not with arrests, only with preventing incidents.

There is increasing use of these services because they are effective. Business is using private sector security more than ever, often in capacities once performed by the public police, such as employee or customer protection or escort service to parking areas. In this way, private security does not supplant the public police—it supplements them. Through this supplementation, the private sector of the criminal justice complex manifests an ever-increasing number of private security personnel. As a matter of fact, private security people are now more numerous than all state and local police. This is particularly apparent in urban areas, where private police often outnumber public police by four to one or even more.

As public forces suffer from insufficient funds and private forces increase enormously, a loose, undefined, and totally unofficial partnership—or, at least, a division of labor—seems to be emerging. For example, with the restriction of beat cops or prowl cars, wealthy individuals and neighborhood groups are now engaging private police to perform the patrols that fell victim to cutbacks in the public sector. No formal agreements forge this public/private relationship. The police were forced to cut back services, and the private firms were able to provide these services to businesses and groups of individuals with common property interests. Private security in various parts of the country is also sharing an expanded role in public building protection, residential neighborhood patrol, traffic control, parking enforcement, crowd control, and court security.

There are many other areas of public/private cooperation, and even closer ties may be anticipated. The cooperation between these elements will increase through economic necessity and through the growing realization that the two are complementary, not competitive.

INDIVIDUAL CRIME PREVENTION EFFORTS

Individual efforts have been successful in providing protection from crime. Similar programs to those that follow may be useful in your neighborhood:

- *Residential security surveys*—A residential security inspection offers a practical and simple solution to security evaluation. It usually consists of a thorough examination of your residence to identify its security deficiencies. The survey determines the required protection and shows how to minimize criminal opportunities. Studies have shown that such surveys reduce your chances of victimization.

- *Property-marking programs*—Citizens borrow marking equipment, often from the police department or a civic organization, and engrave permanent identification numbers on portable property. The numbers are then recorded with the police. Program participants post decals on their doors or windows indicating that their property has been marked. Marked property is less appealing to a thief, and in the event of a theft, your personal property may be identified and returned to you. This prevention program has enjoyed much popularity over the last few years and has been shown to reduce burglary rates (see Chapter 2).

Individual crime prevention efforts may be as simple as replacing a burned-out light bulb for an older neighbor, thus increasing his or her nighttime security. They may be as neighborly as asking a neighbor to accompany you when you go shopping. In so doing, you add to that person's well-being, as well as your own, through doubling your protective capabilities.

Take your older neighbor to the bank to deposit a Social Security check, and while you are there, point out the advantage of electronic mail deposits to eliminate the possibility of mailed checks being diverted to criminals.

If you're going to the grocery store, offer to pick up a few items for a neighbor, and reduce the likelihood of an attack. If you transport a neighbor to his or her place of worship, your neighbor will be delighted to return the favor when you cannot find a baby-sitter and you must show up at the boss's Christmas party.

A nosy neighbor can be a neighborhood treasure who will tell you when your floodlight is out, remind you that you have allowed the vegetation to grow too high around your trash can area, or advise you that you failed to lock your garage. If you reciprocate, and advise your neighbors of security shortcomings at *their* homes, you have the beginnings of a crime-fighting neighborhood organization.

Still another valuable service, which even a senior citizen can provide, is to serve as "block parents" who can offer guidance or shelter for neighborhood children who may need assistance. On a more formal basis, McGruff Houses perform these and other services, and have the additional advantage of being a part of a nationally advertised endeavor to provide for neighborhood children. This is a most important consideration, because today's parents are often both engaged in breadwinning.

CRIME PREVENTION THROUGH ENVIRONMENTAL DESIGN

Because the physical environment directly affects criminal activities, changes in the structure and design of the environment tend to reduce opportunities for crime. Proper physical design of buildings and landscapes makes your environment safer and may motivate you to engage in additional crime prevention behavior.

Increased surveillance may be accomplished by eliminating places of concealment, such as dense shrubbery, overgrown hedges, unpruned trees, garbage accumulations, and dark, isolated parking lots, alleys, hallways, elevators, lobbies, and stairwells. Increased lighting in streets, parks, and sidewalks also helps. With greater visibility, you and your neighbors can look out for each other and perhaps offer assistance if needed.

Environmental design can make it easier to distinguish between people who belong in an area and those who don't. Common lawn areas can be divided into private yards or patios, using small picket fences, well-trimmed shrubbery, or concrete curbing. In effect, these measures extend the social control of residents from their houses and apartments into nearby common areas. This approach can be further enhanced by limiting the number of public access points to the area and by providing the remaining entrances with adequate lighting, visibility, and security.

The environmental design of streets also may be modified to reduce crime. Traffic can be rerouted so that the residential character of neighborhoods is preserved. Certain avenues can be narrowed, and selected streets turned into cul-de-sacs to avoid through traffic.

Improving the appearance and attractiveness of your house, property, and any shared areas will promote a sense of responsibility among you and your neighbors. Decorative painting, lighting, installation of benches at strategic spots, and careful landscaping will motivate neighbors to care for each other's welfare and safety. These steps also will tend to intensify the use of streets, parks, and surrounding land structures by local residents. Criminals are less likely to commit crimes in attractive neighborhoods than in run-down, deserted areas.

Many experts recently have examined personal security from the perspective of the perpetrator. Criminals form mental images of potential targets often based upon nonverbal cues given off by the target. These messages convey meanings about opportunities, risk, and convenience for committing crime. Social psychologists suggest that burglars weigh five sets of questions before committing a crime:

1. Am I detectable? For example, where are the doors and windows positioned, and what is the distance from the street to the house?
2. Are any meaningful barriers present? Does the structure have a gate, strong locks, or an intrusion alarm?
3. Are there any signs or symbolic barriers like Neighborhood Watch or private patrols that define territoriality and vigilance?
4. Are residents active in the streets and yards? Are lights on in the homes, and are newspapers still lying in the driveway?
5. Is there a positive social climate in the area? Are people suspicious of me, staring at and questioning me, or can I go about my business without interference?

These issues provide deep insights into the criminal mind that can be used for environmental design that offers maximum security.

Neighborhood Crime Prevention: A Checklist

1. Join a cooperative crime prevention program in your neighborhood. Programs include block watches, citizen patrols, and anticrime campaigns.
2. Participate in all community programs tailored for individual crime prevention, including residential security surveys and property-marking programs.
3. Organize a citizen crime prevention program if none is available in your neighborhood.
4. Even simple crime prevention acts are useful, such as replacing a burned-out light bulb for an older neighbor, accompanying your neighbor on a shopping excursion, or driving your neighbor to the bank to deposit a check.
5. Design your residence and its surrounding area to reduce the opportunities for crime.
6. Design your house in such a way that visibility out into the street is increased.
7. Reduce places of concealment for criminals by cutting and trimming overgrown bushes, trees, and shrubbery.

8. Increase lighting in parking lots, alleys, corridors, lobbies, elevators, and stairwells.
9. Divide common lawns and areas into private yards and patios.
10. Limit the number of public entrances to your apartment building or condominium.
11. Route heavy traffic away from your streets so that the residential character of your neighborhood is preserved.
12. Provide adequate maintenance for your property, and continuously upgrade its appearance.

30
Consumer Fraud, Con Artists, and Con Games

"Mrs. Smith, my name is Sylvester Fox," said the caller, "and I represent the Holy Tabernacle Publishing Company. Your late husband—and may I offer you my sympathy in this your hour of loss—your husband, Thomas, ordered this lovely Bible for you not two weeks before he died. You can see it has been inscribed with your name, and I'd like to collect, including everything, a hundred seventy-six dollars and eighty cents."

"Just a moment," said Mrs. Smith. "Let me get my checkbook."

CONSUMER FRAUD

Most businesses are honest. However, there are always those that will try to cheat you if they think they can get away with it. It is usually safer to do business with a firm that has been recommended to you by relatives or trusted friends. Before contracting for a service or making a major purchase, check the reputation of the company by calling a consumer service bureau, such as the Better Business Bureau. The local office of the Federal Trade Commission may provide information on types of businesses, if not the actual firm. Remember, even though a business may be licensed, there is no guarantee that its personnel are honest or that it provides quality work.

Unscrupulous Contractors
Before you authorize any work from a contractor, obtain a *written estimate*. Later ask the contractor to itemize each item of cost before you sign it. If you need clarification, do not be ashamed to ask questions or to consult an attorney.

Retail Swindles

Beware of consumer rip-offs when shopping in retail establishments. Signs such as "Lost Our Lease" or "Everything Must Go" may be used to lure shoppers into the store. When paying by check, make the draft payable only to the company, not to an individual employee of the store.

Always have a secondhand car checked by a mechanic before you buy. Used-car dealers are skillful at hiding the defects of their wares.

At a supermarket, watch as the checkout clerk rings up each item. Price mistakes are often made unintentionally as well as deliberately.

When making a major purchase, such as an air conditioner or microwave oven, shop around and compare warranties. Some warranties offer full service, while others provide minimal coverage on certain parts of the product. Ascertain who guarantees performance under the warranty *and* the ability and resources of the guarantor to meet the contractual obligations. Save all receipts, and note the installation date. It is possible that you will wish to file a complaint against a company, and this information is essential. Describe to the person who has the authority to resolve your problem what is wrong with the merchandise and what you want done about it.

If you aren't satisfied, you may want to take the matter to court. Small-claims court sessions are held at night in many jurisdictions, and often you will not need to hire a lawyer. Payment of a small filing fee will usually assure that your case will be heard in one month.

Mail Fraud

One area of widespread fraud is termed mail fraud. Frauds of this type are invariably categorized as legitimate business transactions—and as a matter of fact, some of them technically are. The fraudulent element in these types of swindles is often overpricing or inappropriateness. Some transactions involve actual lies, and their promoters rely upon inertia on the part of their victims—that is, they figure that instead of going to court, their victims will just chalk their mistakes up to experience.

Mail fraud can include insurance offers (especially health insurance); debt consolidation; magazine subscriptions; land, property, and condominium offers; securities and oil leases; franchise deals; work-at-home plans; publishing your own books; home improvements; medicines and miracle cures; chain letters or similar pyramid schemes; and discount purchasing clubs.

Not every mail offer for these goods or services is fraudulent—most are legitimate and respectable. Suggestions for determining which is which are found in a subsequent section of this chapter, "Protect Yourself."

CON ARTISTS AND CON GAMES

The con artist is sometimes glorified in movies and literature, presented as a wholesome cross between W. C. Fields and Robin Hood. In the real world, he or she is a despicable criminal, preying on the uninformed and elderly, often taking their life savings and leaving them to blame themselves for a life of privation and despair. Even worse than to rob people of their money is to rob them of both their money and their self-respect.

Stranger at Your Door

This book repeatedly cautions you not to admit anyone into your home unless you know who the person is and why he or she wants admittance. One of the many good reasons for this advice is that the person could be a confidence man. Here are a few of the ways in which con artists operate.

One of the simplest cons is initiated by a person who knocks on your door and asks for a glass of water. As he or she is ushered into the kitchen, an accomplice sneaks in and steals money, jewelry, credit cards, or other valuables.

Another particularly vile con involves the "funeral chaser," who reads the obituary notices and shows up at the home of the deceased with highly overpriced merchandise that the deceased ostensibly ordered. Of course, it isn't true, but the salesperson can be most persuasive, often threatening to tie up life insurance proceeds and employing other such tactics.

On another occasion a caller claiming to be a bank examiner requests your help in trapping a dishonest bank employee. You are asked to withdraw funds to be used as a test of the suspect's honesty. Unfortunately for you, it's the phony bank examiner who is a crook.

Other Common Swindles

Another ingenious swindle involves a caller who says he has inexpensive new appliances for sale. You are requested to meet the salesperson at the loading dock of a retail department store. He or she meets you there, asks you to back your car up to the platform for delivery, takes your money, and is never seen again.

In another very effective swindle, a person approaches you in the street and says you can buy a case of expensive liquor at a low price. You are taken to a store and told you are to wait until he or she returns with the liquor. You are asked to pay for it at that point. Your "friend" enters the store, never to return with either your money or the goods.

Another scheme, this one principally to bilk the elderly, is the pigeon-drop. It is usually worked after a person has made a deposit into a savings account and is leaving, passbook in hand. A stranger, approaching the victim, will flash a wad of money, indicate that it has just been found, and ask what should be done. The mark, predictably, will answer, "I don't know." A "passerby" (actually another confidence crook) states that a friend at a nearby bank would know what to do, and agrees to telephone the banker. Upon returning from the phone booth, the group is informed that the money should be split among all of them, providing that it isn't claimed by the real owner by the end of the day. The problem, however, is that a $2,000 fidelity bond is required, "to protect the bank."

The pigeon is prevailed upon to provide the bond (with the promise of half the windfall) and awaits the return of the conspirator who claimed to have a banker friend. Of course, no one returns at the end of the day.

Another swindle, one common in large cities, is the multiple rental scam. The con artist leases an apartment, using an assumed name. Subsequently, the apartment is relet to as many as fifty other people, and the confidence cheat receives a month's rent and a security deposit from each of them.

One other confidence game, "three-card monte," is a standby on the streets of New York, and other cities as well. It is ostensibly a game of skill, in which the dealer rapidly moves three cards, and the player attempts to pick a target card from among the three that the dealer lays out. Seldom does a player select the proper card. It may be the result of a great deal of skill and dexterity on the part of the dealer, or it may be that the dealer has palmed the target card and the player is playing a can't-win game. It is an interesting show, with lots of action and occasional excitement.

But that isn't all. Frequently, pickpockets mingle among the players and spectators around the dealer and players.

One veteran New York policeman estimates that the street con artists annually steal more money than bank robbers. One authority estimates that, in New York City alone, $3.5 million is bilked by street sharpies each year.

Real Estate Con Games

Real estate is fast becoming a favorite of the confidence man. The attraction of real estate lies in the fact that the stakes are high. Measured by numbers of six or seven digits, real estate could be quite a haul for a trickster. One con works this way. The con artist will stand in an upscale residential area, on a busy thoroughfare. He or she will stop people on the street, saying, "Excuse me, but are you the Mr. Green who is to meet Mr. Black here?" Most will say no, but occasionally one will answer, "Why?" The con artist will zero in on his or her prey.

He or she will give the victim a business card, which bears the name of a well-respected real estate firm. (In actuality, the con artist stole the cards from one of those plastic bins that salespeople sometimes situate on their desks.) He or she explains to the mark that he or she was to meet Mr. Green, who was to sign a contract to purchase "that particular house" on the corner. It must be sold on that day, by order of probate court, so that the estate can be dissolved. If the intended victim expresses any interest, the con artist will say that the property could be bought at a most attractive price, because with the estate closing that afternoon, there wasn't sufficient time to contact others who had shown interest in the property.

The conversation continues, and the prospective purchaser is inveigled into giving the con artist a certified check as earnest money. He or she receives the crook's promise that the closing attorney will meet with him or her at his or her office two days later. Only then does the bargain seeker realize that greed has cost him or her a great deal of money.

Repair or Rip-Off?

Other common rip-off schemes include "repairmen" or engineers who offer you repair work at unbelievably low prices. A phony engineer might inspect your home and determine that the heating, plumbing, or chimney needs repair. You might be asked to sign a contract and give a down payment, but you never see the "repairman" again. An individual might say he or she has enough material to blacktop your driveway or repair leaks in your roof. The work is done with black oil that never dries, but you have already paid cash, as requested. A "gardener" offers to cover your property with topsoil. Later you learn it is sawdust mixed with motor oil.

One very common con involves people in cars who look for autos needing bodywork. They offer these repairs at a low price, and only later do you discover that the materials used disintegrate after a short time.

PROTECT YOURSELF

Advice on this subject is easy, but implementing it is much more difficult. However, if you can follow a few simple rules, you ought to be safe from the smooth-talking con artist.

Older people are special targets of swindlers and should be on guard against the unscrupulous criminal who would turn another's disadvantage into his or her advantage. Always look a gift horse very hard in the mouth. Never be rushed into any investment by a smooth talker. Any investment with merit can stand thorough investigation.

Never give any money to a stranger offering you a once-in-a-lifetime deal. Walk away from anyone who approaches you with money to share with you. Never withdraw any money from a bank and turn it over to a stranger. Entrust your repair work to reputable companies or repairers recommended by friends or relatives. Remember, the fraud will exploit your weakness—your desire to get a "good deal." A stranger who approaches you with a great deal probably has a great deal to gain from you. Chapter 31 discusses a variety of financial scams and methods for your protection.

CHARLATAN LOVERS

The ultimate con involves a man or a woman who pretends to love you but whose heart is focused on your dollars. It usually begins when your "lover" asks to borrow a little money and ends when your credit cards, jewelry, home, business, and life savings are taken. All of a sudden your lover has disappeared, whereabouts unknown. This type of operation has typically ripped off dozens of partners, usually women. If you happen to locate the imposter, usually you are too heartbroken, poor, and demoralized to pay the legal fees required for prosecution.

Common sense, caution, and sound judgment can save you from this painful experience. Experts propose the following signals as a warning that you are dealing with a charlatan Romeo or Juliet:

- The man or woman appears slick, too perfect. He or she is extremely attractive and a perfect dresser.
- Your partner rarely if ever talks about him- or herself, displaying excessive interest in everything about you. This tactic may be flattering, but it is also unrealistic.
- Your partner proceeds rapidly with the relationship emotionally, intellectually, and physically.
- You can't pin your partner down on a home or business address.
- You learn that your partner has a history of avoiding commitments.
- Your partner has no visible means of support and is vague about job and personal resources.

Your best defense against such a partner is a strong offense. Always take care of your personal property yourself; do not be lax or careless with your money or jewelry. Never loan money to a partner whom you have known for only a short period of time and whose history and background have not been definitely revealed. If you decide to invest in your partner's business, go through your lawyer or a business adviser.

Should you be conned, report the crime to the police or the office of the district attorney. Also, immediately report any credit cards that have been stolen. Above all, do not shy away from pursuing the case; your former "lover" will be someone else's Romeo or Juliet tomorrow.

Consumer Fraud, Con Artists, and Con Games: A Checklist

1. Obtain references from friends, relatives, or a consumer service bureau before you contract for service or major purchases. If you decide to use a service, obtain a written estimate first.
2. Retain receipts, warranties, and other related materials in case it becomes necessary to seek replacement, repair, or adjustments of contracted services or merchandise or to file a complaint.
3. Be especially aware of strangers who approach you on the street with schemes for making quick money.
4. Thoroughly investigate all get-rich-quick schemes before you invest. If a business transaction requires your immediate attention, pass it up.

31
Investment Fraud

"Ten Accused of Commodity Schemes"

"Five Charged in Texas in Savings Inquiry"

"Jail Term Set for Fraud in Tax Shelters"

"Seventy-Five Lose 1M in Coin Scam"

"Ex-[Brokerage] Official Gets Five Years in Fraud"

"U.S. Says [Businessman] Was Mastermind of $40 Million in Fraud Schemes"

"Jilted Investors Tried to Steer Boesky Sentencing"

"Shareholders of Texas Bank Accept $1.5 Billion Bailout"

"Broker in [Reporter's] Case Is Sentenced"

Numerous criminal acts of fraud within the investment community resemble those in the descriptive headlines. They include widespread insider trading among respected, if not revered, figures in the investment arena; misappropriated funds at major brokerage houses; noncollateralized or seriously undercollateralized loans among major money center banks; new-venture underwritings for nonexistent products; diversion of trust funds by attorneys for their personal use; malpractice and malfeasance at savings and loan associations; and misappropriation of client funds by investment fund operators. In the last year or two alone, enough cases could be cited and analyzed to fill volumes.

Many of them are so infamous that you have undoutedly already read or heard of them. In one spectacular case, a twenty-three-year-old financial wizard just out of college persuaded experienced investors to give him a total of $10 million for investment in selective stocks. He even sent his clients official-looking statements that resembled those of honest brokerages. Instead of investing the money, the young financial "genius" used the funds to purchase two homes, luxury cars, and expensive paintings.

In yet another swindle, seventy-five investors lost more than $1 million in a coin scam advertised on radio talk programs including WABC and on cable TV's Financial News Network. The fraudulent company "guaranteed" investors in rare coins 15 percent annual return and even promised to repurchase the coins in a year. In fact, the coins were worth only a fraction of their sales price to the investors. Most investors, including a blind seventy-two-year-old man, lost much of their life savings.

To avoid similar swindles, you must be very careful when you decide to invest your hard-earned cash.

BLUE-SKY NEW VENTURES

If it has not happened already, one of these days your phone may ring, followed by a pitch of this kind: "Good afternoon, Mr. Wilson. This is Mike Lee of Blue Sky International Securities, Unlimited. Your account representatives at another reputable firm indicated that you are a savvy investor who can spot and act on a great opportunity when you see one. As an established investment firm, we have brought many new ventures public and have made unusually large profits quickly for those privileged to get in on the action before the public offering is completed.

"We are currently consummating a deal with what I believe will be our most extraordinary underwriting, a firm called Integrated BioComputerology Services. I don't have to tell you how hot this field is and the overnight fortunes that have been made by outfits like Apple, Compaq, Borland, Lotus, and others that started on a shoestring. We are letting a few select clients in on the deal before the public offering is completed the day after tomorrow.

"We are inviting special customers like you to participate at our own insider underwriters' and founders' cost of ten cents per share, and we are even absorbing the customary commission. At the opening, the public's price will be fifteen cents, and if this exciting offering goes anything like the many other high-tech firms that we have taken public, the price will quickly rise to thirty cents or more.

"I enjoy dealing with astute, seasoned investors like yourself and would like to establish a long-term relationship and prove myself and my firm to you. Let me put you down for just ten thousand shares, a modest commitment of only $1,000. I really want you to have a piece of this action, not simply for the sake of making some important money on this sensational stock, but for what you will come to know as a most rewarding long-term relationship. To beat the opening public-offering prices, you'll have to get a check for $1,000 out to me by tomorrow, preferably by Express Mail. You don't want to take the chance of missing this one!"

Pitches like this come from fast-talking, smooth telephone solicitors in an office crammed with phones and called a boiler room. The first contact that you receive is typically made by a low-paid individual called an "opener." Once you express interest in the pitch by actually committing the $1,000 or requesting more information, you are turned over to a much more accomplished high-pressure sales artist called a "loader." He or she will frequently add to the preliminary pitch some exciting, confidential embellishments that will make the offer seem very plausible and irresistible, and the loader will try to convince you to extend your commitment even further.

You discover too late, after your money is committed, that the entire undertaking was a fraud and there is little hope of ever recovering your investment. The fact is that under current Securities and Exchange Commission (SEC) regulations, such individuals can solicit by phone without disclosing all the facts in the written offering prospectus. That document need only accompany the first written communication, usually with the order confirmation. Only occasionally does the SEC catch a broker doing a number on a client, whereupon with sufficient evidence, the broker, the firm, or both may be put out of business.

According to the New York State Attorney General's Office, few penny-stock investors who have been defrauded agree to prosecute after losing even substantial sums. Sometimes they don't wish to reveal just how imprudent and foolish they were, sometimes they want to avoid the expense and time required by litigation and possible countersuits, and— not the least—sometimes they recognize that most of the really damning evidence is only word of mouth. Thus, in New York alone, it is estimated that large numbers of investors lose hundreds of millions of dollars through deceit and outright fraud.

During 1986–1987, an infamous New Jersey brokerage firm was

eventually convicted of fraudulent practices. In the course of testimony, it was discovered that almost all the firm's deals resulted in deep or total losses for many unwary investors the firm had bilked throughout the country. Except for a few very favored customers, it is unlikely that even if profits are to be made, they will be made overnight, as many are led to believe.

SHELL GAMES

A close relative of the new venture is an existing corporation without any substantial assets—frequently a relatively new business gone sour, as the familiar statistic about five-year survival rates indicates most new firms do. These nearly bankrupt firms have gone through the significant earlier expenses and delays of SEC registration and underwriting. The essentially dormant company, not yet having taken the formal steps for dissolution, thus becomes a marketable asset in itself, appropriately referred to as a "shell."

Such shells become the basis for many multimillion-dollar swindles in the following way. Stock fraud con artists acquire the company, apply for a name change through the secretary of state, and then install management figureheads who have clean criminal records. The next step after the takeover is to reduce the equity of the shareholders of the original corporation. This is accomplished by declaring a reverse stock split—for example, one new share for each one hundred original.

Using appropriately formulated telephone pitches, like those illustrated earlier, brokers aggressively try to foist the fundamentally worthless stock upon unwary investors. With a really good pitch, the investor base may increase geometrically, with the worthless stock continually rising in price. The fraud is completed when the shares held on behalf of the criminal backers is completely liquidated. At this point, the price quickly plummets, leaving the investors holding the worthless stock. Alternatively, the criminal manipulators may manage to pass off the valueless stock in exchange for really valuable assets, or as collateral for a loan.

Numerous scams like this eventually come before the SEC. Although it promptly halts trading in the shell's stock, for most victimized investors the action comes too late to return any of their investments. Most often the "financial advisers" abscond with the fortune, spend all the money, or end up in prison.

A particularly famous case involved a firm called Texas Uranium

Corporation, which after three years of operation went bellyup. After ten years of dormancy, the corporation was acquired in 1967 to support a shell con. Texas Uranium was particularly attractive because it still had the legal authority to issue five million shares of its stock. After the criminals got control, numerous bogus acquisitions were quickly assigned extremely inflated asset values, amounting to over $5 million, on the shell's balance sheet. As the news spread regarding the quickly rising book value of the company and aggressive acquisitions, the stock price moved sharply higher. By the time the SEC halted trading in 1968, the con artists had liquidated their shares and amassed a fortune.

FAST-BUCK COMMODITIES FUTURES

Not just the well-heeled, but increasing numbers of amateurs are being lured into commodity futures trading. The attraction of these contracts for the future delivery of exciting commodities like gold, silver, platinum, and the like is that they are highly leveraged. Relatively few investment dollars can control sizable sums. By their very nature, futures exercise an almost irresistible appeal to the greedy, get-rich-quick investor. The problem is that unbeknownst to the average investor or novice in this medium, futures trading is a real sucker's bet, with the likelihood of turning a profit well below 10 percent.

As in the earlier securities fraud examples, commodities fraud is frequently perpetuated by slick, savvy, professional-sounding operators in boiler rooms temporarily located at prestigious Wall Street addresses, or the equivalent at other financial centers. Therein lies part of the danger to the investor: legitimate commodity futures brokers also operate by phone and have similar addresses. Among other advantages of these con artists is the typically limited grasp of the inexperienced investor in this financial arena. Also balancing the scales in favor of fraud is the complex array of factors that dictate the future price of the commodity underlying the contract. Thus, it is possible to play on the investor's ignorance by identifying a couple of well-known recent events that common sense suggests should make the future price of the commodity worth gambling on.

Of course, the words *gamble* and *risk* never arise in the salesperson's pitch; rather, the solicitor will practically guarantee immense profits. As in the earlier scams, things move very quickly. Lest the hot opportunity be lost, the con artist urges the investor to have bank funds wired to the fly-by-night brokerage firm, with the usual promise that informational literature will be immediately forthcoming. The scam centers on the fact that a genuine futures contract, like those regulated by the Chicago Board of Trade, is not what the investor will be getting. Instead, the investor will receive—if anything at all—an *option* on the touted commodity, that is, a so-called deferred-delivery contract. Unfortunately for the investor, such contracts were banned in 1978 and no longer exist in U.S. futures markets.

Other painful variants on commodities futures fraud also exist. Through a pyramiding scheme (and a so-called ponzi fraud), the investor may be beguiled into committing further hard-earned capital (and spreading the word of his or her success to friends) by quick profits on some initial trades through the criminal operators. In effect, the con artists are operating a "bucket shop" in which they invested funds of initial speculators. Some investors are used to pay off others to set them up for much bigger kills.

Another approach is that employed by some fully licensed but dishonest brokers in which buy orders are intentionally not executed. If the commodity price then falls, the faked loss is posted to the investor's account, and the broker pockets it. Should the price rise, the broker declares that a clerical error resulted in the order not being processed.

Finally, a consortium of investors can operate over a period of time to manipulate certain futures prices, but this takes a level of sophistication and cooperation between brokers and traders that goes well beyond the two simpler schemes just described. As with insider trading, however, the wary investor should never dismiss the possibility.

BURNED BEFORE YOU KNOW IT

Almost everyone is likely to experience a ponzi scheme or hear an irresistibly enticing investment offer pitched by phone from a boiler room operation. Perhaps the phone pitch will even be followed by a written prospectus with pronouncements and disclaimers. By the time you recognize the realities of your investment, the horses will have bolted the barn, leaving you with a significant void in your pocketbook. The account agreement that you long ago signed but barely read—the one with the pro forma, finely printed clause buried on the back, indicating that you would not sue your broker, but subject all claims to an arbitration board dominated by the investment community—has left you up the creek with little effective recourse.

LAND FRAUDS

Frauds come in many varieties, but perhaps the most enduring of all are land frauds. The United States is a great agrarian nation, and we are conscious of the land. It is no wonder that we have this great attraction for land, nor is it any wonder that the frauds and sharpies gravitate to land-based enterprises.

One typical fraudulent operation offered coal-mining rights on land in a southern state. Promoters had promised as much as three thousand tons of coal on each of the lots sold. In reality, there was no coal in the field. Part of the success of the operation was due to the efforts of a shill. This person was introduced to potential investors as a satisfied customer who was pleased with his investment and impressed with the reputable management of the operation. Mining rights were sold throughout the United States and overseas. This scam netted the organizers upwards of $3 million.

An almost identical swindle involved supposed coal fields in another Southern state. This entrepreneur operated on a grander scale, raking in more than $10 million. The presiding judge termed this the largest fraud he had seen during his tenure on the bench. On a charge of racketeering, the defendant was sentenced to twelve years of a possible twenty-year maximum.

THREATS AND COUNTERMEASURES: SOME META-RULES

As you can see, there are numerous threats and pitfalls to your investment security. The deceptive practices of some investment dealers and brokers, as well as the outright fraud of the criminal, are relatively easy to conceal, because even legitimate investments are complex and relatively uncertain. The already ripe context is enriched by the inherent avarice of the prey. Most investors prefer getting much richer to a little richer, and most prefer it much sooner to a little later. Accordingly, the scams are legion, and not merely a feature of recent history.

And contrary to what most believe, the regulatory agencies such as the Securities and Exchange Commission, the Federal Deposit Insurance Corporation, and the various states' attorneys general and consumer fraud agencies cannot protect you and your investment. These agencies primarily serve to make sure that full and accurate disclosure of all the relevant investment information is publicly available. They cannot protect you against devious financial schemes, they cannot tell you what is likely to be a sound or unsound investment, and even when you've actually been criminally victimized, they can only help after the fact and generally in a way that attempts to enhance as a whole the future fairness of the investment markets to which we are all exposed. For you in particular, this is hardly solace—your money is gone.

Some investors are not deterred from undue risk by even the severe disclaimers of the Securities and Exchange Commission: "These securities have not been approved or disapproved by the Securities and Exchange Commission nor has the SEC passed upon the accuracy or adequacy of this prospectus—any representation to the contrary is a criminal offense. These securities are highly speculative, involve immediate substantial dilution, a high degree of risk, and should be purchased only by persons who can afford to lose their entire investment."

What is remarkable is that in the face of powerful warnings and such powerful regulatory agencies as the SEC, significant numbers of investors regularly lose large sums through frauds that would make the typical robbery or burglary pale by comparison. And embarrassment, the threat of countersuits, and your earlier agreement to pay all litigation costs should you lose your appeal—and you probably will since it's largely your word against theirs—will even keep you from becoming a statistic in the complaint records of the criminal courts, regulatory agencies, or consumer protection agencies.

AVOIDING PITFALLS

To appreciably reduce your likelihood of falling prey to investment fraud or deception, you need a set of guidelines on investment security, one that will discipline you to be more prudent and cautious. Do not, on the other hand, be so restrained that you become paranoid and miss important, legitimate opportunities to enhance your future net worth through astute, carefully considered investment.

What you should remember, to protect yourself, is what you already knew before the "blue sky" and greed took hold: if it looks too good, it most probably is! You should realize that the markets are ordinarily too large and efficient to allow financial bargains to be anything but highly adventitious and transitory—in short, you usually get what you pay for!

As in life itself, risk inheres in any investment. Coupled with the aforementioned guidelines, a strategy that diversifies by institution, by investment type, by issuer within these financial alternatives, and by commitment over time (rather than as lump sums) should go far in significantly reducing your chances of losing your investment nest egg.

In addition to these general protective rules, you should remember two more: If the investment yield is inconsistent with the general market for that investment risk, then someone probably is misrepresenting the facts. Centuries of lending experience, through wide variations in interest rates and prevailing inflation, have taught us that people can expect about a 3 to 4 percent real annualized return on their investment after taxes and inflation; anything more than that should alert you to undisclosed risks.

A FAIR WARNING

The scams that have been perpetrated on the unwary investor are seemingly without bound. The criminal's inventiveness has produced investment frauds that could fill volumes and keep TV series like "Dragnet" running forever. Every year, FBI statistics on reported crime reveal that no one is too rich or poor, sophisticated or uneducated, old or young to escape the clever and persistent con. This truth prevails whether the con artist involves stocks, new business ventures, commodities or land fraud, bogus franchises, invention "marketing," talent "promotion," dead-end "work at home for profit" schemes, religious/medical/charity frauds, and so on.

RESOURCES FOR REDRESS

Should fortune not continually shine, and should you believe that fraud has befallen you, you may wish to seek redress through some of the following agencies or their counterparts in your state:

Assistant Attorney General in Charge
Consumer Frauds and Protection Bureau
Office of the Attorney General
Two World Trade Center
New York, NY 10047
212-488-7450

Securities and Exchange Commission
Regional Office
26 Federal Plaza, Room 1102
New York, NY 10007
212-264-1636

Federal Trade Commission
Regional Office
2443-EB, Federal Building
26 Federal Plaza
New York, NY 10007
212-264-1207

Commodity Futures Trading Commission
Regional Office
One World Trade Center, Suite 4747
New York, NY 10048
212-446-2068

Although it is impossible to construct an exhaustive set of guidelines that will anticipate every possible investment risk, the examples and safeguards described in this chapter and the following checklist should serve to reduce your vulnerability to many of the threats posed by fraud.

Investment Fraud: A Checklist

1. If an investment sounds too good, it likely is; do some research before committing your dollars.
2. Never commit funds based on a cold call from an unknown broker or brokerage; it may well be a boiler room operation.
3. Beware of the deal that requires a quick response on your part.
4. Be skeptical of securities offered at substantial discounts from the prevailing market investments of comparable type.
5. Be alert to transactions that involve secretive foreign aspects such as off-shore financial institutions.
6. Watch out for unusual delays by brokers in making delivery of your securities or your investment proceeds; you may be caught in a "bucket shop" operation or in the misappropriation of your assets.
7. Never leave your securities with the brokerage firm, but have a certificate issued in your name and sent to you. Even if the brokerage house is insured, a bankruptcy could cause crucial delays in getting and liquidating your investments.
8. Be suspicious if transaction confirmations do not arrive promptly.
9. Keep an eye out for evidence of excessive buying and selling by your broker; periodically check through your trades of the past couple of years.

10. Never forget that brokers are in business for themselves first. Even though it would appear that their long-run interests are best served by retaining customers, you are easily replaced by the disgruntled customers of yet other brokers!

11. Whenever possible, manage your own securities and deal with discount brokerages and no-load funds; no one will care as much as you about your precious investment dollars, and at least the substantial up-front fees will be in your pocket.

12. When approached by a mutual fund salesperson, watch out for the statistics being touted; usually highly favorable epochs are cited to make their best case; look at performance in down markets, remember that few managers consistently do better than the Dow Jones 500-stock average, and realize that an average annual 9 percent return is historically about all you should expect without exposing yourself to excessive risk.

13. Always check the financial soundness of the issuer of fixed-yield investments in Standard & Poor's, Moody's, or similar references, whether the instrument be a bank or S&L CD, municipal or corporate bond, or other investment.

14. If the net real return from a fixed-yield investment is beyond 3 to 4 percent, examine the investment very carefully before jumping into the water.

15. When buying stocks, determine whether your account representative is a broker or broker-dealer; the latter buy and sell for their own accounts and therefore have a vested interest that may seriously bias the advice you are getting.

16. When first opening an account, obtain the firm's recent financial statements and be cautious of doing business with those having net capitalization of under $1 million.

17. In regard to new accounts, always request evidence that both the firm and the broker are licensed; inquire as to the number of years in business as well as the experience of the broker and/or lesser-known firms. Get bank references, and check with regulatory agencies.

18. If the brokerage also has an investment banking division, find out the firm's policy about recommending any stocks where there is potential for conflict of interest; inquire not only about the institution's underwritings, but also about senior partners who may serve on the boards of various companies having publicly traded stock.

19. Although deposits in banks and S&Ls are insured by the FDIC and FSLIC, it is wise to obtain a copy of the institution's recent balance sheets, since the government auditor's roster of "problem banks" is not readily available. Certainly split any joint accounts over $100,000 into separate ones if at the same bank.

20. In regard to the "penny stocks" of new ventures, insist on seeing the written prospectus, no matter how sweet the deal seems or the sense of urgency that you are given.

21. When you receive the prospectus, look to see if a substantial portion of the underwriting will be siphoned off to pay expenses accrued by the promotors/principals before going public, to pay excessive salaries, and so forth. Look at the intended use of the funds and the associated planning horizon to see if additional offerings or debt instruments will need to be floated soon.

22. Examine not only salaries but also the compensation in the form of stock to be given to officers; it should not be excessive, be capable of rapid exercise, or result in the substantial dilution of existing market shares in public hands.

23. Scrutinize the experience of the officers, directors, and promoters; determine their track record in similar deals and in comparable markets. Invest only with well-established investment managers with proven long-term track records.

24. If not in the prospectus, any especially alluring claims about the deal should be backed up in writing by the underwriter/broker; look for not only what is said, but what is not.

25. In new, diversified investment trusts, watch out for the possible unloading into the trust portfolio of one or more "dogs" previously held by the trust organizers; again, obtain and evaluate the prospectus first.

26. Remember that no matter how sophisticated the offering and associated financial jargon may sound, any nitwit or criminal with enough perseverance can float a public corporation.

27. Remember that in most states, anyone, including a charlatan, can call him- or herself a financial adviser (with or without a newsletter), since few states have licensing procedures like those for stockbrokers, real estate brokers, tax attorneys, CPAs, and the like. Whether dealing with a licensed individual or not, be hard-nosed and base your investment decisions on recent historical results, not simply reputation.

28. Remember that the key role of agencies like the SEC, Federal Reserve Board, and so on is to try to minimize flagrant abuses in their respective jurisdictions. They cannot prevent you from being imprudent or criminally victimized. Their concerns are more sweeping and strongly biased in favor of firming the public's confidence in the investment markets and banking system.

PART FOUR

SOME SPECIAL SECURITY PROBLEMS

32
Planning for an Emergency

A snow and sleet storm crippled a broad area from Wyoming to the Great Lakes and spun off a tornado in the Texas Panhandle that leveled 150 buildings in one town. The blizzard was the second to hit the upper Midwest this week. Emergency work crews are attempting to clean up the area, but it is estimated that some homes will be without power for as long as ten days.

No one knows how he or she will react in an emergency, but giving some advance thought to different possible situations can help many of us cope better with the unexpected. Personal security in an emergency situation is largely a matter of being prepared.

NATURAL DISASTER

Sophisticated early-warning systems and advanced communications systems have taken much of the danger out of natural disasters. For example, hurricanes take fewer lives now because residents of a danger area may have days of warning to evacuate the area before a big storm hits. Tornadoes, though much more random and harder to track than hurricanes, also pose less of a threat than they once did, simply because we have become better at recognizing conditions might lead to them and can rely on extensive media communications to pass the word if conditions become serious.

If you live in a hurricane- or tornado-prone area, you should have emergency supplies on hand. These include a battery-operated radio, spare batteries, a flashlight, candles and matches, a clock or watch, and some drinking water.

283

Where should you go if threatening conditions are sighted? If you have a basement, that is an excellent retreat. Otherwise, go to any interior room on the lower floor of your house, apartment, or office building. About twenty years ago, thousands of fallout shelters were built in this country. Many survive to this day as storm cellars, and they provide ideal protection. If possible, get under a heavy piece of furniture, which would afford some protection against falling objects. If you're in your house or other building, open some windows to equalize air pressure.

BLACKOUTS

To be properly equipped during a power burnout or blackout, always have at least two working flashlights in your home, plus your trusted battery radio. Don't open refrigerators or freezers—in fact, tape or tie the doors closed to avoid accidental opening and spoilage of the contents.

The criminal element is likely to be out in full force during any extended blackout, so be careful to establish your personal security at such times. Remember, the police won't be able to offer you as much protection as they would under normal circumstances. They will be tied up keeping traffic moving and keeping other vital services functioning.

FIRST AID

Everyone should have at least a rudimentary knowledge of first aid. If you've never had a first-aid course, take one. This discussion introduces the basics, touching on only those procedures that will enable you to save a life.

Stop Bleeding

If bleeding isn't severe, it poses little immediate problem. The most serious concern is arterial bleeding, characterized by bright red blood escaping in a pulsating, pumping manner. Steadily flowing blood is not arterial bleeding, and often its treatment can wait.

Apply pressure directly over an arterial wound. Use the cleanest available cloth—possibly your shirt. Do not apply a tourniquet unless you are absolutely unable to stem the flow and are unable to get qualified medical help within a very short period.

If you must apply a tourniquet, tie a handkerchief around the affected part of the body between the wound and the heart. Tighten the knot, using a stick stuck through the handkerchief and turning it like a faucet handle until the flow of blood stops. Do not remove the tourniquet. On the victim's limb or on a note pinned to the victim's garment print the time that the tourniquet was applied. This will be valuable information once professional help arrives.

Start Breathing

The most effective way to revive breathing is mouth-to-mouth resuscitation. It isn't difficult to do. Simply tilt the victim's head back, pull his or her jaw open, pinch his or her nostrils closed, and breathe air into his or her lungs. You will see the victim's chest rise and fall. Wait three or four seconds (two or three for a child), and breathe in air again. Wait again. Breathe in air again. Keep this up until the victim begins respiration independently or someone relieves you.

Stop Choking

Choking is among the leading causes of accidental death and, in the home, is the leading cause for infants under age one. You can identify choking when:

- The victim cannot breathe or speak because no air can pass through the airway or vocal chords. The victim may grasp his or her throat to indicate choking.
- The person turns blue from lack of oxygen in the body.
- The choking person falls unconscious because oxygen is not reaching the brain.

Remember, when a person's airway is obstructed, fewer than four minutes remain before death. A choking person cannot wait for a physician, paramedic, or ambulance.

Do not put anything else in the victim's mouth that he or she might choke on—not water, food, or your hands (you might well lose a finger). Let him or her cough up the obstruction. If this fails, use the widely recognized Heimlich maneuver or hug. Here is what to do:

If the victim is standing or sitting:

1. Stand or kneel behind the victim.
2. Wrap your arms around the victim's waist.
3. Make a fist, and place the thumb side against the person's abdomen just above the navel but below the rib cage.
4. Hold your fist with your other hand, and with an instant upward thrust, press into the person's abdomen. You may have to repeat this procedure several times to eject the object.

If the victim is lying down:

1. Be sure the victim is on his or her back. Turn him or her over if necessary.
2. Face the victim, and kneel by his or her hips.
3. Put one of your hands on top of the other, and then place the heel of your bottom hand on the victim's abdomen just above the navel and below the rib cage.
4. Press the victim's abdomen with a quick upward thrust. Repeat this procedure several times, if necessary.

Treat Poisoning

If the victim has been poisoned, try to find out what has been ingested. If the container is at hand, follow its instructions in case of misuse. Alert the nearest hospital or police or fire station, or contact a physician for instructions by phone.

Give the victim as much liquid as he or she can hold to dilute the poison. Try to induce vomiting, except in cases of poisoning by acids, alkalis, or petroleum products. Vomiting may be induced by giving the victim a half-glass of water in which a tablespoon of salt has been dissolved. If this isn't effective, a finger forced deep into the throat will activate a gag reflex and probably bring on vomiting. Treat for shock after vomiting has subsided.

If you can't determine what the poison is, make an educated guess. If there are burns and blisters around the victim's mouth, it is likely that a corrosive liquid caused the poisoning, and vomiting should not be induced. If you smell an odor like lighter fluid, motor oil, or gasoline or a basically "oily" aroma, vomiting should not be induced.

Treat Burns

If a burn is caused by exposure to heat or flame, cover the victim with a thick layer of clothing or blankets to protect him or her from further injury, and await qualified medical attention. If the burn is caused by exposure to some corrosive chemical, flush it with water, and cover it with a dressing to prevent contamination. Treat for shock if the burns are severe.

Treat Shock

Shock is a natural defense mechanism, which enables the human to avoid excruciating pain by lapsing into an unconscious or comatose state. Some animals that "play dead" when injured or in danger of death are actually in a state of shock. Shock is characterized by unconsciousness, pallor, loss of body heat, and extremely shallow (sometimes indiscernible) respiration. Severe shock can be mistaken for death—no discernible breathing, a deathly pallor, a deep state of unconsciousness in which the victim might not react to stimuli, and a cold, clammy feel to the skin.

To treat shock, elevate the victim's feet to let gravity assist in the blood circulation process and to bring oxygen-carrying blood to the brain. Cover the victim lightly to conserve body heat, but don't let him or her become overheated. If he or she is breathing, even in a shallow fashion, fine. Otherwise, resuscitate. It is better not to attempt to restore consciousness until some color and warmth return. Wrists and ankles should be rubbed to stimulate blood circulation.

HOUSEHOLD EMERGENCY PLANNING

Keep lists near all your telephones with the numbers for police, fire department, ambulance service, key physicians, and a poison control center, as well as any other emergency phone numbers that might be relevant to your family or your area. Know the locations of the nearest hospital emergency room and all-night pharmacy, and be familiar with the most direct routes to them. Always carry your hospitalization insurance card with you.

Hurricanes, tornadoes, blizzards, windstorms, cyclones, and earthquakes have at least one thing in common. Any of these catastrophes can result in destruction of homes and other structures, long periods without power, the unavailability of medical assistance, and the distinct possibility that the only food available will be what you have on hand.

For such emergencies, it's clearly necessary to keep a first-aid kit on hand. However, it's common for home first-aid kits to be depleted, leaving a roll of gauze and little else.

What should a reliable kit contain? First of all, an instruction booklet. The first-aid materials in this chapter are excellent and can help you save the life of a loved one. In addition, your booklet should contain suggestions for coping with situations that aren't life threatening.

Your emergency medical stores should include plastic bandages, individually packaged cleansing pads, a disinfectant like bacitracin, adhesive tape, gauze in rolls and in individual sterile packages, scissors, aspirin or other analgesic, laxatives, tweezers, and preparations to control diarrhea and to induce vomiting.

One excellent method of reminding yourself to make certain that prescription medicines will be available to you in times of crisis is this:

When your supply is down to two or three days' worth, place that in your emergency kit. The next time your supply is low, use what is in your emergency stores, and substitute the fresher items. Repeat this process each time your supply runs low. In this way, you will have your needed medicine available, and it will be fresh if you have taken the time to make the periodic switches.

Medicines that you are likely to overlook are wetting or cleansing solutions for contact lenses, petroleum-based lip protectants (such as ChapStick), denture adhesive, burn ointment, and antacids.

Other nonmedical items that might improve the quality of life in a crisis are a razor with spare blades, insect repellant, toilet tissue, a magnifying glass, your eyeglasses, a sewing kit, paper cups, toothbrushes, and toothpaste. A rechargeable flashlight in your emergency area would be of great assistance to your family on a pitch-black night, as would a portable radio—especially if you remember to replace the batteries periodically.

Invariably, you will find that you don't have something that you really need. Household ammonia can be used in place of smelling salts, chlorine bleach makes a satisfactory disinfectant when diluted, baking soda can be used as a dentifrice, and hydrogen peroxide makes a satisfactory disinfectant and mouthwash.

It is possible that your emergency haven is in a storm cellar or basement. If this area of the house is not used and cleaned on a regular basis, you will probably find spiders and insects there. Many of the items suggested for use in the shelter—rubbing alcohol, ammonia, and chlorine bleach—will kill insects. However, some insects may survive your pest control endeavors, so it might be necessary to treat daily or even more often. Boric acid, in powder form, is widely used for control of roaches, and, according to one nationally syndicated columnist, ants will not cross over a sprinkling of talcum powder. Similarly, another source advises, snakes will not crawl through sulfur, a valuable piece of information if rising water forces these pests from the lowlands.

Fire extinguishers should already be in the home, in the kitchen, near the furnace, and close to any storage areas used to safeguard flammable liquids.

Gas and water mains often rupture when structures are damaged. It could be necessary to turn off these mains to avoid explosion or flooding. Make certain that a pipe wrench and an adjustable crescent wrench are handy for this purpose.

Know where and how to cut off electrical power. This may be accomplished easily if circuit breakers are installed. They operate like a light switch. Pull-out cartridge fuses are rectangular devices with a folding handle. Power may be interrupted by simply pulling the fuse by its handle until it can be removed from the fuse box. Some older circuit-breaking devices utilize round fuses, which resemble the threaded portion of a light bulb with a round glass porthole on top. To disable a circuit, just unscrew it.

Tall heavy furniture could fall and cause injury or damage. Secure these items by attaching them to wall studs. Hot-water tanks may be secured against strong structural members with flexible metal strapping.

Removing the rollers from refrigerators or other heavy appliances will keep them in place. Unstable, heavy items of furniture, such as china cabinets and freestanding bookcases, should be so situated within a room that, if these items fell to the floor, they would not block exits from the room. Window-unit air conditioners can shake out of the window in a storm or earthquake. It is essential that you avoid injury or damage by carefully selecting what, if anything, is placed directly below these windows.

Fire is often a complication of a crisis situation. The great San Francisco earthquake of 1906 was not as destructive as the fires it spawned. To prevent fires, you may give the integrity of gas lines in the home an assist with flexible connectors. The give in the connector could prevent the gas lines from being torn out.

WHEN AN EARTHQUAKE HITS

A major earthquake begins with a gentle rocking sensation and almost instantly sends you tumbling to the floor. Sometimes it will be impossible for you to move, so severe is the motion.

Do not leave the house, unless you see fire or smell gas. If possible, you should position yourself under a stout table or in a doorway (which is more steadily braced than a wall); avoid chimneys and anything made of glass (windows, mirrors, china cabinets, and the like). If you're in the kitchen, turn off the stove, then take cover.

If you are outside, get away from trees, buildings, power lines, and anything else that could fall on you. In a crowded building, don't run for the door, since you run the risk of being trampled by all the others heading in that direction.

In a high-rise building, your actions should be similar to those suggested for a single-family home: avoid glass, get under something sturdy, and be alert for heavy items that may be moving toward you. One thing you should *not* do is attempt to use the elevator. An obstruction or a crisis-related elevator dysfunction could leave you trapped in the car, and with all of the activity going on in the building, you would probably have a long wait for rescue.

If you are in your automobile, pull to the side of the road, and wait it out. Avoid overpasses, power lines, and bridges.

When the Shaking Stops
After the earthquake, first attend to those critically injured. Remember, lifesaving first aid is (1) stop bleeding as necessary; (2) start breathing if someone has stopped; and (3) treat for shock (elevate feet, cover with blanket).

Wear shoes, and avoid broken glass. Check gas, water, and electric lines. Shut off any of these services that aren't operational. Once gas is shut off, don't attempt to restore service. Wait for the power company. Avoid downed power lines.

Check sewage lines before attempting to use toilets. In this way you may prevent wastes and refuse from contaminating an area in which you may be forced to live for a while. To prevent backup from the sewer lines into the house, insert bathtub and sink stoppers firmly into position, and, time permitting, add weight to them.

Check the building, inside and out, for damage. Rope off areas that may be hazardous (for example, below a partially destroyed chimney). Assume that the instant a closet or cupboard door is opened, all the items inside will fall on you. In this way, you may avoid injury and minimize the loss of stores that you might need before the crisis ends.

Battery-operated radios and automobile radios may enable you to keep in touch with the rest of the world, but strive to preserve battery power. You don't really know how long you will be in a crisis, and you must ration wisely. Avoid use of your automobile, except in serious situations. To do otherwise could hinder emergency crews.

BEWARE THE HUMAN JACKALS

In any crisis, opportunistic thieves may be expected to assemble to loot. You may remember the looting that followed the assassination of Dr. Martin Luther King, Jr., in 1968. One of the looters, before a national TV audience, opined that it was unfair that the younger looters were taking the quality merchandise, leaving the less desirable goods for the others.

You may be faced with the prospect of defending your home and family against a wanton, avaricious mob at a time when the ranks of law enforcement and other emergency forces may be stretched tenuously thin. You may wish to add a firearm to your emergency cache, or you may not. It is not a decision to be taken lightly.

HAZARDOUS MATERIALS

Hazardous materials are not only a health and safety issue, but also potentially a concern of law enforcement. Not only are large companies and government agencies often guilty of wrongdoing, but believe it or not, even you can violate the law by failing to dispose properly of community and household items.

The federal government and more and more states have enacted laws making it a crime to dispose improperly of some sixty thousand hazardous substances covered by the Occupational Safety and Health Act. These hazardous materials are found nearly everywhere, including your home, your office, and even supermarkets.

Currently, the government spends about $70 billion annually on pollution control. Still, hazardous wastes manage to pollute the air we breathe, the food we eat, and the water we drink. The Environmental Protection Agency (EPA) lists more than twenty-five thousand potentially hazardous waste sites throughout the United States. Recently, one of its testing programs revealed that 23 percent of one thousand water wells were contaminated by organic chemicals. Also, an ever-increasing number of rivers and waterways are becoming polluted. The recent dumping of pollutants into the Ohio River forced the cutoff of water service to hundreds of thousands of residents along the river's course below Pittsburgh.

Not only wastes but materials used in various industrial processes have proven to be extreme hazards. A 1988 EPA report disclosed that 733,000 public and commercial buildings and 35,000 schools contained asbestos in potentially carcinogenic form. Over 500,000 businesses had asbestos installations. A major tragedy occurred in Bhopal, India, in December 1984, when an accidental release of methyl isocyanate fumes from a Union Carbide pesticide plant resulted in the deaths of over 2,000 individuals and at least 200,000 injuries.

Take Action

If you suspect that you and your family are suffering from dangerous contaminants, above all don't be frozen by panic. Instead, visit your neighbors to determine if they likewise are suffering from the same pollution. Then if there is a hot line in your area dealing with environmental problems, call about the problem. In the meantime, organize your neighbors into separate groups or a coalition, and write to the source of the pollution. Perhaps your letter will move the culprit to action.

If there is a toxic spill, follow the instructions of the police and other safety professionals. Don't stay around if they ask you to leave. Then do not return until the area has been declared safe by authorities.

The Office
If your office is toxic, take similar steps. Find out whether your co-workers have similar problems, for how long, and when and where they occur. Next report your evidence to your employer, and request that a specialist certified by the American Board of Industrial Hygiene be brought in to evaluate the potency of possible contaminants.

You can also contribute by acquiring one or more easy-to-grow foliage plants like philodendrons, spider plants, and peperomia. These plants reduce levels of indoor pollutants, including formaldehyde, which is found in many building materials. Incidentally, these plants are beautiful and will brighten your workplace.

Physical Condition
Maintain your body in top physical condition, because a strong body can withstand the effects of many chemicals. Rid yourself of any excess weight, because human fat cells are storage depots for some chemicals. A careful and nutritious diet and above all limiting cigarettes, alcohol, and saccharine (better yet, eliminating them altogether) will improve your health.

Read the warnings on products, and if you have doubts about their effects, don't buy them. In many areas, a special hot line will provide information about toxic substances in food products.

If you recently gave birth, have your breast milk tested before feeding your baby. Chemicals are also contained in a mother's milk.

Household Items
Be sure not to store toxic household items such as gasoline, kerosene, used auto parts, paint, and old pesticides in your home. These can cause genetic damage, cancers, birth defects, and even death. The National Institute for Occupational Safety and Health reports that symptoms include headaches, persistent fatigue, skin irritations, flulike symptoms, and stinging eyes, nose, and throat.

Some household substances may be disposed of by washing them down the drain or wrapping them properly and carefully and placing them in your trash can. More hazardous materials should be saved for communitywide collection days or taken to a toxic waste depot. Recyclable materials should be taken to a recycling center. Reliable information is available from your local OSHA office and waste management officials.

Arts and Crafts

Arts and crafts promote physical and mental skills in both children and adults, but can also present significant health hazards. Creative work materials often are toxic, and inhaling large quantities can produce brain damage and even fatalities. Exposure to lead found in paints, ceramic glazes, and solder may lead to permanent injuries. Be certain that very young children use only water-based paints and apply protective masks when using aerosols or other potentially dangerous inhalants. Above all, check labels on play materials to ensure they do not contain toxic elements.

OTHER EMERGENCY PLANNING

List all the possible catastrophes and emergencies that you might encounter; then sit down and discuss with your family what all of you should do in each situation. Put your plans in writing, and make contingency plans. For example, if both mother and father are at work and the children are at school, would each member of the family know where to go and what to do? What if public transportation facilities aren't operating? If your home is severely damaged by natural disaster, would every member of the family know where to meet? Knowing what to do is 90 percent of the battle when an emergency does present itself.

Planning for an Emergency: A Checklist

1. Plan for natural disasters.
2. Have a first-aid kit.
3. Have a battery radio and extra batteries.
4. Select a place to wait out a storm or other calamity.
5. Provide drinking water.
6. Have flashlights and candles on hand in the event of a power failure.
7. Post a list of emergency telephone numbers by every phone.
8. Locate the emergency room entrance of your nearest hospital.
9. Carry the policy number and name of your hospitalization insurance carrier with you.

10. Locate the nearest all-night pharmacy.
11. Know some basic first aid.
12. Make a list of all emergency situations into which you might be thrust. Plan your actions in the event of each such emergency.
13. During an emergency, remain calm, be sure to secure yourself, and then administer aid to those in need.
14. If you suspect pollution hazards, check with your neighbors to determine if they are suffering from the same symptoms.
15. Call the special hazardous-waste hot line in your area if you suspect a toxic waste problem.
16. Organize a letter campaign to notify the polluter of the problem.
17. Always follow the instructions of police officers and other safety personnel at the scene of a toxic-substance emergency.
18. Check with your co-workers and then notify your employer concerning pollution in the office. Request that a specialist certified by the American Board of Industrial Hygiene evaluate the situation.
19. Use houseplants to reduce levels of indoor pollutants.
20. Maintain a nutritious diet and good physical condition, because a healthy body can better withstand the effects of certain chemicals.
21. Limit your consumption of alcohol, cigarettes, and saccharine.
22. Do not store toxic household items such as gasoline, kerosene, used auto parts, and old pesticides in your home. Learn the proper methods for their disposal.
23. Recyclable materials should be transported to a recycling center.
24. Try to avoid toxic materials for arts and crafts, but when they are utilized, apply proper safeguards.

33
Security in a Crisis Situation

Fire destroyed a large part of the Van Hoffman residence at 345 Elmhurst Drive late last evening. Mr. Van Hoffman is credited with safely getting all the family members out of the burning home. "I panicked at first," he confessed, "but fortunately we had talked about this kind of thing before, and everyone had a pretty good idea of what to do."

A crisis calls for a prompt and proper reaction, so the recommendations in this chapter are brief and to the point. If faced with any crisis situation:

1. Take a second to gain your composure.
2. Consider your emergency plan. Chapter 32 gave some suggestions for emergency planning.
3. Act on your plan. Move and perform in a logical, sensible manner.

A crisis may befall us at any time, and only occasionally do we have advance warning. Weather forecasts can warn of blizzards or hurricanes, giving us a head start on coping with a crisis. But no one can yet predict an earthquake. While people have tamed some of the wild rivers, built walls in places to hold out the sea, and generally learned to coexist with nature, we still have a long way to go before we can feel safe from natural disaster. Trains and trucks carry extremely hazardous materials through our communities each day. Accidents requiring widespread evacuation are seemingly daily occurrences. Convoys carrying nuclear waste material sometimes travel our roadways, amid the fanfare of publicity. What should worry us isn't the occasional nuclear load; what most threatens us are the loads they don't tell us about.

And even as we bring nature under control, we are creating new hazards with our own technology. This year, in the space of one week, three separate incidents requiring the evacuation of nearby residents occurred in one Southern city. One of these was a chlorine leak from a water treatment plant; the second, also a chlorine leak, was the result of a fire in a home in a low-income neighborhood. Fire officials were at a loss to explain the presence of the cylinder of chlorine in the residential setting. The third evacuation was occasioned by a leaking tank car of liquid carbon dioxide.

FIRE CRISIS

Early Stages of a Fire

If you're awakened by smoke at night, or smell smoke but don't see the fire, pause to collect yourself, consider your plan, and then act. Locate the fire, get everyone out, and call the fire department.

In locating the fire, feel a door before you open it. If it's hot, you have located the fire, so go in the other direction.

If you have been alerted by smoke rather than by flame, you may discover a small fire—one you feel you can handle. Resist this do-it-yourself impulse. First call for help, and then start counting to twenty as you try to fight the fire. Once you reach twenty, look for a way out. A fire can spread very quickly, and you will want to have a safe evacuation route available to you if you need it. Don't get so involved in saving your possessions that you lose your life.

Fire Extinguishers

Portable fire extinguishers are intended for use during the early stages of a fire. They should be conveniently located, and all members of the household should be familiar with the proper use of the equipment. A fire extinguisher is only a stopgap protection—one to be used until the arrival of the fire department. Do not forget to call the fire department before you use a fire extinguisher.

Fire extinguishers should be selected on the basis of reliability, ease of use, the types of fires most likely in the areas you want to protect, and the probable size, intensity, and speed of travel of a fire in the area. Once an extinguisher is purchased, it must be serviced periodically to assure that it is in satisfactory operating condition.

The National Fire Protection Association has classified fires into four types, and only the appropriate fire extinguisher should be used for each type of fire. Refer to the table on the facing page.

Class of Fire	Type of Fire	Type of Extinguisher
A	Combustible material (e.g., paper, wood, cloth plastics, textiles, and rubber)	Water, dry chemical, water solutions
B	Combustible liquids or flammable gases (e.g., paint solvents, gasoline, grease, oil, thinners, and flammable chemicals)	Carbon dioxide, foam
C	Live electrical equipment (e.g., appliances that are plugged into sockets, transformers)	Sodium bicarbonate, potassium bicarbonate, ammonium phosphate
D	Combustible metals (e.g., sodium, potassium, magnesium, and titanium)	Various heat-absorbing substances not reactive to burning metals, including special dry chemical powders (which may be stored in barrels)

Advanced Stages of a Fire

If you see flames in your home, get everyone out, call the fire department, and do not return unless you can save a life. You should have previously arranged—and practiced—two separate ways out of the house from any room. If possible, these evacuation routes should involve one door exit and one window exit. Remember that smoke, heat, and combustion gases rise. It is better to crawl than to walk, since the air will generally be more breathable closer to the floor.

All upstairs bedrooms should be equipped with rope or chain ladders, to allow for an alternative emergency escape route if the main staircase is blocked by the fire.

An outside staircase is even better than a rope or chain ladder, especially if there are very young or elderly people in the house. (But because such devices would also provide second-story access to a burglar, the affected door or window must be fully protected.)

If you don't have an outside staircase or a ladder for emergency

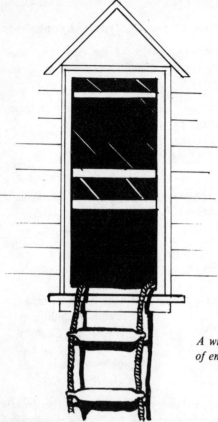

A window ladder provides a means of emergency escape.

escape, improvise. Tie together rolled (for strength) sheets, blankets, drapes, and bedspreads to form a rope; tie one end to a piece of furniture large enough not to be pulled through the window; and lower yourself down through the window. Put the bed sheets on the end of your escape rope nearest the ground, because they are the most likely to tear under the weight of your body, and the nearer they are to the ground, the shorter the distance you will fall.

As for phoning the fire department, use a neighbor's phone—or better yet, get the neighbor to call. You may be so distraught that you will not be able to remember your address. Move your car well away from the house, so that it won't interfere with emergency vehicles, and have one member of the family stand by to direct the fire fighters to the nearest fire hydrant if necessary.

If a pet has been left in the house, don't go back in and attempt to save it, but break out a window on either side of the fire and call the animal.

Car Fire Crisis

If your car catches fire, get out of the car. Touch, then open the hood. Rip burning wires loose, and extinguish the flames if possible.

Your first impulse should be to get out and, if the fire is at all advanced, to get away. On leaving, unlatch any interior hood lock, but touch the hood carefully before opening it, not only to prevent burning your hands but to avoid an outward swelling of flame if the fire is burning beneath the hood.

If there is no great flame but wiring is burning, pry or rip it loose with a handkerchief protecting your hands. If there are flames, smother them if possible. A CO_2 or dry chemical extinguisher (marked for use on Class B or C fires) is ideal and should be carried in the car, but you can use dirt, an old blanket, or even your shirt. If you are unable to make any headway and the fire gains on you, retreat to a safe distance and call for help.

STALLED CAR CRISIS

If you are driving with passengers along the expressway and your car stalls, get the car completely off the roadway. Get the passengers out of the car and away from the road. Signal for assistance. Attempt repairs if you are qualified, but do so away from the road traffic.

A more or less universal signal that you need assistance on the road is to display a square piece of cardboard or a flag that can be seen from a passing auto. A white cloth tied to the radio antenna is another widely used emergency signal. Leave lights on at night, utilizing emergency blinkers or turn signals to warn oncoming traffic. A raised hood will also signify that caution is in order and assistance is needed.

Two very common causes of a car stall are vapor lock and loss of battery power. With a vapor lock, the starter will attempt to turn the engine and will make noise, but the engine won't start. A little time will generally cure this ailment, as the engine will cool off.

If no power, or insufficient power, is being made available from the battery, you won't hear the starter motor when the starter switch is engaged. Shut off the radio, heater, air conditioner, and lights, and try the starter again. You may hear no sound, or you may hear a metallic click. Either indicates a lack of battery power, for which the remedy is a battery charge or a new battery.

There is one thing, however, that you might try. Often a fully charged battery cannot deliver power because accumulations of corrosion block the passage of current from the battery. Gently rapping the bolts securing the cable attached to the positive battery terminal (usually marked "pos" or "+") with a hammer, or even the heel of a shoe, will move the cable slightly. In many instances, this will dislodge enough corrosion to permit passage of current.

If you are alone—especially a female alone—and it is dark, your instructions for handling a disabled vehicle are somewhat different. Get the car off the road. Stay inside, and lock the doors. Signal for assistance, and wait inside the car until help arrives.

Exercise some common sense concerning the assistance you may be offered. Don't unlock your doors for anyone other than an emergency service vehicle or a law enforcement officer. Decline all other offers of assistance, but add that you would appreciate the highway patrol's being notified.

IF YOU SEE A CAR ACCIDENT

If you see an accident and help has not yet arrived, call for assistance, then go to the scene. Assure the victims that qualified assistance is on the way. If you are positive that there is no peril to you personally, offer assistance. Signal oncoming traffic by activating light blinkers. Discourage smoking if gasoline is spilled. Don't move any victims unless they are in danger, and don't attempt to render first aid unless you're qualified to do so, except to save a life.

If you are a compassionate human being, you will want to extend a helping hand to a fellow human in distress. Unscrupulous criminals are known to have staged accidents to lure unwary good Samaritans to a spot where a robbery or assault might be perpetrated. So, regardless of the extent of your compassion, remember that you can best serve your fellow human in distress by getting qualified medical or other emergency assistance to the scene as soon as possible.

WATER ACCIDENT CRISIS

In the case of a water accident or a drowning, don't attempt a swimming rescue of a bather in trouble. Use a spare tire, log, long stick, or other buoyant item to rescue the victim, even if you must swim it into position. Then pull the bather to shore.

Once the victim is on land, attempt to clear water from his or her lungs by placing him or her on the stomach, elevating the waist, and gently tapping the back. If breathing has ceased, turn the victim over, and start mouth-to-mouth resuscitation immediately. Keep it up until you are relieved or respiration begins again.

Your own principal hazard lies in the rescue attempt. Don't try swimming to the victim and grabbing him or her. In the bather's panic, he or she may restrict or disable you and place both of you in danger. Use something that floats; don't try a rescue without such an item. If at all possible, send for help before you jump in. If you can't swim, throw a tire or life preserver to the victim, and go for help.

ELECTRIC SHOCK CRISIS

If you see someone being electrocuted, insulate yourself before giving assistance. Your first obligation is your own safety, so at all costs avoid contact with the source of electric power in working to save the victim— you can be of no assistance if you are knocked unconscious.

Watch where you step; then break the contact, preferably with an on-off switch if you can find it; if not, with a long, dry stick. Don't use anything metal or anything so short that you risk contact with the power source.

Move the victim away from any area of danger if additional shock is a possibility. Then, if necessary, begin your efforts to start the victim's breathing.

Security in a Crisis Situation: A Checklist

1. In every crisis situation:
    a. Take time to compose yourself.
    b. Consider your emergency plan.
    c. Act on your plan.
2. In a fire crisis:
    a. Locate the fire.
    b. Get everyone out.
    c. Call the fire department.
    d. Attempt to control or extinguish a small blaze with an extinguisher suitable for that particular fire.
3. In a car fire crisis:
    a. Get out of the car.
    b. Touch, then open hood.
    c. Rip burning wires loose.
    d. Extinguish flames if possible.

4. In a stalled car crisis:
   a. Get completely off the roadway.
   b. Get passengers out of the car and away from the road.
   c. Signal for assistance.
   d. Attempt repairs, if qualified, but do so away from traffic.
5. In a stalled car crisis, alone and at night:
   a. Get the car off the roadway.
   b. Lock all doors, and signal for assistance.
   c. Wait in your car for assistance.
6. In a car accident crisis:
   a. Call for qualified assistance.
   b. Assure victims that help is on the way.
   c. Offer direct assistance if aid is coming and if there is no peril to you.
   d. Activate light blinkers to warn other motorists.
   e. Discourage smoking, especially if gasoline is spilled.
   f. Don't move the victims unless absolutely necessary.
   g. Use first aid only to save a life—for instance, to stop bleeding or reactivate breathing.
7. In a water accident crisis:
   a. Don't attempt a swimming rescue.
   b. Use a buoyant item for rescue even if you must swim.
   c. When the victim is on land, clear his or her breathing passages and resuscitate if necessary.
8. In an electric shock crisis:
   a. Protect yourself.
   b. Break electric contact, consistent with self-protection.
   c. Resuscitate the victim if necessary.
9. In every crisis situation, your first obligation is your own safety. Only then should you attend to the needs of others.

34
Security for Children and Teenagers

A sixteen-year-old boy was shot to death at 5:30 P.M. yester-
day after an argument near his home. Police said a fifteen-
year-old neighbor was arrested and charged with the death.

Our young children and our teenagers are special individuals with
special problems that must be faced. The very youngest are the most
helpless. Weak in body, without adequate judgment and totally without
guile, they are both victims and the accomplices to many safety and
security incidents. Since they are far more apt to be the victims of an
accident than a crime, that problem is the first focus of this chapter.

SAFETY FOR TODDLERS

To protect toddlers, you must start at the bottom. Go through every
room in your house—on your hands and knees, if necessary—and look
for potentially hazardous items that little fingers can reach. Here is a
room-by-room description of some of the hazards you should look for.

In dens, living rooms, and family rooms, remove delicate china,
ashtrays, and other ornaments from low coffee tables. Use metal, heavy
glass, plastic, or other materials that don't break easily into small cutting
fragments. Place straight-back chairs or rockers near walls to prevent
children from falling backward when they climb on them. Avoid placing
brightly colored, irresistible items where they might be reached by
children using a chair as a stepladder. Get cord shorteners for lamp
cords.

There are inexpensive childproof closures available for unused electric
outlets. These are a must in every home.

Grounding plugs on electrical appliances are there for a good reason.

If you don't have grounded outlets in your home, use the adapters, and use them properly. A healthy adult might be able to withstand the shock from a shorted electrical appliance, but that doesn't mean a child can.

Be careful about locating ungrounded appliances—particularly radios, stereos, and TVs—near gas or water pipes, commodes, sinks, tubs, basins, radiators, floor furnaces, or other natural grounding items in your home. A short circuit in an appliance can deliver a fatal shock through the body, particularly if the person is grounded.

Your kitchen is probably the most hazardous room in your home. There are knives that cut, stoves and heaters that burn, and probably enough chemicals under the sink to kill or injure a whole neighborhood. For example, most oven cleaners are made of lye, which can cause severe burns. Ammonia or ammonia-based cleaners emit fumes that can damage eyes and nasal passages. Ammonia mixed with chlorinated scouring powder can release poisonous chlorine gas. Read the labels on cleaning materials, and provide locked storage for insecticides, herbicides, swimming pool chemicals, and other common household poisons. Heavy cans should be stored low down, where they have a shorter distance to fall.

Bathrooms also have their share of hazards. Place nonslip materials in tubs and showers. Hide or lock up all medicines. Throw away unused portions of prescription drugs. Don't give children access to adult-strength pain relievers, cough medicines, or other strong medications. Be extremely wary about the use of bathroom electrical appliances. Dispose of razor blades safely, and keep razors where children can't get at them.

Bedrooms are best secured by minimizing the child's access to things that are easily broken, by securing wires he or she might trip over, and by protecting unused electrical outlets.

When you furnish a child's room, make absolutely certain that safe, nonlead paint is used, especially on a baby bed. If in doubt, strip it to the bare wood, and repaint it yourself with lead-free paint. Furniture used in children's rooms should have rounded corners. Use wall-to-wall carpeting, which doesn't have loose edges to trip little feet and which also provides for a soft, cushioned landing.

Bookcases, some buffets, and any items of furniture with plate-glass doors can be very hazardous to children. Place such pieces out of the way, or set a chair or some other piece of furniture in front of the glass to prevent a youngster from falling or running into it.

All firearms in the home should be made secure against accidental discharge. Use a trigger lock if a weapon is a part of a collection. If it is used for decorative purposes, remove the firing pin altogether.

If there are stairs in the home, equip them with handrails. To protect toddlers from a fall, use expanding accordion types of gates with spring latches at the tops of staircases.

Finally, if you have a swimming pool, make sure it is fenced against youngsters' wandering into your area by accident or design. Even when your pool is properly enclosed, bear in mind that its presence is a twenty-four-hour hazard for all children who can't swim.

SECURITY EDUCATION FOR CHILDREN

Children should be taught certain things early in life, such as to avoid unnecessary contact with strangers and to withhold all personal information from the same. They should learn to use the telephone to call for assistance. Tell them which neighbor to go to if they are threatened, and remind them to be extra careful in opening doors to anyone they don't know. By age five, a child should be able to use a telephone and know how to dial the operator for assistance. He or she should also know his or her full name, address, and telephone number, and where his or her parents work.

In addition, the FBI makes these suggestions for the self-protection of children:

- Travel in groups or pairs.
- Walk along heavily traveled streets, and avoid isolated areas when possible.
- Refuse automobile rides from strangers, and refuse to accompany strangers anywhere on foot.
- Use city-approved play areas where recreational activities are supervised by responsible adults and where police protection is readily available.
- Immediately report anyone who molests or annoys you to the nearest person of authority.
- Never leave home without telling your parents where you will be and who will accompany you.

SOME ADULT CRIMES AGAINST CHILDREN

The most serious—and, fortunately, least frequent—peril the child might encounter is victimization by an adult. Most adult crimes against children and young people are crimes against property. Adults may steal a child's bicycle, usually because the child didn't take steps to protect it when he or she wasn't riding it. Strong-arm robberies of expensive bicycles are definitely on the increase. A good lock, a good chain, and a lamppost offer the best protection for an unattended ten-speed bicycle (see Chapter 11).

Rape, kidnapping, and child molestation are constant parental concerns. Depending on their relationship to the children, molesters use a wide variety of tactics to lure children. A family member might feign love and affection; a teacher, member of the clergy, police officer, or baby-sitter might use his or her position of authority; an older friend or companion might utilize games or pornography; a stranger might try bribery, requests for assistance, or citing an emergency. By teaching your youngsters about the schemes, tricks, and ruses of molesters, you may save them from horrible injury and even death.

Each of us must take the necessary steps to swing the odds more heavily in our favor. Strong preventive measures such as securing the home and car, taking care in the street and in stores, and teaching children caution with strangers and how to report trouble will help keep crime statistics down.

LATCHKEY CHILDREN

A recent phenomenon or, to be more precise, a label for an older one is occupying a great deal of media attention. That phenomenon is latchkey children. These are children who have working parents who leave them alone after school without adult supervision.

According to librarians, many working parents find it convenient for their youngsters to roam the library stacks for hours. Estimates of the number vary considerably. In a poll conducted by a respected public opinion sampling firm, it was determined that 12 percent of elementary school children are left alone after school each day. U.S. government researchers cite a lower total, 7 percent of the five- to thirteen-year-old school children. Other estimates range as high as 15 percent. Whether the total number of these unattended children is five million or fifteen million, great numbers of them are unsupervised and ripe for trouble.

There are a number of things which parents can do to increase the safety margins for their children. They should, for example, investigate organized after-school care centers for at least the younger children (grades one to four).

Protecting Latchkey Children

Your child's school maintains certain information as a matter of course. This should include: photographs, personal and medical history, and descriptive information. If any of these items are not included in the school's files, provide them to the principal, and request that they be placed with your child's records.

Inform the school of those individuals authorized to pick up your children at the end of the day. Likewise, inform your children that they should leave school only with persons you designate. Make certain that each child knows exactly who has your approval.

Alert the school if the safety or life of a family member has been threatened.

Advise the school of the details of your children's before- and after-school care.

Inform the school, with as much advance notice as is possible, when the child will not be present.

Advise schools of the names, addresses, and telephone numbers of persons to contact in emergencies. Also explain the relationship of the emergency contact.

Have a clear understanding with your children of the route they should follow when going to or coming from school.

Do not permit your children to walk to or from school alone.

Suggest to your children ways of dealing with circumstances or people in whose company they are uncomfortable.

If you are divorced or separated, provide the school with a copy of the applicable court order.

Before a child enters school, teach him or her your phone number (with area code), how to use the telephone, and how to get assistance from the operator. At the earliest possible time, teach the child the use of 911 or your local emergency number.

Know your children's friends well enough to anticipate where they might be at any given time.

If a child tells you that he or she prefers not to be in the company of some person, especially if that person is an adult, pay heed. Don't precipitate a confrontation, but remain aware of a potential problem.

Establish a "secret word" with your children. Make certain that they know *not* to go with any stranger who doesn't speak the secret word.

A stranger is *anyone* who is *not* a friend of the child's parents or guardians.

Each morning, make a mental note of the clothing worn by each of your children that day.

Do not use large letters when labeling your children's books or other belongings. Your children might answer a stranger who called them by name, which could be read on a book.

Set up a rendezvous in the event a child gets separated from you while shopping. The best way is for the child to go to the nearest clerk, say that he or she is lost, and ask for help in finding you.

Fingerprints on file with your local police can help identify a child when the child is very young or is incapacitated.

It is advisable to have the same person pick up a child every day, if practical.

Work with your neighbors toward the establishment of safe houses, McGruff Houses, or other havens for a child who is frightened or in some real or imagined trouble.

Above all, listen to your children. Even more important, take what they say seriously. What they tell you may be the wildest flight of fancy imaginable, in which case, you'd probably be amused. It might be a veiled recitation of a dire physical threat, in which case your belief in your child could avert tragedy. If threats prove baseless, you could allay the child's fears.

MISSING CHILDREN

Most missing children return safe, sound, and unscathed, having been so engrossed in what they were doing that they simply lost track of time. If a child is missing or unduly late returning home, there is seldom reason for panic. Notify the police; they have the resources to find a lost child. (They may also have the lost child and be trying to locate his or her parents.) Then enlist the assistance of neighbors and the child's associates. If this effort locates the missing youngster, or if he or she turns up, remember to notify the authorities so that the police search may be terminated.

HALLOWEEN

Halloween should be a fun time for you and your children. Yet every year, incidents, often tragic ones, occur. Some include children who bite into apples laced with psychedelic drugs or containing razor blades. Dark-costumed children are struck by motorists, and small children who stray too far from home are unable to find their way back.

To help assure that this day is safe, take precautions. Do not let children go trick-or-treating alone. Make sure there is a responsible person with the group.

Check your child's costume. It should have adequate holes for your child's eyes, nose, and mouth. In addition, it should be light enough in color to be seen at night. Pin your name, address, and phone number on the costume of a very young child.

Know where your child is going. Instruct him or her to stay in the neighborhood. Warn your child not to ring the doorbells of any houses where the lights are out. Keep your own house well lighted, and make sure that someone is home.

Set and enforce a curfew for your child, and make certain a responsible person is at home at this prearranged time. Inspect all candy, fruit, or other goodies that a child brings home. Throw out anything that is unwrapped or looks suspicious.

TEENAGERS

Children are probably never so troublesome as when they are in their teens. When a child reaches puberty, the changes that alter his or her body often proceed too fast for the child to make proper adjustments. Awkward, clumsy, or gawky describe the not-quite-adult adolescents. As the body changes from childlike to adult, it does not progress in orderly fashion. "Fits and starts" is more descriptive. Unreliability of larynx is a plague for adolescent males, whose voice might switch from basso to soprano in midsyllable.

As many as 90 percent of all young people, male and female, have committed at least one offense for which they could have been brought to juvenile court—although few are. Only one in nine (one in six if you consider only males) is referred to juvenile court for nontraffic offenses prior to the eighteenth birthday.

According to FBI statistics, those under eighteen accounted for about half the arrests for larceny, burglary, auto thefts, and arson made in the United States during 1979. Another third of such crimes involved those eighteen to twenty-four years old. Arrest rates were higher for the fifteen- to seventeen-year-old group than for any other group, and this group also had the highest incidence of arrest for "property" crimes— larceny, burglary, and vehicle theft. The eighteen- to twenty-year-old group led all others in being arrested for the personal crimes of murder, rape, robbery, and aggravated assault.

When this book was first published, in 1975, the under-eighteen group accounted for:

- One of every twelve homicide arrests
- One of every five rape arrests
- One of every three and one-half robbery arrests
- One of every seven aggravated-assault arrests
- One of every two burglary arrests
- One of every two larceny arrests
- One of every one and one-half auto theft arrests

The eighteen- to twenty-four-year-old group accounted for:

- One of every four homicide arrests
- One of every two and one-half rape arrests
- One of every one and one-half robbery arrests
- One of every four aggravated-assault arrests
- One of every three and one-half burglary arrests
- One of every five larceny arrests
- One of every four auto theft arrests

By now, those under eighteen account for:

- One of every eleven and one-half murder arrests
- One of every six and one-half rape arrests
- One of every four robbery arrests
- One of every eight aggravated-assault arrests
- One of every three burglary arrests
- One of every three larceny/theft arrests
- One of every two and one-half auto theft arrests

The eighteen- to twenty-four-year-olds account for:

- One of every three murder arrests
- Three of every ten rape arrests
- Two of every five robbery arrests
- Three of every ten aggravated-assault arrests
- One of every three burglary arrests
- Two of every seven larceny/theft arrests
- One of every three auto theft arrests

There is a commonly held, but not well substantiated, belief that a good half of all crimes—minor traffic violations excepted—are due to drug abuse. Property-oriented crime is increasing, however, and drug users seem to be a significant factor in this increase. It can also be demonstrated that the relatively high incidence of drug abuse among the young is a significant factor in juvenile crime.

For a parent, all this leads to a first, and most important, recommendation when it comes to protecting your teenager from crime, either as victim or criminal: know where your children are, what they are doing, and with whom. Your child is just as likely to be bad company as to be with bad company, and if you are too quick to spring to your offspring's defense, you may be an unwitting accomplice. Admit that your child could run afoul of the law, and plan for this possibility with your teenager.

If possible, take one or more teenagers to visit a jail. Let them see what goes on inside those walls. If you can convince them that they could be incarcerated, they may be deterred from the temptation to commit a crime. At least keep the lines of communication open—this may help to head off teenage problems before they get too serious.

Teenage crime is often spawned in an atmosphere of poverty, hopelessness, drunkenness, squalor, frustration, idleness, and adult crime. It is a function of nobody giving a damn, especially not parents; of school absenteeism and dropping out; and of peer-group pressure. However, juvenile delinquency is not the exclusive province of the ghetto. The greatest growth in the crime rate is found in the suburbs. Rates of increase in the commission of serious crimes are much greater for females than for males, especially for juvenile females.

Of the ingredients for spawning crime, only poverty seems to be an exclusive characteristic of the ghetto. The suburban juvenile delinquent is less deterred by possible consequences, because he or she is much more likely to get off scot-free, or at least to draw a suspended sentence, than is the ghetto offender. Idleness is a problem as common in suburbia as in the city. A part-time job is excellent for combating idleness and for building self-confidence.

Open lines of communication between parents and children are wonderful, and although the teenage years are probably too late to start to establish these, you have nothing to lose and much to gain by trying. You need to make a teenager belong. A teenager who doesn't feel a sense of belonging at home will surely look for places and groups where he or she can have that feeling.

CULTS

The unhappy teenager may be attracted to cults. The formation of a cult is not in itself a violation of the law, but the way many cults conduct their activities is. There is evidence, verified by police and medical authorities, of child abuse, neglect, beatings, and other acts of violence. Ex–cult members have reported being slapped, being forced to make public confessions, having their food spat on, and being forced to eat pet food off the floor. Members of some cults have engaged in prostitution, and have encouraged both incest and sexual abuse of children.

Cults may not routinely abduct babies, but they snatch minds and spirit. The worst crime so far associated with a cult was the massacre in 1978 at Jonestown, Guyana. A cultist dictator managed to establish total control over hundreds of followers, convincing them all—men, women, and children—to kill themselves by drinking cyanide mixed in grape drink. Armed guards made sure no one disobeyed orders. Most of these cult followers were dead within five minutes.

How Widespread?

Recent estimates point to more than 2,400 cults in the United States. These groups differ widely in size and nature, ranging from Sun Myung Moon's Unification Church and Hare Krishna to Rama, Jon-Roger and his MSIA Group, Trungpa (a Tibetan guru), the Manson family, and Divine Light Mission. Some grow to a very large size. The group led by the Swami Muktananda at one time had 140 centers in the United States.

Causes

Don't delude yourself that only the poor, disenfranchised, and desperate are susceptible, and that your loved ones are exempt and safe from cults. Typical "draftees" to a cult are children of fathers with high-stress occupations, read newspapers regularly, and are satisfactory students. All youngsters who are searching for meaning in life or spirituality are vulnerable. Many join cults because of frustration with established religion. Some are desperately searching for acceptance. The cultist group becomes their surrogate family, and the masculine cult leaders, their father figures. Remember, the cult also serves the specific needs of its followers. Recruits are not usually passive targets overpowered by mind controllers.

Prevention

Once your youngster has joined a cult, it usually is too late for successful action. Prevention is the best, and perhaps only realistic, approach. Never allow your home to be a meeting place for the cult's persistent recruiters. And keep such recruiters out of schools and off its grounds.

Communication

You must broaden the channels of communication with your loved ones. Be open-minded, tolerant, and willing to discuss sensitive subjects. As described in Chapter 18 on teen suicide, you must learn to be an active listener by being totally attentive and not interrupting or imposing your ideas before your youngster has finished transmitting complete thoughts. Help your youngsters ask appropriate questions and think for themselves.

Youngsters vulnerable to cults often are unable to evaluate and choose among various options. They perceive cults as the only available alternative. As their parents, you should help them develop the art of critical thinking, to discern between productive and nonproductive choices, to make decisions, and to solve problems. Above all, be a proper role model, and instill in your young people confidence and self-esteem. Should your children seek to detach themselves from a cult and be willing to return home, provide them with love, warmth, and professional counseling.

JUVENILE DELINQUENCY

Children under eighteen may be responsible for offenses that the general society considers unacceptable. Some of them may be general violations of the law; other actions may be criminal only when committed by the young. A college student may cut class and be guilty of no crime. A junior-high student cutting class could be charged with truancy. The only difference is that the junior-high student is a few years younger. Besides truancy, these status violations, as they are called, include curfew violations, tobacco or alcohol violations, loitering, and being a runaway. These young people may also be called unmanageable, incorrigible, or "in need of supervision."

Since the end of World War II, rates of juvenile delinquency have increased dramatically. It is probably no coincidence that juvenile malfeasance is tied in with increasing movement of both parents from the home to the work force, with a correspondent lessening of supervision over children.

Juvenile delinquency was once the virtually exclusive province of males. Now, however, females are rapidly closing the gap. While male delinquents tend toward theft, females are more likely to run away and commit sex offenses. Of those who have been incarcerated for juvenile offenses, only one-third are the product of two-parent homes. But even growing up with both male and female role models is no guarantee of adult stability. Whereas a happy home is less likely to produce delinquents, an especially strict one tends to have the opposite effect. Homes headed by alcoholic, maladjusted, or sociopathic parents can be breeding grounds of delinquent behavior.

Socioeconomic Effects on Delinquency

A lower position on the socioeconomic scale militates toward delinquency. For several reasons, this tendency intensifies in a slum or ghetto environment. First of all, the opportunities available in the slums are fewer than in other parts of a city and certainly fail to keep pace with aspirations. The desire of the young to achieve a better life makes the young people increasingly less satisfied with their lot. The traditional avenues out of the ghetto (education, public service, the military) may be closed to them, sometimes for lack of educational achievement. The ghettos generally have the city's highest rates of illiteracy. Ghetto schools frequently are characterized by general disruptive behavior, exacerbating an already next-to-impossible learning environment. It is little wonder that the slum-poor often feel themselves to be outside society, and not amenable to its rules and ideologies.

THE YOUNG AND REGRETFUL

Perhaps the single problem with most potential for long-term concern is the ever-increasing numbers of pregnant teens. In many homes of pregnant teens, the mother-to-be may be the third generation unmarried. A generation or so ago, if a young girl became pregnant, her father would confront the family of the fathering child and arrange for either support from or the marriage of the young man.

More recently, sexually active young women avoided pregnancies by taking birth control medication or other precautions. Today, there is a distinct change in pattern. More and more young unmarried people are becoming parents. Part of the reason is *machoism*. Fathering children elevates one's status among peers, according to some observers. Also, many teen mothers receive public assistance, which tends to increase the standards of living in the home. In fact, there is a widely held belief that many complete cellular families choose to live apart (or at least maintain separate living accommodations) in order to maximize income from public sources.

Regardless, there are a half-million children born to parents who are, themselves, children under the age of seventeen. Virtually every one of these girls (96 percent) elect to raise their children. While their motives are noble, the reality is frightening. Forty percent of single-parent female-headed households live in poverty, according to 1986 statistics.

VIOLENCE AND THE MEDIA

Parents, researchers, and politicians have long expressed a concern over violence in the media: how is it affecting children and their perceptions of the world? In many forms of entertainment today, including television, motion pictures, and music videos, violence is commonplace. Often, the more graphic the violent scenes in a program, the more it is sought after. A series of *Rambo* movies, which were box office hits, focused on physical and firearm violence. Among popular music videos, 60 percent flaunt some violent act.

Television reaches a huge population of viewers and has become the center of attention in many American homes. VCR ownership alone has increased by 234 percent between 1984 and 1987. A study by the Annenberg School of Communications at the University of Pennsylvania found that TV viewers are exposed to sixteen acts of violence in each evening's prime-time programs. Weekend daytime children's programs, especially cartoons, contain three times more violence than prime-time programs, with over twenty acts of violence each hour.

As children begin to accept the persistent images of violence as a standard form of behavior, they become desensitized. Even though they understand that what they see on TV is made up, they may nevertheless believe it. Evaluating the actions and characters on TV independently of the whole show, children may view violence as an acceptable way to solve problems. They imitate what happens around them, and violence on the screen may serve as a model. Children exposed to violence in cartoons have shown an increase in loss of temper, fighting, kicking, selfishness, and cruelty to animals.

Television depicts violence as the way to obtain power; violence makes people do what you want. To justify these types of programs, networks argue that while some shows contain violence, they also express positive images. Children, however, do not watch entire shows, but engage in much channel switching. Any moralistic message intended to balance out the violence is lost because children are not interested in following a plot. They tend to most remember, and even imitate, the violent actions from the shows they watch. In Arkansas, a ten-year-old boy was shot in the neck by a friend imitating a commercial for a toy laser-gun game in which players shoot at each other.

Some parents, ignoring the negative effects of violence in the media, argue that they see no obvious difference in their children's behavior. Perhaps they do not understand that desensitization is a gradual process. Or, more likely, they simply do not welcome the prospect of monitoring their children's viewing and enforcing their decisions.

The most important thing you can do as a parent is to supervise program selection. In cartoons, videos, and other programs, it is important to limit the viewing of role models that you would not want your children to imitate. Be consistent in this monitoring, and do not hesitate to enforce the viewing rules you set down. Giving in to arguments only proves to children that they can have their own way if they apply enough pressure. Discussing characters and their actions in the shows they watch may help them make sense of what happens, and may provide any opportunity to discover how your children see the world.

Parents should also express their views to their government representative, and especially to other parents. Putting pressure on local TV stations, movie theaters, and cable and national networks will advertise that parents are concerned about what their children are watching, and that they will not accept violence as the norm. Voicing a desire to see more constructive children's programming may encourage the replacement of violence as a main attraction.

These concerns are given more attention when delivered by a group of parents acting as a coalition. Many parent groups, calling for a national violence rating system for all television programs, advocate a compromise with networks, rather than strict censorship of programs. All children deserve to see the world as more than an ugly, fearful place.

Security for Children and Teenagers: A Checklist

1. Make the home as accident-proof for children and elderly people as possible.
2. Start at the floor of each room, and look for hazardous situations; place breakable items high and out of reach.
3. Check for child hazards, such as easily broken glass, easily dumped chairs, lamp cords, unguarded electric outlets, short circuits in ungrounded electrical items, knives, scissors, stoves,

heaters, cleansing chemicals, insecticides, herbicides, other poisons, medicines, razors, razor blades, sharp-edged furniture, rugs that can slip or trip, lead-based paint on baby beds, plate-glass doors, firearms, staircases, and so on.

4. Teach children security lessons early in life.

5. Protect your children after school until you return from work by designating a secure place for them to stay under adult supervision.

6. Be sure teachers and supervisors are thoroughly familiar with your children's daily routine, transportation patterns, and personal habits in the event of an emergency.

7. Teach children proper methods for protecting their property, especially bicycles.

8. Teach children to avoid involvement with strangers, to avoid walking or playing in unsupervised areas, to run and yell if threatened, and how to contact police and neighbors in the event of an emergency.

9. Instruct teenagers to let parents know where they are, what they're doing, and with whom.

10. Recognize that teenagers get in trouble, and plan for it with your child.

11. Impress on teenagers the importance of respect for the law.

12. Encourage teenagers to hold jobs.

13. Prevention is the best strategy for protection from cults.

14. Keep cult recruiters out of your house and school.

15. The best protection from cults is open communication and understanding between you and your youngster.

16. Provide your children with support and professional counseling when they decide to leave a cult and return home.

17. Assist your children in the art of critical thinking and choosing properly among competing options.

18. Be a positive role model for your youngsters.

19. Monitor all programs and movies that your children watch.

20. Do not permit them to view violent or negative role models, including those in cartoons and videos.

21. Consistently supervise children's viewing habits. Hold fast to any rules you impose.

22. Do not give in to complaining over restrictions on programs.

23. Openly explore the characters and actions in programs, and explain any situation that may be unclear to or misunderstood by your children.
24. Express your concerns about violent images to government representatives, TV stations, and movie theaters. Enlisting the support of other parents by forming a coalition will give strength to your opinions.

35
Special Occasions Mean Special Risks

"I'm still in shock," declared Lucia Whittlesby yesterday evening. She had just given a bridal shower for a neighbor, and the guests had recently left. "The silver tea set is missing, and I don't even know what else is gone. I can't imagine who would do such a thing—and to think that I invited them here!"

The special occasions in our lives can also be the source of some rather special security problems. Any occasions that are covered in the local newspapers present special problems, as do any social get-togethers.

FUNERALS AND WEDDINGS

A death in the family will result in an obituary in the press, listing the time and place of funeral services. It is expected that every member of the deceased's household will attend these services, and burglars know it. Arrange for a friend or neighbor, or a contract security guard, to house-sit while you are attending funeral services.

A wedding is one of the most important days of one's life and is also a momentous occasion for the father and mother of the bride. Make certain that this special day is not spoiled by a burglary during the ceremony. A wedding notice in the newspaper is not the burglar's only tip-off—he or she may have been alerted by banns of marriage being published at your church, or by an employee of your caterer, florist, jeweler, or someone else providing services or goods who happens to double as a "bird dog" for a burglary ring. Even a passerby seeing a man leaving the house in a morning coat with a daughter in a bridal gown can inform a burglar of the valuable wedding gifts on display inside. Protect them with a house-sitter or guard.

EVERYDAY SPECIAL OCCASIONS

Occasions don't need to be too special to offer a burglar the chance to rifle your house. If you are seen leaving the house with your golf clubs, a burglar knows there will be hours to work undisturbed. The burglar has only to ring the bell to determine if anyone is left at home.

While it isn't practical to get a house-sitter every time you play nine holes of golf, you can arrange with a neighbor to keep an eye out for any unusual occurrences. From the vantage point of security, a nosy neighbor is a jewel. Of course, you should be ready to reciprocate when your neighbor leaves with his or her bowling ball or tennis racket in hand.

HAVING A PARTY

If you're having a big party at home, take some precautions, especially if you don't know all your guests well. Resist the impulse to show off your collection of gold coins. There is nothing wrong with the host's and hostess's enjoying their own party as much as the guests do, but your party planning should include some commonsense security planning. Check out any help you hire, and take the precaution of safeguarding small, easily portable valuables. You might count the silver, too, after everyone has left.

Hosting a party with a guest list that includes persons not known to you, such as an author's reception or a political fund-raiser, can be a great deal more expensive than you anticipated at the outset. Thieves attending these gatherings are certain to be on the lookout for small, easily concealed items to steal. They may also rifle guests' handbags. As Chapter 13 urges with regard to shopping, you should be in tactile contact with your handbag at all times, unless it is protected in locked storage. Furs, too, are highly sought-after items, and can be removed by concealing them under other garments. Through a window or fire escape, a thief could drop valuable commodities to an accomplice waiting on the street below.

Protecting your guests' property requires a bit of planning. You shouldn't use a room easily accessible from outside, for reasons mentioned in the preceding paragraph. You probably shouldn't select your own bedroom either. If you're like most people, you tend to keep your own valuables near at hand for protection, usually in your own bedroom. Your best bet would be a spare bedroom or a youngster's.

A FRIENDLY GAME OF CHANCE

At what point does your friendly Friday-night poker game become a professional gambling operation? More than a few such games will be invaded by robbers this year, and some will be raided by the police as well. High-stakes poker games do constitute gambling and, therefore, are an attraction to robbers. The potential for trouble increases if one member of the poker crowd has gotten in over his or her head and might be capable of nonsporting means of getting even.

It is generally best to avoid high-stakes games. But if you'd rather not avoid them, at least take some precautions, such as using chips rather than currency and settling at the end of the game by check instead of cash.

GOING TO THE MOVIES

When you go to the movies, it is not enough to choose the film of your liking, but you must also pay full attention to ensure that the movie theater is in a safe neighborhood. Try to avoid sitting near boisterous or suspicious individuals, and never tell a fellow moviegoer to stop talking or to refrain from smoking cigarettes or something else. Have an usher conduct these distasteful tasks. Above all, be sure your children are properly supervised whenever you allow them to go to the movies.

THINK SECURITY

This chapter barely touches the surface of the many special occasions that might require special security measures. The main point is to realize that your security hazard increases anytime you're out of your home or whenever anyone else is in it. Some situations, of course, are more hazardous than others, and only you can properly match resources against risks. If, however, you train yourself to think in terms of potential risk in advance, you will be prepared to take the appropriate protective steps.

Special Occasions Mean Special Risks: A Checklist
1. Assume that your security needs increase whenever you're out of the house or whenever someone else is in it, and take adequate protective steps.
2. Arrange for a house-sitter when you and your family attend a

funeral, wedding, or other event that may have been the subject of newspaper or other publicity.

3. Establish agreements with your neighbors to keep an eye open on your behalf whenever you're away from home. And, of course, be ready to reciprocate.

4. Guard against pilferage of small valuable items if a group of strangers or casual acquaintances is invited to your home. Investigate any part-time help engaged for special occasions.

5. If you are hosting a social gathering, protect your guests' coats and other belongings in a room that is secure from burglars.

6. Don't carry large amounts of money to a high-stakes poker game or similar activity. Use chips while playing, and settle debts by check at the end of the game.

7. Select a movie theater in a safe location, avoid boisterous individuals, and, if required, seek assistance from the theater's staff.

36
Moving to Another City

The Blake family moved to another city because of a job change. One week later, their house was burglarized, the family car was stolen, and someone tried to sell their children marijuana. Unlike the place they lived before, their new neighborhood and school were in a high-crime area, where the children were assaulted by young toughs in school.

Nearly forty million Americans change their residences each year, and anyone who has moved can tell you that this complicated process requires careful planning. A high priority on your moving list should be protection from crime. Nothing is more disheartening than moving from a stable low-crime area to a neighborhood high in crime and where drugs abound.

The first item on your agenda should be to determine the incidence of crime, including the levels of violence and theft, in your new neighborhood. Go to the library and look up the *Uniform Crime Reports* published annually by the FBI. If you are unable to find it, ask your reference librarian for assistance. This publication contains useful and interesting information on the levels of crime and the number of police officers for most cities and towns in the United States. For your city or town, look up how many homicides, rapes, aggravated assaults, robberies, burglaries, and auto thefts occurred over the last year. Then compare the numbers with similar crimes in cities nearby of comparable size. For your convenience, population figures are provided for each city.

You can also determine how many officers your new city's police department has, compared with other cities in the same category. This effort should not last more than half an hour if you can manage to tear yourself away from the fascinating statistics and crime descriptions provided by the FBI. It is well worthwhile, because you will protect yourself and your family for many years to come from places with high crime. You might as well choose a location close to your job that has a low, rather than a high, incidence of crime.

FIELD WORK

Walk or drive around your potential new neighborhood, especially at night or on weekends, and look for signs of crime. These may include undesirables, young toughs, youth gangs, drug addicts, prostitutes, panhandlers, and derelicts. Beware of visible gambling, like three-card monte, or other forms of street betting. Also, determine if there are bars, saloons, off-track betting parlors, drug dens, "smoke shops," or similar crime hazards in your new neighborhood.

Try to determine whether people routinely use the streets during the day and night, or if they are afraid to venture outside. Are the streets deserted and isolated? Ask the same questions about nearby parks. Next, check the lighting in the neighborhood. Is it adequate for the nighttime? Is there sufficient lighting outside of your new home?

Also, examine the exterior of your new house or apartment building to see whether it is surrounded by untrimmed shrubbery or foliage, excellent hiding places for criminals.

Make sure there is convenient and efficient transportation. You do not want yourself or your family to walk a mile through deserted streets to the bus stop and then wait an hour for the bus, especially late at night or very early in the morning.

SCHOOLS

Check the level of safety in your youngsters' new school. Reread "School and Campus Security" (Chapter 20), and discuss with your family the security and safety measures needed to assure maximum protection. Be certain to check the incidence of racial and religious hate crimes on school property and in your new city. Newspaper accounts and the annual report by the local police often provide this information. You might even contact the public relations unit of the local police for information on this highly dangerous crime.

Racial and religious hate crimes have been increasing over the last several years. In Los Angeles, for example, the number of reported crimes involving bigotry and prejudice increased from twenty-six in 1980 to 115 in 1987. These crimes included hate literature, disruption of religious services, assaults, vandalism, graffiti, arson, cross burnings, and gunshots. More than 10 percent of these acts occurred on school property.

ESSENTIAL INFORMATION

Before moving to your new destination, obtain the following emergency, information, and referral phone numbers. They may save your life or the life of a loved one. If you can't obtain these numbers before you move, make sure they are recorded as soon as you arrive at your destination. You might use the space on this page to enter the proper telephone numbers.

Police Department...

Fire Department...

Poison Center...

Suicide-Crisis Hot Line.......................................

Emergency Medical Service.....................................

Rape Hot Line...

Arson Hot Line..

Child Abuse or Neglect Hot Line...............................

Elderly Abuse or Neglect Hot Line.............................

Wife Abuse Crisis Center......................................

Runaway House...

Drug Abuse Referral...

Alcoholics Anonymous..

Al Anon...

Alcohol and Drug Council......................................

Toxic Waste Hot Line..

FBI...

Physician...

ENVIRONMENTAL POLLUTION

While searching for crime hazards during your tour of the prospective neighborhood, also be alert for problems arising from toxic wastes. Is the town dump nearby, and does the wind blow in the direction of your building or home? Is the water supply fully protected from the town dump? Are there odors from service stations, manufacturing plants, or other commercial establishments? Do these companies dump their wastes nearby? Is there a frequently used railroad in the neighborhood giving off constant smoke and noise?

Unless you check these hazardous-waste and pollution problems very carefully, you might find yourself a victim of hazards more devastating even than the crimes listed in the FBI *Uniform Crime Reports.*

MOVING TIME

Don't expend so much energy checking crime and pollution that you forget to properly plan your actual move. Above all, read a copy of *When You Move: Your Rights and Responsibilities,* a pamphlet published by the Interstate Commerce Commission (ICC). It covers in detail what you should know about selecting a moving company, mover's liability, procedures for complaints, weight, setting a date, method of payment, and mutual responsibilities for you and the moving company.

A reliable moving company is of critical importance, because of the hazards of thievery when movers and packers roam around your house. Also, reliable companies are less likely to experience robberies from moving vans. Remember, all agreements must be in writing.

If you move within the same city or state, make sure your moving company is authorized by the appropriate *state* regulatory agency, usually the public utilities commission. Don't forget to notify your post office, banks, relatives, friends, business acquaintances, and credit card companies of your change in address. The U.S. Postal Service provides cards designed specifically for this purpose.

After you have planned carefully and completed all these steps, you are ready for your move. Best of luck and success in your new home.

Moving to Another City: A Checklist

1. Determine the expected incidence of crime, including the extent of violence and theft, in the city or town to which you intend to move. Compare these numbers to places nearby with a similar population.
2. Determine the amount of police coverage at your final destination compared with nearby cities of similar size.
3. Spend several hours walking around the neighborhood to which you intend to move, and observe such indicators of crime as drug addicts, prostitutes, derelicts, street gamblers, youth gangs, and neighborhood toughs. Also note area crime hazards like bars and drug dens.
4. Observe how neighborhood sidewalks and streets are utilized. They will usually be deserted in high-crime areas except for criminals, street people, and young neighborhood toughs. Employ similar criteria to determine safety in nearby parks.

5. Be sure lighting is adequate on your neighborhood streets and outside your home.
6. Make certain that your new destination is near safe, reliable, and convenient transportation.
7. Walk around your new neighborhood to determine whether it is threatened by toxic waste, excess noise, or other forms of pollution.
8. Obtain emergency and essential phone numbers before you move.
9. Notify your post office, relatives, friends, business associates, bank, and credit card companies of your new address.
10. Be sure to put all conditions involving your move in writing.
11. Obtain the Interstate Commerce Commission publication *When You Move: Your Rights and Responsibilities*; follow all instructions.

PART FIVE

SECURITY FOR BUSINESS EXECUTIVES AND FOREIGN TRAVELERS

37
Kidnap/Extortion Problems

The kidnappers of Gianni Vitelli, an heir to a jewelry fortune, demanded a record $16 million ransom for his release, according to police sources. The request came through a note written to the family by a terrorist and delivered by the kidnappers to a friend. Authorities refused to disclose the name of the friend or how she received the message.

Corporate executives, bankers, the well-to-do, and members of their families have been prime targets of extremists, kidnappers, and extortionists in Europe and Latin America for many years. Hostage taking has been recently referred to as "the pest of modern times." Now that these crimes are also occurring with more frequency in the United States, basic information on how to prevent and deal with them should be included in this book.

Even if you aren't particularly well-to-do, don't skip this section of the book, because you—or more particularly your family—may be the victim of a kidnapping for reasons other than financial. Rapists, child molesters, and other sex criminals frequently abduct their victims and, as an afterthought, sometimes add extortion to the offense. Kidnapping may also be politically motivated, with the extortionist attempting to gain some nonmonetary kind of ransom.

THE EXTORTION CALL OR LETTER

If you receive an extortion letter, handle it as little as possible, and alert law officers at once. If you receive a phone message that one or more members of your family has been taken hostage, stay as calm as possible. The caller will be extremely nervous and should not be pushed into rash action.

331

Take detailed notes of the entire conversation—or better yet, make a tape recording. Recordings are extremely valuable to investigators. Even if only an office dictating unit is available, keep it close to your phone at all times. If you can't make a recording, note the exact time of the call, the exact words of the caller, any characteristics such as a regional or foreign accent, and any background noises or music. Have a form handy to help you gain as much information as possible.

If you are at the office, notify your secretary while the call is in progress, and have him or her attempt to trace the call. Ask your local telephone company, in advance, for recommendations regarding the immediate tracing of calls.

Indicate complete willingness to cooperate with the caller. Note each instruction in detail, and even if you are recording the conversation, repeat instructions back to the caller to assure they are clearly understood.

If the call is being traced, keep the caller on the line as long as possible. This will help the phone company in its efforts to trace the call. Ask any plausible question to prolong the conversation: Who is calling? Is this a serious call or just a joke? How do I know it's not a joke? Why have you picked on me in particular? When will I get more instructions?

Ask further questions about the hostage: What is he or she wearing? Is he or she all right? Can I speak to him or her? What exactly is wanted?

If money is demanded, ask in what denominations the bills should be. Where should the money be delivered? When? If the money is to be dropped off, ask how to get to the drop-off point even if you know the route. If money is to be given to someone, ask how to recognize that person.

On the first phone call, try to arrange the simultaneous exchange of money and hostage. If the caller insists on a drop-off point, tactfully try to arrange a person-to-person payoff. Point out the risk of a third person's intercepting a drop-off.

Any ransom money paid should include a minimum of 5 to 10 percent "bait money." The safest type of bait money is probably bills the serial numbers of which have been recorded.

Offer the caller a code word for identification purposes so that cranks and other potential extortionists are unable to exploit the situation if it is publicized. After the call is completed, notify the Federal Bureau of Investigation and the local police department, regardless of instructions to the contrary. Maintain absolute secrecy, and do not permit any of the

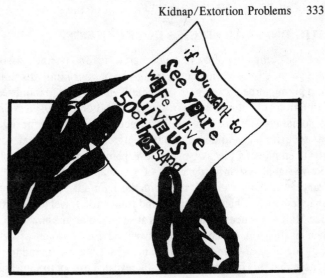

Responses to a kidnap note must be carefully planned.

facts regarding the kidnapping or demands for ransom to be known to anyone outside the immediate family except the investigating officers.

Don't handle letters or communications demanding the payment of ransom. Turn these over to law officers as soon as possible. Don't touch or disturb anything at the scene of the abduction. Minute particles of evidence that are invisible to the naked eye may be destroyed.

Be calm, and strive to maintain as normal a routine around the home and office as possible. Place full confidence in the law enforcement officers who are investigating the kidnapping. In addition to obtaining photographs and a complete description of the victim, these officers must have all facts relating to the personal habits, characteristics, and peculiarities of the victim. When kidnappings occur, the first concern of the FBI and other law enforcement agencies is always the safe return of the victim.

The taking of a hostage by the attackers is not the beginning of this crime. Weeks, even months, almost certainly have been devoted to learning as much about you as possible. If you frequently appear in newspapers or other media, they will have followed your every move, figuratively speaking. A little later, they will literally follow your every move, to learn how you live your life, with special attention to routines. During this time, they will determine the where and the how of their proposed abduction.

ANTIKIDNAP STRATEGIES IN THE OFFICE

As a basic company policy, instruct secretaries and business associates not to provide information concerning you or your family to strangers. Avoid giving unnecessary personal details in response to inquiries from information collectors for use in such publications as business directories, social registers, or community directories. Review your organization's security plans to determine their effectiveness, and make certain that all employees are aware of these plans. Establish a simple and effective signal system in the event of a kidnap attempt.

Vary your daily routines to avoid the habitual patterns for which kidnappers look. Change the times and routes you travel to and from the office. Refuse to meet with strangers at secluded or unknown locations. When leaving your office or home, always advise a business associate or family member of your destination and what time you intend to return, but insist that this information never be revealed except to someone with a legitimate need to know it.

PROTECTION OF CHILDREN AT HOME

Make sure that outside doors, windows, and screens are securely locked before you retire at night. Be particularly certain that the child's room is not readily accessible from outdoors. If your home has an intercom system, leave the transmitter in a child's room open at night, or keep the door to the room open so that any unusual noises may be heard. Since leaving the door open removes some fire protection, an intercom is preferable.

Never leave young children at home alone or unattended, and be certain they are left in the care of responsible, trustworthy people. Children should learn early to keep the doors and windows locked and never to let in strangers. Teach children how to call the police if strangers or prowlers hang around the house or attempt to get in.

If you do leave the children at home for a short time, keep the house well lighted and the garage doors closed. Instruct household employees not to let in strangers or accept packages unless they are positive of the source. If you are expecting a package, alert household help to that fact. Try to discourage your children from publicly discussing family finances or routines, and remind yourself not to permit advance publicity for business trips or other occasions when you will be away from your home and family.

PROTECTION OF CHILDREN AT SCHOOL

Arrange for your children to be escorted to school, and if you feel especially susceptible to kidnapping, do not let them take taxis or public transportation.

Your prime consideration in selecting a school for your children will be scholastic, but the FBI does suggest a few security policies to check out prior to enrollment. If your child's school doesn't have such policies, bring pressure to bear for their adoption through parent groups, the school administration, or trustees.

Among the policies that the FBI suggests is a rule that before releasing a child to anyone except his or her parents during the regular school day, a teacher or administrative official should telephone one of the child's parents or guardians for approval. When a parent requests by phone that a child be released early from school, the caller's identity should be confirmed before the child is permitted to leave. If the parent is calling from home, the school should check the request by a return telephone call, with the child identifying the parent's voice. If the call is not being made from the child's residence, the caller should be asked questions about such things as the child's date of birth, the courses he or she is studying, or names of teachers and classmates. If there is any doubt, the child should not be released.

Teachers should be alert to suspicious-looking people who loiter in or near the school. If there is no logical explanation for their presence, the police should be notified immediately.

The obligation of schools is primarily education. It is unrealistic to expect schools to develop a high degree of protection for students. Nevertheless, the schools have some custodial obligations. It is realistic to expect them to provide minimal security. They should maintain information about students, including address and phone number; identification of, and phone number for, legal guardian; previous school attended; a photograph no more than one year old of each student; and the name, address and phone number of an emergency person, designated by the legal guardian, who would be able to offer assistance if the legal guardian cannot be contacted. Other information that would prove valuable in an emergency is the name and address, of the family physician or minister, priest, rabbi, or other spiritual leader.

Other information that would be valuable in the event of problems includes fingerprints, descriptions, shortcomings of vision, speech, or hearing, and other characteristics, including hair and eye color, birthmarks, or moles. But it would be unrealistic to expect schools to maintain all this information, and some of it is not even permitted in certain jurisdictions.

ADDITIONAL ANTIKIDNAP STRATEGIES

Employers can be of tremendous assistance to police investigating kidnappings by keeping confidential files of personal information about each executive. Such files should be available to designated company officers, including the security officer, at all times, including weekends and holidays. Each file should include the following information:

- Name of the executive (and nickname if applicable)
- Home address(es) and telephone number(s)
- Spouse's and children's names and nicknames
- Addresses and phone numbers of children's schools
- Name, address, and telephone number of spouse's employer
- Names, addresses, and telephone numbers of the family's nearest neighbors on all sides
- Family cars—year, make, color, license number, name of person who usually drives each car
- Domestic employees—names, addresses, telephone numbers, hours of employment
- Regular social activities of each family member—with name, location, telephone, and also the number of any person who could give information about such activities
- Current color photo of each member of the family
- Description of clothing usually worn
- Medication required regularly by members of the family

DEALING WITH THE PRESS

After a kidnapping occurs, the press will no doubt be seeking information as soon as the police are notified. While being as cooperative as possible, be sure not to release information that could jeopardize hostages or witnesses or hamper the police investigation. Only you, or a specifically designated alternate, should speak to reporters, who should be asked firmly but politely to protect the identities of any witnesses. The press should not be permitted to enter the home or office or to examine the scene of the abduction.

Appropriate information to release might include name, age, and relationship of the victim; time and method of the kidnapping; if the police concur, a description of the kidnappers; valuables or other items stolen in conjunction with the kidnapping; and victim's illnesses or required medication. Don't say a word about the names and addresses of witnesses; serial numbers or denominations of any ransom money; cash or other valuables overlooked by the kidnappers; or details of any security procedures that the kidnappers overcame, whether or not they were in use at the time.

STRATEGIES FOR THE KIDNAP VICTIM

If you yourself are kidnapped, there are a number of things you can do that may save your life. Remember the previous instructions for crisis situations: take a moment to compose yourself; consider your plan; then act on your plan.

Above all, stay calm. Don't threaten anybody. Kidnappers may well be mentally unbalanced, perhaps dangerous psychotics, so don't push them into anything rash. Never fight physically with your abductors—they have probably planned your abduction carefully and will have sufficient manpower to handle you. If your abductors direct you to talk to someone—your spouse or employer, for example—don't attempt heroics.

Cooperate with your abductors as well as you can, but do not tell them what actions might be taken by your family or employer. Assume that you will get out of this situation alive and that everyone connected with your abduction—family, police, and the FBI—is, first and foremost, working with that objective in mind. Recovery of ransoms or apprehension of offenders is a secondary consideration until the victim is returned safe and sound.

Upon your release, you can best see that justice is served by providing detailed information to the police. So try to determine where you are and to remember everything you can about your abductors and their methods.

In today's political climate, your kidnappers will in all likelihood be young idealists, probably more interested in furthering their cause than in obtaining a ransom. Their commitment may lead to taking risks that a more prudent person would find unacceptable.

Having thoroughly researched you, and having spent a great deal of time in planning the abduction, they will not give you much opportunity to escape. They will transport you to a previously prepared location, designed for the purpose of holding you as long as they see fit. You will almost certainly be prevented from knowing where you are being taken, and it is quite possible that you will be forced to make part of the journey in an automobile trunk.

Particularly if you are held in a dark car trunk, you will require all your concentration and attention to avoid panic. One helpful tactic would be to gather as much information as your confinement will allow. Utilize which of your five senses are available to you. Hypothesize where you might be going. You will be able to hear and detect odors, and once you are released, these might be of importance in finding those responsible.

And the odds are great that you will be released. Nine out of ten kidnap victims are. If you have the opportunity to leave evidence at the kidnap site (a monogrammed pencil or a business card, for example), you may provide the information that will ultimately result in your freedom. If you are caught in your duplicity, however, it may prove unfortunate. But you are valuable currency to the kidnappers, so there is the distinct possibility that your life will be spared, as long as you represent monetary or idealistic value to them.

Keep your mind active. Attempt to keep track of time. Even if you are unable to see outside, you may be able to differentiate night from day by temperature patterns or the apparent mealtimes of your captors.

Personalize your area of captivity. Keep your space clean, and insofar as you are permitted, yourself as well. Designate part of your space as a bedroom and sleep there; eat only in your "dining room." If your captors permit you to have the personal items from your billfold, display snapshots of your family.

THE STOCKHOLM SYNDROME

Finally, the time will come when you will no longer be a captive. You may escape, you may be ransomed, your captors may be diverted to more important activities, or you may be freed by the police. Far from being relieved by the end of your captivity, you may experience extraordinary reactions. Quite possibly, you will find yourself viewing your captors as your allies, and the police as a threat.

Remember the interesting circumstance of a newspaper heiress who was taken hostage. After not being heard from for some time, she was suddenly back in the news, allegedly participating in a bank robbery and admitting being involved in a personal relationship with one of her erstwhile captors. This is a frequent reaction following a prolonged period of captivity. This set of phenomena is termed the Stockholm

Syndrome, after the effects observed in 1973 among a group of hostages released from a five-and-a-half day siege following a failed bank robbery in Stockholm, Sweden.

Often hostages will be released to reporters or other representatives of the media. Sometimes, the newly released captive will make unfortunate statements, praising the assailants and criticizing the law enforcement personnel who were responsible for the release. Again, this is a manifestation of the peculiar psychological reactions of kidnap victims.

SPECIAL ANTIKIDNAPPING STRATEGIES FOR BANKERS

A kidnapping or extortion plot involving a bank or a banker requires special handling. If hostages are taken and the banker is brought to the bank by a criminal, do not trip the alarm. Instead, a prearranged signal—indicating that an extortion is in progress—should be given to another employee. This signal should be well rehearsed and so disguised that the criminal will not be able to intercept it.

The employee recognizing the extortion signal should immediately contact police or the FBI and give them the address of the hostage's family. If this cannot be reported safely while the criminal is in the bank, it should be done immediately after the criminal and hostage leave.

All employees aware of the extortion signal should follow bank robbery procedures regarding observation, preservation of fingerprints, and so on (see Chapter 28).

Ransom money should be paid as directed by the criminal, making certain that decoy money is included. After ransom money is paid, a much higher amount should be publicized, because this will often provoke dissension among gang members.

Kidnap/Extortion Problems: A Checklist

1. If an extortion call is received:
   a. Stay calm.
   b. Tape or take notes of the conversation.
   c. Attempt to have the call traced.
   d. Cooperate with the caller.
   e. Have all instructions repeated, even if you understand.
   f. Repeat the instructions.
   g. Keep the caller on the line as long as possible.
   h. Ask pertinent questions to assure that the hostage is, in fact, being held.
   i. Speak to the hostage if possible.

    j. Determine what, how much, and to whom payoff is to be made.

    k. If possible, arrange simultaneous exchange of ransom and hostage.

2. After the call is received:

    a. Notify the police and the FBI, regardless of the caller's instructions to the contrary.

    b. Keep all the details of the call secret except from family and police authorities.

    c. If a letter, rather than a phone call, was the means of demand, do not handle it unnecessarily.

    d. Do not disturb the scene of abduction.

    e. Maintain normal routines insofar as possible.

    f. Trust the law enforcement officers involved, and cooperate completely. Their primary concern is the safety of the victim.

3. Have a form handy to help you to obtain as much information as possible from the extortion call.

4. Arrange signals to advise that an extortion call is in progress.

5. Guard against the release of personal information.

6. Be alert to strangers.

7. Always advise someone when you are to be expected, but not in such a manner that this information might be compromised.

8. Vary your daily routines, so that you do not establish regular behavioral patterns.

9. Refuse to meet strangers at remote or unfamiliar locations.

10. Do not leave children alone in the home. Leave them in the care of trustworthy people.

11. Teach children good security habits.

12. Avoid obvious indications that children may be at home alone.

13. Be careful about children en route to and from school.

14. Work for secure practices at your children's schools.

15. Maintain personal information files.

16. Don't release information to the press until the kidnapping victim is returned. If this is impractical, release only information approved by the police.

17. If you are a kidnap victim, cooperate, and remain calm. Do not offer your abductors information, but gather all details that might assist in their apprehension and recovery of any ransom after your release.

18. Remember to keep your mind active, keep track of time, and concentrate on details.
19. Upon release, refrain from praising the assailants and criticizing the law enforcement officers responsible for your release.
20. In kidnap/extortion threats involving bankers:
    a. Don't trip the alarm if there are hostages.
    b. Signal so that the police and FBI can be notified.
    c. Don't disturb evidence.
    d. Include bait money with the ransom.

38
Overseas Travel

Motivation, health, linguistic ability, and family circum-
stances—these are some of the traditional criteria multina-
tional corporations consider when screening candidates for
overseas positions. Today, a new criterion, the psychological
ability to cope as a hostage . . . may be equally critical.
—Management Review *(January 1981)*

Travel abroad is not what it used to be. These days you may be greeted overseas with shouting, jeering, anti-Yankee slogans, verbal and physical harassment, even threats on your life. Increases in terrorism, violence, and crime dictate that you must be prepared for any contingency. Careful preparation and common sense are your most important weapons.

PRECAUTIONS

The ordinary traveler should avoid known trouble spots and be familiar with any problems in a particular region. A list of countries dangerous for Americans may be obtained from the State Department or your local passport office. A travel agency or airline can provide additional information, but it may not be precise and up-to-date.

Information you should try to gather includes the frequency of terrorist acts against U.S. installations or businesses, whether American travelers have been attacked or threatened, and whether an active propaganda campaign exists in the underground press. Talk to travelers who have recently returned from the area, and ask about such things as demonstrations, strikes, and threats.

Language Problems

Don't assume that wherever you travel someone will be able to communicate with you in your own language. Learn at least enough of the local language to be able to ask for assistance, report a crime, and find out if your language is spoken. Portable dual-language dictionaries can be helpful. If you need help with the language, be sure you obtain it from a trustworthy individual.

Some of the people you encounter, though quite fluent in your language, will act as if they have no idea of what you are saying. Some do this simply to be difficult. For reasons of their own, they dislike Americans, and they are merely being contrary. Others, though, want you to speak English very much, particularly if you are with another who is speaking your language. Still others pretend not to comprehend in order to lull you into a false confidence that you can speak English without being understood. If you are bargaining with a foreign shopkeeper and at the same time discussing prices in English with a companion, you may be undermining your bargaining position. You almost certainly will end up having paid more than you should.

Automobiles and Driving Regulations

Driving regulations and traffic laws in other countries often differ substantially from those in the United States. One American tourist was involved in a routine accident in Mexico and was detained in jail for months while investigation and proceedings were completed.

Find out as much as possible about local traffic rules and regulations, and make sure you are adequately insured and have the correct papers. Personnel managing border-crossing points can be particularly helpful regarding this kind of information.

Choose an inconspicuous car, and do not display any identifying information such as corporate names or distinctive license plates. Don't put your name on a reserved parking place.

Money

As is the case when you do any traveling, you are faced when going overseas with the necessity of carrying more cash than you feel comfortable with. Be sure to use traveler's checks, and don't keep all your money in one place. It's a good idea to keep your funds and important papers in at least a couple of safe places so that if one stash is wiped out, you are not completely helpless.

Be familiar with the exchange rates and physical appearance of any foreign currencies you are likely to handle. Also, don't exchange your money for local currency on the street or at your hotel. Go to a bank for this purpose.

Accommodations

Your hotel can be a citadel when you're away from home, or it can be a trap. Look for accommodations in the middle of things, where you can blend into your surroundings. The availability and response time of police services are necessary considerations. The size of a hotel is important—in general, bigger is better, certainly for anonymity. The staff of the hotel—particularly at night—is important, as is the clientele. The staff should be large enough to provide a modicum of protection, and the clientele should not include an all-night procession of hookers, drug pushers, and other undesirables. The composition and capability of the hotel's security staff—as well as the screening procedures for prospective employees—are something that, if possible, you should determine in advance.

Most important, consider the construction of the building. Look for a hotel with few entrances, and with entrances that are constantly monitored. The section of sleeping-room floors should be defensible. Fire escapes should let you out but no one else in, and doors and windows should be secure against undesired entry. Ideally, you should select a hotel room on the fourth through seventh floors. In all likelihood, this would place you high enough to avoid most of the street noise. A more important consideration is your safety. In the event of fire, your only means of escape could be out the window of your sleeping room. The aerial ladders used by fire departments rarely reach heights higher than the seventh floor of a new hotel. In older structures with high ceilings, the fifth or sixth floor might be safer for you.

IN A FOREIGN LAND

Once you have settled in, try to befriend local residents who can apprise you of the political situation and its dangers. Register with the nearest American consulate or mission. If there is no American representation, contact the embassy or consulate of the country designated to handle U.S. interests. In the event of an emergency, such as sudden evacuation or riot, these contacts could be vital; more usual assistance includes replacement of lost passports, cables home in case of illness, and resolution of minor communication problems.

Ordinarily American representatives will not make travel arrangements, replace airline tickets, lend funds to stranded travelers, or, more significantly, intervene with local law enforcement officials. You must abide by the law of the host country, and if you get into trouble, you will be judged according to local law. Your U.S. representatives will be limited in power and influence, but they can arrange for representation by a local attorney, and they will notify your family of your plight.

Beware of Drugs

Drug laws in foreign countries can be very severe. Avoid drugs, addicts, or pushers at all costs. It is estimated that about 1,600 Americans are in foreign jails, one-half on drug charges. Most are males under thirty. Many have been detained for long periods without trials, in primitive and unsanitary facilities. A conviction on charges of drug use or trafficking abroad could result in a long prison term and even a death sentence.

Third World and Soviet Bloc Countries

Be particularly careful when visiting Third World countries or nations with Communist leanings. These countries often prohibit actions that we take for granted. For example, there may be strict bans on taking pictures in certain areas. Authorities may arrest or harass travelers who violate these rules.

Third World countries can be especially difficult. There may be customs officials or local police who like to throw their weight around. The best advice is to be careful and use common sense. Be aware of the sensitive nationalism of Third World officials, and assume that they are going to be more sensitive than many Americans would be in similar circumstances.

Ground Transportation

Ground transportation in many overseas destinations is more modern, reliable, and functional than in the United States. Except in the Greater New York City area and a very few other locations, privately owned transportation is the principal American means of getting from one place to another.

In Europe and most of Asia, mass transportation carries the bulk of the load. Because they are the main means of getting from place to place, overseas transport systems often have amenities that are unavailable or less available in the United States. This is particularly true for the disabled traveler. A journalist involved in advancement for the physically disabled has been quoted as saying that travel for the disabled is much easier in Europe because more money is spent there to provide technologically advanced transportation for them.

Sending Postcards Home

In some places, it is more difficult than one would imagine to send postcards home. A syndicated columnist received a letter from a reader who mailed a large number of postcards from Brazil. Not one of them was delivered to its destination. Apparently the mail personnel removed the stamps from the cards and cashed them.

Fortunately, other locations have better delivery records. Costs of mailing a postcard vary considerably. However, in 1987 it cost twenty-three cents to mail a postcard to the United States from Mexico. Sending a card from Canada costs thirty-two cents; England, forty-two cents; West Germany, forty-eight cents; Italy or Spain, fifty-three cents; France, fifty-six cents; and Japan, seventy cents.

THE BUSINESS TRAVELER

The business traveler, especially the executive, must be careful, because he or she is particularly vulnerable to acts of terrorism. The business executive must practice all the general tips for the typical overseas traveler, but in addition, special precautions must be taken because corporate officers are special targets for terrorists.

The first precaution is to maintain a low profile. Do not broadcast your travel plans and itinerary. Provide information about your schedule only on a need-to-know basis. Some executives visiting a hostile country may even travel under assumed or modified names and make reservations in several hotels. Try to avoid repetitious patterns, and vary the days, hours, and routes you take. Plan your trip carefully to minimize the time you actually spend in the foreign country. Prepare your itinerary carefully, and give it to a trusted colleague or to a member of your family. In case of an emergency, this information will be helpful in locating you, and it may even save your life.

Avoid shady establishments, including seedy hotels and restaurants. Do not leave valuable papers in your hotel room; check them into the hotel safe or a safe-deposit box. Avoid rooms on the first floor or those easily accessible from the outside. Try your best not to be paged. Avoid traveling alone, especially at nighttime, unless it is absolutely necessary; try to travel in a group. Your luggage should not display your name, home address, or company logo, although the company address is usually all right. Finally, do not display large sums of money or expensive jewelry.

Overseas Travel: A Checklist

1. Avoid known trouble spots.
2. Prepare all necessary precautionary measures before you travel to an area.
3. Register with the American consulate or mission.
4. Abide by all laws of the host country.
5. Learn enough of the local language to be able to ask for assistance or report a crime.
6. Learn local traffic laws before driving in a foreign country.
7. Be familiar with local exchange rates and the physical appearance of foreign currency. Traveler's checks are safer than cash.
8. Select a hotel with adequate security.
9. Avoid drugs, drug abusers, and drug sellers.
10. Be particularly cautious in Third World countries or nations with Communist ties.
11. Be sure to have a valid passport; record its number in a separate place, and bring along a copy of your birth certificate.
12. The business executive should maintain a low profile.
13. Do not advertise your itinerary and schedule.
14. Avoid taking the same route each day at the same hour.
15. Leave your itinerary with a member of your family or a trusted colleague.
16. Avoid shady establishments, including seedy hotels and restaurants.
17. Never leave valuable papers in your hotel room.
18. Avoid rooms that are easily accessible from the outside.
19. Avoid being paged.
20. Try not to travel at night, especially without a companion.
21. Your luggage should not advertise your name, home address, or company.
22. Do not show large sums of money or expensive jewelry.

39
Bombs and Bomb Threats

Five years after Sinclair Larchmont was killed by a bomb that had been placed under his automobile, the authorities say they will never be absolutely sure of the motive for his killing.

Bombings are by far the most common incidents perpetrated by terrorists. About two-thirds of all terrorist attacks employed explosive or incendiary bombing devices. Bombings and bomb threats are occurring with ever greater frequency. In New York City in 1981, after a bomb had exploded at La Guardia Airport, 170 bomb threats in all types of locations were recorded in a single day. The most common targets are private residences and commercial buildings, although bombs have also been exploded in crowded office buildings, banks, post offices, apartment houses, cars, schools, jammed streets, and even police stations.

Bombs do not discriminate among victims and usually injure more innocent bystanders than intended targets. According to the FBI, 30 persons died and 133 were injured as a result of 1,142 bombings in a recent year. Property losses were more than $67 million. This figure omits the losses resulting from irrecoverable working hours and the psychological damage to the victims.

BOMB PRECAUTIONS

Be on your guard for suspicious-looking packages, objects, or people that do not belong in an area. If you spot an unusual parcel or similar item, do not touch it. Call the police, the fire department, or the company security force, and then—from a safe distance—warn others about the possible danger.

Look for unusual objects or wires before unlocking or opening the door of your car. Be alert for anything unusual or out of the ordinary, such as the hood of your car's being slightly ajar or a window left open when you know you closed it. Another step you can take to protect yourself is to examine photographs of common bombs.

THE BUSINESS EXECUTIVE

A businessperson needs additional protection. It is imperative that you maintain a low profile. Do not display your name in building directories, on mailboxes, or in any other place accessible to the public. Have an unlisted telephone number. Never display your name or title on a reserved parking space.

Your car should not stand out. Simple, typical, nondescript standard-model cars are preferable to conspicuous limousines with protective gear. Your vehicle should not display corporate logos, distinctive license plates, or other types of identification.

Ninety percent of terrorist attacks take place while the intended victim is in an automobile. A firm that specializes in arming vehicles for high-profile, high-risk individuals increased its business by more than 375 percent in two years. Arming an automobile can save money for the executive who is paying costly ransom insurance premiums. One major international insurance broker provides such discounts. But even an armored car will prove ineffective unless you practice other standard precautions to reduce your vulnerability. Look for occupied vehicles parked nearby, check to see if you are being followed, and lock your car after each use.

MAIL BOMBS

A mail bomb (also called a letter bomb) is a favorite implement of fear utilized by certain terrorist groups. While other bombs are undiscriminating, the mail bomb is quite discriminating. It is usually addressed to one individual, who is quite likely to suffer injury, sometimes even death.

Several years ago, two such bombs were delivered in London, apparently the work of the same person or organization. One was addressed to the prime minister, the other to the U.S. Navy's European headquarters, also located in London. The Navy headquarters bomb detonated, slightly injuring a Navy petty officer. The bomb addressed to Prime Minister Thatcher was defused without incident. However, a similarly addressed bomb did explode several months earlier, slightly injuring an aide.

Not all letter bombs are as benign as these examples. In 1973, an

Israeli attaché in London received a parcel slightly smaller but thicker than an ordinary envelope. When opened, it detonated. The force of the explosion destroyed the desk at which the attaché was seated. Splinters, some of substantial size, flew throughout the room like shrapnel. A number of these missiles struck the attaché, causing severe bleeding. Shortly thereafter, he died. Three or four ounces of what was believed to be plastic explosive were sufficient to take that man's life.

The insidious nature of a postal bomb is that one person may murder another from halfway around the world, at little more expense than the price of a stamp.

MAIL-SCREENING PROCEDURES

Any unusual mail situation is worthy of caution. Look for the following clues that something is amiss:

- Foreign mail, airmail, and special delivery
- Restrictive markings ("confidential," "personal," etc.)
- Excessive postage
- Poor handwriting, sloppy typing, or unusual handwriting style
- Incorrect titles or titles used alone without names
- Misspelled names or words
- Oily stains on the envelope or package (which may be caused by explosives)
- No return address
- An excessively heavy, rigid, or thick envelope
- Envelopes that are uneven or lopsided
- Unevenly distributed weight
- Extreme amount of masking tape or string on the envelope
- Mail with an unusual odor
- Sealed enclosure within the outer mailing envelope
- Damaged pieces of mail
- Any unusual occurrence or peculiarity

These precautions are equally applicable to home or office. Large companies may check all mail carefully with electronic scanning devices.

If you spot a suspicious-looking piece of mail, don't touch or move it; leave it alone. Open all windows and doors in order to reduce the effects of any blast. Notify the police or security personnel, leave the room, and don't return to your home or office until it is absolutely safe to do so.

Bomb threats are complicated problems that often require the advice and expertise of trained consultants.

Bombs and Bomb Threats: A Checklist

1. Be on guard for any suspicious-looking packages; they may contain bombs.
2. Call the police or fire department if you suspect a bomb.
3. Warn all people nearby of the danger.
4. Examine your car for unusual objects, wires, or any peculiarities before opening the door.
5. Examine photographs of bombs to familiarize yourself with this danger.
6. Keep a low profile if you are an executive or another likely target for a bomb. Keep telephone numbers unlisted, and don't call attention to your car or parking space.
7. Learn how to screen suspicious-looking mail.
8. Do not touch or move suspicious-looking mail.
9. In buildings, open all windows and doors to minimize the impact of the explosion.
10. Evacuate the building as quickly as possible.
11. Notify the police without delay.

40
Terrorism

On a routine business trip to Central America, Mr. Bernard Collins was invited to dinner at one of the cities' finest restaurants. The group never finished its meal. Terrorists avenging the death of a comrade by government security agents machine-gunned the executives, killing them.

TERRORISM IS ON THE INCREASE

No one knows with certainty the rate of incidence of terrorist acts, but it is certainly growing quite rapidly. FBI statistics estimate that acts of international terrorism in this country and in U.S. overseas installations are increasing. According to a recent U.S. government statement, international terrorist incidents surged from 500 in 1981 to approximately 800 in 1985, an increase of 60 percent. In 1986 more than eighty nations experienced terrorist attacks, resulting in nearly 2,000 casualties.

The U.S. Department of State's Office for Combating Terrorism provides this breakdown of terrorist attacks against the United States and its citizens. Of almost one thousand incidents over five years, 47 percent were bombing attacks. It is important to realize that these included the attack on the U.S. Marines barracks in Beirut and the attack on the U.S. Embassy in Kuwait. Almost 260 persons perished in these two incidents alone.

In a recent year, most of the terrorist attacks against U.S. citizens, 46 percent, occurred in Western Europe. Latin America was the site of the next most frequent attacks against the country, 29 percent of the total. Other areas in which Americans were attacked by terrorists were the Middle East (13 percent), Asia/Pacific (9 percent), and sub-Saharan

Africa and North America, which were tied at 1.5 percent each.

Of these attacks, bombings were the most frequent, followed by arson, armed attack, kidnapping, hostage taking, assassination attempts, sabotage, vandalism, theft, extortion, harassment, intimidation, and hijacking.

AIRCRAFT HIJACKINGS

Since 1931, when statistics were first assembled, 151 successful hijackings of U.S. aircraft have occurred. Seventy-nine percent of the hijackers were taken to Cuba. As a result of the stringent passenger preboarding procedures initiated by the airlines, these hijackings all but ceased.

But events of the last several years have proved that the airliner is still a favorite target of the terrorist. Once you have boarded a plane, you become a potential target of any terrorists aboard. With a little advice, however, and a lot of common sense, you may be able to avoid the terrorist's wrath.

AVOID TARGETING YOURSELF

Actually, your exposure to peril begins well before you board the plane. When you awaken on the morning of your departure, you must begin your antiterrorist routine. You should appear and deport yourself in such a manner that you become "invisible." Your appearance should be as nearly like that of the other passengers as possible.

At the same time, avoid looking "American." You shouldn't wear your Princeton sweatshirt or your Hard Rock Cafe T-shirt. Nor should you wear diamonds on every finger. Looking like a Wall Street investment banker could increase the amount of your ransom.

In short, avoid anything in your appearance that would attract attention. Just blend into the background. You will wish to avoid being confused with a hippie or a punk rocker. On the other hand, your hair should be long enough that you won't be confused with a military person traveling in civilian clothes.

A travel agent, the State Department, or the consulate of the nation you are visiting will be able to advise you of what you may anticipate in that country. You will probably wish to avoid national holidays that focus on great military victories—or on humiliations, too, for that matter.

If you travel extensively throughout the world, you will have a passport full of visas. Someone might think you are an espionage agent. After several pages are filled, you should get a new passport. You must appear to be what you are, a harmless tourist.

Military personnel on leave overseas should obtain a passport and use it rather than a military ID for identification. Remember, in one hijacking, the only casualty was an American military man in uniform.

Write down your passport number, the issuing office, and its expiration date. Place a copy in your billfold and in your baggage. Use your office address and telephone number on baggage and for hotel registration.

Before departure, you will want to make certain that you have left behind a detailed itinerary; make certain your affairs are in order, just in case. If your insurance coverage does not cover you overseas, add that protection.

If possible, avoid airlines flying the flags of nations involved in hostilities, or noncombatant nations supporting those which are at war.

Your bags should be locked and free of travel stickers. A bag is easily opened, so the locking will not protect you from a determined thief, but knowing that the bag had been forced could warn you that someone had planted a bomb there.

Carry only your passport, credit cards, and a driver's license in your purse or billfold. A little money, of course, is also necessary, but remember to change your U.S. currency to local money as quickly as is practical. In addition to branding you as an American, your dollars may place you in danger of arrest for violating laws forbidding possession of foreign currency.

Proceed through the passenger screening checkpoint as soon as possible after arriving at the airport. Spend as little time as possible in airline ticket areas, cocktail lounges, preboarding screening areas, departure gates, and anywhere in the terminal that is adjacent to large plate-glass windows. These areas are either favorites for terrorist attack, or are likely to be high-injury locations in the event of explosion or gunfire. The various airline club lounges offer excellent services. In addition to the convenience of a restful place to wait, these clubs usually provide another level of passenger screening, an important consideration for a potential terrorist victim.

Once in the aircraft, you will have sufficient time to carefully examine the immediate area of your seat. Check the seat pockets, and look under your seat cushion, in the overhead storage bins, or anywhere else that explosives or firearms could be concealed.

In the air, avoid intense, serious discussions, particularly of religion or politics. Napping or reading is a much less provocative way to spend time. And, if it should happen that one of the passengers on your flight is to be marked for execution, it probably won't be the innocuous, "invisible" man or woman.

Once at your destination, get your bag handler to find a taxi for you rather than trying to do it yourself. Blending in with other travelers is the ideal camouflage. When you arrive at your hotel, don't let your baggage out of sight. First of all, something may not be there when you need it, and on the other hand, something may *be* there that you most certainly don't want to be there—a bomb, for example.

Request a hotel room at the back of the building away from the main entrances. Ideally, your room should be no higher than the seventh floor, this being about the highest an aerial rescue ladder can reach.

Your hotel can be a safer place if you will do a few little things. Leave your room neat and orderly. If your possessions are disturbed, you should be able to notice the difference, and this will put you on your guard. If you leave a TV or radio playing when you leave, it is likely that you will have no uninvited visitors. They'll assume you are in for the evening. If you avoid Americanized bars and restaurants, you will certainly be safer, probably will spend less, and will be able to enjoy the authentic local cuisine.

If you feel the need to relax with a cigarette after enjoying your meal, make certain it is a local brand. In this particular instance, cigarette smoking could be decidedly hazardous to your health, for your smoking preference could easily identify you as a stranger.

JAMES BOND ARSENAL

The average traveler doesn't have access to the special superspy arsenal available to upper-level executives. Some sophisticated devices include a pocket fountain pen that signals in the presence of hidden bugging devices, a portable scrambler for telephone conversations, a bomb sniffer, a high-intensity flashlight that blinds an attacker for fourteen hours, sophisticated transmitters that fit into a wallet or a watch, a laser gun that can record human speech from the vibrations made on glass windows, an electronic handkerchief that can transform a man's voice into a woman's, and a briefcase that can filter out background noises like those of trains and airplanes.

Most terrorist attacks are made against automobiles, so the trip to the terminal should be made as inconspicuous as possible. Avoid a commercial travel agency, unless you have conducted a recent and thorough investigation of all of the firm's personnel.

A personal (or spouse's personal) credit card, rather than a company card, would be a more secure means of paying for airline tickets. Cash is even more secure. Avoid mentioning your firm's name or your position to others traveling with you.

Vary your routes to and from frequently visited cities, just as you vary your driving route to and from work. It's also a good idea to travel tourist class.

Terrorism: A Checklist

1. To avoid being a target of terrorism, appear and deport yourself in such a manner that you become "invisible." Act and dress like other travelers, avoid looking American, and blend in with the local population.
2. Before making the trip, leave a detailed itinerary with someone you trust.
3. Carry only your passport, credit cards, and a driver's license.
4. Spend as little time as possible in airport areas accessible to the public. Airline club lounges offer good security and excellent services.
5. Once in the aircraft, fully examine the immediate areas of your seat for explosives, bombs, or firearms.
6. Avoid intense discussions with other passengers. Topics to avoid include religion and politics.
7. Avoid bars and restaurants that Americans or other visitors frequent.
8. Thoroughly investigate the accommodations you will use while traveling.
9. Avoid use of travel agencies, as a general rule.
10. Use cash or a personal, rather than company, credit card for travel tickets. Consider tourist-class travel.
11. Take care in disclosing personal data to other travelers.
12. Vary travel routes and flights to make your travel plans less predictable.

41
Computer Crime

A board of education computer programmer was recently arrested and charged with using the school computers to create a racetrack betting system.

If noted bank robber Willie Suttom were still plying his trade today, he would be a computer criminal. Why? For the same reason that he robbed banks in days past: because "that's where the money is."

Anyone with access to a computer can commit a computer crime. Recently, a prisoner serving a thirty-year sentence for embezzlement tampered with computer records at the state penitentiary in order to get an early release. The prisoner also managed to use the institution's computer system to sell 100,000 pounds of cotton grown at the prison for $20,000. The proceeds went to friends of the inmate.

THE COST OF COMPUTER CRIME

According to government experts, the average computer crime nets nearly $500,000. The traditional embezzler, stealing from a manually maintained set of books, nets only about $20,000. Bank robbers, by comparison, do little better than $10,000 for the serious risks they take of being shot.

Computer-related activities employ perhaps ten million people, a number that is certain to increase as time passes. In addition, in all types of offices and businesses today, it is not unusual to have desk after desk bearing personal computers. And there are likely to be many other larger computers that the outsider never sees, linked to these by telephone lines.

Through such networks, these millions of computer-savvy people could conceivably gain access to the contents of a firm's central com-

357

puter and the valuable files it holds. For a few thousand dollars, these individuals can purchase a home computer identical to the one they use at work. The central computer cannot tell where a message is coming from, only that the access codes are proper. By equipping their home computer with a telephone link, these people could possibly gain access to the computer's information and assets for questionable or illegal purposes.

Certainly the firm will have initiated security measures to protect against the loss of its intellectual and tangible assets. But what if the computer whiz is more sophisticated than the measures used to protect the integrity of the system?

Far-fetched? Not in the least. Several years ago, separate groups of teenagers were able to gain access to data in a number of computers throughout the country. They introduced the term *computer hacker* into the general vocabulary. In a relatively short time, they entered more than sixty systems, where they read files, scanned individual medical records, destroyed data, used long-distance telephone lines free, and even "paid" one person's hospital bill. In the fall of 1987, a group of European hobbyists were able to enter a NASA scientific network, where they spent three months sifting through the files. These hackers confessed their activities, but only after they had reason to believe that they were on the verge of being discovered. A communiqué issued by the group indicated that they had become involved in "industrial espionage, economic crime, East-West conflict, Comecon embargoes, and the legitimate security interests of high-tech institutions."

COMPUTER CRIMINAL PROFILE

Studies show that the typical computer criminal is eighteen to thirty years of age, bright, and highly motivated. This person views crime as a challenge and the computer and company as impersonal objects. Computer criminals are likely to be well dressed, courteous, ambitious, and hardworking—unfortunately, not with the best interests of their employers in mind.

COMPUTER ABUSE TECHNIQUES

There are an unbelievable number of ways that a computer can be criminally abused. A partial list follows.

Sabotage is one of the easiest ways to attack a computer system. Disgruntled programmers, supervisors, clerks, competitors, political extremists, or terrorists may attempt to destroy the main physical parts of the system or critical circuitry or programs. The sabotage may be executed by use of explosion, fire, excessive water, or simply sophisticated programming.

A new form of sabotage is computer "viruses" that, like their biological counterparts, can infect computers and destroy their programs. A virus may be created by a programmer who writes a code that modifies a part of the system software. These viruses are highly contagious in the sense that they easily pass to other computer systems, destroying all their programs. You may protect your computer from viruses by utilizing only software or programs with which you are thoroughly familiar. Never copy any software unless you know and trust its source. These procedures should be effective, because viruses depend upon software for propagation.

Theft of computer services is extremely common. Persons may use the computer at someone else's expense. A programmer may have a private business on the side and have the computer mail out his or her bills, for example.

Computers may be programmed to steal property from the company. The programmer may direct the computer to place orders for merchandise and direct it to be sent to a planned location. Similarly, a programmer might order the computer to transfer negligible amounts from each transaction to his or her own account.Computer personnel may simply steal data in the form of computer programs or output. This may involve copying printouts, programs, mailing lists, or other data that would be of interest to a competitor.

Of course, computers can be used for much more sophisticated theft, such as complex financial swindles. False companies can be established, or misleading information can be provided to investors.

The problem with computer security is that there are many ways to penetrate a system without detection. The computer is particularly vulnerable to electronic penetration. Wiretaps and bugs can gather information from lines serving the computer. The list is endless.

EMPLOYEE SCREENING

Basic safeguards to assure at least a minimum of protection for a computer system include careful procedures for screening employees. Determine character and integrity as well as an applicant's technical qualifications. In-depth interviews, background checks, and fingerprinting are valuable aids for employees who will have access to secured or sensitive information or software.

DIVISION OF RESPONSIBILITY

Set up procedures for a division of responsibilities. No one person should have access to all areas, nor should one programmer have authority to run and modify programs that access sensitive files. A computer operator should not serve as a programmer, nor should a systems manager work as an operator. Rotation of personnel is also helpful. Suspicious interruptions of the day-to-day computer operation should be logged.

COMPUTER CENTER ACCESS

Access to the mainframe computer system or sensitive data by employees should be limited to authorized personnel and only on a need-to-know basis. All personnel should be given identification badges.

Public tours should be kept a reasonable distance from the equipment to minimize the chance of accidental or malicious damage. Logs recording the time of each visitor's entry and departure should be maintained. Overcoats, luggage, and briefcases should not be allowed in the computer area.

A course in computer security should be a requirement of all employees who have to implement these procedures.

UNAMBIGUOUS POLICIES

All instructions to personnel should be in writing. This will reduce errors in communications. An annual security briefing should be required for all employees. This not only serves as a refresher course but also demonstrates in a highly tangible way that your company is concerned about computer security and that it will not tolerate abusive practices.

Formulate a code of ethics for people working with computer systems and software, and establish penalties for violators. A written code of ethics is an excellent preventive step for a dishonest employee who may argue, "I did not know that 'playing' with the computer was against company policy."

PHYSICAL SECURITY

Your main computer facilities should have good physical security. This includes locks, guard systems, alarms, adequate lighting, and few windows. The facilities should be in a relatively isolated area.

The computer facility should be constructed of waterproof and fire-resistant materials and have flood-control devices. Materials made out of wood, for example, should be avoided whenever possible.

A complete security audit and review should be conducted at least once a year. This should include identification of assets and an analysis of vulnerability.

DISASTER PLANS

Disaster recovery plans should be established and periodically tested. Experience shows that even a minimum of training and drilling may prevent a disaster.

You should develop a backup system in case the primary computer system fails. This system should include alternate power sources and alternate computer equipment.

Use special computer safes to store computer tapes, disks, and print-outs. Arrange off-site storage facilities for backup tapes and disks. These facilities should be fire-resistant and waterproof. Emergency shutdown and recovery procedures for quick start-up should be developed well in advance. This should include practice alerts and dry runs through the emergency procedures.

MANAGEMENT RESPONSIBILITY

Computer security should be the responsibility of management. Periodic rotation of managers will discourage fraudulent schemes and make the job more interesting.

ELECTRONIC PROTECTION

Electronic security devices should be utilized—including closed-circuit television systems to prevent placing electronic bugs. Also carry out physical inspections for listening and other interception devices.

CODES AND PASSWORDS

Security codes, passwords, scramblers, and cryptographic devices should be used to screen out unauthorized users and increase computer security. All codes and passwords must be changed periodically without the user's taking any initiative to do so.

REMOTE TERMINALS AND NETWORKS

Use of remote terminals and networks may be limited by special computer programs. Develop special programs to block unauthorized personnel from using remote and inactive terminals. Prevent employees from accessing your firm's central files and also outside telephone lines from the same terminal or personal computer.

DISPOSAL AND STORAGE

Prepare plans for disposal of stored information, printouts, records, tapes, and disks. Paper shredders and burning procedures are recommended.

Arrange for special computer insurance, because regular insurance policies usually are inadequate for computer protection. Study all legal aspects that may arise as a result of the computer system. This includes computer contracts, leasing, privacy matters, and trade secrets.

HOME COMPUTERS

As mentioned earlier, a telephone link can make it possible to access the office computer system from home. When employees must access a computer from off-site locations by calling on modems (telephone links), password protection can be assured by using callback modems or by installing hard-wired security codes on the home computer.

REPORTING COMPUTER CRIMES

You should establish procedures for reporting criminal acts to the police, district attorney, and other proper authorities. Failure to develop such procedures might delay the reporting process and, in turn, may provide time for the criminal to destroy essential evidence. Investigate all security breaches and suspected criminal acts immediately.

Always prosecute offenders. Failure to press charges and prosecute will only encourage others to commit similar acts.

In the past, computer thieves have not been required to "pay the price" as other criminals are. In part, this freedom from punishment has been computer mystique, a tendency of those who don't fully understand the computer to ascribe near-magical qualities to a machine that is, in reality, probably less sophisticated than an automobile, just harder to understand.

One of the nation's leading experts in computer security estimates that the probability of prosecution in a computer crime is only one in twenty-two thousand. Even if indicted and found guilty, the computer criminal will, in all likelihood, get off with a ridiculously light sentence. One computer thief, for example, who stole more than $21 million, was sentenced to probation for less than twelve months.

Someone who hears such reports might be taken in by them and be tempted to couple his or her knowledge of the computer with an intimate knowledge of the firm for which he or she works. This person might decide to enjoy the singular position of diverting assets from others to him- or herself. However, the nation's jails are filled with those who have said, "They're not going to get me, because I won't make mistakes." Computer security is getting tighter, and those who fight computer crime are getting as smart as those who commit it. The would-be computer criminal may join the long list of kings and queens, presidents and dictators, tycoons and executives, and even average citizens who have pitted their abilities against the established order and have paid the price of their vanity.

Computer Crime: A Checklist

1. Establish selection procedures for screening all new employees and in-depth probes for employees who will have access to confidential information.
2. Develop procedures for separation of work responsibilities.
3. Carefully log all suspicious interruptions of computer operations.
4. Only authorized personnel should have access to the computer.
5. All employees should take a special education course in computer security.
6. Write down all instructions to computer personnel.
7. Formulate a code of ethics on computer operations.
8. Be sure your computer facilities have good physical security.
9. Construct your computer facility out of fire-resistant and waterproof materials.
10. Conduct an annual security audit.
11. Establish disaster recovery plans, and test them at least once a year.
12. Develop alternate equipment and power backup systems in the event the computer fails.
13. Store all computer tapes, disks, and records in special computer safes.
14. Develop emergency shutdown and recovery procedures.
15. Introduce periodic rotation of computer personnel.
16. Use electronic security devices to prevent electronic penetration.
17. Utilize security codes, passwords, scramblers, and cryptographic devices to prevent unauthorized use of the computer.

18. Block employees from accessing your firm's central files and outside telephone lines from the same terminal or personal computer.
19. Limit the use of remote and inactive computer terminals. Use callback modems or install hard-wired security codes when employees must access computers from off-site locations.
20. Destroy all unneeded computer records and printouts.
21. Acquire special computer insurance.
22. Investigate all suspicions of computer abuse.
23. Press charges and prosecute offenders in all cases.

PART SIX

THE CRIMINAL JUSTICE SYSTEM

42
The Criminal Justice System: Victims, Witnesses, Jurors

The Citizens Crime Commission of New York, a nonprofit organization financed by business, has urged that bail procedures be changed to protect the public from crimes committed by suspects while awaiting trial. The panel pointed out that one-quarter of the new arrests in Manhattan were for crimes committed by people who were out on bail for other crimes.

So far this book has concentrated on personal security and crime prevention. This chapter focuses on something nearly as important: what you may experience after a crime has been committed. You may be involved as a victim, witness, or juror. You will find that your life has changed as a result of the experience.

Most people are unfamiliar with the workings of the police, prosecutors, and courts. The average law-abiding citizen has misconceptions and fears of criminal justice proceedings. At some point in your life, you will probably have a firsthand experience with the criminal justice system, and you should be prepared for this often difficult and complex encounter. Your role as an informed complainant, witness, or juror is a vital one.

THE COSTS OF CRIMES

One authority has estimated the annual cost of crime at $100 billion. Of this loss, $75 billion is what the criminal takes. These figures include stolen merchandise figured at cost plus all markups, insurance, and the losses suffered by the victims of crime. The remaining $25 billion is the cost to the nation of fighting the inroads of crime.

THE CHRONOLOGY OF LAW

To combat this enormous cost of crime, society has two major weapons:

laws and those who enforce them. Over centuries, a highly complex system of legal justice has evolved, requiring constant response to changing conditions. New laws are enacted, new interpretations are made by judges, and new modes of operating within this environment are developed by lawyers and enforcement officials.

This criminal justice system moves through four distinct steps: (1) crime to prosecution; (2) prosecution to trial; (3) trial to disposition; and (4) disposition to sentencing.

Crime to Prosecution

Assume you are walking down the street, and a car stops. The driver demands money from you. You surrender your purse or billfold, and the robber departs. Your neighbor, seeing your difficulty, calls the police at once and gives the information they request. The police see a car matching the description of the one driven by the assailant, and return with the suspect to the scene of the crime. You make an identification, and a search discovers your property in the robber's possession. The police return most of your belongings to you and give you a receipt for the others, which will be used as evidence against the suspect.

You may be photographed for evidence of the physical assault upon you. When practical, you will be asked to repeat your story for the prosecutor's office, if the police feel that there is probable cause that a crime was committed by the person in custody.

Should the police decline to arrest the individual, the matter would almost certainly be dropped. You couldn't sue the police and force them to arrest the person. You might make a citizen's arrest, but in so doing, you might open yourself to charges of false arrest.

Prosecution to Trial

There may be a number of reasons why the prosecutor's office may decline to prosecute. One might be that the act was not a violation of the law, but you were both robbed and assaulted, so there's still a case.

A second reason—one all too frequently resulting in a dismissal of charges—might be that the arresting officers lacked sufficient cause to arrest, or otherwise violated the suspect's rights.

Another reason that prosecution would not be pursued could be insufficient evidence, or that there are other cases more deserving of the attention and the available resources in the prosecutor's office.

Possibly your attacker might not be brought to trial because he or she has an excellent reputation and no previous criminal record. First offenders frequently are not tried.

Another reason for inaction might be the prosecutor's self-interest. Perhaps he or she is up for reelection or election to a higher office, and feels that vigorously prosecuting a particular suspect may damage his or her career.

A final reason that might prevent your case's coming to court is the possibility that the attacker might be a prominent individual who is owed favors, or is a close relative or associate of such an individual.

Trial to Disposition

Since the time that this book was first published, there have been some major changes in the way that trials are conducted and concluded. More than 300 victim/witness assistance programs have been established. Whereas persons accused of crimes have a number of rights, victims and witnesses are not extended as much protection. The victim/witness assistance programs are intended to lessen the impact of crime and judicial procedures upon the innocent, while maintaining the constitutional guarantees for those accused.

Among the support services that these assistance units provide are accompanying victims and witnesses through the confusing and sometimes frightening labyrinth of offices and bureaucracies; apprising the innocent of what may be done to help speed justice; possibly providing protection if intimidation is attempted to deter the victims or witnesses from testifying; interceding with employers when the victims or witnesses are required in court; allowing victims and witnesses to have input into bail hearings; often providing information concerning the outcome of the trials; and providing transportation to and from court.

Other assistance that may be provided through victim/witness programs consists of recovering property used as evidence, paying witness fees, providing notification of parole hearings, and notifying victims and witnesses if a convicted criminal escapes.

Disposition to Sentencing

Trials are disposed of in several ways. Among them are verdicts of guilty or innocent and plea bargaining. Many trials end in sentencing by the court. Victims may (or may not) be given the right to enter into the court record a statement of the impact that the crimes have had on their lives. Traditionally, victims testify at the trials and bail hearings, but sentencing input is a relatively recent concept. These newer concepts are usually permitted at the discretion of the court and may not be allowed in every jurisdiction or courtroom.

VICTIMS AND CRIME

If you are a victim of crime, you should remain calm. If you have been injured, go to the nearest emergency room for treatment. Then report the crime. You may be afraid, but remember that the only way to assure the arrest of the offender is to call the police.

The probability that the offender will be arrested will increase by about 10 percent if you call the police within two minutes of the crime. If more time has elapsed, notify the police anyway.

Find out if your state has a victim compensation or restitution program. Many programs pay you for loss of earning power, property damage, support, medical expenses, and burial and funeral expenses. In most states, you are eligible for an award if you are totally innocent and did not contribute to your victimization. Some states allow compensation to victims who suffer undue financial hardship. Generally the offender does not have to be convicted for you to receive payment. You may consider bringing a civil suit against the criminal, but most people convicted of crimes do not have enough money to pay any damages that the courts may award.

In Court

Now you are ready for your day in court. This will not be an easy task. You may have experienced apathy, aloofness, and bureaucratic behavior on the part of the police, and you very well may be in for more of the same once judicial proceedings begin. You will arrive at a large, strange building, perhaps with many entrances, with many people walking around. You may even encounter the criminal who victimized you, nervously pacing up and down the court corridor.

Whatever you do, avoid contact with the defendant, and do not get involved in conversation. Criminal defendants or their friends and relatives have been known to intimidate, threaten, and harass victims. If this occurs, report the incident to the prosecutor immediately. Threats away from the courthouse should also be reported to the prosecutor, the police, or both.

One of the most depressing and infuriating aspects of your court experience is the ease with which your trial may be postponed. You may take off from work, arrive at the courthouse, wait around for hours, and then learn that the proceedings have been delayed. This may occur over and over again during the trial, and it may last for months.

Lesser problems include difficulty with parking, finding your way around inside the courthouse, and uncomfortable waiting conditions. You might even find it difficult to determine the status or progress of your case. Try to find someone in the prosecutor's office who is willing to update you on your case. This may be the best single way to mitigate frustrating experiences. Otherwise, contact your victim/witness assistance program for help and support.

The Witness Stand

Now you are ready to testify. Your evidence can make or break the case. Review your testimony before your court appearance. Picture in your mind what occurred, so that you recall details. You may make notes, but do not memorize your testimony because it will appear staged.

Remain alert and calm, and never lose your temper. Your testimony will have greater impact if you maintain your composure. Think before speaking, and answer all questions slowly and in a loud and clear tone. If you do not fully understand a question, ask that it be rephrased or explained. Always tell the truth, and never exaggerate. Remember that you are under oath. Courts are interested in facts, not opinions; the more objective your testimony appears, the greater its value.

Taking the witness stand is not an easy matter, especially if you are unaccustomed to public speaking. But if you follow these simple instructions, you may be sure that your testimony will be greatly improved.

Victim Assistance

A relatively new but useful development is block clubs or Neighborhood Watch groups that provide assistance to victims. According to the National Institute of Justice, one of the finest programs of this sort is the Philadelphia Block Watch. This program provides many support services for crime victims. These include reassuring the victims, staying with victims, listening to their fears and anxieties, extending practical experience like lending victims money or baby-sitting, accompanying victims to court or to local services, aiding victims in obtaining the proper type of help, helping victims make informed decisions, explaining the criminal justice system and what to expect from it, and providing liaison with the police and the prosecutor.

A similar program to aid victims can be established by any community with inspired leadership, motivated block watches, and dedicated police officials.

Jurors

Many people are neither victims nor witnesses of crime. Instead, they are called to serve on a jury. When you are called for jury duty, be punctual, and follow instructions carefully. If for some reason you are unable to serve on the jury during the scheduled time, notify the jury commission, which may be able to postpone your jury duty or excuse you. Try to get some idea of how long you will have to serve—two to three weeks is not unusual.

Before serving on the jury, you will be screened by the attorneys for both sides. Don't be insulted if you are rejected by one of them. The defense attorney and prosecutor both attempt to select jurors who are likely to sympathize with their side.

After you have been selected for the jury and the trial begins, concentrate on the proceedings and try to follow the case. Listen to and weigh all underlying conflicts; above all, be objective. Never discuss the case with anyone (even other jurors) until the judge instructs you to reach a verdict. Don't read newspaper stories about the case, listen to radio commentators, or watch TV news programs; this could result in a mistrial.

Although you will be paid for serving, the fees are usually very low. Therefore, try to make arrangements with your employer to share the financial burden.

The Criminal Justice System: Victims, Witnesses, Jurors: A Checklist

1. Always report a crime, even if you are only a witness.
2. Seek medical treatment if you have been injured.
3. Remember as many details as you can about the crime scene and the criminal, including all unusual occurrences and characteristics.
4. Try to record the names and addresses of all potential witnesses.
5. Record exactly what property was lost, stolen, or damaged.
6. Note the name and shield number of the investigating police officer, and also record the special police report number assigned to your case.
7. When a suspect is apprehended, be sure to press charges.
8. Be careful when preparing your written complaint.
9. If you are unable to appear at the trial on the scheduled date, notify the prosecutor's office immediately.

Makeovers have

Mickey Mouse is said to be one of the best known "faces" in the world. The cartoon mouse is recognized in most countries.

But Mickey has changed through the years. His eyes are no longer huge circles as in 1928 or pie-cut as in 1934. His nose is shorter, and his teeth have disappeared.

Some things have not changed. For instance, the cartoon Mickey still has four fingers on each hand.

Mickey Mouse was such a hit when introduced in 1928 that he was featured on toys made the next year in the United States and abroad. European toymakers did not pay for rights and made unauthorized toys featuring a five-fingered Mickey who had teeth.

Those old toys are scarce and expensive today. One tin toy, which recently sold for more than $15,000, features a ratlike Mickey and Minnie on a motorcycle. It was made in 1931 by Tipp and Co. of Nuremberg, Germany. The company, which was founded in 1912, made many tinplate toys, especially cars, planes and military toys until 1942. It started to make toys again after World War II but went out of business in 1971. The company used a "T.C." mark.

I just bought a pair of triangular "smoking tables" at an auction. The tables are 18 inches tall and ha

RALPH & TERRY KOVEL
Antiques & Collecting

the ashtrays are marked "Tiffany Studios, New York." Could the tables have been made by Tiffany?

"Tiffany" is linked with glass, lamps and a retail shop. Louis Comfort Tiffany's businesses also made furniture, metalwork, pottery, silver and jewelry. Many of Tiffany's table designs reflected his fascination with the Orient. Tiffany Studios was founded in 1902.

Your tables probably were made between 1920 (when smoking tables became popular) and 1932 (when Tiffany Studios filed for bankruptcy).

The bottom of my Royal Worcester figurine, First Dance, is marked "Modeled by F.G Doughty." Who was Doug

Freda Doughty w daughter of Charles D British travel write Her mother wa Freda and her began work

the poison ivy itch

"Leaves of three, let it be," is the best advice for avoiding poison ivy and the terrible, itchy skin rashes that may result from contact with the plant. Calamine lotion and IvyBlock are some of the products used to combat exposure to poison ivy.

By Dave Darnell

You don't even have to go outside to get poison ivy. Many people get it from their pets.

"A dog or cat runs through poison ivy and then people pet the animal and they break out," said. Pets rarely react to

first exposure is mes from burning ecause the toxin actions i

about 4 inches long. In the summer they are bright green, but turn yellowish or reddish in early fall and then bright red.

They produce green berries that turn white.

10. Find out whether your state has programs for victim compensation or restitution and whether or not you are eligible for benefits.
11. Notify the prosecutor's office or the police if the suspect or the suspect's associates attempt to threaten or intimidate you.
12. Be sure to contact the prosecutor's office or special victim/ witness hot lines to find out whether your case has been delayed or postponed.
13. Try to establish a steady contact in the prosecutor's office who can inform you about the proceedings.
14. Prepare your court testimony carefully.
15. Retain your composure, and never lose your temper on the witness stand.
16. Speak slowly and in a loud and clear voice when presenting testimony.
17. If you do not understand a question, ask that it be repeated.
18. Your testimony should be precise, objective, and truthful.
19. Always appear in court at the scheduled time if you have been selected for jury duty.
20. Notify court authorities if you cannot serve on the jury on the scheduled date.
21. Be alert and listen to all the trial proceedings.
22. Do not discuss the case with anyone or be exposed to news items about the trial, because this could cause a mistrial.
23. Make arrangements with your employer to assist you financially, because fees paid to jurors are relatively low.

PART SEVEN

THE FUTURE OF CRIME

43
Crime in the Twenty-First Century

Crime in the twenty-first century actually began in the summer of 1987, when the Federal Bureau of Investigation issued the *Uniform Crime Reports* reflecting the nation's crime experience during 1986. The news was not good. Increases in reported crimes were the largest in six years, up 6 percent from the 1985 levels. What is worse, violent crime had increased 12 percent. That is the key fact in the report. If we are interpreting the information correctly, we must conclude not only that crime is becoming more widespread, after a very short decline, but that it is also characterized by increasing violence.

Crime is not, however, the only problem that concerns late-twentieth-century Americans. It probably isn't even the most serious concern.

By the summer of 1987, the one factor that most concerned Americans was AIDS. That year, 48 percent of Americans found AIDS the single most serious threat. Particularly frightening to many observers is a feeling reported by half of Americans that any action necessary to control this disease should be taken, even if it abridges the rights of some citizens.

In the past, many mass crimes have been committed in the name of maintaining society's integrity and welfare. Plague carriers were slaughtered, and yellow-fever victims were abandoned to die, lest they infect their neighbors. State-organized exterminations of other people have occurred throughout history. Russians attempted genocide against Jews in the 1800s, and in World War I, the Turks attempted total slaughter of the Armenians. The exterminations perpetrated by the Nazis in the 1940s, officially to protect the "Aryan race" from contamination, are too recent to require cataloging. At this writing, ethnic wars are smoldering in Sri Lanka, Kashmir, and many other parts of the world.

We now see the same fears expressed toward the carriers of the AIDS virus. Should a vaccine not be developed at near-geometric rates, victims could find themselves in serious peril, not only from disease, but also from their fellow humans.

The wandering garbage barge that experienced so much difficulty in finding an off-loading point in 1987 underscored another concern of humanity as it rounded the corner and headed for the twenty-first century. The dissipation of our natural resources, and the difficulty of replacing them, worries us. If we cannot or will not manage our waste, we most certainly will be buried beneath it.

We are additionally concerned about crowding in the skies above our airports, and we are even more concerned about the near misses that threaten passenger confidence and the safety of those in the air and on the ground below.

We are concerned about our continuing rape of our environment. Our ransom of the future of our children is given many names—acid rain, vanishing ozone layer, and the ever-increasing temperatures that threaten to turn our planet into one gigantic greenhouse.

Another cause of concern is our disregard for the well-being of our neighbor. Shooting in cold blood a person who may have cut in front of you on the freeway is much more than irresponsibility; it is insanity. But it is also a clear manifestation of the violence that is pervading our moral fiber.

In other places, these pages have told of the effects of the Baby Boom generation on the nation's crime experience. It is the largest generation in the history of our planet, and in a world made uncertain by global war, a threatening peace, and the awesome specter of nuclear weapons, it became history's most pampered generation. Sociologists and criminologists thoroughly documented the Baby Boom group. They found that a small number—one-sixth of the total—was responsible for a disproportionately large fraction of crime: two-thirds. Researchers also found that those with extensive juvenile crime records were responsible for 75 percent of serious crimes (described as those involving injury, theft, or damage) and 80 percent of all other crimes.

Researchers then compared the Baby Boom generation with their children, the "Baby Boom Echo" so prominent in the weekly newsmagazines. The term *Baby Boom Aftershock* is much more descriptive of this very violent group. Criminals of this generation began their crime careers earlier, have been involved in crime longer, and are destined to be more criminally active. It is these young criminals who may well propel our rates of violent crime to dizzying levels.

This group, which is preparing itself now for a career of crime, is much different from the present generation or any of the preceding ones. Although the criminals of this group entered their life of crime at about the same rate as their earlier counterparts, they manifested violent tendencies at a much earlier age. Their crimes are much more violent than those of their predecessors, and a great deal more likely to cause serious, even fatal, results.

Furthermore, these criminals are more likely to commit second and subsequent crimes of violence, as well as other crimes, all prior to the age of eighteen.

If we are to successfully survive the Baby Boom Aftershock—indeed, if we are to survive at all—we must have a great deal of assistance from our legislators. According to the nation's premier criminologist, we would be remiss to continue to allow criminally active juveniles to enter adulthood at eighteen with a clear record and past offenses ignored. He maintains that juvenile records should certainly be considered in efforts to deal with criminally violent adults. Already, the incarceration of juvenile offenders is widespread and, as research indicates, should prove most effective in reducing crime to more satisfactory levels. If we are to survive well into the twenty-first century, we must place our problem criminals in custody, and they must remain incarcerated until they become a significantly lesser threat to society.

Hand in hand with the career criminal is the drug dealer. Hordes of these criminals are bringing dope and dealers to our shores, and they are killing us, with the overdose of crack or, just as certainly but a great deal less humanely, with a lifelong addiction to the drugs that deprive us of our dignity, our careers, our families, and, finally, our lives.

There are now about 250 million people in the United States. In the world, there are 5 billion. By the year 2000, there will be 268 million Americans and over 6 billion people crowded together on this planet, vying for its resources. Inevitably, there will be conflict as nations and individuals struggle to survive. This struggle will reach one of two ends: survival of the fittest, following an exercise of arms or intimidation, or the survival of the wisest, who gained the desired ends through coexistence.

Crime in the twenty-first century will be widespread and all-encompassing. None of us will be able to ignore it. The struggle may pit class against class; it may match the very ill against the healthy; it could be nation versus nation, Moslem versus Infidel, Jew versus Gentile, or young versus old.

What we today call the emerging nations will have a clear superiority in population. That is a foregone conclusion, barring, of course, some sort of intervention, when we consider present-day birth rates.

Intervention, there will be, however. It might take the form of the apocalyptic Four Horsemen—the biblical Fire, Famine, Plague, and Death—or it may pattern itself into an enlightened respect of one person for the other, and through worldwide cooperation, we may cast aside our differences and focus on our similarities, learning to live in harmony with ourselves, our neighbors, and our environment.

Crime protection strategies for the twenty-first century require long-term planning unlike the immediate direct action described in previous chapters. At present, individuals are most immediately affected by crime and, therefore, responsible for avoiding or preventing it. But in the twenty-first century, the business community and government officials will be as vulnerable, and consequently must more than before add their efforts to those of private citizens.

In doing so, they can benefit from the studies of delinquency by Professor Marvin Wolfgang and the future prognostications of crime by criminologist Georgette Bennett. Their work has been refined to apply to the issues involving safety and security as far as the year 2025. According to Georgette Bennett, criminal offenses in the twenty-first century will consist of much more white-collar crime and computer crime than is perpetrated today. Women and the elderly will commit more of these crimes.

WHITE-COLLAR CRIME

An upsurge in white-collar crimes can be expected to begin around the turn of the century and continue well into the first quarter of the twenty-first century. In the 1990s exceptionally intense violence will be due largely to the Baby Boom Aftershock, but this same unwholesome cohort will enter the turn of the century in their thirties, an age highly susceptible to white-collar crimes. Over the next fifteen years, an additional six million people are expected to swell this most crime-prone age group.

White-collar crime will soar around the turn of the twenty-first century and remain at its highest level for about ten years: a double shock attributable to the large numbers of individuals highly vulnerable to white-collar crimes resulting from overlap of the two unusually large cohorts (one the Baby Boom born after World War II, and the second their children). During the 1990s they will be well into the ages most vulnerable for commission of white-collar crimes, and they will continue to be at high risk for this type of crime at least for the first few years into the twenty-first century.

The evidence of this trend is already on the record. Since the early seventies, arrests for white-collar crimes have increased up to 90 percent. Such cases are the most frequently filed in U.S. district courts, accounting for almost 30 percent of the volume. The upward trend is likely to continue over the next several decades.

Theft of Information

A new and special form of white-collar crime, theft of information and technological secrets, will surge. Trade secrets and development plans, rather than tangible assets, will be the most valuable corporate assets and, therefore, the main concern of criminal justice by the turn of the century. As litigation over the past ten years involving stolen technological information increased by at least 500 percent, court decisions quadrupled and now exceed 200 a year.

The cost of information theft runs to billions of dollars. Yet it is increasingly difficult to prevent, let alone detect or curtail. Use of technology to counter these crimes is less than efficient. Briefcase checks, lie-detector tests, surveillance of copying equipment, wiretaps, and antibugging devices are increasingly expensive, raise complicated civil liberties issues, and often are unreliable.

In one far-out case recently reported by the *Wall Street Journal*, students in an MBA course on marketing were hired by competing companies to gather proprietary technological information, including inventory levels, sales volumes, and potential new products, from various companies. These degree candidates misled the targeted companies by giving the impression that they were collecting data only for their university assignments. They even used university marketing department stationery to engage in this industrial espionage. The companies supplying information never dreamed it would be transmitted to competitors.

Medical Fraud

As the population ages, medical quackery invariably increases. Older citizens, requiring more legitimate remedies, drugs, and the services of physicians, will also be lured by bogus treatments and inadequately tested drugs, poured onto the market by unscrupulous companies. Perhaps the most widespread problem will involve medically related insurance fraud, where a physician may treat one family member but bill all present; charge for expensive services never performed; provide unnecessary treatment; and engage in fee splitting.

Personal Computers

There has been a tremendous surge in ownership of desktop computers. (Chapter 41 examines implications of this mammoth expansion.) It is predicted that by 1990 one out of fifty Americans will own personal data-processing equipment. Together with the expansion of computers in private industry and government, these machines will increase the opportunities for theft. Using new software for the personal machines, electronic bandits will be able to enter decentralized data systems through interlocking telecommunications systems. Few supervisors and managers will have the expertise to monitor expert operators.

TERRORISM

Most frightening will be the increased interest of terrorists in computer systems and installations. According to criminologist Marvin Wolfgang, terrorism is certain to surface as one of the most heinous types of crimes in the twenty-first century. The fear of street gangs will be replaced by the terror of theological-ideological groups of international terrorists. Small bands of fanatics, acquiring miniature nuclear weapons with tremendous destructive capacity, will control enormous power. They will attempt to poison the major water supplies, burn down key buildings, and even engage in local forms of chemical and bacterial warfare. Some of the more hearty bands, taking control of small developing countries, will use them as bases to threaten the superpowers. Even outer space will not completely escape the damage due to crime. Satellites will be damaged, dislodged, and even stolen. In this universe, humankind will experience no respite nor find anywhere to flee.

Overall, crime will become ever more internationalized because of the drug problem. Even street robbery, burglary, and larceny will have an international character. Money from these crimes is likely to be used for purchasing drugs, especially cocaine and heroin from South America and Asia.

FEMALE CRIMINALITY

The Baby Boom Aftershock will also produce more crime by women during the decade of the nineties, at least up to the turn of the century. The high concentration of female teenagers and young adults ages fifteen to twenty-four will result in their committing more crimes.

Although only about one in ten arrests for violent crime involve women, this figure represents an approximate increase of 22 percent between 1971 and 1985. This contrasts with an increase for violent crimes over that same period of only some 5.5 percent for males. Additionally, the number of arrests of women for larceny, auto theft, burglary, and arson increased more than 50 percent between 1971 and 1982, while over the same decade, arrests of men for the same offenses increased by only 29 percent. Over the next twenty-five years, we can expect substantially more crime by women.

Singleness

The shortage of men since World War II, postponement of marriages by men and women, the high divorce rate, and a general tendency for women not to remarry after divorce will generate large numbers of single women, many with children. In 1960, some 4.5 million women were living alone; today this figure has increased to nearly 13 million women who are on their own.

The combined excess of women and shortage of men will diminish the incentive for men to honor commitments and fulfill the responsibilities that accompany fatherhood and marriage. Women will suffer emotionally and financially. Out of frustration, jealousy, fear of losing a relationship, and poverty will emerge thefts, robberies, domestic violence, aggravated assaults, and homicides.

Feminism

The feminist movement is an important factor in the increase in crime by women. Ironically, greater freedom in general and expanded opportunities in the work force tend to produce more crime. Whereas in the 1950s only one-third of the work force was female, today nearly one-half of all employees are women. Greater numbers create greater opportunities for embezzlement and other crimes.

The jobs traditionally held by women in assembly and manufacturing have gone to foreign shores, where labor costs are far less than in the

States. American women have therefore moved into jobs in .ous other sectors: service, finance, insurance, and real estate. Hospitals, retail stores, hotels, and motels are largely staffed by women. These positions provide tremendous temptation and opportunities for theft, especially for economically deprived women.

Many women are in managerial positions in the nation's corporations, in department stores, in law and accounting firms, and in financial institutions. These patterns of employment, likely to grow over the next decade, also provide greater opportunities for crime in the workplace.

THE ELDERLY AND CRIME

The ranks of the elderly will swell during the first quarter of the twenty-first century and give rise to an increase in offending by senior citizens. In a few more years, one of every four Americans will have reached age sixty. Around the year 2000, the number of people eighty-five and older will increase by two-thirds, and by 2010, the number of elderly aged eighty and above will have doubled to twelve million.

Unfortunately, even venerable oldsters, including septuagenarians and octogenarians, commit crimes. By far the most prevalent offense committed by older citizens is larceny, especially shoplifting. Since the early 1970s, the arrest rate among the elderly for larceny has increased by 25 percent, or twice the rate of increase among the general population for the same crime. But older people also engage in violence, especially domestic disputes. Sex crimes like molesting children also are relatively common among the elderly. Also, the leadership of organized crime consists mainly of older men.

Investment fraud will rise as older people seek myriad more advantageous ways of investing their savings. And as the number of work years is lengthened by legislation outlawing mandatory retirement, older people will have more opportunities to commit white-collar crimes, including fraud, embezzlement, forgery, and counterfeiting.

Causes

Analyzing the kinds of objects stolen by the elderly reveals that they are not motivated only by poverty or survival. Expensive cuts of meat, high-priced cosmetics, and gourmet cheeses are among the objects pilfered. The main cause of crime among the elderly seems to be that their lifestyle induces a state of "drift," relatively free of the social controls and responsibilities that anchor most adults in our society. The elderly often change residence, lose mates, experience the passing of good friends, suffer side effects of drugs, undergo biochemical alterations, and—probably most important—have no meaningful work. Free time with an emphasis on play and leisure leaves them just like juveniles, who often find themselves in a similar position of drift. Boredom, impatience, loneliness, irritability, frustration, and a feeling of meaninglessness then often set the stage for crime.

A volcanic eruption of violence is therefore expected in the 1990s, while white-collar crime is likely to explode around the turn of the century and continue unabated for the next twenty-five years. It is not too early for individual citizens, corporate executives, and government officials to prepare for the inevitability of these events. In the fight for survival in the war against crime, the information provided in this volume is just one step toward the protection and safety of every citizen in the nation.

Crime in the Twenty-First Century: A Checklist

1. Anticipate crimes you will experience in the future, and begin preparing personal plans, such as saving money to acquire locks, window guards, alarms, household safes, lighting, and dogs.
2. Familiarize yourself with personal computers so that you are less likely to be victimized by criminals that utilize them.
3. Institute planning and measures now to prevent theft of information.
4. Learn more about your own medical treatment to prevent medical fraud.
5. Establish citizen crime prevention programs now that address the violence expected in the nineties.
6. Make plans now for long-term crime prevention through environmental design.

About the Author

Protection of people and their property has been a lifelong career for Ira A. Lipman. As chairman and president of Guardsmark, Inc., one of the world's largest security services companies, he directs an international network of protection professionals. Guardsmark personnel are responsible for the security of thousands of people and billions of dollars in assets. Following many of the procedures personally developed by Mr. Lipman, the firm serves many leading multinational corporations and institutions, protecting such diverse operations as manufacturing plants, oil refineries, banks, hospitals, and corporate offices.

Known throughout the industry for his innovative approach to security problem solving, Mr. Lipman is frequently sought as a source of information on crime prevention techniques. He has been editorially praised by the *New York Times* for his leadership in disarming the security industry, and his and Guardsmark's achievements have received acclaim in such publications as the *Wall Street Journal*, *Reader's Digest*, *Business Week*, *People*, and *U.S. News and World Report*. He is also publisher of *The Lipman Report*, a monthly newsletter for executives that focuses on security problems ranging from terrorism and sabotage to computer crime, drug abuse, and employee theft.

Mr. Lipman was principal force in the formation of the Committee of National Security Companies and currently is Chairman of the Executive Committee of the National Council on Crime and Delinquency, and National Chairman of the National Conference of Christians and Jews. He and his wife, Barbara, divide their time between residences in New York and Memphis. They have three sons—Gustave, Joshua, and Benjamin.